JANE BROWN is the author of *Gardens of a Golden Afternoon*, the story of the partnership between Edwin Lutyens and Gertrude Jekyll, which has become a much-loved classic to garden-minded readers all over the world. Her other books have included *Lutyens and the Edwardians* and the gardening biographies of Vita Sackville-West, Lanning Roper and the American landscape gardener, Beatrix Farrand. Believing that writing, like gardening, is an 'art of place' she has recently pulled up her Hampshire/Surrey roots and transplanted herself to Cambridgeshire.

The Pursuit of Paradise

A SOCIAL HISTORY OF GARDENS
AND GARDENING

JANE BROWN

HarperCollins*Publishers*

HarperCollins*Publishers*
77–85 Fulham Palace Road,
Hammersmith, London w6 8jb

This paperback edition 2000
1 3 5 7 9 8 6 4 2

First published in Great Britain
by HarperCollins*Publishers* 1999

A catalogue record for this book
is available from the British Library

Grateful acknowledgement is made to the following to reproduce
copyright material: Messrs John Murray Ltd., for
John Betjeman's 'Middlesex', *Collected Poems* (1958); and
Messrs Chatto and Windus for Wilfred Owen's
'When late I viewed the gardens of rich men',
The Poems of Wilfred Owen, ed. Jon Stallworthy (1993).

ISBN 0 00 638867 1

Set in PostScript Linotype Adobe Caslon by
Rowland Phototypesetting Ltd, Bury St Edmunds, Suffolk

Printed and bound in Great Britain by
Omnia Books Limited, Glasgow

To adventurers in garden history everywhere

CONTENTS

LIST OF ILLUSTRATIONS

17 *Runner Bean*, design for machine-printed cotton by E. Q. Nicholson, c.1950. (By kind permission of Tim Nicholson)
18 *Golding Constable's Kitchen Garden* by John Constable, 1815. (Ipswich Borough Council Museums and Galleries)
19 Cedric Morris's garden at Benton End, Hadleigh, Suffolk, c.1944. (By permission of the Trustees of the Cedric Morris Estate and Firstsite, The Minories, Colchester)
20 Garden made for Sir Frederick Gibberd at Marsh Lane, Harlow, Essex. (The author, by kind permission of Lady Gibberd)
21 *The World Turned Upside Down* by Bernard McGuigan at The Garden Gallery, Broughton, Hampshire. (By kind permission of Rachel Bebb/The Garden Gallery)
22 *Dragonfly* by Jeff Hisley at The Garden Gallery. (By kind permission of Rachel Bebb/The Garden Gallery)
23 Retaining wall by John and Andrew Dejardin at Wingwell, Wing, Rutland. (Dejardin Design)
24 Rose Dejardin's nursery ground, Wingwell. (Dejardin Design)
25 *Iris Seedlings* by Cedric Morris, 1943. (Tate Gallery, London)
26 *The Royal Family at Windsor* by Rex Whistler, 1939. (The Royal Collection, © Her Majesty The Queen)
27 John Claudius Loudon's layout plan for villa and gardens for *The Suburban Gardener and Villa Companion*, 1838. (John Gloag, *Mr Loudon's England*, 1970)
28 London, garden city, 1559. (P. D. A. Harvey, *Maps in Tudor England*, 1993, by kind permission of the Museum of London)
29 'The Manor of Paston divided and planted into Rural Gardens' by Stephen Switzer from *Ichnographia Rustica*, 1718. (J. D. Hunt and P. Willis, *The Genius of the Place*, 1975)
30 Plan of Stowe, Buckinghamshire, published by Sarah Bridgeman, 1739. (G. B. Clarke, *Descriptions of Lord Cobham's Gardens at Stowe*, 1990)
31 Bayleaf, a Yeoman's property of c.1500, at the Weald and Downland Museum, Singleton, West Sussex. (By permission of Dr Sylvia Landsberg)
32 & 33 Maps of Higham Ferrers, Northamptonshire, 1591 and 1789. (M. Beresford, *History on the Ground*, 1984)
34 Aerial photograph of Higham Ferrers. (Cambridge University Department of Aerial Survey)
35 *Back Garden at Bardfield* by Edward Bawden, 1933. (Towner Art Gallery and Local Museum, Eastbourne. © Estate of Edward Bawden 2000. All Rights Reserved, DACS)
36 *Garden Path* by Eric Ravilious, 1934. (Towner Art Gallery and Local Museum, Eastbourne. © Estate of Eric Ravilious 2000. All Rights Reserved, DACS)

ILLUSTRATIONS IN TEXT

ACKNOWLEDGEMENTS

For the last twenty years or so I have been a spectator, only occasionally drawn into the fray, of the rise of interest in garden history. Almost everyone I know or have known in that world has contributed to this book in thought, word or deed. I hope they will accept my thanks and admiration, and make allowances for what may sometimes seem my cursory or cavalier sweep through their particular area of expertise in order to conjure so large a subject into the convenient and desirable object that we call a book.

I would like to acknowledge, with gratitude, all the sources for quotations and illustrations, which I have made every attempt to credit accurately in the text, the notes and the lists of illustrations. To a great extent this book reflects my own collection of books and papers gathered together over the years and now all familiar treasures: their wide-ranging and sometimes surprising subjects are brought to the light of reference here to acknowledge the obscure corners into which the social historian of gardens needs to forage. Too few of these sources, but some of the best, are listed for further reading. I would like to add my particular appreciation for the illustrations in this book, in colour and black and white, and as line drawings in the text, which are all images of my affection and regard, and often constitute a story in themselves.

My particular thanks are offered to the following people: to Kay Sanecki for her memoir of the founding of the Garden History Society and to Ted Fawcett for prompting others to write theirs; to Philip White for the wonderful job he has done with the Hestercombe Gardens Trust; to Peter Stanford for encouraging me to explore the missing legacy of Catholic England; to Barbara Oakley for her recollections of Constance Spry; to Mark and Liz Robinson for informing and inspiring my chapter on the military garden; to Richard Lewis for researches for my science chapter; to Ros Wallinger for being named for Rosamund Clifford as well as for the inspiration of her garden at Upton Grey; to

Alison Kelly for her revelations of the remarkable Eleanor Coade; to Jonathan Lovie for taking me to Henrietta Luxborough's resting place; to Colin Brown for his family memories of En Tout Cas; to David Wheeler, whose *Hortus* has pursued the social aspects of garden history for years; to the Revd. Mervyn Wilson for an insight into his gardening philosophy; to Patricia Jaffe for her original introduction to Newnham College and her knowledge of engraving and engravers; to Patricia Reed for her encyclopaedic knowledge of the Nicholsons and taking me to Ditchling Museum; to Todd Lonstaffe-Gowan for pioneering Georgian town gardens; to Kate Perry, archivist at Girton College, and Biddy Marrian for asking me to write *A Garden of Our Own*, the story of Girton's garden, which has naturally filtered into this book; to Wendy Titman for handing me her archive material on school gardening (it is now for her to write the definitive book!); to Christopher and Stephanie Taylor for bringing garden and landscape archaeology into the perspective of friendship in my newly-adopted Cambridgeshire; and lastly, for here, to Beth Chatto for gardening as I do in my dreams.

It has been especially exciting to watch the growth of county gardens trusts and how they embrace all kinds of conditions of people into their folds – this is where the social history is truly being discovered, written and made. My book has benefited from contacts with the trusts in Sussex, Hampshire, the Isle of Wight, London, Surrey, Devon, Cornwall, Warwickshire and Hertfordshire and from the three that are now my local trusts, Leicestershire & Rutland, Northamptonshire and Cambridgeshire. My personal thanks go especially to Gilly Drummond, Diana Ford and Lucille Ashdown of Hampshire, Brenda Lewis, Russell Morris and Denise Todd of Surrey, Pamela Paterson of London Historic Parks and Gardens Trust, Noreen Jardine of Warwickshire, Shirley Evans in Cornwall, Grant Pitches in Leicester, Jenny Burt of Northamptonshire and John Drake and Audrey Osborne of Cambridgeshire. My thanks also to many professionals in landscape and garden design whose work informs this book including Andrew Wilson of the Inchbald School, Rosemary Alexander of the English Gardening School, John Brookes and the Society of Garden Designers, John and Rose Dejardin, Rachel Bebb, Edward Hutchison and Dominic Cole. My long-standing lecture dates at the Architectural Association Garden Conservation Course have taught me much – my thanks to Ted Fawcett and Gordon

Acknowledgements

Ballard, to Carole Newman, Pamela Paterson and Charlotte Johnson amongst many other former students, and salutes to the new régime of David Jacques and Jan Woudstra.

This catalogue of my much-appreciated encounters of the last twenty years has to end with the inevitable fear that I have left so many people out, but I am grateful to them all the same. This is my first book written in Elton and I extend my appreciations to friends and neighbours especially Linda and Brian Guest, Bill and Verna Emmerson, Tim and Jane Cummins, Joan Wiley and Peter Hamill.

No book of mine would ever be written without the initial encouragement of Caradoc King and Sam Boyce of A. P. Watt, nor without the treasure-trove of the London Library and its staff. I am also grateful for the helpfulness of the staff at Peterborough Central Library. My final thanks go to Michael Fishwick and his team at HarperCollins to whom I extend my warmest admiration for their commitment and professionalism: Michael, Rebecca Lloyd, Kate Johnson, Vera Brice, Annie Robertson, Betty Palmer, Caroline Hotblack and Julie Cass have worked especially hard to transform my ideas and words into one of their beautifully-crafted company of books.

FOREWORD

The dam of pompous, political history was breached by the publication of George Macaulay Trevelyan's 'popular and nostalgic' *English Social History*, in America and Canada (for the war effort) in 1942, and here in 1944. It fell upon starved minds and sold four hundred thousand copies in the first five years, was constantly reprinted and has now appeared in an illustrated version. Professor Trevelyan invented our history, as most of us are not prime ministers or generals, and all of us have been taught in his benevolent shade. Some of his page headings picked at random are: village church music, Highland emigration, censorship and press, state of the roads, the game laws, women's labour, sanitation, cheap gin, building fashions, house decoration and gardens. He powered our cult of personal worth, our desire for roots and local history, and for a history of food, farming, football and every everyday subject that can be conceived. The tentative beginnings of garden history were carried forward on this wave, and have now become a degree subject. But garden history has been overly aristocratic, as if only the great and the good had gardens: what follows is an attempt to redress the balance, to outline a history of gardens that is also popular and nostalgic.

Introduction

The opening sound for this tale of garden history is the small familiar scratching, then twang! as it hits a stone, of a garden hoe. It is an everyday, unimportant sound, and yet a universal one. The elevation of the hoe into a solo is prompted by an advertisement which recently fell through my front door for the latest edition of 'a lavish, state-of-the-art pop-up following the classic tale of Peter Rabbit, with interactive flaps and tabs, beautifully illustrated pop-up scenes, bright illustrations, and even a sound effect from Mr McGregor's hoe'.

With a nod to Humphry Repton for his popularization of the 'interactive flaps and tabs' in his Red Books of two hundred years ago, it is the sound effect of Mr McGregor the gardener's hoe, that catches interest. It has been heard in almost a century of children's imaginations, equally familiar on the remotest African veldt farm or Birmingham allotment, in leafy Melbourne suburbs or back gardens from Osaka to Amstelveen, so widely has Peter Rabbit been translated and read. The sound of the hoe is an introduction to the cultural idea of the garden.

Beatrix Potter's first book of Peter Rabbit's adventures among Mr McGregor's lettuces was published privately in 1901, and taken up by Frederick Warne & Company in the following year. Miss Potter fell in love with her publisher, Norman Warne, and they were about to marry when he died in 1905. To comfort herself, she bought Hill Top at Near Sawrey, in the Lake District, the kind of 'homely place' that had fuelled her imagination for Peter's adventures, or so one version has it. She eventually married in 1913, becoming Mrs William Heelis, and a very successful farmer, sheep breeder and owner of thousands of Lake District acres; she gave a great deal of land to the National Trust, including Hill Top, where the garden has now been restored to bring alive her illustrations, using photographs of it in her time. Hollyhocks, sweet williams, lamb's lugs and other old-fashioned flowers jostle with the gooseberry 'Wynham's Industry', the very variety in whose netting Peter Rabbit was ensnared.[1]

However, there are at least two other claimants to the soil of the scratching hoe. Beatrix Potter's journals were written in code – a code broken by Leslie Linder who published them in 1966 – and these reveal the Peter Rabbit characters to have been modelled on people and animals Beatrix knew on annual holidays at Dalguise House at Birnam ('Fear not, till Birnam wood Do come to Dunsinane') in Perthshire.[2] Perthshire Tourist Board have made a Beatrix Potter garden in Birnam village, where Mr McGregor in bronze presides, and have a summer exhibition on her in Birnam Institute, which she knew well. (Perhaps it is the vision of the warlike Malcolm and Macduff and their tree-girt hordes tripping over Squirrel Nutkin and Mrs Tiggy-Winkle that is most alluring?)

The almost-royal and definitely regal novelist Dame Barbara Cartland also claims her garden in Hertfordshire as Mr McGregor's. Her home is Camfield Place, outside Hatfield, which once belonged to Beatrix Potter's grandparents. Beatrix wrote that Camfield was 'bound up together in fact and fancy, my Dear Grandmother, the place I love best in the world and the sweet balmy air where I have been so happy as a child'. Dame Barbara's literary imagination naturally enjoys the ghost of the young Beatrix composing her diary code in the drawing-room, and she finds, 'When I walk in Mr McGregor's Garden at Camfield Place and look at the door in the wall which Beatrix Potter's "fat little rabbit could not squeeze underneath" and down the Nut Walk which, when I came, was full of pretty red squirrels, I think that just as it was the most perfect place on earth to Beatrix, so it is to me.'[3]

Seldom can a scratching hoe have uncovered so many powerful passions and ideas. Rabbit royalties and family wealth funded Mrs Heelis's Lake District acres and her support of the National Trust and the Friends of the Lake District. They in turn (and with a little help from William Wordsworth) created the Lake District National Park and a phenomenon of this tourists' age. Potter's mythic garden embraces the children of the world and seems to cross all social divides but when turned into a reality it invites commercial rivalries and competitiveness. Gardeners have an ideal that draws them on to spend on plants, gadgets and potent mixes, and this ideal seems to have been instilled in early life; merely digging, and growing cabbages and roses, baby broad beans, is curiously not enough for many. The little garden becomes the key to a world of wonders and delights, of fabulous riches and wealth. The power of the garden is this duality of growing and dreaming, of digging and daydreaming, of the future's possibilities allied to the nostalgic past.

In the world of gardening today, class means as much on the flower show bench as amongst people. The classical Greeks had a complex hierarchy of gardens, but they were pleasure gardens and labour in them was despised, presumably carried out by invisible slaves (a system maintained in grand British gardens until the 1920s). The orchatos, or chortus, or hortus, where fruit and vegetables were grown were the lowest status of all. These divisions were carried into history, the pleasure garden being noble, the kitchen garden bucolic. But the classically despised labour, or at least a little of it, was soon discovered by emperors and queens to be rather fun. George III's original charter to the Royal Horticultural Society is crowded with lords and baronets plus a bishop, though some good gardeners had to be added for efficiency's sake. These days we have all learned the joys of baby carrots and broad beans, and though the lords are still prominent in the horticultural world, they are likely to lose their places to politicians and pop stars who 'want to be remembered for their gardens'.

The real divide is meretricious, between the Experts and the rest of us; Vita Sackville-West was terrified of experts (professional nurserymen like Clarence Elliott) and yet she is universally regarded as one of the great gardeners of the twentieth century. And the moral of *that* is, as the Duchess in the Red Queen's garden used to say, that experts are only human. But even today snobbery runs deep. Ever since the 1940s, when it was necessary to encourage digging for victory, the BBC and some magazines and newspapers have cultivated the horny-handed son of the soil; last spring (when the garden subjects are dusted off in time for the Chelsea Flower Show) the Radio Four flagship *Today* included an argument about daffodils between two kinds of gardener: the clipped, educated, posh voice in favour of sweeps of miniatures, the *Narcissus bulbocodium* which Wordsworth saw, because these are in scale with the landscape, pitted against the bucolic growler wanting the biggest and brightest trumpets and doubles. Here is the cut and thrust of garden debate, for have not the worthies of the RHS Narcissus committee, with legendary names like Barr and Backhouse, been working for years to produce the biggest trumpets, the doubles like ballerinas' tutus, the many-headed 'Cheerfulness'? The size of daffodils is just one of the pitfalls. By thy taste in plants thou shalt be known!

Gertrude Stein's a 'rose is a rose, is a rose, is a rose', could not be further from the truth, and roses have come a long way recently.[4] By the early 1950s some 700 varieties of bush hybrid tea were on sale in Britain, from Continental, American and British breeders, developed specifically for the small garden, sturdy bushes carrying porcelain-like blooms: the symbolic 'Peace', yellow with pinky shading 'very large and full' with as many as forty-five petals; or the rich coppery orange-salmon 'Mrs Sam McGredy', all giving of their best set 2–3 feet apart in well-manured beds, on their own. Hybrid tea popularity can be judged by membership of the National Rose Society, founded in 1876 when 'the Queen of Flowers had fallen on evil days', with a few thousand members in the 1930s, 20,000 in 1949, 45,000 in 1955 and almost twice that number by 1960. Lovely as hybrid teas were, there had in the 1930s already been a backlash, on the daffodil principle that the flowers were large and garish. Constance Spry's 'favourite hobby' was growing old-fashioned roses in her orchard and Edward Ashdown Bunyard of Allington Nurseries near Maidstone (home of the apple Allington Pippin) published *Old Garden Roses* in 1936. They were both keen to rescue the shrub roses which could be grown in a mixed border or the semi-wild; Mrs Spry loved her 'Cardinal de Richelieu', the fine white moss rose 'Blanche Moreau' and the pink mosses 'Salet' and 'Madame Louis Levêque'. At Sissinghurst Vita Sackville-West also had the 'Cardinal', and her favourite hybrid musks bred by the Revd Joseph Pemberton, 'Cordelia', 'Felicia' and 'Moonlight': she would not have a hybrid tea in the garden.

After the war Graham Stuart Thomas wrote of 'fulfilling a kind of mission' when he used his petrol ration to scour the British Isles for remnant collections of old damasks, mosses, bourbons and Provence roses, but he was proved to be right in his revival of these marvellous plants.[5] I still have the tattered black-covered Manual of 'Wild Species, the Old French and New Hybrid Roses for growing *as Flowering Shrubs*' from his first collection at James Russell's Sunningdale Nurseries in the 1960s.[6] When Sunningdale was sold to Waterer's in 1968 Graham Stuart

Thomas went to the National Trust and was to fill the walled garden at the Trust's Mottisfont Abbey in Hampshire with his collection. Their cousins were planted at Castle Howard by James Russell, the damasks, centifolias and their mossy sports beside long walks in Lady Cecilia's Garden, underplanted with dianthus, phlox, sages, peonies, thymes, lavenders and hardy geraniums.

The more commercial side of the 'old' rose revival passed into the hands of a young farmer from the West Midlands, named David Austin, who also disliked hybrid teas and floribundas for their unpretty flowers and lack of scent, but wanted their garden-worthy vigour allied to some of the old species. In 1961 Austin produced a hybrid from the Le Grice pink floribunda, 'Dainty Maid', and a nineteenth-century pink gallica 'Belle Isis', which he named 'Constance Spry'. A second hybrid, of Le Grice's velvet red 'Dusky Maiden' with the crimson gallica 'Tuscany' produced a new rose, 'Chianti': 'Chianti' and 'Constance Spry' were the basis of Austin's new English roses, deliciously crinkled and cupped flowers of taffeta pinks and apricots like can-can skirts, with abundance of scent and good foliage. English roses, such as those named after 'Gertrude Jekyll' (rich pink), 'Heritage' (blush pink) and 'Graham Thomas' (tea-scented yellow) have bridged the rose divide, winning National Rose Society medals and Chelsea Show plaudits in abundance.[7] But the Royal National Rose Society have not been idle either, and have decreed that roses are no longer 'hybrid tea' and 'floribunda' but are now 'large flowered' and 'cluster flowered' instead; and varieties of miniature (patio) and ground-covering roses have now multiplied.[8] The mountain range of taste that divides Watford from Winchester and the large and clustering roses in the 'World's Leading (& friendliest) Plant Society's' garden at Chiswell Green from the National Trust's collection of delicate and ancient shrubs at Mottisfont Abbey is only safely breached by ramblers and climbers, which are, on the whole, loved by everyone.

The rose and daffodil partisans are only a fragment of the garden population though, and there are endless other divides: rhododendrons are a battleground between species and hybrids, old hybrids and new; and azaleas, both evergreen and deciduous, are suspect by all (though beloved in royal gardens). Azalea hatred is a relic of the nadir of plant taste, the 1960s, the decade of ground cover, which also blights Japanese

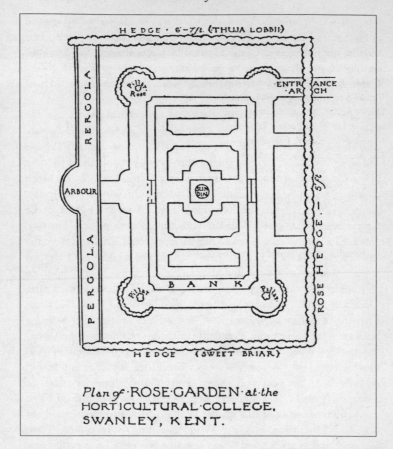

Plan of ·ROSE·GARDEN· at the
HORTICULTURAL·COLLEGE,
SWANLEY, KENT.

The Rosarian's Rose Garden, 1899: plan of an enclosed rose garden for Swanley Horticultural College in Kent from *Our Gardens* by Dean Samuel Reynolds Hole. Dean Hole was one of the founders of the National Rose Society, of whom the secretaries were Revd H. H. d'Ombrian (page 68) and Edward Mawley: Mawley and Gertrude Jekyll wrote *Roses for English Gardens*, 1901, which summed up the Victorian taste for Hybrid Perpetuals and Teas which was about to give way to the new Hybrid Teas, of which the first 'La France' (pink) had appeared in 1867. The variety and colour of roses for such a garden was a personal taste, but the bushes for these beds and the bank were to be chosen from the accepted favourites, many of them also available as climbing roses for the pergola.

Introduction

The Rosarian's Roses, c.1900:

Hybrid Perpetuals (developed in the early 19th century from *Rosa chinensis* and *R. damascena* for more than one flowering during June and July and favourites from 1840):
'Baroness Rothschild', pink but no scent
'Charles Lefebvre', dark crimson, fragrant
'Doctor Andry', crimson exhibition rose
'Duke of Edinburgh', scarlet crimson
'General Jacqueminot', fragrant crimson
'Her Majesty', pale rose, scentless
'Louis van Houtte', dark crimson
'Margaret Dickson', creamy white
'Marie Baumann', carmine-red
'Mrs John Laing', rosy pink
'Ulrich Brunner', cherry red

Tea Roses were named for their scent which was reminiscent of tea chests from China and *Rosa moschata*, the musk rose: Teas were the first yellow shades but fragile and not easy to grow, needing most shelter:
'Anna Olivier', pale buff
'Catherine Mermet', pale pink
'Comtesse de Nadaillac', peach/apricot
'Doctor Grill', rosy fawn
'Madame Hoste', yellow
'Maman Cochet', pale rose
'Niphetos', white

Hybrid Teas, from the crossing of the beautiful, delicate, scented Teas and the vigorous but generally unruly Hybrid Perpetuals: the earliest popular varieties were
'Augustine Guinoisseau', blush white
'Bardon Job', crimson
'Captain Christy', blush white
'Caroline Testout', pink
'Gloire Lyonnaise', lemon white
'Gustave Regis', yellow
'La France', pale rose
'Mrs W. J. Grant', rosy pink
'Viscountess Folkestone', creamy white

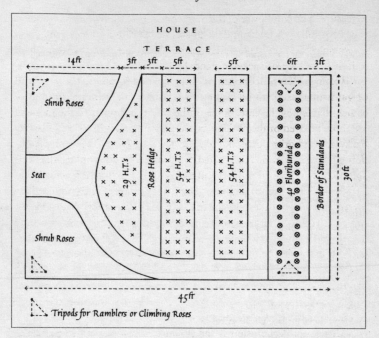

HOUSE

TERRACE

14ft · 3ft · 3ft · 5ft · 5ft · 6ft · 3ft

Shrub Roses

Seat · 29 H.T.'s · Rose Hedge · 54 H.T.'s · 54 H.T.'s · 40 Floribunda · Border of Standards · 30ft

Shrub Roses

45ft

⌐⌐⌐► *Tripods for Ramblers or Climbing Roses*

The Rose Enthusiast's Garden, 1958, a plan reproduced from F. Fairbrother's *Penguin Handbook on Roses* for a garden 45 feet by 30 feet devoted to Hybrid Teas, Floribundas and Standards planted in rows in bare earth beds. This plan too indicates changing fashions, with the introduction of the rose hedge so that not all the beds are seen at once, and the areas for Shrub Roses which can be underplanted with spring bulbs, daffodils, scilla, crocus and grape hyacinths. In 1958 the 'old-world charm' of the Shrub Roses was just returning to favour: the Hybrid Teas, Floribundas and Standards for this layout were mainly the mid-twentieth century introductions that we still use today.

cherries, small spiky and crawling conifers, sheets of heather and aberrations in gilding such as the overly golden elaeagnus, aucuba, *Euonymus* 'Emerald n' Gold' and even *Robinia* 'Frisia', which cause plant connoisseurs to reach for their dark glasses. There is a general rule that anything new, large and covered with flowers – especially delphiniums, larkspurs, lupins, gladioli and their kind, are bad taste, whilst the 'wild' and small-flowered are desirable: no garden of taste will tolerate frilled or large-flowered cyclamen but tiny white or purple *Cyclamen coum* are a treasure. The cult flower of the moment is the snowdrop, which addicts travel for miles in freezing dark to admire, kneeling in frost and snow to worship the minuscule variations in white and green, with perhaps a dash of yellow, of spur and pendant and cups.

Taken to logical conclusions these divided loyalties, the very stuff of gardening, seem to be leading to a fashionable minimalism, but of course that is not the case. Some of the smartest flowers of the moment are those beloved of the old florists, the single-species breeders of smoky backyards and grimy greenhouses: the double golden *Cheiranthus* (wall-flower) 'Harpur Crewe', the 'pasted' laced auriculas, the crinkled dianthus and ruched and frilled peonies and poppies. The distinction actually lies between the old (good) and new (bad), a rejection of the commercially forced and falsely iridescent for the sake of old varieties, driven by the rise of environmental consciences and historical appreciation. Au fond it is the difference between gardening, which is as old as human civilization, and horticulture, which is comparatively new. It is a symbolic and therefore potent distinction for a society that has perfected nostalgia; like the parable of the Prodigal Son, a sophisticated embrace awaits that which was lost, or nearly so, as against a chilly glance for conscientious labours that have been steadfastly with us all the time.

This state of confusion is the product of history, but in particular of the rise of garden history, which warrants some explanation. A nice beginning can be made with the forsythia, arching golden racemes against a cold blue sky, originally named by the Dutch botanist Martin Vahl for William Forsyth, George III's gardener and one of the insti-gators of what was to become the Royal Horticultural Society. Forsyth senior and his son, William Forsyth junior, were both in the original twenty-eight members of the society, present at the third meeting on 28 March 1804, but Forsyth senior died later that year.[9] Forsyth junior had written a modest *Botanical Nomenclature* in 1794, but he is credited with the first definitive draft of a history of gardens, which appeared, however, not in his name but as George William Johnson's *History of English Gardening* of 1826. Johnson was a barrister, the first of a grand flush of canny lawyers who easily adapted to gardening, and the acquisi-tion of Forsyth's researches made him into a garden writer; he published *A Dictionary of Modern Gardening* in 1846, then joined the magazine-market scramble with *The Cottage Gardener* in 1848. Though castigated for his 'cottages', all seeming to have a double coach-house attached, he resurrected forgotten histories of old London nurseries and market gardens.[10]

An interesting paradox arose with the arrival of the Prince Consort: Victorian popular gardening almost seemed to reflect the happy young Queen's discovery of 'the lore of plants and bees' and the beauteous scents of lilacs in the moonlit gardens of Windsor, under the tuition of her beloved bridegroom.[11] Albert the scientific was a great support to what was still the Horticultural Society of London, which had suffered a series of setbacks and scandals as the founding members faded and died. He engineered the charter to 'The Royal Horticultural Society' prior to the opening of the Society's new garden in Kensington Gore in June 1861. Prince Albert was accompanied by his royal children, who helped to plant a wellingtonia, but indulgent sighs at this pretty picture must have turned to scowls when he spoke of reuniting gardening with her sister arts of architecture, sculpture and painting.[12] This was not at all what the horticulturists wanted, but they were comforted by the splendid and brilliant displays of azaleas, orchids and pelargoniums. Goodness knows how history would have been changed by the Prince Consort's premature invention of the artist-gardener (though his words were almost certainly heard by the eighteen-year-old Gertrude Jekyll who was to become just that some thirty years later) but of course he was dead by the end of the year. Grief-stricken, the Queen asserted 'her peculiar and personal patronage' to the garden where Albert had wielded his spade; her subsequent seclusion made this but a gesture, but it was to institute a closeness, a royal cachet of approval of horticultural taste, that was to gild the horticultural lily down the years.[13]

The Victorian gardening juggernaut wanted neither history nor art, but a hybrid of the two; they wanted styles, styles which could be learned from popular manuals. Thus, a yard or two of bulbous balustrade and perhaps a fountain created an Italianate garden; some rocks, a tiny bridge, a lantern, maple and weeping willow was a 'Japanese' or 'Willow pattern plate' garden (which inspired the persisting impracticality of a weeping willow, a large and thirsty tree, in small gardens). French parterres, Elizabethan knots, the Alhambra re-born at Elvaston in Derbyshire, China and Egypt at Biddulph Grange, and 'Ye Herbe Garden' spelled out in clipped santolina at Broughton Castle, as well

Introduction

as the pioneering Lamport gnomes, all were part of the eclectic band-wagon of which we are the horrified heirs.

To confront this chaos two large and ebulliently forceful men emerged, one an architect, the other a gardener. The architect was William 'Topsy' Morris who founded the Society for the Protection of Ancient Buildings with his friend Philip Webb in 1877. Morris and Webb preached architecture with all the whims of design left out, a return to vernacular traditions, the hand-crafted, native ways of doing things rather than the foreign, imported or 'learned formation'. His interest in textiles led Morris to research dyes made from plants (he was habitually dressed in indigo-dyed cottons and wools) and study old herbals, Leonard Fuchs' *De Historia Stirpium* of 1542 and John Gerard's *Herball or Generall Historie of Plantes*, for his fabric designs, especially Sow Thistle, Black Poppy, Daisy, Eyebright, Wild Artichoke and common Willow (the native *Salix alba*). His other great designs featured notable garden pests, 'Strawberry Thief', 'Brother Rabbit' and 'Wood-pecker'. Morris, with his Arts and Crafts beliefs and socialism was against the grain of Victorian high gardening: he introduced a left-wing bias to conservation which was always to mark radical romance. In *News from Nowhere* he enshrined his reverence for the refuge of the old, historic garden, '. . . the picture of the old house by the Thames to which the people of this story went', Kelmscott Manor: at the end of their journey when they reach the door in the wall, 'my companion gave a cry of pleasant surprise and enjoyment; nor did I wonder, for the garden between the wall and the house was redolent of the June flowers, and the roses were rolling over one another with that delicate superabundance of small well-tended gardens which at first takes away all thought from the beholder save that of beauty. The blackbirds were singing . . . the doves coo-ing on the roof ridge . . . and the swifts wheeled whirring about the gables. And the house itself was a fit guardian for all the beauty of this heart of summer.'[14]

Morris awakened the appeal of the dignified old garden. His Art Workers' Guild fellows, John Dando Sedding (*Garden Craft Old & New*, 1891) and Reginald Blomfield (*The Formal Garden in England*, 1892) did the field work, seeking out the seventeenth-century stone glories of Haddon Hall, Montacute, Brympton d'Evercy, Edzell and Balcaskie, old gardens which had mercifully been spared the attentions of 'those heaven-directed geniuses' – as Sedding dubbed 'Capability' Brown and Humphry Repton. There just might have been an alternative agenda, not purely historic, by claiming gardens as the rightful realm of architects: garden architecture took on a weighty meaning as exemplified by Robert Lorimer and Edwin Lutyens, with the latter's dictum 'that there was no such thing as a free curve' allied to Gertrude Jekyll's love of 'sanity, serenity and sobriety' in old gardens. But her planting, added to the architectural geometry in Lutyens's gardens, was of the highest artistry – and not for the first time the shade of Prince Albert must have had cause to smile.[15]

Morris's ebullient alter ego was a young Irish gardener, a garden boy who had slaved at washing pots and potting up, at planting out and clearing away, named William Robinson. He came to think the whole performance a waste of time and plants, and betook himself to London where he was employed by Robert Marnock at the Royal Botanic Society's garden in Regent's Park to collect native plants. After travelling on the Continent and to America as a journalist, including writing for *The Times*, Robinson published *The Wild Garden* in 1870, and sank his savings into starting *The Garden* magazine the following year. While he was not against exotics and imported plants, he was against their domination: Robinson was the environmental complement to Morris's artistic belief in history, and in his writing, especially in *The Wild Garden*, he revealed plants in habitats where they thrived: Cheddar pink, arabis, viola and saxifrage on stone walls, ferns in wet ravines, spring bulbs at the margin of the wood, and double crimson peonies blowing amongst long summer grasses – seen 'to fine effect' in the garden of a friend. In a 1983 reprint, Richard Mabey welcomed *The Wild Garden* into 'its late inheritance', so closely did it foretell the aims of a generation of 'green' gardeners and conservationists who had emerged almost a hundred years after it was written.[16]

In the late nineteenth century Morris and Robinson's radical views were only aired to a liberal fringe: Robinson was too efficient an editor to allow them to compromise his magazines' popularity. *The Garden* was published weekly from 1871 until 1927, the chief competitor to the older (1841) *Gardeners' Chronicle* which had close affiliations with the Royal Horticultural Society: both magazines were aimed at professional gardeners. (In 1879 Robinson also launched my own favourite periodical

Gardening Illustrated, of 'middle class' appeal and lasting until 1956 in the *Country Life* stable.) Surprisingly it was the *Chronicle* which on Saturday, 29 September 1894 led with an article on fifteenth-century gardening. The article debated the meaning of obscure words such as Flos campi (*Lychnis coronaria*), 'dyllys' (dill), and 'parrow', 'pympernold' and 'mouseer', which had been found in a book of poetic instruction in the library of Trinity College, Cambridge, by the Hon. Alicia Amherst while researching her *History of Gardening*. Published by Bernard Quaritch the following year, this was a landmark book, highly readable and with an immense bibliography from libraries at Hatfield and Kew (where an outline for a general history by Sir William Hooker of 1821 had been found) as well as from Cambridge and the library of the author's father, Baron Amherst of Hackney. It revealed the linguistic and scientific demands of garden history, the need for an academic's care and yet an artist's appreciation of the broader pictures of history and geography, as well as a philosopher's insight into human nature. This was not something for *Gardeners' Chronicle* readers to dabble in on a wet afternoon. This was a serious subject.

Despite the seventy years between Johnson's *History* and Alicia Amherst's, the time was not yet right. The gardens of the 1890s were all too gloriously thriving in a most prosperous present. Why would they need a past? The National Trust was founded also in 1895 to protect the 'wild' like the Lake District fells, and rescue small and ancient vernacular buildings, like Alfriston Clergy House; these were under threat, but gardens were safe, secure and private.

One example has to carry the story forward from here, for garden history is above all specific, all gardens are different and it is their individual encounters with history that bring it alive. Coombe Abbey is in the middle of England, to the south-east of Coventry, and tells a splendidly typical story: it was a Cistercian abbey, dissolved by Henry VIII, sometime the home of the young Princess Elizabeth, where she played with her aviary and 'fairy farm' (*Plate 4*). Later it was the home of Lucy Harington, Countess of Bedford; a gardener, worshipped incidentally by John Donne, she sold it to pay her gambling debts in 1622. Under the new owners the Cravens, Coombe entered the catalogue of splendid formal gardens, *Britannia Illustrata*, with a bird's eye view of its walks and avenues by Knyff and Kip, though an eighteenth-century

Craven called in Capability Brown to sweep all this away. 'He has ruined old avenues and not planted in their place half enough,' commented Viscount Byng on his travels in 1789. Brown had made a lake and carriage drives through the parkland, and the deer were able to take titbits from the house windows for another hundred years, until the 2nd Earl Craven, flush with good fortune, called in William Eden Nesfield to re-medievalize the once-medieval abbey in high Victorian fashion. Nesfield dug a moat and used the spoil to level off a terrace on the south front of the house, and called in his father, William Andrews Nesfield, the doyen of formal revivalists, to design some fancy fan parterres.[17] At this point a young man, perhaps a garden boy still, named William Miller, started at Coombe where he was to work for forty years; the 2nd Earl died in 1866 but gardening had enslaved the Cravens, and work carried on for the 3rd and 4th Earls, their resources refreshed when the latter married the sixteen-year-old daughter of a New York millionaire in 1893. The great garden at Coombe was completed for the young American countess in the year of Queen Victoria's Diamond Jubilee, 1897, a Victorian overlay of some 180 acres of ornamental gardens and woodlands, on a park of 650 acres, set in an estate of 7000 acres. We can see Coombe in all this glory because William Miller – who had risen to head gardener and retired to become a landscape gardener – put down his pen one day in that year of 1897 and applied his name stamp to a magnificent watercolour plan he had made, and which survives.[18] Miller's plan shows the forty-acre garden of avenues and carriage drives, interspersed with walks, shrubberies, flower rondels, a bowling green, beds for display, wild flowers and spring bulbs in grassy meadows and planted islets in the lake. Though this was a pleasure garden for the Abbey, its heart was the head gardener's kingdom, the walled garden with his house, the bothies, greenhouses, hotbeds, vegetable and cutting gardens, and even a paddock for the pony that mowed the lawns. This was forty years of labour, a life's work, brought to entire and perfect completion in the most glorious year of the Queen Empress's reign.

Tragedy struck at Coombe Abbey, as it did everywhere else, with the First World War. The Cravens' eldest son was wounded and gassed serving with the 3rd Battalion of the Hampshire Regiment; in July 1921 the 4th Earl was drowned from his yacht *Sylvia* at the Cowes Regatta. As the now 5th Earl was incapable of coping with the demands of death duties and necessary reorganization of the estate, it was decided to sell.

Coombe's plight was far from unique; hundreds, if not thousands of gardens with 700 or 800 years of history, were in a similar plight, and in the 1920s and 1930s, though the conservation movement was forming, there were many other demands. The Council for the Preservation of Rural England was founded in 1926 to fight urban sprawl and the despoliation of the countryside. The Institute of Landscape Architects (1929) were anxious to establish themselves in the line of inheritance from Brown and Repton but to convert rather than restore historic landscapes. The Georgian Group, founded by Robert Byron and Lord Rosse in George VI's and Queen Elizabeth's coronation year, was intended to fight the destruction of eighteenth-century buildings. On the garden side, Marie Luise Gothein's two-volume *History of Garden Art*, translated from the German by Mrs Archer Hind, was published in 1928; and valuable research was published by the prolific Eleanour Sinclair Rohde, a bookish heroine interested in herbs and medieval gardens, who published *The Story of the Garden* in 1932 and catalogued Colonel Leonard Messel's antique library at Nymans before it was largely destroyed by fire in 1947.

The Coombe Abbey estate was auctioned in several lots in 1923 and bought by men of substance who prized its status and privacy, and perhaps prevented it from becoming a building site, but also treated the garden as treasure trove, selling off every movable feature without compunction. Mighty Stowe, 'A Work to wonder at' according to Alexander Pope, endured a similar fate in the 1920s, its fabulous statuary snapped up by men of new wealth such as Sir Philip Sassoon (Trent Park and Port Lympne) and Lord Fairhaven at Anglesey Abbey who were making their own garden-symbols of status. In far away 1974, Miles Hadfield was to write in the catalogue of the SAVE exhibition 'The Destruction of the Country House' that 'surely we can trace the decline [of gardens] to the outbreak of war in 1914' – but in all that time no one ever did.

The Royal Horticultural Society gained its familiar locations in the early 1900s, with the Vincent Square headquarters and the exhibition (Old) hall, as well as the garden at Wisley; the second (New) hall was built in 1928. At first, the Society was elitist and elderly, many clerics and sprightly octogenarians trotting up to the imposing entrance in

Vincent Square to an unchanging routine of specialist committees on orchids, narcissus or 'the floral', at which they put on spectacular displays and awarded themselves medals. Though the Society began the century as one of many large societies up and down the country with active memberships, the centrifugal lure of London and a national remit was attracting more and more nurseries and exhibitors to the fortnightly shows, which the public could pay to see. From the 1950s, the RHS enjoyed spectacular commercial and popular success.

There were two subtle but powerful influences which were affecting historic gardens and conservation, a matter which came to the fore with the National Trust's wartime scheme to assess the 200 best country houses with a view of saving at least some of them. This inspired the formation of a National Trust and Royal Horticultural Society joint committee to save important gardens and fostered the climate for the Garden History Society. In retrospect this tremendous initiative was influenced by a love of rhododendrons and the rediscovery of Capability Brown: though oddly enough it was Vita Sackville-West, who hated rhododendrons and had little time for Brown, who was asked to make a broadcast appeal for support and funds for the Gardens Committee, of which she was a founder member, and she was also influential in the decision that Hidcote Manor (neither rhododendrons nor Brown) was the first garden to be saved.

The National Gardens Scheme, through which private gardens opened to raise money for charity, had started in 1927 and it was through one of the founders, Mrs Christopher Hussey at Scotney Castle, that the saving of gardens became one of the causes to benefit. Christopher Hussey, who was architectural editor at *Country Life*, had written his book on *The Picturesque* (1927) from his understanding of his grandfather's creation of the romantic and rhododendron-filled landscape garden at Scotney, and from 'his appreciation of the link between the view from the window in the library . . . and the books on its shelves'.[19] Hussey was a powerful voice in the Georgian revival and through his interest *Country Life* published a string of books on houses and gardens open to the public in the late 1940s and early 1950s. Dorothy Stroud's *Capability Brown*, delayed by the war, eventually appeared in 1950, with an introduction by Hussey who noted that it filled a gap 'in the history of national art that has been as regrettable as it can now be perceived to be large'.[20] This was the redemption of Brown, who had been so hated by the Arts and Crafts believers for sweeping away the old formal gardens they loved.

Not surprisingly, the small and fairly close-knit group who formed what we would call the 'conservation lobby' possessed similar opinions, and the National Trust's early preponderance of eighteenth-century houses is matched by large, romantic gardens, usually with rhododendrons: these include Bodnant (the home of 2nd and 3rd Lords Aberconway, both Presidents of the RHS), Nymans, Sheffield Park, Rowallane and Mount Stewart in Northern Ireland, Trengwainton and Glendurgan, Trelissick in Cornwall, Scotney Castle (on the tragically early death of Christopher Hussey in 1960) and Cotehele (in springtime one wonders if there can be any Cornish cove bereft of rhododendrons?), Wakehurst, Stourhead, Cragside and Plas Newydd.

It was perhaps in protest at too many rhododendrons, but definitely because of another important book, that the Garden History Society was started in 1965. The book was published in the best promotional traditions of the Shell Guides, in response to the popularity of garden visiting. A small and copious nugget (the first garden history book I ever owned) the *Shell Gardens Book* was edited by Peter Hunt in 1964. He had drafted in as contributors landscape architects and horticulturists as well as gardeners Margery Fish, Christopher Lloyd and Graham Stuart Thomas, and some of the developing breed of garden-biased historians, Miles Hadfield, Edward Hyams, David Green and Barbara Jones. Small, intense, black-and-white pages bulged with information on people, styles and features from Oxbridge medieval to Robinson and Jekyll, with the first county by county list of historic gardens. The tremendous effort of getting everyone and everything together for the *Shell Gardens Book* gave Peter Hunt the idea of a society.* 'In the summer of 1965,' remembers Kay Sanecki, 'when I was his p.a., we talked about (a society) over tea . . . in the Charing Cross Hotel', near the publisher's office in Bedford Street, Strand. As a result Peter Hunt telephoned Miles Hadfield, Kenneth Lemmon and Anthony Huxley 'and one or two others', which resulted in a circular letter, an enthusiastic response, and a meeting

* The Georgian Group's support for eighteenth-century buildings had been extended by the Victorian Society, founded in 1958 by the Countess of Rosse, with support from John Betjeman and Christopher Hussey, with the gift of Lady Rosse's grandfather's Linley Sambourne House in Kensington, so 'groups' were in the air.

in November 1965 at Vincent Square. Between forty and fifty people turned up, the landscape architect Frank Clark took the chair, a society was agreed, a committee elected and Kay Sanecki ('I was the girl with a pen in my hand') found herself the secretary. She remembers going home with a three guinea subscription from thirty-seven people and opening the bank account the following day: Oliver Dawson was the first treasurer, shortly followed by Denis Wood, of Woods of Taplow, the most prestigious landscape gardening firm of the day.[21]

The young Garden History Society applauded Betty Massingham's biographical resurrection of Gertrude Jekyll, but preferred to find their *raison d'être* in earlier times under the academic influences of John Harvey (who always admitted to stopping at 1800), Christopher Thacker and Ray Desmond (both of whom could be persuaded to the end of the nineteenth century). This view was justified by the first triumph in restoration, when the National Trust asked for help with the mysterious Dutch-inspired water garden at Westbury Court on the shores of the Bristol Channel, in the late 1960s (*Plate 3*). Serious academic restoration first proved its worth here: the foreignness of the long-legged pavilion, which seems to have walked out from *The Game of Ninepins* by Pieter de Hooch, the austere hedges flanking the straight canal topped by jolly yew pyramids and holly balls and, most evocative of all, the elaborately espaliered apples, Court Pendu Plat of 1613, Calville Blanc d'Hiver even older (1598) and Golden Reinette and Catshead, known in the mid-seventeenth century (*Plate 2*).[22] Westbury Court gave garden academics a heady impression of Lazarus-like resurrection, and with a change of chairman and secretary in 1972 to Ted Fawcett and Mavis Batey they 'chose to campaign'.[23] During the 1970s and early 1980s there was a terrific raising of the historic garden profile by the efforts of a devoted band, and what the subsequent chairman Keith Goodway nicely called 'a network of kitchen tables around the country'.[24] The redoubtable Mavis Batey fought her planning inquiry battles with a velvet-gloved toughness in defence of ancient acres or avenues, in the name of Painshill or Levens (which Loudon had once defended from dahlias), and took her persuasive powers to Whitehall, where it was promised that outstanding parks and gardens would have protected status, provided that the Society could justify them. So the Society set out to list, county by county, the best historic parks and gardens in the land.

It was a Pandora's Box, sparking a myriad of responses from local historians and local authorities, such as Hampshire County Council, who started to assess history on the ground, as well as in bricks and mortar. But how do you say a garden is outstanding when it is merely a wilderness of brambles, tumbled pavilions and leaking pools? This is the subject of endless debates and comprises the essential fascination of garden history – a great garden may be fragmented into other people's gardens (as at Claremont and Esher Place) or it may have become a nature reserve (as Ellen Willmott's Warley Place). Often it is in institutional ownership (and the caring professions and religious institutions are the worst), or part of an hotel or a school. As a result gardens became of interest to a broad spectrum of the burgeoning environmental lobby: the Countryside Act of 1968 gave local authorities the powers to buy sites for country parks, which allowed many mouldering giants to be adapted to public use. This was what happened to Coombe Abbey, so much a part of fashionable design history for almost five hundred years. It had declined so far by the 1960s that it was overlooked, but was rescued by Coventry City Council in 1964. It now entertains all-comers and exuberant children and picnicking travellers can enjoy its spaciousness, magnificent trees and sense of history, and indeed it is part of a nationwide network of such caravanserai for the historically-minded, along with Charles Barry's Italianate Trentham country park in Staffordshire, and the curious Elvaston country park outside Derby, which includes the remains of Beau Petersham's bower of Mon Plaisir for his beloved Maria Foote, and many of William Barron's fantastic clipped yews.

Back in the 1970s the idea of historic gardens caught all sorts of imaginations. The little church of St Mary at the gates of Lambeth Palace, which had the tombs of the Tradescants in its tiny churchyard was (strangely, on the Archbishop of Canterbury's doorstep) threatened with demolition: it was rescued by the remarkable energy and persuasive charm of Rosemary Nicholson, who set up the Tradescant Trust in 1976 under the patronage of the Prince of Wales and the Marchioness of Salisbury. St Mary's is now restored and carefully converted into the Museum of Garden History, a friendly and thriving oasis of exhibitions and information for visitors to London. A little farther to the west, at about the same time, gardens took the fancy of the flamboyant director of the Victoria & Albert Museum, Roy Strong, who won sponsorship from ICI and the Sainsbury Family Charitable Trust for a mammoth 'One Thousand Years of British Gardening' exhibition, showing during the summer of 1979. The exhibition sparkled with Sir Roy's application of his own expertise in Renaissance art and history to gardens of that period (this was, and is, unique amongst notable historians) and made the Royal Horticultural Society, the National Trust, the Royal Botanic Garden at Kew and the Royal Institute of British Architects' drawings collections and library, turn out their treasures, some of which they did not know they had. It also did no harm to the saleroom value of garden art and antiques. Perhaps the dusty recesses of the Lindley Library in Vincent Square yielded the most amazing accumulated evidence of Victorian gardening which had long lay unregarded: a young Canadian scholar with a deliciously dry sense of humour, named Brent Elliott, had just arrived at the RHS and, as part of a series of garden history commissioned by Sir Brian Batsford, he wrote *Victorian Gardens*, which 'a general consensus', he discovered, thought 'was the nadir of British gardening'.[25]

The intellectual pollination of any small world brings people to the right places at the right time, and garden history clearly excels at this. Roy Elliott, a distinguished member of the Alpine Garden Society and the RHS, and an original contributor to Peter Hunt's *Shell Gardens Book*, was concerned that old cultivars and varieties of garden plants were fast disappearing, and also that any survivors might not be recognized in old gardens being demolished or those enthusiastically restored. Thus the horticultural contribution to this mania for the past came about with the formation of the National Council for the Conservation of Plants and Gardens in 1980. The NCCPG, also under the Prince of Wales's patronage, was an agent for dispersal as well as collection, and has to date set up thirty-nine county-based groups and almost 600 national collections of individual genera. Garden historians find fellowship (and sometimes cross swords) with botanists, botanical artists and 'collectors' – a wider spectrum of talents and interests – over this most precious and ephemeral of the nation's treasures. Graham Stuart Thomas's collection of roses at Mottisfont Abbey now does double-duty as the NCCPG's national collection of pre-1900 shrub roses; spectacular Leeds Castle in Kent holds collections of monarda and nepeta; but collections are also held by private individuals and sometimes in very small gardens – mother and daughter Charis Ward and Sarah Sage have euphorbias and sedums at Abbey Dore Court in Herefordshire; and to watch the modest and slight figure of Noreen Jardine ushering her foxglove charges between her own tiny garden and the Jephson Gardens in Leamington Spa is to see a connoisseur at work.[26]

It was also in the 1970s that the landscape architect Bill Mount persuaded Somerset County Council that they owned a national treasure in the garden of the County Fire Service Headquarters at Hestercombe, outside Taunton, with its spectacular terraces and garden buildings by Sir Edwin Lutyens (*Plate 6*). The complete planting plans for the beds and borders by Gertrude Jekyll had been carefully kept by a former gardener: thus the first really complex planting restoration, using old named varieties, was set in motion and, in the wake of Betty Massingham's biography, it was this that launched the Jekyll revival. Bill Mount moved to Sussex, where he found a generous patron for the first County Gardens Trust in John G. McCarthy, and another early restoration project was funded for the old garden at Brickwall, Northiam, the former Frewen family home. The beginnings of garden trusts can be found in the Garden History Society's need for local help with county-by-county lists and in the NCCPG's county groups searching out plants in old and ruined gardens, when they found that they had enough to do rescuing the plants without being involved with the fate of the gardens as well.

Two new varieties can now be added to the collection of garden historians: first, landscape architects who quite rightly felt it would be profitable to brush up their historical techniques in order to manage restoration projects as consultants and, secondly, private owners who realized they just might have a national treasure outside their windows. When the first spoke to the second there were often eruptions, sometimes of a magical kind, as when Hal Moggridge, landscape architect and heir to Brenda Colvin's practice, took Mrs Maldwin Drummond of Cadland in Hampshire, a small Brownian gem of a landscape devised for her husband's family in 1778–9, to a conference he felt might interest her at Blenheim. Of course some landscape architects, notably Ralph Cobham and Hal Moggridge, had been thinking historically for some time, and the 1983 conference held by the Garden History Society in the riding school at Blenheim was both to mark the bicentenary of the death of Brown, and also air the early stages of the preparation for a management plan to carry Blenheim into the next millennium. Mrs

Drummond heard Dorothy Stroud on Brown, showing that garden history began with geography and archaeology: she heard David Green, historian of Blenheim for almost forty years, on his beloved palace and unique understanding of Vanbrugh, Hawksmoor and Henry Wise;[27] and she heard what was to be done with history, and how this most triumphal landscape of history could be enjoyed and funded in the present, for the future.[28] She went home to Hampshire and – with the enlightened support of the County Council – she established Hampshire Gardens Trust, a partnership of public funding to support the organization of voluntary interest and work for the care and sometimes restoration of local gardens and parks 'at risk', for the education of children through improvements to school grounds and for the creation of new green places. Hampshire Gardens Trust drew upon a natural constituency of wide interests, it was an idea that quickly caught on in other counties and spread like wildfire, an enthusiasm reflected even in the corridors of power, where Dr Christopher Thacker was now established as the inspector of historic gardens and landscapes at English Heritage.

And then came the little matter of a wind. A tornado had been recorded at Wisley in 1965 and there was a damaging squall in 1990, but between these was the Great Storm of 1987, which scooped all these burgeoning projects of garden history up into the air and scattered them. The garden establishment of Britain was about to be transformed, when, in the early hours on the morning of 16 October 1987 the channel ferries ceased operating in the face of an unbelievable immediate weather warning. The storm growled and crashed its way across southern England, from Dorset to Norfolk for four or so dawn hours; some thought it was a nuclear attack, many could not believe their eyes as pine trunks and garden buildings whirled about their heads, salt spray could be tasted in north Surrey, and views unseen for two hundred years were opened up to astonished eyes. The storm unravelled a century of sentimentality and lax management of trees, simply felling the frail and old and shallow-rooted ruthlessly.*

* I write this with some shame, having been absent during these appalling hours, at the end of a lecture tour in Boston, in a party which included John Bond, Keeper of the Savill and Valley Gardens in Windsor Great Park; the first news came at breakfast when we learned that John had been summoned home in the middle of the night, Boston time, to rescue his royal charges.

Introduction

It was an ill wind, but it found garden historians ready: questions about reparation were asked in both Houses of Parliament and the shock and horror of the storm made the government realize that historic gardens must have public funding. The English Heritage inspectorate was enlarged and funded to cope with claims for restoration schemes, and evidence of both historical research and future management, usually with some arrangement for public access, were the conditions of grants. Grant-aid, with all its drawbacks and opportunities, thus arrived in the garden, as it had so long before in the worlds of the other arts; it encouraged a great sorting of priorities (just how many Brown or Repton parks or even Lutyens/Jekyll gardens were vital to posterity?), it drafted in private donors and sponsorship, and it fostered a small but vital world of professional expertise, supported by the post-graduate diploma courses in Garden Conservation offered in London at the Architectural Association and in York at the King's Manor Institute of Advanced Architectural Studies. Many of the postgraduates for both courses come from the continent, where there is a network of visits, exchanges and conferences, including a European Gardens Scholarship financed by Nancy McLaren in the name of her late husband Martin McLaren, who was Gertrude Jekyll's grand-nephew.

In all these post-war years, whilst garden history was invented on kitchen tables around England and great winds blew, the Royal Horticultural Society – mostly facilitated, I suspect, by the expertise among its governing body of merchant bankers who were also keen gardeners – had been re-inventing itself and assuming the most splendiferous guise, one of which Sir Joseph Banks would have been inordinately proud. Prince Albert's smiles over the resurgence of gardening as an art would have turned to rollicking laughter had he been able to see a splendid exhibition at Sotheby's in January 1987 celebrating 'The Glory of the Garden', or – as all the exhibits came from friends and supporters of the RHS and were definitely not for sale – how very many rich and cultured friends the Society had now. Gardens had reached the dizzy heights of Bond Street at last – fantastic paintings of gardens by Thomas Robins the Elder, by Elgood and Parsons, flower-wreathed furniture painted and embroidered, silver flowers, botanical paintings by Ehret, van Huysum and van Os and Eliot Hodgkin's tempera *Twelve Months of the Year*, flower-sprigged Spode and Swansea creamware and, as a relief, curious gadgets: a cucumber slicer and nineteenth-century aphis brushes. Best of all were the whimsies, the eighteenth-century Chelsea china pea pods lent by HM The Queen Mother, the fruit paintings, the plant labels, and some of the vast collection of *cartes visites* Brent Elliott had brought out of dusty graves – a nineteenth-century portrait gallery of nurserymen, botanists and gardeners by the dozen, the back-bone of the Society.

No reason for this exhibition was given, and it is tempting to suggest that the Society was simply displaying the fact that it too had a historical appreciation; or was there a sense of farewell to the old RHS as most of us had known it? In the 1990s one could not open the now large and commercially colourful *The Garden* (a title appropriated in 1975 from William Robinson's defunct magazine of that title to popularize the RHS Journal) without wincing at the battery of advertising: Wisley was no longer simply the garden; its status was shared with two (frankly) not even mediocre places, Rosemoor and Hyde Hall. At Wisley somewhere behind the veil of commercialism – the best garden bookshop in the world (if you could negotiate the china and table napkins) and the 'best plant centre' somewhere between these and a pretty good restaurant – was a garden, which for most people seemed to be almost irrelevant. Chelsea Flower Show, since the war the very heart of the competitive bartering of plants and garden-making contracts, has become more of a media event than anything else: when something potentially more spacious and useful emerged in the shape of the Hampton Court Show, the RHS promptly took it over. Those three little letters RHS have become inescapable, spreading across the country on a new network of bumper flower shows, on garden activities from Logan to Trebah, on seemingly every vaguely horticultural outlet they can find (and someone has been carefully searching them out) from Exbury to Holden Clough.

The new RHS will, I predict, find itself about as popular as the Football Association or the English Test Cricket Board. The message of my book is that there is an alternative to commercial mayhem, and that the way to keep a haven of pleasure and peace (as opposed to what Robin Lane Fox has finally dubbed Exterior Decorating and a horticultural hell of instant plants in psychedelic colourways) is to enter the magical world of garden history. Its study reveals abundantly why we should protect and preserve the substance of the really great works of art, such as Stowe or Sissinghurst, retaining their essence by planting them according to their place and time. It teaches us to treasure all kinds of plants, even those with delicate, small and usually heavily scented flowers, so that they can be used in historic places to invoke the *genius loci*. It fosters a historical perspective that takes exception to the many ugly and barren places in everyday lives (ironically these are too often school grounds and children's formative landscapes), and encourages something to be done about them. And it encourages the making of gardens in urban settings.

The story of the Victoria Garden in Farnham demonstrates this point. The Garden now occupies a small but sensitive site in the centre of Farnham, next to the Sainsbury's car park, the site of an open air swimming pool opened to celebrate Queen Victoria's Diamond Jubilee in 1897 (*Plate 5*). The site had been fought over for many years until eventually the antagonism was such that only a garden could placate all the vested interests. Fund raising skills were harnessed to design and planting skills to create, not a bland, park-like public desert, but an exquisitely pretty small garden, formal, hard wearing, but wreathed in clematis and roses and scented with lavenders, a garden, immaculately cared for and now well into its third summer, which though open all the daylight hours has never been vandalized.

The realization of history on the ground informs and enriches the present and the lives of everyone involved in a remarkable way. A final example of the creative present that the past can inspire is the restoration of Hestercombe's Lutyens and Jekyll garden. It remained a flagship of restored delights throughout the 1980s, and in 1987 was one of the gardens which was filled with visitors on a fine summer afternoon to celebrate the 60th anniversary of the National Gardens Scheme. Every-one thought that the Lutyens celebration of stone building crafts and geometry, graced with Jekyll flowers was wonderful, but there were occasional rumblings about another garden, this one an eighteenth-century garden behind Hestercombe house, made by Coplestone Warre Bampfylde. One day, on a visit, a young man named Philip White literally opened a Lutyens doorway and glimpsed the overgrown valley beyond; he fell in love with this wilderness of old dreams and allowed it to change his life. With his wife's agreement, he gave up his job, mortgaged their home and acquired the Crown lease on the valley. He gathered a band of helpers and they set about clearing, discovering the lake and its rills and waterfalls, the old pathways and bridges, the foundations of temples and ornaments, other temples in ruin, until finally the whole romantic valley garden, made by the accomplished watercolourist and poetic friend of William Shenstone, was revealed. Through imagination and hard work Hestercombe now has two places in history, an eighteenth century and an early twentieth century, two gardens of contrasting characters and philosophies, a doubled sense of place that informs everything that happens there (*Plate 7*).

CHAPTER ONE

⊱⊱⊷❄❄⊶⊰⊰

The Purest of Human Pleasures?

Gardens and pleasure seem inextricably entwined, tied together as in a lovers' knot. Some historians hold that the only gardens worthy of the name are pleasure gardens, an understanding derived from the complex hierarchy of orchards, gardens and groves enjoyed by the Greeks.[1] These were all places associated with notions of the divine, of bliss, fertility, happiness and pleasure, invariably induced by the presence of gods and goddesses – Aphrodite, Tantalus, Epicurus – whose very names still carry pleasurable connections. For the Greeks the growing of vegetables was the lowly province of the poor: Pliny the Elder's 'chortus' are the fields of the poor. We have discarded this attitude, which comes with a classical education, for more catholic pleasures, shared by everyone who has grown, dug, cleaned and cooked the first new potatoes or harvested even the most lackadaisical lettuce with inordinate pride. There are many pleasures in gardening but this chapter is devoted to searching out the most deeply embedded, the sensual and sometimes sexual pleasure that is implicit in all ancient gardening traditions. Something other than pride or duty keeps us plodding up and down the lawn on a hot afternoon, something other than tidiness fires an onslaught on the couch and ground elder. Where do the hazy fantasies – that perhaps imagine the dance of the seven veils on a suburban terrace – come from?

That Elizabethan wizard Sir Francis Bacon must take some of the blame. Despite the bubble of his reputation having been pierced and re-blown so many times, and though he has been accused of the vilest crimes and perversions, his *Essays* remain unsullied and sublime. 'On Gardens', the most printed piece of garden literature – strangely bedfellowed with 'Vain Glory', 'Simulation and Dissimulation', 'Death' –

scribbled off in the long quietnesses of afternoons amongst the tapestries and flowers of his beloved Hertfordshire home at Gorhambury, with a breathtaking facility and ease, opens with thunder: 'God Almighty first planted a garden' and continues with a lilting breeze . . . 'And, indeed, it is the purest of human pleasures.'[2]

The purest of human pleasures. This phrase has become something of a mantra. Bacon had an enviable gift for memorable phrasing – he deals in allurement, in weaving silken webs around darker notions. Being human, we are hardly likely to derive too much pleasure from too much purity. Bacon's garden was certainly a refreshing respite from the intrigues of the Elizabethan court, but no garden of pleasure has ever been entirely pure (look at Eden, after all). No, he is fooling us; pleasure in gardens is rather more robust, it is sensual, physical, sexual, and we shall have to look elsewhere.

We shall have to begin at our beginnings, with the help of one of the most remarkable painters of modern times. The American artist Georgia O'Keeffe, who was born in 1887 and lived well into her ninety-eighth year, has been called 'the greatest painter of flowers in the history of Western art'.[3] Her images of giant peonies, irises, convolvulus, nicotiana, roses – in all she made over 200 flower paintings – leave the merely botanical far behind. They transport us to fantastic places, through virgin petticoats of double white peony or rose, down the deep, dark throats of purple irises. O'Keeffe said that she painted flowers for people in cities who never looked at them, but she painted 'as if we humans were butterflies' and on regular trysting terms with calyx, corolla and stigma. Her flowers are also deeply feminine, the work of a woman and artist 'in full bloom'. She seems to have divined the age-long lure of peony, iris and rose and jogged some primal memory in our minds. Perhaps it is the memory of the first journey we make, though I have never heard that anyone remembers the journey from our mother's womb to emerge from that soft cave between her legs. With her flowers O'Keeffe celebrates riotous colours and exquisite forms, but the strangest and most brilliant thing she does (that has caused most alarm and controversy) is to reveal them as our natal familiars.

When washed and swaddled and laid in our mother's arms, these familiars – huge coloured blossoms as big as our own heads – arrive as votive offerings at the bedside. They please our mother and make her smile, and the equation of flowers and pleasure is confirmed: the pungency of daffodils, or the heady sweetness of lilies, passes into infant sensory memory as good, synonymous with well-being and happiness. From the very beginning the fortunate child (and would it were the birthright of all children) put out to doze beneath the blossom trees, becomes quite naturally a creature of the flower world, a child of the garden. It is an existence endorsed in a hundred ways: 'Round and round the garden, like a teddy bear' sings some well-intentioned giant, and the rest is drowned in tickled laughter, and all-round congratulations. 'Mary, Mary, quite contrary, How does your garden grow?'; 'the maid is in the garden hanging out the clothes'; where can the magic beanstalk grow but in a garden? Where can poor Cinders be found when she is to try on the slipper that will make her a princess? There are flower fairies and 'Ring-a-ring of roses' . . . age-old images endlessly re-illustrated and renewed. And new garden familiars constantly appear: Bill and Ben the Flowerpot Men, Worzel Gummidge, the Herbs, Raymond Briggs's Snowman, perhaps even the Teletubbies and many more that creep into the infant heart and mind. Those grand viziers of nursery-rhyme land, Iona and Peter Opie, in their *Oxford Nursery Rhyme Book*, confirm that chanted rhymes and repeated friendly visions do, at some point and earlier than adults might think 'fire the fancy, charm the tongue and ear, delight the inward eye', as Walter de la Mare believed:

The Little Old Cupid

'Twas a very small garden, The paths were of stone,
Scattered with leaves, With moss overgrown;
And a little Old Cupid Stood under a tree,
With a small broken bow He stood aiming at me.

The dog-rose in briars Hung over the weeds,
The air was aflock With the floating of seeds;
And a little Old Cupid Stood under a tree
With a small broken bow He stood aiming at me.

The dovecote was tumbling, The fountain dry,
A wind in the orchard Went whispering by;
And a little Old Cupid Stood under a tree,
With a small broken bow He stood aiming at me.[4]

Robert Louis Stevenson created a classic of comfortable childhoods, for the children of the empire, *A Child's Garden of Verses*, where the familiar garden becomes a world of adventure, a field of dreams:

> Here is the sea, here is the sand,
> Here is the simple Shepherd's Land,
> Here are the fairy hollyhocks,
> And there are Ali Baba's rocks.

And the flowers 'all the names I know from nurse:/Gardener's garters, Shepherd's purse/Bachelor's buttons, Lady's smock/And the lady Holly-hock'. Stevenson, the adventure writer, created the garden as a beloved home but a stepping stone to adventure too: when the children longed to escape, as all children do, the whole magical universe awaited beyond the bedtime story:

> How many miles to Babylon?
> Three score and ten . . .
> Can I get there by candle-light?
> Yes, and back again.[5]

Infant expectations are not disappointed, and the land of fairytale opens wonderful gardens of long ago and far away. Hans Christian Andersen's stories exploit garden imagery in a way that the Brothers Grimm's do not. Andersen's tale of the Rose Elf introduces the myth of Isis and Osiris with the gruesomeness that fascinates exploring minds. The Rose Elf lives in the garden's most lovely rose, but coming home late one evening he finds the petals closed against him. He takes refuge in another rose, this one warmed open by the kisses of a girl who is in the garden bower with her lover. The Elf's sharp ears pick up their sad parting vows, the rose is given to the lover, and both Elf and rose find themselves on a journey. The lover meets a jealous brother, who kills him, and the outraged Elf returns home, hidden in a leaf in the mur-derer's hair: helplessly he watches the girl mourn, she goes to her lover's grave and retrieves his severed head, together with a sprig of jasmine growing nearby. Finding the largest flower pot she puts the head into it, covers it with earth and plants the jasmine sprig, watering it with her tears before she creeps away to die. In time the jasmine flowers and in each flower is a spirit; they discuss the dark deed with the Rose Elf, 'We know it, we know it,' they cry. The wicked brother takes the flowering jasmine to his room, and at night the Elf and his flowery witnesses leap out and kill the wicked murderer with poison darts.[6]

The garden can be the stepping stone to adventure but it remains a benevolent place, with the power to protect against the evil which may be found there, and even to redeem evil people and deeds. The lover's severed head in the flower pot is a pervasive image (and suggests a new aspect to Bill and Ben the Flowerpot Men) evoking the pagan head of the Green Man found in so many Christian churches, and the legendary Gardens of Adonis in which pots sown with wheat, barley, lettuce, fennel and flowers were carefully tended by the women of ancient Greece: after eight days these 'gardens' were carried in procession with images of the dead Adonis and flung into the river or sea to please the gods of rain and good harvest.[7]

Redemption of an evil garden owner is the moral of Oscar Wilde's 'The Selfish Giant': the giant will not let the poor children play in his lovely garden, he locks them out, and spring fails to come. Not only spring, but summer and the harvest fail; winter and frost reign within his garden walls, until one day the children creep back through a hole in the wall, and the trees and flowers blossom once more . . . all except one tree, beneath which stands a little boy in tears. The giant sees this from his window and walks out; the children scatter, except for the little boy whose tears have temporarily blinded him; the giant lifts him into the tree, which breaks into bloom. The giant is transformed: '"It is your garden now, little children", he says.' The wall comes down, the children play and the garden blooms. But the little boy has disappeared, and despite everyone else's happiness, the giant is heartbroken; generations of children play in the garden, but the ageing giant still mourns the boy. One winter's day he looks out to see the tree in blossom, and the little boy standing beneath it again. He rushes out to the child, and is pained to see the wounds on his hands and feet. '"Who art thou?" he asked, and fell to his knees. And the child smiled on the Giant, and said to him, "You let me play once in your garden, today you shall come with me to my garden, which is Paradise."' And in the wintry afternoon, the children came and found the giant, dead, all covered with blossoms.[8]

It may be said in passing that many of the best writers for children have purveyed the image of the garden as a place of innocent pleasures, a refuge from the difficulties of growing up. Wilde, Lewis Carroll,

Kenneth Grahame (especially in *Dream Days*, the forerunner to *The Wind in the Willows*), Arthur Ransome, Walter de la Mare, A. A. Milne and James Barrie have all been revealed to have more than a little in common with Milne's dormouse, blissfully happy in his bed 'Of delphiniums (blue) and geraniums (red).' The demands of adulthood, like the tutting Doctor determined to 'cure' the dormouse by teaching him the adult pleasures of 'endless chrysanthemums (yellow and white)', oppressed all of them in subtly differing way, but gave them all their wizardry with words.[9]

The worst nightmares of childhood can be eased in the garden. Andersen's 'Little Ida's Flowers' seeks to persuade the child that her flowers are not dead, but exhausted after a fabulous ball. Despite the daylight logic of planting seeds and watching the flowers reborn, the imaginative child demands a more flamboyant resurrection: that night Ida dreams of the Nutcracker Ball and how the flowers waltz, and one of the greatest spectacles of fantasy is born, Tchaikovsky's ballet music leading to Disney's *Fantasia*. It is all so wonderful that the death of the flowers is perfectly bearable, and Ida takes them solemnly out into the garden for decent burial, knowing they will return.

Much more important than absolute scientific accuracy in these garden tales, is the chance that somehow, somewhere, the child's real life will touch the fairytale. For me, in retrospect, it is the memory of a soft blue velvet cloak, worn over a prickly organdie dress, sprigged with forget-me-nots. I only wore the finery once (except for dressing up) when I was taken to a performance of *Nutcracker* at Bournemouth Pavilion, by my godmother, a large and gently humoured aunt named Ida, and we watched as the flowers waltzed.

The adult companion, the storyteller, is vitally important, for no matter what terrible things may happen in the garden, the love that comes with words and pictures obviates the evil, even makes it tantalizing and exciting. This becomes of greater importance the farther we wander (and it goes without saying that the television or video 'storyteller' falls short in providing such loving companionship). For the goal of childhood is of course Babylon, where all the best garden stories come from: Husain Haddawy, a recent translator of *The Arabian Nights* remembers his own childhood in Baghdad. 'I would go to sleep, still living with magic birds and with demons who pursued innocent lovers and haunted my dreams, and often dreaming, as I grew older, of a face in Samarkand that glowed with love and blessed my waking hours.'[10] Thus his grand-mother, his storyteller, guided him through the rites of passage, through the most sinister and scary nights, into adulthood. The *Nights*, the stories that Scheherazade tells (and she too becomes a beloved storyteller in the process) come from the most ancient garden culture; the whole motif of the epic is of a sacred garden, violated, and returned to fidelity again. The passion of the *Nights* may come as a shock to prudish, post-Victorian parents but the versions expurgated for Western sensibili-ties have weakened the power of the stories, and of the garden. Leaving out the sexual implications was to trick growing children, denying them an essential aspect of humanity that the children of the east took for granted. The new translations tell the whole story and the 'pleasures' of the gardens – which we suspected were there all the time – are openly revealed.

The stories were first set down in the tenth century; the prologue sets them in the Sassanid dynasty of Persia (c. AD 211–651) with two brothers ruling, one in northern India, the other in Samarkand. The younger, distraught at discovering his wife's infidelity, visits the elder, who is called Shahrayar, and is royally received and housed in a splendid pavilion in the garden. The garden, *chahar bagh*, is walled, with four water channels, imitating the four rivers that flowed from Eden. Pining from remorse the younger brother refuses all entertainments and remains in his pavilion. While his brother goes hunting he is amazed from his window to observe his sister-in-law 'strutting like a dark-eyed deer', entering the garden with twenty attendant slaves. The 'slaves' disrobe to reveal they are ten men and ten girls, who proceed to copulate zealously, whilst the lady avails herself of the vigorous Ma'sud, who has leapt over the wall to her. At noon they all bathe, re-robe and leave the violated garden. The watcher feels much better, quite cheerful in know-ing that he alone is not a cuckold, but Shahrayar has to be told of what took place in his absence, and in his fury he vows to take a different woman to bed each night and kill her in the morning. To stop this massacre of innocents, the Vizier's intelligent and educated daughter, Scheherazade, who has read history, philosophy, poetry and medicinal lore, volunteers to restore his faith in women by keeping Shahrayar listening night after night, and keeping faith with him. The gardens of the *Nights* are spectacular: 'the water flowed from a large pond to a smaller one, surrounded with sweet basil, lilies and narcissus in pots of inlaid gold . . . thickly intertwined branches were heavy with ripe fruits, so that whenever the windy host passed through them, the fruits dropped on the water, while birds of all kinds swooped down after them, clapping their wings and singing. To the right and left of the pond stood couches of sandalwood covered with silver.' With such blandishments the clever Scheherazade kept her listener wanting more . . . and it was invariably another garden of pleasures . . . the Garden of Delight, with a bower of trellised boughs hung with grapes like rubies, where the birds sang all kinds of songs, the trees were laden with all kinds of fruit, apples sweet and wild, Hebron plums 'whose colour no eyes have seen and whose flavour no tongue can describe'.[11]

Scheherazade, in winning her life and redeeming the angry Shahrayar and the beauty of his garden, reveals to the western world the glories of the Middle East, where gardens are so precious as to be truly Paradise. Such gardens, and their pleasures, hang suspended in our imaginations because of these tales or their many derivations; to western children so far away, even to present-day children in the Middle East (perhaps especially so in some countries) the drab fabric of real life is transformed by the gossamer of those distant romances.

Present-day children's books may give the impression that the garden is too tame for modern adventurers. Library shelves now offer the under-fives *A First Green Book*, and a growing choice of reading on the ozone layer, acid rain and saving whales. Novels and stories are set in space, in C. S. Lewis's Narnia, beyond Tolkien's Misty Mountains, in the wild landscapes of William Mayne and Alan Garner. The home garden, the emblem of modest security as the Hobbit's garden at Bag End, is left behind, for the grand adventure of growing up. But, it is as well to remember that, unlike other fantasy regions, the garden waits for the traveller to return.

There are many ways to rediscover gardens in youth, but it seems that to read just one book, or see one film, can be sufficient. Frances Hodgson Burnett's *The Secret Garden*, writes Alison Lurie, has become the most popular book in her courses on children's literature, and a cult amongst American college students for the last thirty years. The book, or rather its author, says Lurie, works nothing less than a psychological 'miracle' in transforming Mary (with her odd private games and cold indifference to her parents' deaths, who might be diagnosed as 'pre-schizoid') and the bedridden Colin (with his imagined hunchback, 'a classic hysteric with conversion syndrome').[12] The real miracle-worker is the garden, based upon the walled garden that still survives at Great Maytham, at Rolvenden in Kent, where Mrs Burnett wrote the story. The garden takes some of its magic from *The Arabian Nights*, for 'every-where were touches or splashes of gold and purple and white and the trees were showing pink and snow above [Colin's] head and there were fluttering of wings and faint sweet pipes and humming and scents and scents'. Mary and Dickon stared at Colin sitting in his wheelchair, who 'looked so strange and different because a pink glow of colour had actually crept all over him, "I shall get well, I shall get well! . . . Mary! Dickon! I shall get well! And I shall live forever and ever . . ."' And later, finally, the planting of the rose: 'The thin white hands shook a little and Colin's flush grew deeper as he set the rose in the mould and held it while old Ben made firm the earth. "It's planted!" said Colin at last . . . and with help he stood up as the sun went down . . . "I want to be standing when it goes, that's part of the Magic", Colin was standing on his own two feet, laughing.'[13]

The power of *The Secret Garden* is extreme; gardens do not have to raise Lazarus to win our affections. Rather the contrary: although the power of plants can often work instant miracles on distressed souls, the garden has by now firmly lodged itself in our minds as a place, readily available to most of us, where dreams can be fostered and just may come true, where there is always a second chance, a tomorrow.

The more adult pleasures come tumbling out of the pasts of the gardens of the Middle East: in fact the pleasurable images predominate in what we know of those gardens, the earliest in our garden heritage (the knowledge of Chinese gardens did not come to the west in any depth until the late nineteenth century). New translations of 'The Song of Solomon' reveal it not as the prim poem of the King James Bible, but an erotic evocation of love in a garden:

> How green
> our bed of leaves,
> our rafters of cedars,
> our juniper eaves.[14]

35

Pleasure gardens were the prerogative of great, and invariably despotic, power, and that rarity made them almost sacred, a precious rendezvous dedicated to the sensual gratifications of beings who were almost gods. The most fabulous gardening dynasty of Mogul emperors began with Babur, who was born in 1483. One of his Samarkand gardens, called Heart's Delight, had an avenue of white poplars leading to a turquoise gate in the wall; in Herat was a white garden with a summer 'joy-house'; and his favourite garden in Kabul was the Garden of Fidelity. Babur kept a diary, and the years ripple away in reading his entry of October 1519 from Kabul: 'the days of the garden's beauty: its lawns were one sheet of trefoil; its pomegranate trees yellowed to autumn splendour.'[15] Emperor Babur died in 1530 and was buried in the garden tomb he had designed for himself. The gardening passion passed lightly over his son, Humayun, but was reborn in his son Akbar, who succeeded in 1556 when he was only thirteen. Akbar famously stopped to wonder at the view of Lake Dal and the carpets of wild flowers whilst he was conquering Kashmir in 1586, but he was also the builder of the fabulous Fatepur Sikri where he gave garden banquets of surpassing wonder: honey breads and spiced vegetables on golden plates, dishes of lambs' brains and testicles, sea tortoise cooked in red chilli, mounds of saffron rice covered in beaten gold, all cooled off with sherbets, lemons, water melon and passion fruit and washed down with teas flavoured with cardamon and cloves.[16] Akbar's tomb at Sikandra is set in a *chahar bagh*, walled and minaretted, with four river rills. His son Jahanghir wrote memoirs, translated in the west in 1909[17] telling of the flowers of Kashmir, of 'mead after mead' of narcissi, violets and 'strange flowers', which turned out to be tulips. Jahanghir's wife was Nur Jahan, a poet, soldier, crackshot – shooting tigers from her howdah – textile designer, also a gardener, and perfumier. Nur Jahan noticed the oil on the pool water from the overhanging roses, ordered it to be collected, and so Attar of Roses was discovered. Jahanghir's greatest garden, Shalimar on Lake Dal, was completed by his son, Shahjahan, who succeeded in 1627; it was he who built the Taj Mahal for his wife Mumtaz Mahal who died bearing their fourteenth child. When William Daniell painted the Taj in 1789 it was framed by trees in garden plots, by planes, holm oaks and *Cercis siliquastrum*, which we have called the Judas tree. Edward Lear's diary for 16 February 1874 elaborates on the garden setting of the Taj:

'What a garden! What flowers! . . . the accompaniment and contrast of the dark green of cypresses with the rich yellow green trees of all sorts! And then the effect of the innumerable flights of bright green parrots flitting across like live emeralds; and of the scarlet poincinannas and countless other flowers beaming off the dark green . . . Poinsettias are in huge crimson masses, and the purple flowered bougainvillaea runs up the cypress trees . . . aloes, ferns and palms . . .' Lear concluded, 'let the inhabitants of the world be divided into two classes – them as has seen the Taj Mahal; and them that hasn't'.[18]

Undoubtedly, to western eyes, the ultimate pleasures of the Mogul gardens were centred upon the tantalizing secrets of the harem. The watcher in the garden, to some extent the voyeur, from the prologue to the *Arabian Nights*, is a constant theme. All too soon travellers from the west were watching the watchers: Sir Robert Ker Porter writes with steaming pen of the Shah's summer court at the Negauristan, the pool of clearest water with roses and other pendant shrubs growing near, throwing 'a beautifully quivering shade over the excessive brightness of the water'. Around the sides of the court are the chambers of the harem, and the ladies came out to bathe, often remaining in the water for hours, sometimes 'when the heat is very relaxing, come out more dead than alive'. The Shah would take his noonday repose in an upper chamber 'and if he be inclined, he has only to turn his eyes to the scene below to see the loveliest objects of his tenderness, sporting like naiads'.[19] We of the west have been the most determined watchers in the garden, most obsessed by these mystical arts of love, which we have attempted to emulate, often in ignorance of the fastidious codes of behaviour that ruled them. The young girls of the harem were condemned to life in a glamorous nunnery devoted to their earthly god: they strolled in closed and guarded gardens, eating sweetmeats, 'shooing away monkeys that scampered down to steal trinkets', playing chess, admiring the caged birds so like themselves or planning festivals to alleviate the boredom – for new year full moon the garden court was scattered with red earth and mica grains so that it glistened, the fountain water was coloured and the dancing girls' ankles were tied with bells.[20] We see the walled *chahar bagh*, with its rills and pools and delicate pavilions through a scented haze of jasmine, frangipani and narcissus, through eyes misty with covetousness of the harem ladies, their hands and feet patterned with henna, lips reddened with beeswax, hair scented with sandalwood smoke and braided with jewels, and in their flimsy silken garments. The erotic zenith of our imaginations sees them covering their bodies with oils, spices, almonds and rose petals, brushing this off for a fragrant sheen on the skin, painting their nipples, rouging the hollows of their breasts, spreading henna between the favourite's thighs to cool her premature ardour, or administering opium, betel nut mixed with lime, hashish and scented tobaccos through a hookah or rubies and emeralds crushed into wine . . .[21] We in the west are still agog that those small, jewelled gardens could contain such high arts of love – often the prerogative of some vastly overweight potentate, with rolling chins and corpulent frame, clad in fabulous furs and flower-sprigged embroidered silks, making the most virile, passionate Hollywood hero look like an amateur.

Although the power of these gardens lies in their aloofness and secrecy, the Mogul tradition physically migrated to the west by way of the exquisite gardens of Moorish Spain. There they enter the mythology of the Crusades and are embroidered with all the sensual trappings of love for things of the Mediterranean. The turbulent Muhammeds, the sons, brothers and nephews of the dynasty of Muhammed I, who died in 1273, made the fantastic gardens of the Alhambra, the Generalife, the Alcazar of Seville and the palace city of Medina Azahara: these were filled with exotic plants, imported from India, 'with scented flowers, singing birds and water wheels with rumourous sound' and remain to us as the remnants of a highly sophisticated garden technology that was established in Spain as early as the tenth century. The legendary Court of the Myrtles was built and its garden laid out for Yusef I, who reigned from 1333–54, and the Court of the Lions for his son, Muhammed V: they remain two of the most sublime, most worshipped gardens in the world, of exquisite proportions and magical lights. In his book *Medieval Gardens*, John Harvey records that at the same time as the Courts were made, one of the great garden books of Moorish Spain was being written, a poem about soils, water and levelling, manures and labours, by Ibn Luyun. He gives the basic rules for the creation of a pleasure garden of the warm south: it must have a south aspect, a shaded wall and watercourse, a pavilion in the centre with views, surrounded by flowers, fruit trees, with vines along the boundaries on arbours and pergolas.[22]

The Alhambra and Generalife were captured by Ferdinand and

Isabella, who entered Granada in triumph on 4 January 1492. Having captured, the west worshipped and was bemused by these gardens: Victor Hugo wrote ecstatically,

> L'Alhambra! Palais que les Genies
> Ont doré comme un rêve et rempli d'harmonies.

'It is difficult not to pile on the hyperboles . . .' Raleigh Trevelyan has written, 'evanescent, floating disembodied, sensuously exotic, luminous, a delicate cluster of soap bubbles, a rose preserved in snow, domes of heaven, kaleidoscope, terrestrial paradise, web of petrified lace, pearls in an emerald setting.'[23] In view of nearly 800 years of violent history, a succinct example of the redemptive powers of gardens.

It is only from the perspective of the Mogul and Moorish gardens of delicacies that it is possible to consider Versailles as clumsy, a blundering overblown extravagance of stony vistas, deafening fountains and exhausting proportions. But Le Nôtre's gargantuan masterpiece was the European response to the Eastern gardens of love. Versailles was also the expression of overweening power (the garden inspiration to be explored in the next chapter) and though its 100 hectares of avenues, diagonals, parterres, *bassins, tapis vert, bosquets, galeries, bains,* pyramids and potagers, and other endless vanities, have filled acreages of design analysis, it was also a garden of love. Love, not sequestered, scented and sensual as in the pleasure gardens of the harem, but love on a large scale, a society pastime, *les liaisons dangereuses.* The acres of design analysis usually fail on this essential, but Nancy Mitford's biography of Madame de Pompadour comes straight to the point: 'the real purposes of Versailles were the three pastimes of pleasure, love, gambling and hunting', and the less pleasurable, except for those who loved posing, the official entertainments. 'Love was played like a game' which had nothing to do with marriage, children or family, but was a daytime amusement: what could Versailles be designed for but endless promenading and fluttering of fans, kisses stolen behind enormous vases, love made in the arbours, tears dropped into the fountains? After dark, by the light of a thousand torches, the games continued through masked balls: with a cast of thousands (no one was ever refused admittance to Versailles if they were correctly dressed) and everyone bent on pleasure, it is not difficult to imagine how a whole uproarious tradition of French farce was born. In

February 1745 King Louis XV hosted one of Versailles' most splendid events – even in an existence devoted entirely to splendour – a masked ball to celebrate the marriage of the Dauphin to Infanta Maria-Thérèse Raphael. The King was determined to remain incognito, and when the doors of the royal apartment were opened 'a very curious procession lurched blindly into the ballroom; eight yew trees, clipped like those in the garden outside in the shapes of pillars with vases on them'. The Dauphin and his bride were recognizably dressed as a gardener and flower seller, but one ambitious court lady, thinking she knew which clipped yew was the king, nestled happily into its branches and into a dark corner. Imagine her shock when she returned to the ballroom, smoothing down her skirts, and realized that the king was unmasked, and had been conversing there all the time. Beware of topiary lest it is not always what it seems![24]

It was perhaps a small but significant sign of the times that French society and social climbers, as long as they were appropriately dressed, flocked to the King's pleasure gardens, whereas in England princes frequented pleasure gardens of the people. The Pleasure Garden became a commercial proposition in early eighteenth-century England at the hands of a man named Jonathan Tyers, who opened Vauxhall, formerly Foxhall, Gardens in 1732, a gala event attended by Frederick, Prince of Wales. Vauxhall was the first example of organized pleasure in a garden, the earliest precursor of Disneyland. It was very much a matter of publicity and public perception, and Vauxhall exploited both; Jonathan Tyers and his family, of whom little is known, were commercially astute enough to keep adding new and well-advertised attractions, making Vauxhall Gardens a success for well over a century, until 1859. With the opening of Vauxhall, Pleasure Gardens became a craze, with sixty-four listed in Warwick and A. E. Wroth's *London Pleasure Gardens of the Eighteenth Century*.[25] Ranelagh, opened in 1742 by the man who ran the Drury Lane Theatre, was the most fashionable of them all, with its famous Rotunda, a building exactly like the Round Reading Room in the British Museum, except that the surrounding walls were tiered with boxes for partying and perusing those thronging the arena below.

The potency of Pleasure Gardens was caught in novels, cartoons, and in a song by Michael Arne called 'Invitation to Ranelagh' of 1780, and quoted at the opening of Mollie Sands' classic book of that name:[26]

The Purest of Human Pleasures?

Hither Nymphs and Swains repair,
Quit the baleful scenes of strife,
Leave the rugged paths of care
And taste of joys that sweeten life.

The Pleasure Gardens swung like dazzling baubles before the young, who were mostly buried in rural England. Listen to Smollett's heroine Lydia Melford (in *The Expedition of Humphry Clinker*): 'Imagine to yourself, my dear Letty,' she writes, 'a spacious garden laid out in delightful walks, bounded with high hedges and trees, and paved with gravel; part exhibiting a wonderful assemblage of the most picturesque and striking objects, pavilions, lodges, groves, grottoes, lawns, temples and cascades; . . . adorned with pillars, statues, and paintings . . . the whole illuminated with an infinite number of lamps, disposed in different figures of suns, stars, and constellations: the place crowded with the gayest company, ranging through blissful shades, or supping . . . cold collations . . . enlivened with mirth, freedom and good humour, and animated with an excellent band of music.'[27]

The youth of Georgian England, as well as their jollifying elders, were seduced, in all senses, by the Pleasure Gardens. Being out of doors gave them freedom and appeared to dilute barriers of class and means. Being in a garden which was clipped, ordered, perhaps blossoming, gave them a feeling of luxury, of being pampered, and they were entertained – by music (Handel, Haydn and Mozart all played at Ranelagh Rotunda), masquerades, gossip, the latest war news (there was always that), celebrity-spotting, games, tea gardens, sweetmeat sellers and luncheon booths, dancing and fireworks. Breaking the rules, staying up all night and taking public breakfast at dawn – it was all irresistible. The gardens, with a commercial liberation to exploit the unusual, the curious, the malformed in man and beast, the exotic and blatantly grisly and hideous, were more exciting than the Royal Parks or genteel places like Bath and Tunbridge Wells. The Regent's Park Zoo, founded in 1826 under the scientific wing of the Zoological Society of London, was in the same tradition, displaying animals in ornamental buildings. The frisson of coming into close contact with the strange and rare was a great attraction: this applied to the human species as well, and – as ever with tourist attractions – the 'respectable' loved to rub shoulders with fortune-tellers, tattoo artists, pimps, prostitutes, drug-dealers and pickpockets. The hazards of such places are brilliantly captured by Fanny Burney when she allows the innocent, but not unintelligent Evelina to visit Marybone (Marylebone, which Pepys called Marrowbonez) in the company of the Miss Branghtons. Evelina steps into a nightmare, discovering that if she is in the company of bright young things who love the thrill of being ambushed in a dark allée by rowdy young men, then it will be assumed that she is enjoying it. Fleeing into the arms of a 'gentleman', she discovers him to be of the same opinion, and finally stumbling into two promenading ladies, she descends from bad to worse.[28]

The eighteenth-century pleasure gardens were a safety-valve for a large section of rumbustious Georgian society and were perhaps one of the reasons why there was no British revolution in the French manner. They celebrated the pleasurable possibilities of avant-garde music and entertainments and allowed the bohemian tendency in most people to find a flowering. But they were also commercial operations and, like all fashions, they faded and failed. Mollie Sands mourns their passing and rightly so: Ranelagh was closed and sold in 1805, the land added to the grounds of Chelsea Hospital; much was used for Chelsea Bridge Road and the new Embankment for the Chelsea Suspension Bridge, opened in 1858, but the eastern part of the Chelsea Flower Show occupies Ranelagh acres and perhaps echoes with past laughter.

Pleasure in public gardens was transformed by the Victorians into sober, respectable family entertainment, with nothing to disturb the equilibrium of a crinoline. The gardens' more raffish pleasures were shut away, out of sight, out of mind, into clubs and pubs. The great human urge to promenade in glory found its next expression on the King's Road, Chelsea, in the 1960s, and has remained an element of British youth culture ever since. The musical promenade finds annual remembrance in the BBC's Royal Albert Hall summer season of concerts and its devoted bands of 'promenaders' will always vouch for the informality, foot tapping and swaying (in a kind of Mexican wavelet) that is customarily allowed to some pieces. There are other signs that the formal manner of listening to serious music in concert halls is reverting to raptures out of doors. As Lydia Melford might have been spellbound by the young Mozart's piano at Ranelagh, so I have been by Yo Yo Ma and his cello with the Boston Symphony Orchestra making melting music across the crowded, sunny lawn at Tanglewood. Even the Proms are now relayed in Hyde Park. This last brings us full circle, for the Pleasure Gardens originally protected the Royal Parks from extremes of behaviour, preserving a graciousness amongst the populace that persuaded successive sovereigns to release them by dribs and drabs for public access. The green lungs of London – Greenwich, St James's, Green, Hyde Park and Kensington Gardens, Richmond, Bushy Park, Hampton Court and Regent's Park, were finally handed over by the Crown in 1851. These, too, have been a sop to revolution: Queen Caroline apparently asked Prime Minister Sir Robert Walpole what it would cost to get St James's Park back into private royal use, and his often-quoted reply was, 'Only three crowns, Madam'.[29]

When Samuel Taylor Coleridge conceived hundreds of lines of 'Kubla Khan', including the 'garden bright with sinuous rills Where blossomed many an incense-bearing tree' in an opiate dream, he was coming late, as westerners did, to the lure of hallucinatory drugs that had for so long been part of the East's garden pleasures. Shortly before 'Kubla Khan' (1797) Lord Macartney had undertaken his mission to Peking to persuade China to trade tea for opium (grown by the British in India for the purpose); the Chinese, shamefully drummed into acquiescence by the Opium Wars and the destruction of the Summer Palace in Peking under Lord Elgin's charge, found their trade and customs controlled by the British for forty years, until the Boxer Rising, and during this time travellers' tales of the gardens slowly filtered home. Secrecy and seclusion elaborated the gardens' attractions, a mystique maintained until Maggie Keswick published her book on the Chinese garden in 1978: she was writing from the standpoint of her family's century-long connections with China, as well as her own lifelong familiarity with and affection for China and its people.[30]

Just as in other ancient garden traditions, the Chinese gardens are drenched in sensual pleasures: the earliest description of a garden comes from the fourth century BC, in one of the Songs of Ch'u, where shamans (their 'witch-doctors') tempt the soul of a dying king to stay in his body, promising lightfooted princesses who wait in the garden pavilion, and who can be reached by walking through orchid-scented galleries, past hibiscus hedges and a pool adorned with just-opening lotus flowers and 'purple-stemmed water mallows'.[31] The Chinese garden was the proper territory for the shamans: the landforms, rocks, water and trees were arranged to imitate the natural landscape (a landscape much manipulated by man for flood control, irrigation and terracing) so that the very soul of China could be met with in a garden. The miniature features, the caves, symbolic stones, bonsai trees, rock pools and rivulets represented the abode of the immortal gods: small pierced pottery incense burners were placed so that a scented mist wreathed the rockeries, as it wreathed the unreachable mountains, and the shaman or sensitive being could shrink himself in his mind's eye, and so enter the tiny caves. Shamans could imagine themselves into amorous assignations with supernatural beings, who some thought inhabited a great grotto beneath the earth, imitated in garden symbolism by a water cave, its entrance almost blocked with a huge rock so that only a canoe could pass. Beyond the earthly realm the traveller was lured by lighted torches, by the sound of ten thousand flutes blown by the wind, to slip down a deep, deep hole into a world lit by sun and moon with 'peaceful grasses, harmonious clouds. Birds answer the call of men, flowers listen to visitors. It is a complete other world.'[32]

Swift's Lemuel Gulliver (whose *Travels* were first published in 1726), Lewis Carroll's Alice, as well as factual western travellers, experienced hazily understood Chinese garden mystiques. The prosaic Europeans adopted the trappings of tip-tilted roofed pavilions and latticed bridges (as will be seen in chapter six) but were completely bewildered by the philosophies of design, and have been so up until the present day. The Taoist belief in a seamlessly sensual, physical and spiritual universe inspired gardens that followed the natural forms and features of the sites: the idea of *wu-wei* meant taking no action that was contrary to nature and natural life, leading to what we might now call an eco-empathetic garden. The Chinese garden makers employed the wind and water experts, the Feng-Shui, to discern the forces that ran through a site: a great rockery might be built to block out evil, or a stream re-directed to channel good forces.

The west has inherited only echoes of the Chinese regard for certain trees and flowers, which were elevated to personalities, or perhaps spiritual status, which gave them sacred values. Bamboo was virtuous, because it bent with the wind but never broke, and was the Confucian symbol of a gentleman; pines too were venerated as survivors of long struggles. Willows, valued for tea from their leaves and an aspirin pain-killer from their bark, were planted (by men) next to water as graceful symbols of pliant beauty (women); mulberry fed the precious silkworms, catalpa wood was prized for chess sets, musical instruments, printing blocks and coffins; paulownia also for instruments and for its flowers; persimmon and peach were symbols of spring, marriage and fertility; the pear of good government, the plum the 'friend of winter' blossom. Herbaceous peonies were the flowers of early summer, planted in great beds and borders, the centre of attention when in flower, and left to their own devices afterwards, the Chinese understanding perfectly how they hated to be moved. The tree peony, or moutan, is more rare and sacred, found in the fourth century growing in the wild, cultivated in the late seventh century, with the first blooms wrapped in cabbage leaves, their stems sealed with wax, and despatched in a bamboo cage via flying horseman to the emperor. Moutans were especially worshipped during the Sung dynasty, the poor saved to buy them, and to grow a fine variety indicated a man of taste.

In China the beloved flower of summer lassitude is the lotus, *Nelumbo nucifera*. It is said that at the moment of the Buddha's birth a lotus bloomed, and he stepped into it to cast his gaze in ten directions, from the eight petals and upwards and downwards: for this alone the lotus remains the symbol of uniqueness and predestination.* In China the lotus reflects the joy in seasonal changes: in spring the pools and lakes are glassy clear, but with the arrival of summer the leaves rise high on their curved stems 'to make a new billowing green surface several feet above the water'. Soon the foliage harbours the precious flowers, the jewels of the world no less, and on large lakes paths were cut through the foliage so that punts could glide secretly among the flowers.[33] Even people without gardens grew lotus in large bowls, filled with rich mud and topped with water, which were placed near the most important entrances into the courtyard. It is the opalescent pinkness emerging from mud, whether in lake, pool or pot, that fascinates the Chinese: they love also the purity and modesty of the flower, and most of all, they love the lotus because, like the peony, they have cultivated them for so long. About 1500 years longer than we in the West.

---

* The Hindu god Brahma also surveys the earth from a huge, this time thousand-petalled lotus.

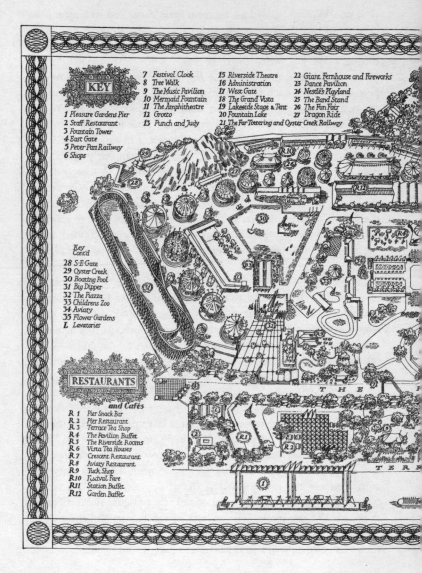

KEY

1 Pleasure Gardens Pier
2 Staff Restaurant
3 Fountain Tower
4 East Gate
5 Peter Pan Railway
6 Shops

7 Festival Clock
8 Tree Walk
9 The Music Pavilion
10 Mermaid Fountain
11 The Amphitheatre
12 Grotto
13 Punch and Judy

15 Riverside Theatre
16 Administration
17 West Gate
18 The Grand Vista
19 Lakeside Stage & Tent
20 Fountain Lake
21 The Far Tottering and Oyster Creek Railway

22 Giant Fernhouse and Fireworks
23 Dance Pavilion
24 Nestlé's Playland
25 The Band Stand
26 The Fun Fair
27 Dragon Ride

Key
Cont'd

28 S·E·Gate
29 Oyster Creek
30 Boating Pool
31 Big Dipper
32 The Piazza
33 Childrens Zoo
34 Aviary
35 Flower Gardens
L Lavatories

RESTAURANTS

and Cafés

R 1 Pier Snack Bar
R 2 Pier Restaurant
R 3 Terrace Tea Shop
R 4 The Pavilion Buffet
R 5 The Riverside Rooms
R 6 Vista Tea Houses
R 7 Crescent Restaurant
R 8 Aviary Restaurant
R 9 Tuck Shop
R10 Festival Fare
R11 Station Buffet
R12 Garden Buffet

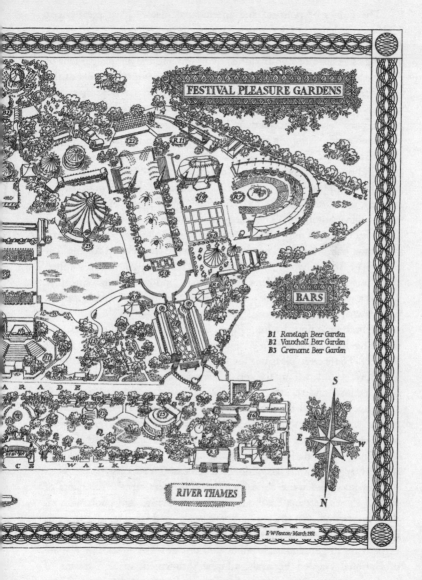

FESTIVAL PLEASURE GARDENS

BARS

B1 Ranelagh Beer Garden
B2 Vauxhall Beer Garden
B3 Cremorne Beer Garden

RIVER THAMES

F. W. Fenton · March 1951

The quirks of political and commercial history have meant that Chinese gardening philosophies have come to the West, in so far as they have come at all, through the age-old filterings of the Japanese. It was the asceticism of Zen Buddhist traditions and the temple gardens of Kyoto that attracted the modern movement artists and designers of the 1930s (as will be found in chapter eight). By that time the phrase 'pleasure gardens' had become commonplace but ever more devoid of meaning. Victorian parks and public gardens had exchanged pleasure for leisure, respectable saunterings on Sunday afternoons to admire the bedding-out or to listen to the band. Park keepers and local authority byelaws forbade any kind of activity that might have led beyond well-corseted smiles or kid-gloved applause: the royal parks of London led the way in decorum, where a child with a skipping rope or a toy yacht was at the peak of pleasurable excitement. The energetic young flocked to their adored Battersea Park, the only place where cycling – all the rage – was allowed.

Some half a century later Battersea's gaiety was revived for the 1951 Festival of Britain, when the riverside section of the park was re-vamped as Battersea Pleasure Gardens. In post-war London these gardens were seen as a wonderland, full of forgotten pleasures: they were real gardens, with lawns, flower beds, and green groves designed by Russell Page, with fantasy buildings by John Piper, Osbert Lancaster and others, and including Rowland Emett's eccentric Far Tottering and Oyster Creek Railway. There were pleasures for all ages, a miniature zoo, roundabouts and rides, a gilded fountain and a crazy clock, a dance pavilion – and one for music and theatre – tea shops, cafés and buffets, places to play and places to sit, all the fun of the fair, and three beer gardens named Ranelagh, Vauxhall and Cremorne. The Festival Pleasure Gardens were based upon these old pleasure gardens; they were intentionally 'finding something which had been lost', bringing both satisfaction and a joy of rediscovery. They were an undoubted tonic and a success.

But now, as I write almost another fifty years on, the remnants of Russell Page's gardens lie about, in ghostly pavings and pools with all their spirit gone, and the park is sporadically used for fetes and festivals of various kinds. We seem to have lost both the need for and the knack of pleasure in gardens both public and private. The 1980s saw a spate of National Garden Festivals, admirably dreamed up as a means of funding the restoration of derelict sites in Liverpool, Stoke-on-Trent and Glasgow respectively. These were hybrids of a flower show and trade fair, intended to spark the British interest in the established continental tradition of summer-long flower festivals, but completely failing to do so. The millennium awaits with more of the same, including the Greenwich dome (a big brother to the 1951 Dome of Discovery) where the pleasures include an exploration inside ourselves or into the wild blue yonder via the technological toys with which most of us work every day. Perhaps we have lost the need for pleasures as they were once found in a garden? Are they left in the mud of the Glastonbury Festival, at the Proms in the Park, to the thrills of Alton Towers (which originally included a fantastic garden, though gardens and thrills are segregated now) or the titterings and giggles behind the fans and masks now *de rigueur* for a National Trust fête champêtre. Pleasures have been dispersed in a thousand ways – into pubs and clubs, gay bars, women-only lidos, to Centre Parcs and outdoor concerts – but the fact is, in the dispersion, the fragmentation, is the reflection of our society, that means we can no longer be attracted to the community idea of a pleasure garden. As to our private gardens, well, there's the nub: the privacy is all, for apart from the occasional scandal around the swimming pool (Cliveden and the Profumo affair being a highlight in pleasure garden history) we now take our pleasures in secret and the social historian will find it hard to know. This precious privacy is the theme of the next chapter.

CHAPTER TWO

✠

The Secret Garden

The secret garden, a hidden place of enchantment and peace, where all our ills can be cured, is one of the most powerful ideas in cultural history. It is a place of submission, of refuge, of sanctuary and of looking inwards for hidden treasures. It is private, but more than that, it is the place for spiritual and soulful conversation, seclusion and once upon a time at least, a place to encounter both God and the devil.

The secret garden steals into our thoughts as the adopted device of the Christian church. The idea of Eden, shown over and over again in medieval illustrations, is of an ugly, naked, oversized Adam and Eve disporting themselves with difficulty in a kind of animal pound, a tiny bare enclosure fenced by a low wicket or wall and bereft of flowers. In a window in Canterbury Cathedral made around 1178 Adam delves with an iron-shod spade in stony ground, with an ungainly and unpleasant-looking Brussels sprout for his labour.

On the other hand, the greatest tribute that the early Renaissance artists could imagine was to place the Queen of Heaven in her own secret garden. *The Annunciation* by Domenico Veneziano is a small image, only 273 × 540 mm, tempera on a panel, painted in the mid-fifteenth century, but it introduces many of the associations of the Virgin's bower (*Plate 10*). The Archangel Gabriel is down on one knee to the left, holding a *Lilium regale* wand in one hand, and with the other he beckons to Mary across a paved and columned court. She stands beneath the colonnade on the right. By placing her in this classical peristyle the artist has elevated her to a place where, in the gardens of the Stoic philosophers, there was 'a place for the easy conversation of intelligent friends' which did not normally include women.[1] The col-

umns of the peristyle are topped with acanthus leaves, the Corinthian
capitals said to have been devised by the sculptor Callimachus of Athens,
who was so moved by the sight of acanthus wreathing the tomb of a
child. Through the central arch of Mary's peristyle is her garden, the
paved four-fold garden of Islam adopted into Christian symbolism, with
roses climbing over an arched pergola which leads to a heavy, barred
door in a high and castellated wall.

All the dreams of the secret garden are encapsulated in this precious
image: the perfect garden, an encounter with an angel, the treasure
within – both Mary herself and the child in her womb – the implied
blessing on philosophic debate, intimations of death and the blind
windows and barred gate which keep the world at bay. There are many
other precious images: Leonardo da Vinci's *Annunciazione* in the Uffizi
in Florence has Gabriel also proffering lilies, kneeling in a flowery mead:
a thousand spangled points of light, usually identified as wild strawberry
(*Fragaria vesca*) with Star of Bethlehem (*Ornithogalum umbellatum*).
Giovanni di Libri's *Madonna and Child with St Anne* is set in a garden,
the two women side by side with the beautiful boy dancing on their
hands, beneath a lemon tree in fruit, on a turf seat which is surrounded
by lattice entwined with leaves. The Dutch school *Virgin in a Rose
Bower* by Stefan Lochner is even more richly exquisite: the roses on the
background trellis are echoed by the jewels in the Virgin's crown, and
she is seated on a turf couch, planted with recognizable violets and wild
strawberries.[2]

The actual sources of these painted gardens were the gardens of a
few earthly queens and many rich monasteries. Additional information
has come across the intervening centuries in illuminated manuscripts,
breviaries and calendars, but these have never been easily accessible and
important research has only ever been done by a few garden historians.
Alicia Amherst's *History of Gardening* of 1895 gave copious and sometimes curious quotations from the records of abbeys and nunneries: the
enthusiastic Anglo-Catholic Sir Frank Crisp (1843–1919), owner of a
fantastic alpine garden at Friar Park, Henley, collected all the manuscript
illustrations he could find into his vast *Medieval Gardens* in 1924. But
the most important work has been done in the last thirty years by Dr John
Harvey, whose *Medieval Gardens*, first published in 1981, has become the
classic source book for a resurgence of interest in this distant period. Dr

Harvey and Dr Sylvia Landsberg have been instrumental in the creation of Queen Eleanor of Castile's garden beside the Great Hall of Winchester Castle and the Shrewsbury Quest garden, related to Ellis Peters' fictional monk, Brother Cadfael. The secret garden enclosed, the *hortus conclusus* of the Queen of Heaven, can be explored by using both the very old images and these new, living gardens: this continual reverberation through time perhaps adds to its emotional and spiritual power.

Just as the Virgin Mary can occupy the sacred peristyle of the Stoics as a kind of honorary man, so she becomes an ambassadress for gardening in the monastic life. In the sixth century St Benedict of Nursia decreed gardening to be worthy and virtuous: chapter twenty-seven of his rules for the Benedictine Order concerned the importance of caring for the tools, the ferramenta, the rakes, spades, scythes, hatchets and flails which were necessary for the monastic gardens. A plan for an ideal monastery layout dating from the early ninth century and found at St Gall in Switzerland, has proved a gift to historians. This remarkably consistent layout, which persists from Fontevraud to the chilly edge of the English fens and the former Peterborough Abbey, shows the cloister, an enclosed and inviolable paved or lawn space, only planted with a cypress or yew to intimate eternal life, on the south side of the abbey church. The refectory was built south of the cloister, adjoining the kitchens, bakery and brewery and convenient for the kitchen gardens to the south-east. Here the hortulan, the lowliest of monastic gardeners, cultivated neat narrow beds of peas, cabbage, onions, garlic, leeks, radish, celery, beet and beans, with some pot herbs, parsley, coriander, chervil, dill and savory. Moving northwards, anti-clockwise around the church, the monks' cemetery did double-duty as an orchard, with apples, pears, medlar, quince, almond and mulberry planted amongst the grave plots; the dead truly succoured the living. At Peterborough the whole east side of the precinct was vineyard and orchard (and survives as such after eight hundred years): the area at the east end of the church was called 'paradise' in the St Gall plan and is the burial ground for abbots and other notables at Peterborough, and with blossoming trees and carpets of wild flowers this echoes the Virgin's flowery mead. The Infirmary is in the north-east corner at St Gall; the Infirmerar's garden grew the medicinal herbs and simples, the handed-down remedies. It was walled

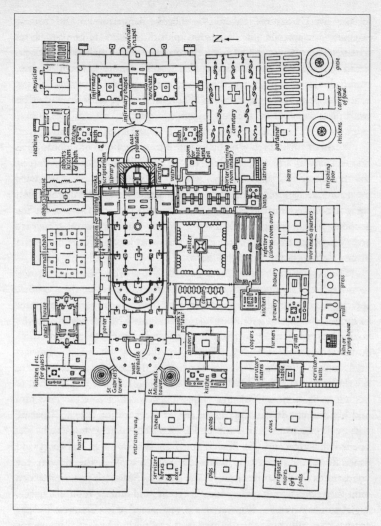

The Benedictine Monastic ideal layout, including gardens, from the plan found at St Gall in Switzerland dating from the early ninth century: Benedictine foundations throughout Europe, from Fontevraud in the Loire Valley to Peterborough on the edge of the English Fens conform to this pattern. (From Geoffrey & Susan Jellicoe, *The Landscape of Man*, 1975)

for here were treasures it would be thought dangerous to find: opium poppies, perhaps the mandrake, an aphrodisiac and demoniac whose screams when it was pulled from the ground would make anyone who heard it mad. The physic garden also held the more benevolent rose, cumin, lovage, fennel, tansy, lily, sage, rue, mint and rosemary, all for aches and pains, fevers and rashes. These were dried for winter use: the word drug comes from the Anglo-Saxon *drigan*, to dry, and the knowledge to do this and administer the drugs conferred prestige and power.

North of the church was the province of the abbot, who would have his own flower and herb garden. In the St Gall plan the west end of the monastery has the visitors' hostel north of the entrance gate, with pens for farm animals extending to the south-west. At Peterborough there are interesting parallels; at the Reformation the Dean took the property on the north side, and the bishop was allotted the farmery area, where the tradition of a model farm, or at least the keeping of the bishop's cows, lasted until the 1920s.

The symbolism of the secret garden with a protected treasure was naturally even more apt in a nunnery, reflected even in their names, such as Mariengaard, meaning Mary's orchard. Nunneries were meant to be secure and sheltered, but history abounds with stories of wealthy young heiresses trying to get out, and others trying to get in. Alicia Amherst relates how William Rufus – perhaps on his way to that last fatal hunt in the New Forest – stopped at the convent in Romsey to see the twelve-year-old Matilda, who was being educated in the care of her aunt, the Abbess Christina. 'The Abbess was distressed to hear him and his knights demanding admission at the convent gate . . . fearing some evil purpose towards the child, made her wear a nun's veil.' She opened the gate and the king entered 'as if to look at the roses and other flowering herbs' and while the king inspected the flowers the young nuns filed silently through the garden. 'Matilda appearing veiled with the rest the king suffered her to go by, and quietly took his leave.'[3]

Another Abbess at Romsey was not so careful of her charges; and she received the following instructions from the Archbishop of Canterbury, telling her to construct a new gate. 'In a Lily garden the Bridegroom is filled with delight and finds pleasure in gathering lilies above all flowers. It is needful therefore to enclose this garden by the defence of shrewd and sharp disciplines . . . lest an entrance be opened to any sower of mischief.

This lily we believe to be the ornament of virginal purity, which by reason of certain matters found in our visitation lately, we desire to protect.'[4]

With all these miraculous images, of lily gardens, veiled virgins, flowery meads, the life-saving physic garden, and the Queen of Heaven's beautiful flowers, it seems not at all strange that for pilgrims and ordinary people, these secret gardens of monasteries and convents could fulfil their visions of paradise. For over a thousand years the religious houses dominated many villages and towns in Britain, and though history represents this as a turbulent relationship, to the majority of the people of Britain they must have been the equivalent of our social and health services, schools and community centres rolled into one. In a thousand years of such everyday closeness it was inevitable that monastic life, benevolent as well as threatening, seeped into our collective cultural memory. The realms of Mary's lilies and healing herbs were magical icons of the annually returning spring to the woods and fields and even squalid yards. They would be seared upon the memory for their beauty and handed down from generation to generation as wondrous visions.

Then, by royal decree, distributed via Thomas Cromwell's dreaded Dissolution commissioners, the Virgin's garden became forbidden territory. The Dissolution of the Monasteries and succeeding Reformation divided more than obedient Protestants from Catholic recusants; 'the stripping of the altars' pervaded all aspects of everyday life. Of concern here is that the people were deprived of the rock of their existence, the pagan cum Roman Catholic calendar which depended upon a sequence of flowery rituals to lighten drab lives, as well as the healing pleasures of the monastic gardens. The history of the Reformation is so wrapped up in theology and politics and one man and his wives, that it seems hardly to touch on this great loss at all. New Protestants felt it best to remain silent, Catholics were silenced for three hundred years, and when they began to speak it was on theology and desperate remedies. Gardens were hardly important enough to mention.[5] The Catholic families retreated behind their walls into little gatherings in isolated country houses, into their secret gardens, and these gardens took on a more sinister secrecy, foreboding betrayal and death. The bed of lily of the valley in a shady corner by the wall, the violets along the path's edge, the summer lilies and roses, these became more powerfully than ever, the Virgin's flowers. But the symbolism stretched: the aquilegia symbolized the Holy Spirit; the single clove pink was called the Nail Flower (because cloves resemble nails); wild pansy or heartsease, three faces in one hood, the Trinity: and the fritillary, Widow's Wail, for Mary's grief. With flowers the Virgin has been transported to the Garden of Gethsemane, the garden of death.

The accepted history of gardens for the period from the 1530s to the death of Elizabeth I is obsessively royal and sycophantic, dazzled by Hampton Court, Nonsuch, Hatfield, Theobalds and Burghley.[6] What the rest of Britain was doing is extremely difficult to discern, but the instinct to preserve the beloved symbolism was so strong that it can be detected still in some gardens that we unhesitatingly call 'old'. As the room of a beloved person is so often preserved after their death, so these old gardens were frozen in time, never exposed to new, and usually Protestant fashion.

With the stripping of symbolism and decoration from the churches and the destruction or 'privatization' of monastic gardens there must have been so much bewilderment, disbelief and hurt that the very framework of life had been snatched away. The calendar of forbidden rituals illuminates this: the dark and cold and terrible strictures of Lent were lightened by Palm Sunday, when branches of yew, box and bursting pussy-willow buds were gathered to be blessed then taken home to impart the blessing upon house and hovel. On Maundy Thursday came the solemn 'stripping' and cleansing, scrubbing with birch and broom twigs, the burial of the Host, the watches kept through bleak and chilly nights, longing for the dawn of Easter Day and the gathering of all the flowers and sweet herbs that could be found to fill the church for the return of Life. From then the spring and summer work was lightened by the continual cavalcade of flowery festivals (the antecedents of modern stylized flower festivals?): rose garlands for Corpus Christi; 'every man's door was shadowed by green birch, fennel, St John's Wort, orpine, white lilies' for St John the Baptist's Eve which coincided with the pagan Midsummer Eve and much dancing around bonfires,

> in everie streete
> With garlands wrought of Motherwort,
> Or else with Vervain swete,
> And many other flowers faire,
> With Violets in their handes.[7]

More flowers were gathered for St Thomas of Canterbury on 7 July and Our Lady's best lilies cut for the Feast of the Assumption on 24 August. Many more local and minor festivals intervened, the whole gloriously rounded with the ritual processions and blessings of fields and gardens for their harvests at Rogation-tide.[8]

It is not hard to imagine that the Virgin's flowers were still gathered and quietly carried to mass in those remote country communities where Catholicism persisted. The imagery of the enclosed garden – sheltering arbours, hedges and walls, the pavilion upon the wall or mount so that a lookout could be kept, the tumbling fountain that masked clandestine conversation – all assumed a heightened usefulness. Secret gardens were a secondary refuge, much nicer than priest holes, when uncertain visitors arrived. In his biography of the Jesuit Edmund Campion, Evelyn Waugh's imagination paints a haunting picture of a nightmare English landscape of ruined churches, monastic buildings reduced to piles of building stone, of Catholic families walled up in their houses, impoverished by recusancy fines and invariably in mourning.[9] Gardens were their only solace. Father John Gerard enjoyed gardening 'for that was much of my recreation in England' he was able to report, after he had escaped: it was also a good disguise.[10]

Secret gardens gain much fascination as remnants of old Catholic England and Scotland, lingering in intangible ways, like the smoke of incense hanging in the air. At Sir Thomas Tresham's Lyveden New Beild, the ghost of his Trinity house still has the tree-grown mount and grassy canals of his unfinished garden in which can be discerned his distant dreams. At Chastleton, a Catesby house before the disgrace of the Gunpowder Plot, there is a curious circular garden, symbolizing the pre-Copernican universe with the earth in the centre, surrounded by planets of topiary. At the other Catesby house, Ashby St Ledgers, there is still the upper room over the entrance arch where the plot was prepared, and Edwin Lutyens (who was highly sensitive to atmosphere) kept some old formality in his design of the Edwardian garden. Other old Catholic houses, Coughton Court, Baddesley Clinton, Grace Dieu, Norbury Park, keep some of the feel of their old gardens.[11]

By their nature and history the Scottish pleasaunce gardens likewise retain their aura. Mary, Queen of Scots is said to have brought many plants from France to Scotland (angelica and French sorrel are two).[12]

In searching out Mary's gardens Christopher Hussey found a description of her child's garden on Inchmahone in the Lake of Monteith: 'You wander through the ruins overgrown with ferns and Spanish filberts and old fruit trees, and at the corner of the old monkish garden you come upon one of the strangest and most touching things you ever saw – an oval space of about 18 ft. by 12 ft. with the remains of a double row of boxwood all round. They are all outgrown and the guidebook calls this Queen Mary's bower, but 'what could the little Queen, five years old and "fancy free" do with a bower? It is plainly the child queen's garden, with her little walk and its rows of boxwood left to themselves for three hundred years.'[13]

In his book on the gardens of Robert Lorimer, Christopher Hussey is looking for the historic background to Lorimer's revivals of the pleasaunce gardens. 'The earliest and most perfect' was (and still is) Edzell's plat, overlooked by the garden house and sheltered by the most fantastic garden walls, with square recesses for the blue and yellow chequer of Lindsey colours made in flowers and carvings devoted to deities, virtues, sciences and humours.[14] The Great Garden at Pitmedden, the home of the Setons, is full of symbolic tribute laid out in boxwood and flowers: the motto '*Sustento Sanguine Signa*', 'With blood I bear the standard', refers to the death of John Seton, fighting for Charles I at the Battle of Brig o' Dee in 1639, and the presiding weathervane shows a cavalier with a flying banner, his crest. The National Trust for Scotland still flies a seventeenth-century Royal Standard over the garden on special occasions.[15] With these and more inspirations redolent of the close associations between Scotland and France, Robert Lorimer accomplished his famed stream of Arts and Crafts gardens in the pleasaunce tradition, at Earlshall, Balmanno and at Kellie Castle, his own family home.[16] Lorimer believed profoundly in such poetic gardens: 'A garden is a sort of sanctuary, a chamber roofed by heaven . . . a little pleasaunce of the soul, by whose wicket the world can be shut . . .'[17]

After the death of Elizabeth I, so conveniently the Virgin Queen, garden symbolism came to serve a dual purpose. The Catholic Henry Hawkins's *Partheneia Sacra* of 1633 is subtitled 'Or the Mysterious and Delicious Garden of the Sacred Parthenes'. His enclosed garden with topiary beasts, arbours and fountains has 'fair, straight and therefore virtuous alleys, covered with the sand of humility', all the Virgin's flowers, together with mounts ('elevations of the mind'), valleys of depression, groves of solitude, vines of spiritual gladness and fountains of the graces. All these to celebrate the Virgin: 'Heer lastly are statues of Her rare examples to be seened, Obelisks, Pyramids, Triumphal Arches, Aqua-ducts, Thermes, Pillars of Eternal Memorie, erected to Her Glorie, in contemplation of her Admirable, Angelical, and Divine life.' Which Virgin was being celebrated was open to interpretation.[18]

The nature of history makes the evidence for Catholic secret gardens difficult to find. One Catholic, Francis Maire, left Cheshire in the mid-sixteenth century to take refuge in his plantations and gardens at Hardwick in County Durham; until 1699 the family kept records of the trees they planted and works in the garden.[19] According to Geoffrey Grigson, the Revd William Turner, the father of English botany, took refuge in botanizing because he found the religious upheavals so disturbing.

For the enduring, perhaps growing, power of the secret garden there is one later corroborative story, the legend of Rosamond's Bower. In the Fan Gallery of the Fitzwilliam Museum in Cambridge is the Fair Rosamund Fan of paper leaf, printed and painted in watercolour, with ivory sticks strewn with painted roses (*Plate 11*). The fan, dated about 1740, comes from a collection made by Leonard Messel and given by his daughter, Anne, Countess of Rosse – both of whom gardened at Nymans. The painting shows a fenced and hedged bower at the royal palace of Woodstock, made by Henry II as a safe house and sanctuary for his mistress Rosamund Clifford. The fair Rosamund is seated with a book, in a latticed arbour, Virgin-like, while another woman approaches, a crown on her head, a dagger in one hand, a cup (of poison) in the other: the parallel being with Gabriel as the bringer of Life, and Eleanor, Henry's jealous queen, as purveyor of death. The fan, like the bower garden, carries a power beyond its size. It has an inscription, 'Oct 26 to ye late Act 1740', which mourns Sarah Churchill's ordering of the destruction of the final remains of the bower garden for Brown's lake at Blenheim.

The fan illustrates a kaleidoscope of myth and legend: Eleanor was actually far away, imprisoned by her husband when Rosamund died, presumably in her bed, at Godstow nunnery in 1176. The rose, *Rosa gallica* 'Versicolor', the striped rose known as *Rosa mundi*, is of ancient and uncertain origin, and Graham Thomas's idea that it may have been found in Syria by a Crusader knight and presented to Rosamund Clifford is difficult to resist. Alicia Amherst noted how 'the halo of romance' hung around the bower, and how Henry III had ordered improvements at Woodstock, 'To make round about the garden of our Queen two walls, good and high, so that no one may be able to enter, with a becoming and honourable herbary near our fish pond, in which the same Queen may be able to amuse herself'.[20] Among Woodstock's ruins the bower in the labyrinth continued to fascinate: Addison wrote, in *Rosamund*, of 'Amaranths and Eglantines with intermingling sweets have wove the particolour'd gay Alcove',[21] John Aubrey sketched the bower's remains, and when the sentimental Vanbrugh came to Blenheim he was determined to save the romantic place.[22] It was his quarrel over the matter with the Duchess which probably made her determined to do the opposite, and most of the evidence was drowned. But visitors still flock to the unprepossessing water spout that is all that survives today.

Recently a footnote to eighteenth-century landscaping history has emerged with Fiona Cowell's work on Richard Woods, who seems to have been the Catholic equivalent to Capability Brown and a preferred designer for secluded and formerly recusant houses, especially in Essex and Yorkshire. Woods, who has been buried in Catholic anonymity, was a friend and neighbour of Philip Southcote at Woburn Farm near Chertsey, another Catholic pioneer and intriguing figure in landscape history, about whom little is known. Woods had a preference for small parks with a 'fondness for rosaries', rusticated bridges, small temples and gothic pavilions, grottoes and waterfalls, all rather reclusive features which perhaps gives the key to his character. His most known work, but that too is 'secretive and unremarked', is Buckland in Berkshire, a park pleasaunce with a planned circuit of delights for Sir Robert Throckmorton: he also worked for the Catholic Arundells, Giffards and Welds and ended his days as surveyor to Lord Petre at Ingrave in Essex.[23]

While the hidden landscapes and gardens of recusancy have been almost lost, the idea of the Virgin's bower, the enclosed garden, has been fostered and has flowered through history as the device of just those Protestants who had rejected her. The 'father of botany', the Revd William Turner, in taking refuge from his worries about the

Reformation, bequeathed a tradition of clerics who tended their gardens as well as their flocks, and made the English rectory or vicarage garden into one of the great historical mythic images.

A century on from the Reformation, during the troubled reign of Charles I, the garden – which could now be appropriated by any part of the community – was turned into the contemplative refuge of the Puritan, William Prynne: Christ 'here on earth did Gardens highly grace . . . Each garden then we see, should still present/Christ to our sight, mind, thoughts, with sweete content'.[24] Another Puritan, George Wither, published his *Emblemes* in 1635; for May a giant hand is watering a costly garden, which cannot be supposed to be the achievement of a day or two, but 'Perswade thee to consider, that, no actions, Can come, but by degrees, to their perfections . . .'[25]

Henry Compton, younger son of a Royalist family but a Protestant to the core, learned his gardening while Master of St Cross at Winchester, soon after Charles II's restoration. The Royal Library at Windsor has the 'curious booke of flowers in miniature' painted by Alexander Marshall, Compton's steward at St Cross, who moved to Fulham Palace with Compton when he was made Bishop of London in 1675.[26] Before long the Bishop fell foul of James II's Catholic sympathies and was suspended, so in refuge at Fulham and forbidden to tend his flock outside his walls, Bishop Compton traded priests and plants with the colonists in America. He was back in favour with William and Mary and made the ultimate sacrifice in letting the King have his gardener, George London, who moved to Hampton Court in 1689. Nothing however won him the archbishopric of Canterbury, so his solace was his plants, 'a greater variety of curious exotic plants and trees than had at that time been collected in any garden in England' as Fulham was described at his death in 1713.[27]

Hanoverian stability encouraged the rectory or vicarage garden to settle itself into the landscape. The endearing Parson James Woodforde, whose diary covers the second half of the eighteenth century (and has been greatly beloved since first publication in 1924) reveals his gourmet's interest in garden and countryside. His pleasure in food is physical – beans and bacon, giblet pie, hashed goose, roasted rabbit with young peas and 'colliflower' load his table for all comers. Christmas dinner is given for bands of village worthies, for pensioners and ploughmen in true Christian manner; he is full of endless solicitations to the poor and the mad, to premature babies and old crones, habitually delighting in the products of his efficient garden and the joy it brings to others and himself. Meals are his entertainment; one magnificent banquet for twenty, given by the Bishop of Bristol, with twenty different delectations in each course, washed down with three kinds of wine, finds the flushed Parson Woodforde gazing fondly on the table decoration, 'one of the prettiest things I ever saw' – a miniature garden with shepherd and shepherdess and a little pavilion wreathed in flowers.[28]

Parson Woodforde shares the obscurity of his own day and fame in ours with Revd Gilbert White of Selborne in Hampshire. Selborne, where he was born and brought up, was White's world, and he learned to wish for no other. After a mildly hectic and controversial youth at Oxford (Pope presented his own edition of the *Iliad* to White at his degree ceremony in June 1743), the perpetual curate accepted that there was nowhere quite like home and settled into his life-long love affair with the curiosities of the Hampshire countryside. White's grandfather had been Vicar of Selborne, and had wisely bought The Wakes, a house opposite the church at the head of Selborne's street, for his family; here Gilbert White took control of the garden on his return and his Garden Kalendar records the adventure of his gardening in detail from 1751–68. With sheer hard work and good organization the garden produced vast amounts, much of it on chalk with 'basons' dug for plants. White never seemed to deal with less than 300 cabbage plants or nine rows of marrowfat peas. Seed was saved from year to year, or triumphantly brought home from excursions, sea kale from a trip to south Devon, and celery, celeriac, peppers, asparagus, cucumbers, artichokes and cardoons were grown as well as all the regulation roots and brassicas. White planted an orchard, prided himself on his soft fruits, grapes and peaches and homemade wines, but his passion was his melon ground: the preparation of the pits, the planting out, earthings up and endless watering, tinkering with the frames and finally the tasting and harvesting, governed his year. The gentle anthropomorphism later applied to Timothy the tortoise was practised on the melons – he cossetted them with hay muffs, feared on their behalf too much sun or rain or wind, or not enough, waited anxiously for them to crack, and then tentatively and finally joyously,

PLATE 1 Haft Paykar (The Seven Portraits) by Nizami: *The Eaves-dropper*, Iranian, *c.*1430, one of many images found in Eastern and European medieval art on the theme of the watcher in the garden. The bearded eavesdropper, or voyeur, can just be seen in the crack between the shutters of the upper window; the two guardians outside the fence seem uneasy, but the pleasures of the garden, the fruit, wine, music and exquisite flowers and blossoms, keep us all spellbound.

PLATES 2 AND 3 Westbury Court, Westbury-on-Severn, the National Trust garden which prompted historically accurate restoration in the 1960s. The long-legged pavilion finds a fellow in Pieter de Hooch's painting *The Game of Ninepins*, dictating the seventeenth-century Dutch formal features; the espaliered fruit trees (ABOVE) are of contemporary varieties. (*see page 18*)

PLATE 4 Coombe Abbey, near Coventry, by William Miller (1828–1909): watercolour plan of 1897 showing every detail of the Victorian layout which had taken almost fifty years to complete. Decay and dereliction set in with the First World War as it did in so many places; some of the paths and trees can still be found in what is now Coombe Abbey Country Park.

PLATE 5 The Victoria Garden, Farnham, Surrey, occupies the site of the town swimming pool, originally opened in Queen Victoria's jubilee year, 1897. Design and planting are historically accurate and the quality of implementation and care achieved, largely by volunteers from local societies, has inspired a community garden that is rapidly becoming a community treasure.

PLATES 6 AND 7 Hestercombe, near Taunton, Somerset: the Dutch garden, restored from Gertrude Jekyll's planting plans, part of the spectacular restoration project which began in the 1970s (ABOVE). Through the gateway, designed by Edwin Lutyens, the view slips backwards in time (BELOW) to the romantic valley of Coplestone Warre Bampfylde's landscape garden, restored by Philip White and the Hestercombe Gardens Trust. (*see page 26*)

PLATES 8 AND 9 Sezincote House, Gloucestershire: Thomas Daniell (1749–1840), pencil, sepia and wash, The Temple of Surya (ABOVE), one of a series of features recorded on a trip to India for recreation in Sir Charles Cockerell's garden (BELOW), c.1810, and still to be seen there. An Indian bridge, guarded by a pair of white Brahmin bulls, originally cast in Coade stone, and a wall of mossy recesses, miniature grottoes of funerary inspiration, were also built from the Daniell drawings.

PLATE 10 *The Annunciation*, by Domenico Veneziano, tempera on wood, painted before 1461, and expressing all the emotive symbolism of 'the secret garden'. (*see pages 50–51*)

PLATE 11 'The Fair Rosamund Fan', an eighteenth century depiction of the legendary secret bower at Woodstock Place that Henry II made for his mistress Rosamund Clifford. The fan, with a painted inscription 'Oct. 26 to ye late Act 1740', commemorates the final destruction of the remains of the bower in Capability Brown's landscaping of Blenheim Park. (*see pages 59–60*)

PLATE 12 Royal Victoria Park, Bath, the display of nineteenth century exotic favourites in flamboyant splendour.

PLATE 13 Ryton Organic Gardens, Ryton-on-Dunsmore, near Coventry, the 'No Dig Garden', one of the series of demonstration gardens.

PLATES 14 AND 15 The National Auricula and Primula Society, Midland and West Section, Auricula Show at Arden School, Knowle, 1997, the florist tradition alive and well: (ABOVE) the worshippers, and (BELOW) the subjects of their worship.

PLATE 16 *Spring in St John's Wood*, by Laura Knight, 1933, painted from the artist's window at 16 Langford Place, London NW8. Ordinary gardens lent the enchantment of realism to between-the-wars British paintings with garden subjects by Gilbert Spencer, D. P. Bliss, Paul Nash and other artists. No longer for 'garden painters' they became legitimate subjects for mainstream artists.

PLATE 17 *Runner Bean*, design for machine-printed cotton by E. Q. Nicholson, *c.* 1950. This design was drawn from her garden, and produced as a furnishing fabric by Edinburgh Weavers and as a wallpaper by Cole & Son.

PLATE 18 *Golding Constable's Kitchen Garden*, by John Constable, painted from an upstairs room in his father's home, East Bergholt House in Suffolk, reputedly on the same day in August 1815 that he painted the *Flower Garden* on the other side of the house. These were Constable's only paintings of a garden, affectionate tributes to his parents, but they extended beyond the fences into the landscape which was to be his artistic homeland. (*see page 220*)

PLATE 19 BELOW Cedric Morris's own garden, Benton End, Hadleigh, Suffolk, painted in its 'Digging for Victory' guise as a wartime garden, *c.* 1944.

PLATE 20 BELOW RIGHT Marsh Lane, Harlow, Essex, the garden made for Sir Frederick Gibberd (1908–1984), architect, landscape architect and town planner, which is generally regarded as one of the finest examples of late twentieth century modern design. This glade, in one of the farther reaches of the nine acres, provides a home for columns and vases removed from the façade of Coutts' Bank in the Strand, London, given a glass frontage by Sir Frederick; now elegantly discarded, they are a mute comment on pomp and circumstance. The garden is now in the care of the Gibberd Garden Trust, and is frequently open to visitors.

PLATES 21 AND 22
The Garden Gallery,
Broughton, Hampshire,
where Rachel Bebb
exhibits the work of
present-day artists in a
garden setting:
(LEFT) *The World Turned
Upside Down* by Bernard
McGuigan and (BELOW)
Dragonfly by Jeff Hisley.

PLATES 23 AND 24
OPPOSITE Wingwell,
Wing, Rutland, where
landscape architects John
and Rose Dejardin have
'work in progress' on their
garden and nursery which
promises exciting and
exquisite 'land art':
(TOP) John Dejardin's
design for a retaining
wall, built by Andrew
Dejardin and (BELOW)
the segmental beds of
Rose Dejardin's nursery
ground in their early
summer glory.

PLATE 25 *Iris Seedlings*, by Cedric Morris, 1943, oil on canvas, purchased by the Tate Gallery in 1981. Painted early in the decade of his greatest successes in iris breeding at Benton End, this is perhaps the most eloquent image of the transforming powers of horticulture: Morris's hand pollination and patient care of these delicate beauties produced many Benton hybrids, most notably the milky-mauve 'Benton Cordelia' of which too few now survive. His passion for irises, depicted here in all their fluttering femininity and alluring shades, fitted in with his amusement with the erotic analogies between the vegetable and human worlds. As an artist he was not alone in this passion, which was shared by Gertrude Jekyll, for whom the iris was her most-planted species, and Georgia O'Keeffe. (*see page 134*)

harvested them. He grew green and yellow canteloupes, Andalusian, Zatta and Romania melons, squashes and succades, he was forever swapping seeds, and at the August harvest he gave melon parties for his neighbours.

White's gardening was so minutely observed, with the same attention to detail that he was to adapt to his beloved swallows and martins, and the whole *Natural History of Selborne*, but he also gives a rare view into middle-sized eighteenth-century garden. He was aware of the landscape fashions, he was able to enlarge his prospect, make paths to the beech-covered hill, the famous Selborne Hangar which dominated his views, and between 1758–61 the highpoint of the garden labouring was the construction of his stone ha-ha, so that visually at least he acquired a small romantic park. The garden now flourishes in many ways that White would recognize, carefully researched and restored by David Standing.[29] It has immense value in giving a clear impression of eighteenth-century gardening, as well as being the domain of a gardening naturalist whose methods are of especial use to us – White was a pragmatic naturalist, in that birds which attacked his garden were shot as examples to their fellows, and though he gave up shooting for sport, he continued to shoot specimens for scientific necessity, sometimes serving them up at table after examination.[30]

White's garden survives because of his great *Natural History*, the 'fourth most frequently published book' in the English language:[31] the events of the 200 years that separate us from him have done a great deal to enshrine the image of the distant paradise of a country cleric's garden into garden history – with some irony in that White never was Vicar of Selborne, but eked out his living on curacies and legacies. In his biography, Richard Mabey has sought to tease out some humanity for White and some logic to the legends; for the former I commend the biography, but the latter must have some place here. After White died at midsummer of 1793, his niece Mary lived on at The Wakes. She was the last of his close family, and when she died in 1833, house and garden were left empty; the 'Captain Swing' riots of farmworkers had reached the village in November 1830, but these were ignored entirely by a journalist of the *New Monthly* magazine who wrote of a place 'almost too beauteous for reality', thus officially beginning, writes Mabey, the 'consecration of book and place as ingredients of an idyll'.[32] The empty house was bought by Thomas Bell FRS, a medical man, amateur marine biologist and co-editor of an 1837 edition of White's writings. Professor Bell enlarged the house, tended and extended the garden, built a greenhouse and planted many trees. He was an excellent steward for almost forty years, by which time White's observances of natural history, his 'weaving of cloth of gold out of straw' had been spun into legend.[33] The Selborne Society was set up in 1885 to preserve this delicate legacy, but White's home fell prey to changing ownerships until the Bibby soap and shipping family arrived in 1910 and stayed until Mrs Bibby's death in 1952. Soon after, an appeal was launched to save The Wakes in the name of the bird lovers of Britain, but this failed to reach its target. This time the rescuer was the Oates Memorial Trust who put up £50,000, and The Wakes Museum was opened in 1955. As the 250th anniversary of Parson White's birth approached (18 July 1970) the garden fund was launched by local supporters led by Kitty McLachlan, who appealed to readers of the RHS journal. This appeal was a success and laid the foundation for the present happy state of the garden. The dual memorial to White and Captain Oates becomes more than the sum of its parts: at first sight they seem a strange pair to march into immortality together, the daredevil young cavalry officer who journeyed to the ends of the earth, and the crabbed cleric with a pony named Mouse, who suffered coach sickness on the shortest journey. One gave his short life for a glorious adventure, the other laboured in peace for sixty years, and yet they might have each acknowledged the other as a kind of hero, and together they heighten the sense of sanctuary of Selborne.

Parsons Woodforde and White were typical minor clerics of the exuberant world of Hogarth and Fielding and the Revd Sydney Smith. The eighteenth-century Church of England was almost universally Oxbridge educated, rather more interested in politics than the welfare of the flock, where some amassed riches from several livings, and others scraped along as tutors or clerical lackeys in some great house. When Parson Woodforde said prayers on Good Friday 1777, he was conducting that particular service for the first time – a service and sermon once a week and communion once a month were the accepted norm. In 1808 legislation and finances changed all this: clergy were obliged to live in their parishes, the government put up a million pounds to build new churches, the ills of pluralism were banished and support from tithe collection instituted. These settled, dutiful clerics, like the fawning, but still keenly gardening, Mr Collins in *Pride and Prejudice*, or the denizens of Trollope's Barchester diocese, inaugurated the heyday of the rectory or vicarage garden, for which White had prepared the way. Perhaps they truly believed that one was 'nearer God's heart in a garden'[34] – even Charles Wesley saw a Cornish garden as a glimpse of paradise. Their gardens afforded a refuge from wives, children, churchwardens or any disagreeable duties; and though the reasons for taking refuge were as numerous as the clerical gardeners themselves, without them garden and horticultural history would be much the poorer.

They continued to be Oxbridge men, and perhaps it is in those two cities that the most nostalgic images survive. In Cambridge the cloistered spaces are haunted by the Church's tormentors, including Newton, Darwin and Wittgenstein. Charles Darwin was introduced to botany by his professor, the Revd John Stevens Henslow, a brilliant mathematician and theologian who was given the botany chair in 1825. Henslow's Walk in the Botanic Garden commemorates his part in setting the garden in its new forty-acre site in the 1830s, officially opened in 1846. By that time Henslow had left his academic privileges for a disreputable parish, Hitcham in Suffolk, where he won souls by founding a school and teaching botany, instituting allotments and flower shows; this was the lot of many devoted gardening clerics. Henslow's son, the Revd George Henslow of Hampton Lucy in Warwickshire followed in his father's footsteps, becoming a significant figure in the RHS. Another Cambridge man, the Revd William Wilks (born in 1843, the same year as Gertrude Jekyll) is one of the most loved gardening clerics; he became curate in Croydon and vicar at Shirley in 1879. It is said that he spotted a curiosity of *Papaver rhoeas* growing with white edges to its petals in a field at the bottom of his garden (Shirley was then still on the edge of open fields) and, marking it and collecting seed, he carefully selected a range from bright scarlet to pure white, with white flakes and edgings, and the Shirley poppy was born. Revd Wilks was beloved in his parish, where his garden was generously shared with his parishioners (and in part still survives) but he also found the energy to rescue and reorganize the RHS. He was appointed Hon. Secretary in 1888, and found the Society in debt and with only a thousand members paying their subscriptions; by drafting in Frank Reader, a master at Shirley Boys' School, to become cashier, he turned around the finances, organized administration and research and instituted what was to become the Chelsea Flower Show, first held in 1913. Wilks was also interested in fruit growing and collaborated on two books with George Bunyard; he was awarded the Victoria Medal of Honour by the RHS, but his loveliest memorial – apart from the Shirley poppies themselves – are the poppy-wreathed gates at the entrance to the Wisley garden, perhaps less noticed than they deserve because they are always open for gardeners.[35]

In her book on Eversley gardens, Rose Kingsley remembers Shilling's Nursery at Hartley Row (on the A30) where her father, the Revd Charles Kingsley, bought daphne, kalmias and hepaticas. William Robinson asked Rose to contribute to the *English Flower Garden* to describe her father's garden at Eversley Rectory – a 'modest and charming and simple type of garden' with soft borders thick with alyssum, saxifrage, pinks, pansies, roses and phlox, a profusion of climbers on the house walls, and roses, ivies, cotoneaster and pyracantha planted around the church walls, so that the parishioners 'should look on beautiful objects when they assembled in the churchyard for their Sunday gossip before service'. Robinson and Canon Kingsley corresponded, sharing a love of California and the giant redwoods – the Canon brought home seeds of wellingtonia, and some of these trees still stand (Scots Pines were also a remarked feature of the area, both Robinson and Rose Kingsley referring to them as the descendants of some planted at Bramshill by James I: Lord Zouche, the builder of Bramshill was a Jacobite sympathizer, and the Scots Pines sent an easily seen signal of a safe house – they were also planted at Chastleton and the Dashwoods' Kirtlington Park in Oxfordshire has similar plantations.)[36] Rose Kingsley became a noted collector of her name flower but she learned her gardening from her father, who with all his vast literary output, academic and clerical duties, found time to be a naturalist and gardener – he composed his sermons and novels pacing a little garden court outside his study – 'the old Persian Yellow, originally from the garden at Bramshill . . . grew there and Rectory rooms were adorned with its vivid golden blooms "mixed with darkest purple pansies on a ground of wild fern"'.[37] Kingsley recommended growing ferns 'as preferable to Berlin woolwork for young ladies'.[38] Canon Kingsley was Rector of Eversley for thirty-one years, from 1844 until his death in 1875; he was beloved in his parish, and the setting of the church and rectory has changed little since his time.*

Roses bring immediately to mind the greatest clerical rosarian, Samuel Reynolds Hole, the Dean of Rochester, who brought his Christian fellowship to the world of gardening, in that he brought together three extremely tetchy people, Gertrude Jekyll, Ellen Willmott and William Robinson, and made them be nice to each other. Dean Hole was a natural diplomat, he wrote many books in a kind of after-dinner-conversation vein – his *Our Gardens* of 1899 takes the reader round his garden alphabetically, arriving at R for the rose garden, 'the palace of the queen, and though she rejoices in the society of her subjects elsewhere, she brooks no rival near her throne'.[39] Dean Hole is the champion of the traditional rose garden and sweeps his reader on into his world: 'Who made you Lord Chamberlain to the Queen of Flowers' he hears his critics mutter, and defends himself as the man who invented rose shows, wrote *A Book About Roses* (1869), was President of the National Rose Society and for fifty-four years had studied roses. Asked if he should not have been tending his flock, the Dean replies 'as regards my ministrations in a small country parish (Caunton, near Newark, Notts., where he was rector for forty years) I always maintained the daily service of the Church, and my daily visits to the school; knew every man, woman and child in the place, and have preached, since I took orders, in 500 churches from the Land's End to the Border.'[40] Some more of the Dean's garden alphabet is irresistible: K is for Kerria – "How can you grow that rubbishy Kerrya[sic]?" I was asked, "every pig-jobber has it in his garden." 'And why,' says the Dean, 'may not the pig-jobber enjoy the bright yellow flowers as much as I do? ... for on the basis of commonality the Laburnum "so familiar and dear to us all" would have to go as well.'[41] By the time he gets to *Prunus pissardii* he has run out of admiring adjectives for his adored plants – admirable, beautiful, charming, delicious, gorgeous, handsome etc., have been played out, and he cannot bring himself to a ripping sweet pea, stunning lily or awfully jolly orchid! The good Dean is nothing short of a gardener's darling – he believed with William Wordsworth that 'Nature never did

* The village is still very proud of him, and two new pictorial memorials – one for Canon Kingsley and the other for the architect John James of Warbrook – have recently been placed in the new church hall.

betray the heart that loved her' and his garden is enjoyment and the stuff of friendship to him. His rose-confederate was the sometime vicar of Westwell in Kent, the Revd Henry d'Ombrain (1818–1905) who founded the National Rose Society with him; d'Ombrain was also founder of The Horticultural Club and was secretary of both for over twenty-five years and, of course, both societies survive today.

The good Dean was also a garden visitor – en route to some of those 500 sermons. In *A Book about the Garden* (1904) he described the wonderful Cornish garden of the Hon Revd John Townshend Boscawen at Lamorran, west of Truro: 'a remembrance of Eden . . . our first glorious home'.[42] Boscawen began his garden about 1850, filling his rocky valley with pines, palms, hemlocks, sequoia and cupressus to shelter precious rhododendrons (which he hybridized), pieris and camellias; and he was one of the first to grow *Cardiocrinum giganteum* en masse – a sight I for one would give a lot to see. Revd Boscawen produced a gardening son, who was never allowed to garden at home, so the Revd Canon Arthur Townshend Boscawen made his vicarage garden at Ludgvan, on the east of the Penzance to St Ives road. Ludgvan rectory looks down on a field – which the Canon filled with anemones – and across the bay to St Michael's Mount. Canon Boscawen had little help but achieved miracles: his anemone experiment founded the Cornish anemone industry. He did the same for broccoli with seeds imported from Germany and played a full part in RHS shows and committees. Yet his church was always well filled and the children regularly taken around the garden to learn their plants. There was much of the Cornish idyll about the Canon's garden and life, which was appreciated by his bishop when he died in 1939: 'his life was a shining example of the combination of personal faith and practical usefulness . . . it will be a lucky thing for Cornwall if his example inspires many others . . . to seek the same paths of sympathetic co-operation with Nature and with their fellow-men'.[43] For such enlightened views the Church of the later twentieth century was to have little use, as we shall see.

It was not by accident that a cleric, the Revd William Gilpin (1724–1804), assisted the more awe-inspiring (sublime) and lugubrious tastes of the Picturesque movement into being. His travels in Wales and the Lake District revealed – when one had dared to venture out of the secret garden – the horrifying grandeur of God's larger works. But Gilpin soon took refuge again, as Vicar of Boldre in the New Forest in 1778, and from then on his journeys to his scattered parishioners in hovels in the woods, enabled him to find the same regressive qualities in gnarled trunks, exposed roots, water-sculpted banks and fallen giants of beech and oak. Gilpin's *Remarks on Forest Scenery and Other Woodland Views* (1791), a landmark of the Picturesque, is a celebration of what designers call 'conceal and reveal' – he revels in the easily parted bough, the dark recess, the skeletal leaf, elegantly hanging foliage and the more 'savage Salvator Rosa aspects' of a . . . 'blasted oak, ragged, scathed and leafless shooting its peeled, white branches athwart the gathering blackness of some rising storm'.[44]

This was the taste of the Gothic novel and quickly found popularity with the middle class: E. W. Bovill's *English Country Life 1780–1830* observed the laburnums and lilacs accompanied by piles of large stones, old roots and trunks, hillocks of flints and fused bricks – and 'one of the greatest of garden horrors' rustic furniture.[45] This fashion for the 'grotesque' rather than 'picturesque' was worst in country retreats: Bovill quotes in horror John Byng's account of a Lincolnshire parson's garden (which was most likely William Stukeley, the antiquarian cleric of Stamford) 'almost cover'd with cloisters, seats, &c, all made of roots of trees, and moss to correspond with an hermitage in the centre, finish'd with curious taste . . . (with) . . . several rooms, recesses and chapels, all light'd by old stain'd glass . . . the ornamental parts of fir cones, tables of polished horse bones, inscriptions worked through the floor in pebbles and doors of fir cones and roots woven curiously together.'[46]

The reverend gentlemen Gilpin, Stukeley and Mason were three eccentrics in any social sphere, but the fact that they were clerics carries the garden of sanctuary into the realm of the Gothic and grotesque. This peculiar fashion – a perfect expression of the self-mocking, less than robust English sense of humour – for grottoes, hermitages, ruins, rock-work and the generally absurd, is irrepressible. It was undeniably popular; Barbara Jones's search for shell-work and grottoes led her to the celebrated places (Woburn, Goodwood, Goldney in Bristol, Oatlands etc)[47] but she concluded that every town in England probably had its example of nineteenth-century grot-work (which is where the word grotty comes from) – a teashop in Brighton, an oyster bar in London, beneath the Blackpool Tower and endless examples in Victorian conservatories up and down the land. Best of all, she found a grotto house in a chalk hillside at Riddlesdown in Surrey faded to a Tea Garden: 'the grotto, entrance ½d., ran tin-roofed up the hill, with dusty memorials to famous donkeys that had given rides on the downs above, and the tombs of pet monkeys from the menagerie, and of cats and dogs, all set into the rock and lava work. Children shouted everywhere, and suitably drank mineral water, and carved their names on the old white paint of the tables or wrote them in very black pencil and purple copying on the open mouths of the shells.'[48] The whole Victorian affair with the macabre is encapsulated in this grimy image, handed down to the mid-twentieth century and now demolished. Out of the incarcerated seashells tumble random associations: the cult of Youngism, from Edward Young's *Night Thoughts*, his two o'clock glooms which produced 'Procrastination is the thief of time' and other worthies under the influence of sleeplessness, depression and drugs. *Night Thoughts* was translated into French – *Les Nuits de Young* – and became the name of a famous Moss rose in 1845, a rose of dark, intense purple maroon velvet flowers.[49] The rose takes its place with the ancient symbols of eternity, the yew, cypress and holly, and is joined by laurel, bay and rhododendron in the secret groves of Victorian shrubberies, those of the rectory sharing the churchyard yews. And any garden visitor will know of the poignant attraction of the pets' graves beneath the laurels. Young in his *Night Thoughts* endorsed the fashion for garden memorials. The empty arches, shell pavilions and rustic obelisks were invariably dedicated to someone, and notable eighteenth-century burials happened in gardens – Jean-Jacques Rousseau who died in 1778 whilst the guest of the Marquis de Girardin at Ermenonville was tucked up in the garden he loved. Rousseau had immortalized Ermenonville as Julie's garden in *La Nouvelle Héloise*, and his burial on the Ile des Peupliers in a massively ornamental tomb caught the romantic imagination of both France and England; foreshadowing, perhaps, the burial of Diana, Princess of Wales, on an island in the ornamental lake at Althorp. In France also, the fashionable Père Lachaise cemetery, designed as an Eden, Arcady or Elysium devoted to 'égalité' and intended to take away the terrors of the catacombs, was tremendously influential: Père Lachaise was seen by William Robinson, whose interest in burials, especially cremation and urn-burial (in the manner of Sir Thomas Browne) was an essential part of his garden writing and thinking. Other far-flung references coalesced – the opinion of Tacitus that virtue belonged in the Stoic garden, which was the place to prepare for death,[50] the garden tombs of the Mogul emperors, Babur, Akbar, Jahanghir and the Taj Mahal, and the growing knowledge of the mysteries of Chinese gardens that made caves and grottoes symbols of the homes of the Immortals. In America (where city cemeteries, such as Laurel Hill, Philadelphia, 1835, had long served dual purposes as parks), lawn and woodland settings with groves and shrubberies had become accepted designs by the end of the nineteenth century. Los Angeles' Forest Lawns (which even dropped the word 'cemetery') was opened in 1906.

It is but a short step, therefore, to Edwin Lutyens's understandably emotive reaction to his first sight of the battlefields of the Pas de Calais in August 1917:

> the obliteration of all human endeavour and achievement and the human achievement of destruction is bettered by the poppies and wild flowers that are as friendly to an unexploded shell as they are to the leg of a garden seat in Surrey . . . It is all a sense of wonderment, how can such things be. Ribbons of little crosses each touching each across a cemetery, set in a wilderness of annuals and where one sort of flower is grown the effect is charming, easy and oh so pathetic, that one thinks no other monument is needed.[51]

In his report to the War Graves Commission Lutyens noted that while it was 'important to secure the qualities of repose and dignity there is no need for the cemeteries to become gloomy or even sad-looking places'.[52] Under his influence, allied to Herbert Baker and Reginald Blomfield, and later Robert Lorimer and Charles Holden, with Gertrude Jekyll's assurances, the war cemeteries became the modern apotheosis of the secret garden.[53] Though many had to be extended for the Second World War, the original designs have been carefully perpetuated: for the cemeteries that Lutyens and Miss Jekyll designed in detail (which set the pattern for all the others) there is the enclosing evergreen (holly or yew) hedge, the symbolic fastigiate oak or Lombardy poplars, massings of the workaday shrubs of the English countryside – blackthorn, whitehorn, hazel, guelder rose and honeysuckle – with the Virgin's flowery meads ushered into soft borders where the headstones stand, hellebores, narcissus, forget-me-not, fritillaries, foxgloves, columbines, London Pride, bergenia, nepeta and roses.[54] These are Arts and Crafts gardens, outdoor rooms of green walls, their vistas ordered and closed by the most sublime stone works, most with book-room pavilions and shelters, all of them laced and imbued with meaning and double meaning, all the mannerist notions of their seventeenth-century forebears. They are echoed in war memorial gardens up and down the land, even all over the world. Interestingly Lutyens came from a military family, and though he rejected so much of this he may have retained some conversation of the legendary Battle of Landen (1693) where William of Orange was badly defeated by the French with many casualties – the summer after 'the earth, saturated with the blood of twenty thousand slain, broke forth into millions of poppies, and the traveller who passed that vast sheet of scarlet might well fancy that the earth had indeed given up her dead'.[55] The longer tradition, that the spirits of the dead returned to life in the fields of corn, came from classical times, requiring the propitiation of the harvest-gods lest that be seen as a double-slaying. Frazer quotes:

> I sometimes think that never blows so red
> The Rose as where some buried Caesar bled;
> That every Hyacinth the Garden wears
> Dropt in her Lap from some once lovely Head.[56]

An elegant ivory-covered volume, *My Lady's Garden* 'planted and grown by Hackleplume' and published in 1921, must be one of the most curious pieces of garden literature. The pen name 'Hackleplume' is from the hackle emblem of the Black Watch and the plume of the Royal Sussex Regiment, and the garden is a series of poems with watercolours by Marjorie Rayner. The copy I have is inscribed by the author 'Kaveh his book' and from the index I see this is Lieut. E. R. Wood of the West Kent Yeomanry:* *kaveh* is coffee blossom, and – like all the names of soldiers and flowers in the book – Lieut. Wood has been worked into a poem:

---

* If any descendant or relative of Lieut. E. R. Wood of the West Kent Yeomanry should happen to read this, I will be happy to return the book.

The Allah Garden

Blossom aromatic, *kaveh* of the East,
Evanescent blossom, fragrant, frail, and white,
In the glow of morning tinged with rose or light,
Later changed to berries – oriental feast –
Coffee, dream of poets – in the Allah Garden.[57]

All the soldiers celebrated in the Allah Garden seem to have been studying at the School of Oriental Studies: most of Hackleplume's subjects seem to be friends who have survived the war; here perhaps should be mentioned the first garden in the book, The Glade of Glory, which is dedicated, like the book itself, to those who did not:

Henderson, Macmorran, whose heroic deeds
Of New Zealand valour swell the glorious list,
Gorringe of the Sussex, Carver – will exist
While our grateful memory eloquently pleads:
Theirs the place of honour in my Lady's Garden.'[58]

This, allied to phrases which follow:

Stricken mothers, weeping, watching, hour by hour
Mourn for loved ones missing from my Lady's Garden.[59]

seems to indicate that they are an informal expression – with much regimental support – of what the War Graves Commission did not allow: the return of the dead for burial at home.

But gardens up and down the land do not require graves to evoke that loss. The contrast between a light and living garden and the unforgettable loss is palpable (at least for me) at How Caple Court in Herefordshire. Here the quality of the fertile, unchanged landscape, with the lichen-covered stone and old timbering of the buildings, standing on a bluff above the Wye valley, inculcates upon a deep peace. The heart of the peace is the garden, once-forgotten elaborate terraces, a huge pergola, a pavilion, statues (which may be shorn of an arm or angel's wing) and trimmed yews. The garden, lately restored, exhibits gentle care and hard work, but it still has all the enchantment of a sleeping garden: it is not difficult to imagine those palmy golden afternoons of Edwardian England in this remote corner of the world, where Lennox Bertram Lee, an amateur garden designer, made his garden and enlarged his house in the Arts and Crafts style, the fashion of the day. The gate from the garden leads into the wildflower-strewn churchyard, which seems to stand on the edge of a golden-enough landscape; inside are the memorials to no less than five members of the Lee family, four brothers and an uncle, killed on the western front. The beauty of this place is full of echoes and questions: voices from the tennis parties, music on a summer's evening, how could they bring themselves to leave? How could they bear the partings? The garden of How Caple Court is not unique: it is just one place in hundreds of thousands, where the garden remembers an inextinguishable sadness in its quiet beauty.

In those still innocent 1890s, readers of the infinitely wise *Gardeners' Chronicle* were given a lesson in the usefulness of a rectory garden with an editorial tour of Dr Bartram's at Wakes-Colne in Essex. The writer, David Taylor Fish, was a gardener turned designer and journalist and his countrywide lecturing and judging had confirmed the rectory garden's healthy survival: 'Modern vicars and rectors, like the older ecclesiastics, are also members of the gentle arts and skilful guilds of horticulture.' At Wakes-Colne the garden had coped with 'modern difficulties' but had not failed in beauty or use. Dr Bartram, who had been headmaster at Berkhamsted School for twenty-four years, taught by example, his three acres crammed 'wherever a foot of space can be found a cordon-tree, bush or plant is packed into it'. Fish considers the interdependence of the life-giving harmony of the garden: the compost and manure from house and stables nurture the garden and orchard, bees and poultry minister to the flowers and pests, and fruit, honey and vegetables are returned to the house in the age-old cycle. 'Waste not, want not' seems written all over the garden; men of God had a special reason (and duty) for demonstrating a benevolent God to their flock – Dr Bartram offered prizes for the cleanest and best cultivated gardens kept by railway or other workers, and widows (the widows always won). Edward Mawley, the rosarian from Berkhamsted, was an old friend of Dr Bartram's and he came over to help judge the roses, which were favourites: 'the whole parish smelt of roses and not a few expert budders were found converting wilding Briars' into garden plants.[60]

The headmasterly Dr Bartram seemed to be holding his position in a changing world. The continuing agricultural depression, the rise of a Nonconformist ministry in new urban areas, even the restoration of a Catholic hierarchy, were threatening the Church of England's traditionally patriarchal ease. The Trollopian world of quiet garden closes was the province of the distinguished and elderly, who held the sway, but not for long, and perhaps it was just because they were so inordinately proud of their gardens, that gardens were marked out as obsolete luxuries.

A remarkable mid-nineteenth-century religious theme park made by James Mellor at Hough-Hole House, Rainow, near Macclesfield, illustrates in a curious way how the garden was to tumble from sacred place to irrelevance. Mellor had been brought up an ardent Methodist, but claimed 'a profound religious experience' in which he had a vision of heaven and a direction to give up 'worldly science' (his family's cotton finishing business) to concentrate on spiritual things. He was also a keen gardener and seems rather cleverly to have found salvation in the unifying theory of natural philosophy propounded by Emanuel Swedenborg (also a keen gardener, who used his garden and a summer house 'with moveable screens and mirrors' for the enlightenment of visitors). Thus allowed to garden 'spiritually', Mellor converted some two acres of paddocks into the Holy Way and all its quandaries, a visitor-experience of Christian's journey to the Celestial City from Bunyan's *Pilgrim's Progress*, complete with a Slough of Despond, Delectable Mountains, Bypath Meadow (which doubled as a tennis court), and Howling House. This last was a summer house with a vaulted room where a sulphurous smoky fire could be lit and an aeolian harp contrived to produce the cries of the tormented. Finally, the Celestial City was the curious and rather bare brick chapel, reached by a spiral stair, where Mellor preached to those who arrived safely.[61]

Though popular with visitors, and administered with the lightness and humour that were apparently characteristic of James Mellor, who lived until 1891 (and the age of ninety-six), surely the garden poses a problem, as a theme park, in that, though amusing, it was the old vision of hell and damnation. Were all such earthly pleasures as a tennis court, the vegetable garden (also the Slough of Despond) and Hill Difficulty beside the arbour, only the prelude to an arid little chapel that promised eternity in dry-as-dust haranguing? If one cares about the garden as a usefully humanist device, which is essentially the thesis of this book, then Mellor's garden provoked confusion as well as amusement. This

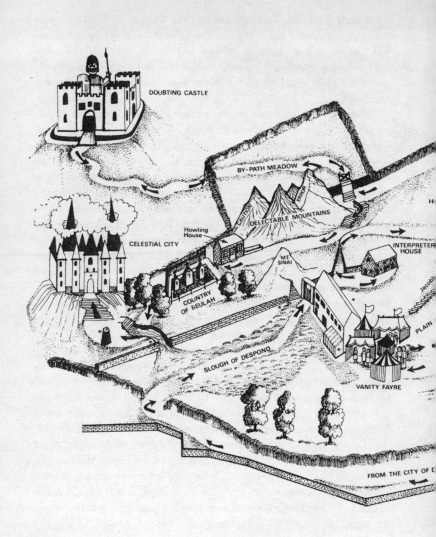

DOUBTING CASTLE

BY-PATH MEADOW

CELESTIAL CITY

Howling
House

CAUTION
ERROR
DELECTABLE MOUNTAINS

'MT.
SINAI'

INTERPRETER'S
HOUSE

H

Jacob

COUNTRY
OF BEULAH

Plain

SLOUGH OF DESPOND

VANITY FAYRE

FROM THE CITY OF D

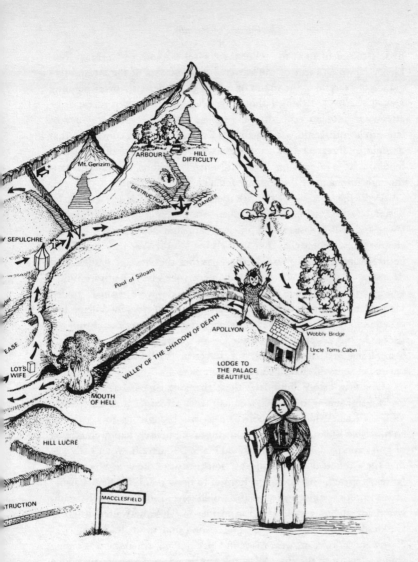

James Mellor's garden at Hough-Hole House, Rainow, near Macclesfield, an imaginatively reconstructed plan drawn by Jean Ashley to show the main features. (From *Garden History*, vol 15, no 2, Autumn 1987).

finds a complement at the other theological extreme, in Cardinal John Henry Newman's fear of the 'extreme deliciousness of the air and fragrance of everything' he found on a visit to dangerously overwhelming Devon ... 'really I think I should dissolve into essence of roses, or be attenuated into an echo, if I lived here'. Was the greatest voice of late-nineteenth-century spirituality so unsure of his own conviction that it could be threatened by a rose? He was very protective of his sisters, living in Rose Mount on Rose Hill outside Oxford, so were gardens the rightful realm of the frippery females of the species?[62]

With the opening of the twentieth century the garden as a useful pastoral device can no longer be taken seriously, and though Trollopian lawns and beds of roses might linger in cathedral closes, for the younger clergy who served as chaplains in the First World War they could only be irrelevant. In hard-pressed urban parishes the vicarage garden, if it existed at all, became increasingly like everyone else's, a private indulgence; in the countryside where Georgian rectories were gradually traded for manageable brick villas the garden might still host the village fête or a garden party or two, but it also became rather precious. From the garden historian's point of view the loss of the traditional English vicarage garden as Gilbert White, the Reverend Wilks and Dr Bartram devised it seems to have been fairly complete.

One man's story illuminates these changing times, that of a much-loved clergyman who reached a constituency far larger than any parish. William Keble Martin was born in 1877 and brought up in a series of comfortable Victorian rectories, enjoying an immensely happy childhood of good companions and country holidays: he knew from an early age that the symbols of the significant moments were the wild flowers that he remembered, and he taught himself to draw them; his first drawing of snowdrops against ivy leaves (he would never mix his subjects again) was made at home at Dartington in Devon while he waited to go to Cuddesdon Theology College. The second and third drawings, *Herb Robert* and *Stitchwort*, were made in Cork in 1899, where he was seeing young men off to the Boer War, the fourth, *Mossy Saxifrage*, was done in the Brecon Beacons, where he helped rescue some climbers. *Jacob's Ladder* marked his engagement and in 1909 he and his new wife, Violet, went to their first parish at Wath on Dearne: they worked hard in a condemned vicarage, gardened to feed themselves and to 'stand shoulder to shoulder' with their mining flock, made their own tennis lawn for their relaxation and were thrilled to see Blériot and the Wright Brothers demonstrating air flights at Doncaster. Keble Martin followed his miners to war as a front-line army chaplain: he later remembered how the canals on the Belgian border looked like flower beds from a distance, crowded with iris, buttercups, meadowsweet and purple loosestrife and how 'we hardly ever met with non-British flowers'. He returned to Wath but after a few years applied to move south for the sake of his children's health: botany was largely forgotten but Violet Martin knew that it was her husband's only solace in times of greatest stress. He drew *Common Meadow Rue* on a holiday in 1923, and then gradually built up his collection, beginning to concentrate upon the flora of Devon, until another war put an end to such luxury. He drew *Sibthorpia* and *Lysimachia cillata* to celebrate outings at the end of the war, and in 1949, aged seventy-two, he officially retired. He neither gave up drawing nor priesting, but allocated them more equal attention; in 1959 his drawings were exhibited at the Royal Horticultural Society in Vincent Square. When his *Concise British Flora* was published six years later he admitted to enjoying every minute of the celebrity status it brought him, and he finished his autobiography, *Over The Hills*, in his ninety-first year.[63]

As if to confirm Revd Keble Martin's lifelong passion, Canon Raven's famous history of *English Naturalists from Neckham to Ray* was published in 1947. This was a 'study in the making of the modern world' and a scientific apologia of weight and scholarship: he traced the study of nature from the mystique of medieval illuminated manuscripts, through the 'scientists' (Abbot Neckham the cosmologist born in 1157; three great Franciscans, Robert Grosseteste, Roger Bacon and Bartholomew the Englishman; and William Turner 'the father of English botany') to the writings of the herbalists Gerard, Parkinson and Culpeper and to John Ray, the 'major naturalist' who died in 1705. In doing so Canon Raven convincingly demonstrated that holy men (which of course they had to be in order to be educated men) had been comprehending scientists throughout history (and long before the advent of Darwin) and also – and perhaps of greater significance – that the study of the natural sciences was implicitly virtuous. (This last draped the mantle of self-righteousness over the movements to conserve flora, fauna and wilderness.)

Canon Raven's book was the Church's only contribution to what might be called the awakening environmental debate outside 'the secret garden'. He followed it with his 1951 Gifford Lectures on science and religion, disowning The Fall and St Augustine's rejection of nature as pagan, and assessing long centuries of wonders and delights in both plants and animals that just might qualify them to be God's creatures.* The argument was valid but it was not to be widely heard, lost in a wave of humanitarian bias, borne on the 'vigour and success' of American religion and philosophy in the modern world.[64]

For the last fifty years the established Church has been almost wholly concerned with internal controversies, to the exclusion of any apparent concern for the natural or cultivated earth that is our home. Church schools, once the beacons of learning in nature study and gardening, have relinquished these subjects to conform to state secularism. Country churchyards – once God's acre, fluttering with wild flowers, butterflies and beneficent ghosts for the comfort of the living – are now mostly burdensome nuisances, a status lamentably dominated by their habitually rough and insensitive maintenance. The majority of town churches have only a tarmac bleakness of convenience, with nothing to support belief in the increasingly irrelevant messages delivered inside them. It is not only the Church of England but all churches in Britain which seem to have forgotten – for one reason or another – that the Mother of Christ belongs in a garden. In so doing they must bear much of the blame for the present schism between town and country, and the modern generations that imagine themselves apart from the natural world. Perhaps the rise of interest in green and woodland burial is the final damnation on the twentieth century's Christian stewardship of Mother Earth, in that their approved abodes for the dead are intolerable for so many of the living.

This conclusion is all the more tragic because there is so much to be done with the notion of the garden of charity and Christian love: far from being an irrelevant luxury or old-fashioned indulgence, the church, rectory or manse garden, call it what you will, could still have an important pastoral role in modern society. It is well known (as the

---

* Revd C. A. Johns' *Flowers of the Field* (two volumes, 1853; 33rd edition 1911) is quoted by Raven in his lectures as one of White's successors. Revd Johns inspired many Victorian gardeners, including Gertrude Jekyll who wore out one copy, 'nearly exhausting two more'.

National Trust will confirm) that gardens win over more hearts and minds and pilgrim feet than bricks and mortar ever will. It is, of course, possible to find religious communities and some churches that find themselves comfortable in the natural world, but to find a rectory garden still performing a pastoral role is rare, so rare that my last garden for this chapter is well-known far beyond its parish. This is the garden of Bulwick Rectory in Northamptonshire, part of a picturesque stone village within needy reach of the post-industrial Corby new town, where for about twenty years the Revd Mervyn Wilson has gardened. Though he regards himself as 'a sort of anachronism' his family tradition of apple growing and gardening and his own belief in a Benedictine legacy – 'a balance for holiness at prayer, charitable work, learning and work with the hands' and making a harmonious setting for life – all supported his persistence.[65] In his previous south London parish of Bermondsey he made a green oasis of part of the old churchyard, despite the rushing traffic, and worked with his parishioners on their allotments in the former Surrey Docks. The garden at Bulwick still entertains annual parties of Bermondsey visitors, of all ages, as well as many people from its own Peterborough diocese: it is a rambling, interesting garden of secret corners, flat lawns for ball games, enclosed spaces for parties, with a folly of 'constructive imagination' with a conical roof that floats above all the hedges. The philosophy is to mix flowers, fruit and vegetables all in several varieties – a range of apples and pears, four sorts of climbing bean, five kinds of potato, avoiding sprays but with occasional winter washes – to create a microcosmic but rich environment in which all forms of life will flourish together. The result is an appreciation of times and seasons, an amazement at the infinite variety of creation seen in detail, and an understanding of the tension between chaos and order that is at the heart of things.

CHAPTER THREE

✦✦✦ ❖ ✦✦✦

The Military Garden

In September 1918, Siegfried Sassoon was summoned to a meeting with Winston Churchill at the Ministry of Munitions, and after an hour spent discussing fox-hunting, Sassoon was offered a job. Much of the time was taken up, however, with Churchill's pacing the room, a big cigar in the corner of his mouth, spontaneously speechifying and vindicating militarism. Sassoon recorded his conclusions of this extraordinary encounter; despite 'the great man' being so likeable and friendly, 'Yet there was no doubt that I disagreed with almost every opinion he had uttered about militarism. Had he been entirely serious, I wondered, when he said that "war is the normal occupation of man"? He had indeed qualified the statement . . . "war – and gardening"'[1]

An exploration of gardening history proves Churchill to have had a point. The British taste for gardening has a great deal to do with a warlike past: fantastic military or embattled gardens were made to reflect war in Europe, or the English Civil War, and so many garden terms come from the arts of warfare – cordon, earthing-up, trench, bastion, the batter of a hedge, palisade, zig-zag, covered way, enceinte. The delight of a garden swing was adapted from a military means of getting a man into an otherwise unattainable position; the ha-ha, the enabling motif of the eighteenth-century landscape style which kept the cows off the lawn, has a military pedigree. The empathy between soldiering and gardening is a persistent human trait. When all these suppositions are explored, the military or embattled garden – warfare by another means – comes gloriously into the full light of a popular tradition. It is this tradition that overlaid the cultivation of plants with the strong desire for order and control, for the demonstration of efficiency through neatness in seventeenth-century gardens. It may even be possible to go farther and suggest that the military traditions, order and neatness, may have been the means whereby men laid siege to, and over-ran the previously feminine domain of the garden.

As with the Mogul emperors and their pleasure gardens, the other great gardeners of ancient history wielded despotic control over their surroundings, though even the despotism seems less terrible when it results in a garden. The miracle oases of the Pharaohs were their most precious perquisites of power, but in the heat and the dust this ancient heritage has dwindled to fragments of evidence. There is the enduring legend of the passionately gardening Queen Hatshepsut bringing home her incense trees from the land of Punt; and her consort Tuthmosis the Third also made gardens with plants won from their joint campaigns in Somalia (Punt) and Syria. Curious artifacts – a wooden model of house and garden found in the tomb of Meketre at Thebes, a strange lotus flower with the head of a child from the Valley of the Kings, desiccated garlands, fragments of tomb paintings, seeds and roots, are being slowly yielded to piece together our distant view of how the Pharaohs loved their gardens.[2]

Cyrus the Second, the Great, who died about 539 BC (and whose empire stretched from the Mediterranean to the Hindu Kush) heads the list of legendary soldier-gardeners: Cyrus was praised by Sir Thomas Browne in 1658 for being 'a splendid and regular planter' who actually dirtied his hands.[3] Recently Cyrus's palace at Pasagardee has been retrieved from the desert sands, revealing a complete structure of stone watercourses 25 cm wide, punctuated at right angles and intervals with 80 × 80 cm square basins, all of which would have brimmed with clear water, controlled by a complex system of sluices. It appears that Cyrus made the first of the ancient four-fold gardens, *chahar bagh*, as he was called the King of the Four Quarters. Cyrus's gardens reveal his omnipotence; his courtiers learned to read his moods by observing his frustration or pleasure in his garden. The site at Pasagardee is completely undefended, a microcosm of a vast, unthreatened empire, a paradise on earth.[4]

The descendants of Cyrus brought their gardens along the southern shores of the Mediterranean – Sicily was taken by the Muslims in AD 878 – and to Spain, where they have already assumed the guises of pleasure gardens. From Sicily the Islamic ideas of gardening travelled up the leg of Italy, to be transformed by Medici princes and warrior cardinals into the fabled villa gardens of the Italian Renaissance. The Medici and their contemporaries were nothing if not power-brokers, and it is sobering to realize that these most beautiful gardens arose out of violence, intrigue and brutality. Their evocative names roll through the memory and garden history – villas Gamberaia, Medici at Fiesole, d'Este, Lante, Castello, Caprarola, the Boboli Gardens in Florence, and so many more – all witness the irrefutable wisdom of making a garden for posterity. The darkest deeds can be erased by the sprinkling of a fountain, the worst reputation burnished by a fine balustrade.[5]

However, the exciting and novel part of the search for the military garden focuses on its more popular origins, in the archaeology of fortifications, and in the collective affinity with spades and mattocks, with trenching and earthing-up, which have been imbibed into our genes from earliest times. Warfare was never the business of an isolated few, but a communal activity. The archaeologist Christopher Taylor has questioned the purely militarist interpretation of embankments and ditches, as at Maiden Castle in Dorset or Clare in Suffolk, as well as on other sites.[6] He suggests that these complex, major structures, which absorbed so many thousands of hours of labour of men with mattocks, could not have been purely for occasional defence, but also served purposes of ceremony, social organization and status, including pleasure in one's surroundings. Common sense also tells us that nature was not much different in first century Dorset or along the Saxon shore from how it is today, and that newly turned and cleared earthworks were soon colonized by wild flowers and herbs, which were undoubtedly gathered and enjoyed. The more enterprising may have grown their coleworts and turnips in the fertile niches where soil was washed down the banks. Human nature, both opportunistic and lazy, was little different either, and having laboured to dig it was only sensible to harvest. This tradition of 'gardening' on fortifications persisted throughout medieval Europe in periods of peace; ramparts and breastworks were colonized as an escape from the disease and stink of the towns and became the notorious sub-urbes, cursed by the commanders who ordered them hastily swept away when the enemy came into view.[7]

Christopher Taylor goes on to suggest that 'defended' but apparently empty spaces on domestic sites, Sulgrave Manor in Northamptonshire and Burwell in Cambridgeshire amongst many, are in fact gardens. Is it not possible that our instinctive love of the fourfold crossing design for a garden comes from the logical grid layout of Saxon towns, the four-gated burghs, rather than from distant Islam? Is not the ruthless consistency of the Roman mind equally evident in the barrack 'terraces', the water rills and hypocausts of the great Chesters Fort on Hadrian's Wall as in the water gardens of Villa d'Este? Dr Taylor also re-examines the motte-and-bailey constructions of the Normans – 'semi-fortified residences of nouveaux lords' – which were often ridiculous and impractical, ill-built and shoddy, but make more sense when interpreted as status symbols in an age when symbols were all. A motte allowed the lord to see what his neighbours were doing, but it was soon ground down by the weather, mimicked in gardens and called a Mount.

The real pleasure of building fortifications is demonstrated by bold Sir Edward Dalyngrigge, who returned from the Hundred Years War at about midway point, in the 1380s, to build his state-of-the-art military fortress at Bodiam in Sussex. Richard II licensed Sir Edward to fortify his manor house 'and make thereof a castle in defence of the adjacent countryside and for resistance against our enemies',[8] but Sir Edward started afresh, on an indefensible lower site, to build himself 'a veteran's toy'.[9] The essential joys of Bodiam are that it fulfils every child's vision of a toy castle, four square, round-towered, castellated, sitting in its lake-like moat, and that it also expresses the luxury of belonging to an island race, of being set apart from these interminable European wars to live in a decorative peace, making garden walks beyond the moat, 'tilting at windmills'. Bodiam, and its contemporary military conceits, Scotney Castle, Kent, and Old Wardour in Wiltshire, are the first intimations that the idea of war (rather than the reality) can thrill our senses and embellish our surroundings to the admiration of our friends.* Bodiam itself, which was rescued from near ruin and restored first by Lord Ashcombe (the builder George Cubitt) and then by Lord Curzon, almost had a higher garden destiny. In 1925, after Lord Curzon's death, it came on the market at £30,000; Vita Sackville-West longed to buy it, 'beloved Bodiam' as she called it, but it was priced wildly beyond her

---

* This idea will of course evolve for about four hundred years, into the sham castles of the Picturesque.

means. If she had had the money there would have been no Sissinghurst Castle garden, and the delicious dream remains of what Bodiam would have become.[10]

From soldiering abroad the British learned 'a wide if ill-assorted' knowledge of fortifications and siege warfare in time for the Civil War; the Royalist Princes Maurice and Rupert and Parliamentarian Generals Fairfax and Goring had all served under Frederick Henry of Nassau at the siege of Breda.[11] The shock as war took hold of the peaceful landscape of mid-seventeenth-century England was compounded by the appearance of the curious constructions of fortification, which sometimes assumed an almost mystical meaning to a stupefied town or village. Most curious were the star forts, great earthworks of jutting ravelins and sloping banks or glacis, like that surviving at Earith near Huntingdon and The Queen's Sconce outside Newark, 'the most comprehensively fortified and most consistently besieged' of battle towns.[12] These star forts, the stuff of old soldiers' tales from the continent, caught hold of the imagination; they were transformed directly into gardens, appearing as a fortified wood at Grimsthorpe Castle designed by Stephen Switzer, masquerading as Paston in his book *Ichnographia Rustica* of 1718 (*Plate 29*). The Stamford antiquary William Stukeley, who had inspected both Earith and Newark defences, sketches the ladies in his Duchess's Bastion at Grimsthorpe in 1736. The walled bastion projected from the woodland, allowing them a view over the park and escape by a stile; a wall and outer ditch prevented the sheep and cattle from getting into the woodland plantation. Switzer uses the ravelins projecting into the wood to dictate the avenues and rides through the trees, each ravelin protecting an enclosed bastion for viewing and conversing, and the whole star fort encased an ornamental garden with pool and central obelisk.

The superstitions that grew from the Civil War and its aftermath is recorded in the diary of Sir Thomas Isham of Lamport, who was staying in Oxford in July 1673: he heard how, during the siege, the Magdalen College walls had formed part of the defences held by Henry Carey, Earl of Dover, and his regiment of scholars, and how they had cut down the trees and built a bastion to command the Cherwell that they called 'Dover Pier'. In 1657 the Fellows had replanted elms to make a shady walk, but these were pulled out after the Restoration because of the taint of being planted 'in the fantastick times' and beeches

replaced them.[13] The terraced embankment on the east side of the
Fellows Garden at Wadham College is also a Civil War remnant. And
at Holywell Mill 'where the scholars do night and day gall their hands
with mattocks and shovells' was the ravelin which was found in excavations for St Catherine's College in the late 1950s. Each side of the
ravelin was about ninety yards long, and the ditch outside about ten
feet wide and eight feet deep; it was a rough affair, the earth bank
spiked with wooden palisades, and the scholars who manned it were
never really put to the test, but it seems appropriate that its form survives
in the boundary of Arne Jacobsen's beautiful modern garden at
St Catherine's.[14]

First among Civil War soldier-gardeners must be Thomas, 3rd
Baron Fairfax of Nunappleton in that soft and watery land of the River
Ouse, just south-east of York. Fairfax embodies the paradox of the
military gardener; he was tall, dark, rather delicate in looks and often
in ill-health, gentle and beloved at home, yet he was brought alive by
military life, displaying an almost manic fire in campaign and battle.
He had been sent to the Low Countries to study war, dancing and
mathematics when he was eighteen, and returned to Yorkshire to marry
Anne Vere; their daughter Maria (Mary) was born in 1638. The following
year, in answering the King's summons to York which was followed by
the abortive march to Berwick, Fairfax began the long campaign which
led him to the command of Cromwell's New Model Army, the victories
at Naseby and Preston, and his bitterly reluctant acquiescence in the
execution of Charles I on 30 January 1649.[15] After all this tumult and
sacrifice, Fairfax returned home to Nunappleton, to his family, his library
and his garden. The garden is known through the words of the tutor
employed for Maria Fairfax, Andrew Marvell, who begins with the
returning General:

> Who, when retired here to Peace,
> His warlike Studies could not cease;
> But laid these Gardens out in sport
> In the just Figure of a Fort;
> And with five Bastions it did fence,
> As aiming one for ev'ry Sense.

Marvell's every stanza plays with military terms and words in a light-
hearted way:

> See how the Flow'rs, as at Parade,
> Under their Colours stand displaid:
> Each Regiment in order grows,
> That of the Tulip Pinke and Rose.

Gradually he veers into a sadness that militarism is no longer just a garden conceit, but has been abroad in England; the poet wishes that Fairfax had not retired from public life:

> And yet their walks one on the Sod
> Who, had it pleased him and God,
> Might once have made our Gardens spring
> Fresh as his own and flourishing.
> But he preferr'd to the Cinque Ports
> These five imaginary Forts.[16]

Thus the soldier's garden, which perhaps began as Fairfax's attempt to re-order the chaos and unnecessary tragedy of the Civil War, is turned by the skill and flattery of Marvell, his 'servant', into a microcosmic metaphor of the larger, unhappy state of England. Marvell loved Nunappleton and its people.

> Bind me ye Woodbines in your 'twines,
> Curle me about ye gadding Vines,
> And Oh so close your Circles lace,
> That I may never leave this Place.

He ends in a celebration of Maria Fairfax: ''Tis She that to these Gardens gave That wondrous Beauty which they have';[17] And, perhaps Lord Fairfax heeded the poet's words, having pondered on his garden state, for upon New Year's Day 1660, by which time Maria was married to the Royalist Duke of Buckingham, he came out of 'gouty retirement' with his Yorkshire gentry to clear the way for General Monck's march to London, his ultimatum to the Rump Parliament and the call for the Restoration. It was Fairfax who led the commission to meet Charles II at The Hague; the King came home, apparently riding to his coronation on a horse from the Nunappleton stable; Lord Fairfax returned to his garden for good.[18]

With the Restoration, the military garden assumes a popular guise; rather as toy soldiers are laid out on the baize, the garden becomes an amusement and spectacle in miniature. Soldiers on horseback in box had been seen in a garden at The Hague[19] and John Evelyn suggested mock fortifications with hedges and trees in his *Kalendarium Hortense*, which was otherwise full of more serious and scientific gardening. On 21 August 1674 Evelyn's diary records an outing to Windsor, where 'In one of the meadows at the foot of the long terrace below the Castle works were thrown up to show the King a representation of the City of Maestricht, newly taken by the French. Bastions, bulwarks, ramparts, palisadoes, graffs, horn-works, counterscarps etc. were constructed. It was attacked by the Duke of Monmouth (newly come from the real siege) and the Duke of York, with a little army, to show their skill in tactics – all without disorder or ill accident, to the great satisfaction of 1,000 spectators. Being night made it a formidable show.' After the siege Evelyn returned to London with Mr Pepys, arriving home about 3 a.m.[20] The ground, now well treed and overlooking sports fields, remained the Maestricht (Maastricht) Garden in popular parlance: just over twenty-five years later Henry Wise recorded the enormous expenditure of £597 on spruce first clipped into pyramids, fruit trees and vines and a 'stockarde' of 41,000 white thorns sent from Brompton Park Nursery in Kensington for planting on the terraced slope, which the workmen called 'Mastrike'. It was, says David Green, in his biography of Wise 'one of the most remarkable small gardens in Wise's career'.[21]

A final vignette from the seventeenth century concerns the doings of another Parliamentarian, Sir Walter Erle, who played a prominent (if slightly quixotic) role in the Civil War in Dorset, and had his garden at Charborough Park near Wareham 'cut into redoubts and works representing the places where he had fought' with correlating maps and siege plans hung on his house walls.[22] Sir Walter's Protestantism persisted, and in 1686, the year after the French revocation of the Edict of Nantes, with fears that James II was going to follow the French path of Protestant persecution, a group of West Country gentry came to Charborough for a secret meeting in the ice house. The ice house, really an underground cavern built in a bank to the north of the house, still bears the inscription, how 'under this roof' a set of patriotic gentlemen 'concerted the great plan of The Glorious Revolution with The Immortal King William etc etc . . .'[23]

Though William and Mary are more usually remembered for the glories of the Privy Garden, the Tijou Screen and the riverside terrace at Hampton Court, King William's first garden in England was more in his soldierly tradition. At Kensington Palace, London and Wise laid out the grounds to the royal taste 'which being entirely military, cut yew and variegated holly were taught ... to imitate the lines, angles, bastions, scarps and counter-scarps of regular fortifications'. The garden 'which was long an object of wonder and admiration' was known as 'the siege of Troy'.[24]

The popular appeal of the Maastricht garden and 'the siege of Troy' allows garden imagery to take its place with what we know of the mood of late seventeenth century exuberance in other arts, music and the theatre. The 'military garden' was an appropriate focus for an age when street talk was dominated by war news from Europe; we can never know how many soldiers clipped in box or green forts flying flags decorated village and town gardens, but we do have the glorious evidence of Laurence Sterne's *Tristram Shandy*, written with the authority of 'good tradition'. Sterne's hero, Uncle Toby, had been wounded in the groin at the three-months-long siege of Namur in 1695 (the capture of Namur was William III's great victory – 'the news came like a thunderclap in London and Versailles')[25] and his faithful servant, Corporal Trim, had been wounded in the knee at Landen, where the French cavalry had defeated the British two years earlier. These two old soldiers were typical of a veteran society, relics of brutal campaigns who were perhaps only fortunate in that they were still alive, and armed with their pride, lived out their lives on the smallest of pensions. The story is set in the 1690s, Uncle Toby's wound has yet to heal properly, and to cheer him Corporal Trim suggests that the map of Dunkirk, 'a poor, contemptible, fiddle-faddle piece of work on paper', could be their summer's task laid on the ground: 'your Honour might sit out of doors, and give me the nography – (Call it ichnography, quoth my uncle,) ... could but mark me the polygon, with its exact lines and angles ... could tell me the proper depth and breadth [of the fosse] – then I would throw out the earth upon this hand towards the town for the scarp, and on that hand ... for the counterscarp ... I would face the glacis, as the finest fortifications are done in Flanders, with sods ... and I would make the walls and parapets with sods too.' In short, all was agreed, and this little Dunkirk garden was laid out on an old bowling green behind Uncle Toby's cottage at Shandy, well screened from view, so the two old gentlemen could hobble around in privacy, overjoyed and chuckling at their game, singing 'Lillabullero', shaping their knots with a penknife, sometimes Corporal Trim in his uniform on parade to wield the spade.[26]

Against the background of happy veterans, the military garden now comes into its own. The first truly professional architect-designer, who is also a soldier, is about to make his entrance, to await the great victory for which the nation would demand the most splendid military garden in honour of its hero.

John Vanbrugh, Glorious Van as he will prove to be, was a child of his time, born in the post-Restoration cheeriness of 1664 and brought up in the garrison city of Chester. He took the King's Shilling and a commission in a relative's regiment but found it too tame, and in seeking adventure he was arrested as a spy in Calais in the autumn of 1688. He was sketching the fortifications at the time, a pastime easily misread (or perhaps not?) with the French and Dutch at loggerheads and William of Orange about to sail to become King of England. Vanbrugh languished in a French prison for four years, writing plays, which he came home to present: *The Relapse* and *The Provok'd Wife* were both performed with their author as the star, but he was only too aware of the hazards of the profession, and he took another army commission. The army gave him routine, subsistence pay, companionship, a steady background to his theatricals and his new-found profession, architecture.[27] The army also gave Van his characteristic dash and verve; he was not afraid to say what he thought (not toadying to grand clients as did other architects and garden designers) and he remained in its embrace until he married when he was past fifty.

Everywhere that Vanbrugh went the landscape became ordered with military precision, and often, as at Stowe, the work was actually done by soldiers.* Vanbrugh's client, Baron Cobham, had been one of Marlborough's chief commanders, and when he married an heiress in 1715 he gave his old sapper regiments work in his new grand campaign of glorifying Stowe. The second phase of work from 1720–25 under Vanbrugh and Charles Bridgeman included a salient, a long, level ridge with the rotunda at its head, dug by the sappers, but all the early

---

* The greatest of military engineers, Vauban, used thirty thousand soldiers to work on his scheme to bring the River Eure by more than 100 kilometres of canal to Versailles in 1685: The Aqueduc de Maintenon remains the 'solitary witness' to this tremendous scheme: the soldiers were recalled to battle in 1688 and the great plan never finished.[28]

eighteenth-century plans of Stowe reveal the 'landscape' garden as an incomplete green fort, with bastions, embankments, ravelins and hornwork (*Plate 30*).[29] Stowe's salients and scarps have softened with years of tempering (and tampering) but the Temples of Venus and Friendship still occupy their green bastions. Castle Howard is still ringed with curtain walls, bastions and turrets, and still invites military phraseology in the grandeur of its 'outworks': Vanbrugh went to great lengths in his correspondence with Lord Carlisle in debating the heights and levels of obelisks and pillars, for there was clearly a nice balance in his mind between vulgar grandeur and a military precision that was wholly desirable.[30]

The military garden has all but disappeared from garden history because it was deemed politically incorrect, a symbol of over-weening, faintly ridiculous power, by the pens, mightier than the swords, of Pope, Addison, Steele and company. Steele's *Tatler* carried a satire on 'tulipomania' of overheard conversation that mentioned Alexander the Great and Ataxerxes, and 'that he valued the Black Prince more than the Duke of Vendome' a rivalry of chronological nonsense. 'I could not conceive; and was more startled when I heard the second affirm, with great vehemence, that if the Emperor of Germany was not going off, he should like him better than either of them. He added, that though the season was so changeable, the Duke of Marlborough was in blooming beauty ... and ... at last one of them told the company, that if they would go along with him, he would show them something that would please them very much. A Chimney-Sweeper and a Painted Lady in the same bed.' Present-day garden historians have fallen too meekly into the satirists' footsteps, so eager to discern the birth of Britain's great moment, the English landscape style, that they have discounted the power of the popular notion of a garden style that embodied soldierly heroism and all the charms of toy soldiers and brightly painted toy forts.

The military garden neutralized the brutality that dominated life in quarrelsome Europe: the way Castle Howard surveys its terrain, the way Stowe is dug in to its landscape awaiting the battalions to battle, the trophies of Claremont that are still to be discovered in and around a twentieth-century housing estate, are soft-spoken veterans in our landscape. War was a landscape art (indeed, horrifyingly so still on the Ypres Salient and in the Flanders trenches; Verdun was after all Vauban's great fortress): making a garden was the most apt tribute to that art. This was deeply understood by Sir Winston Churchill, already quoted on that alliance of war and gardening, and elaborated on time and again in his three-volume exposition of his ancestor Marlborough's life and times. One example, before the battle of Ramillies: 'Marlborough, of course, knew the ground perfectly . . . [he had been more than a month at Meldert, and] was accustomed to keep himself fit and hard by riding every day . . . the whole region was familiar, it had long been regarded as a possible ground of great battles . . . Marlborough rode out, examined every aspect, vista, hump and hillock – he had a marvellous topographical memory (as well as maps from the French engineers, and maps were very accurate, clear and noted every detail of military potential).'[31]

Little wonder therefore, that after his textbook and resounding victory at Blenheim in August 1704, John Churchill, Duke of Marlborough's reward from a grateful sovereign and nation was to be a palace in a garden, or park. Marlborough actually had a beloved home and garden, the now vanished Holywell House, south-east of St Albans, where he gardened, planted trees in ranks of battles and kept his trophies.[32] Fame, however, being no respecter of its victim's affections, deemed he should move to mightier quarters at Blenheim Palace. From an apparently chance encounter at Christmas 1704 with Vanbrugh the team of all the talents for Blenheim was formed under the architect's supervision. The gardeners (a title not to be underestimated) included Henry Wise, armed with a copy of *Allingham on Fortifications*, which was a supplement to the classic Vauban textbook (surely well-thumbed after Kensington and Maastricht).[33] On 18 June 1705 'with rustic junketing and slamming down of guineas',[34] the foundation stone of Blenheim Palace was laid, just where the Duchess would one day look out on her flower garden. Vanbrugh and Wise agreed on the layout of a vast state or military garden on the south front of the palace, 'a 77 acre plot consisting of a 250 yd. parterre, patterned in dwarf box, leading to a formal wilderness called the Woodwork; the whole stretching 750 yards from the Saloon portico towards Bladon Church.'[35] The rectangular parterre and the 'colossal polygon' of the Woodwork had stone-built curtain walls, with eight huge bastions: there was a walk along the walls which gave an overview of the immaculate plantings of yew, hollies, bays and laurels (the plants were measured before leaving the Brompton

Nursery to fit the uniformity of the pattern), or for 'turning about' to enjoy the vistas through the park.

Besides the Military Garden, Blenheim had a flower parterre for the Duchess, on the east front of the palace, with lavender, roses, pinks, rosemary, lilies, jasmine and honeysuckles. Beyond the Woodwork was the kitchen garden, hardly less splendid, with walls fourteen feet high and four bastions each 100 feet wide, enclosing eight acres. The Duke had great faith in Henry Wise, with *Allingham on Fortifications* tucked under his arm, and he wrote, 'I am at ease, being very sure that Mr Wise will be diligent' to the Duchess in May 1706.[36] Marlborough was nervous about his mortality, neurotic about too many people having keys and access to Blenheim, and he urged Wise to plant the largest possible trees for soonest effect. Blenheim must have been Brompton Nursery's finest hour[37] and thousands of plants were supplied, a near-military exercise in planning and delivery. Fruit for the kitchen garden included peaches, nectarines, apricots, cherries, plums, quince, apples, gooseberries, currants and vines. Lebanon cedars four feet six inches high were charged at twenty-five shillings each, and other large standard or pleached limes and hornbeams, pyramidal bay trees, shaped hollies, yews, juniper and laurels – all for the Woodwork – were all mature and costly. The nursery was skilled at moving large trees, and some of the limes and hornbeams which were transported and planted in baskets to protect their root systems apparently looked instantly as though they had been in place for thirty years. Flowers supplied included Brompton stocks, polyanthus, ranunculus, hyacinths (over 5000), violets, carnations, marigolds and 4600 tulips and 100 damask roses.[38]

The Great Duke died in 1722, having only lived in his tribute palace since 1719. The Duchess called in Colonel Armstrong, who had been Marlborough's chief engineer, to militarize the wanderings of the river Glyme through the Park in a last great scheme she thought to please a soldierly heart: the labour of canalization, raising and lowering of water, and a fine cascade echoed Vauban's great Versailles project of almost forty years earlier, but it was not to be.[39]

The kitchen garden had succeeded beyond all Wise's expectations. When Vanbrugh visited in 1716 he declared it 'an astonishing sight', he had seen nothing either in England or abroad to compare. At this point the Duchess of Marlborough fell out with Vanbrugh, who was never

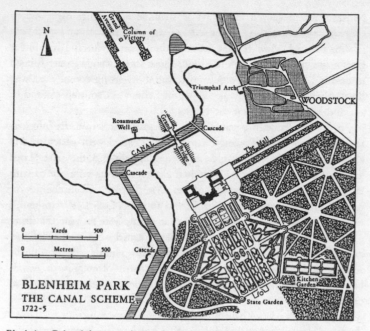

Blenheim, Colonel Armstrong's plan for the canalization of the River Glyme, the final touch to the Military Garden. From Green and Bond, 'Blenheim after Vanburgh' in *Landscape for a Palace*, 1997.

to see Blenheim again; the year before he died, 1725, he returned to look, but was not allowed admittance.[40]

The military garden was left to grow; in 1748 the reporter for Salmon's *County and University of Oxford Guide* paced out the gravel walks at 2200 feet long from the palace, with a cross path 1850 feet long. He walked the terraces from bastion to bastion and explored the vistas kept cut between the large laurels, box and hollies, which were fast growing into a wilderness. Within fifteen years, in 1763, Capability Brown had swept it away, the Woodwork, the military garden, the Duchess's flower gardens and all. In 1925 the 9th Duke of Marlborough commissioned Achille Duchêne to design the water terraces which restore a facsimile formality to the west front, but the military garden, on the south front, remains a cricket field (the levelling had some use after all). The 'colossal polygon' which caused Henry Wise such headaches has disappeared: only the cricketers who saunter out to bat on the smooth and level field of dreams might hear some echoes of the Great Duke and his dinner guests ringing in their ears . . . look, those trees, that was the French position . . . those laurels signify my Right . . . swing round . . . those limes, they are my Left flank . . . we had them . . . so, and so, and so . . . and his voice fades on the breeze.

Brown's Blenheim became famous, a great attraction. In July 1792 the loquacious Lord Torrington found it crowded with phaetons and chaises hired from Woodstock for trundling around the park. Lord Torrington found Vanbrugh's kitchen garden thriving and, armed with an introduction to the head gardener, Mr Shipley, his lordship wins himself a magnificent basket of fruits and another of roses. 'What shock'd me much', he confided to his diary that night, 'was to hear the firing of the guns, and to see a set of Jacobins arm'd against the national guards, – the birds; – Oh fye! – what, for a few cherries, destroy all the songsters? And here will they come to perish. "Stretch forth, Marlborough, thy hand of mercy, and of pity; and let not infamous slaughter prevail".'[41]

Andrew Marvell had rather demeaned Lord Fairfax's lowly gardening, but then Marvell was no gardener. History tells us that truly great generals, like Fairfax and Marlborough, had a softer side to their characters, which made them care for their men and be beloved by them. And what did the daughters of great soldiers do with their fathers' genes? Frances Wolseley, daughter of the diminutive 'model of a modern Major-general', hero of Queen Victoria's African campaigns, and Gertrude Jekyll, daughter of an officer in the engineers, were but two of them that took to gardening.[42]

The evidence of history is that 'gardening' – though undoubtedly subject to much scorn and ribald commentary – was seen as a civilizing and beneficial influence. The flamboyant eighteenth-century adventurer Benjamin Thompson, soldier-spy, was made Count Rumford by the Elector of Bavaria for reforming his army, establishing military gardens, schools for army children, paid occupations in peacetime and making the soldier's life respectable. William Augustus, Duke of Cumberland, dubbed 'the Butcher' for his notorious harassing of the Highlanders

after Culloden, brought his own men south and gave them paid employment in landscaping the southern end of Windsor Great Park. Cumberland was appointed Ranger of the Park in 1746, an office which has meant
responsibility for the Sovereign's most important gardening matters ever
since, with Thomas Sandby, his aide at Culloden, taking the role of
Deputy Ranger and designer of Virginia Water and the Obelisk Pond
and of the planting of this whole area.[43] All the work was done by
soldiers (a Sandby painting in the Royal Collection at Windsor of the
Chinese Bridge shows a large working party in identical undress and
tricorn hats), which included twice rebuilding the Virginia Water dam
when it was swept away by flood. For the final reconstruction, which
survives today, an account records 'the work done by the 23rd Regiment
of Foot from 29th June to 23rd September 1789' moving 26,293 yards of
sand in carts and barrows for just over £600, the sergeants' allowances
for the 12½ weeks costing just over £28.[44]

But the 23rd Regiment of Foot were – by some irony – putting the
final touches to a vast romantic landscape at Virginia Water, for the
fashion had long since changed. Ralph Dutton wrote in *The English
Garden* that the military garden declined with the arrival of the House
of Hanover – or alternatively 'the advent of the romantic garden may
be looked upon as the obscure recompense for the loss of the romantic
House of Stuart?'[45] History seemed to be in the hands of the twenty-
four-year-olds, for William Augustus, Duke of Cumberland, had been
made commander-in-chief and marched to Culloden in his twenty-
fourth year, and down in the subdued south, history had appointed a
young man of the same age named Lancelot Brown, as head gardener
at Stowe. It was at Stowe, in the early 1740s, that the English landscape
style found its greatest practitioners in the trusting relationship formed
between the old soldier, Lord Cobham, and his eminently capable right-
hand man.[46] Brown was grassing over the parterre, breaking avenues,
loosening lawns, planting drifts of trees, much influenced by William
Kent, and not long after Lord Cobham's death in 1749 he was to leave
Stowe and set up on his own account. Brown was a coffee-shop craze,
a phenomenon of the powerful Whig society which competed to be
men of taste: by the time he died in 1783, aged sixty-six (mourned as
'Lady Nature's second husband'), he had transformed thousands of
acres from Northumberland to Sussex, from Holkham in the east to

Widdicombe in the west, into sublime green rolling vistas. With further irony he had replaced the military garden with serpentine greenery by means of a military device: the origin of the ha-ha is variously credited to Vanbrugh's sketches of the Calais fortifications, to John James sketching one seen in France, to Defoe's observations of the Blenheim walls sunk into ditches or to an early example at Duncombe Park.[47]

The eighteenth-century landscape style was undoubtedly an expression of power. Other people's acres were 'borrowed' for the long views, 'inconvenient' villages were razed to the ground (the villagers sometimes housed elsewhere) and great tracts of land once open to all were fenced and guarded. Some of the appeal may have been simply that it was a cheap solution to maintenance problems. Those crisp embankments, which needed too frequently to be hand cut, resting at their precise and steep angles, the immaculate cut of earth mounts like sugar lumps, the formidable canals, all look marvellous in paintings and engravings, but what happened after a wet summer, when slump set in? How costly it must have been to restore cut-glass encirclements like the amphitheatre at Claremont, how much, much cheaper and simpler, to smooth it all out? No wonder Brown was popular with the land-owning class: he must have saved them a fortune. 'Landskip' was much more easily drafted in and out of productive farming, another advantage as no landowner liked to waste usable acres. All in all it was the most convenient of solutions, giving the beefy philistines among the aristocracy a glow of ill-deserved artistic pride: but most of all it puzzled the populace, who could not understand – in a world that still struggled and laboured to tame the 'wild' heath and scrubland, what could be so marvellous about apeing nature.

Landscape gardening, obsessed with the serpentine line and bosky groves of planting, led fashionable taste eventually to 'jungles of plants' and untidiness: very smart, modern notions. It superseded a national pysche forged by centuries of warlike prowess, grand military stratagem (whether we like it or not) and a love of garden order expressing military order and heroic deeds. This is much less celebrated as a garden heritage, and yet there it is, none the less.

Charles Dickens had seen something of this to inspire him to the estimable Wemmick's world in *Great Expectations*: cucumber frame, salad plot, bower, wine cooling in the minuscule lake, pigs, chicken,

The Development of the Ha-Ha: Sketches from J. T. Hyde's *Elementary Principles of Fortification*, 1860, show (fig 101) a common hedge and ditch turned into a breastwork to be defended from the hedge side: (fig 103) 'a good nine-inch brick-wall is musket-shot proof' and if, given time, a ditch is dug in front using the earth to shore up the wall the enemy will be further deterred. Hyde's manual was illustrating techniques from the time of Vauban in seventeenth-century France. Military-minded designers like Vanbrugh, Wise and Bridgeman easily adapted the traditions of fortification into landscape gardens, using the same features, marking the deer and sheep out as the enemy: hence Felix Kelly's delightful drawing of the outcome, from E. Burton, *The Georgians at Home*, 1967.

with 'the smallest house' he had ever seen, awaited Pip in Walworth. The house with sham gothic windows and gothic door, the real flagstaff, the flag run up on Sundays, and the nine o'clock gun on its lattice-work fortress 'protected from the weather by an ingenious little tarpauling contrivance in the nature of an umbrella'. '"I am my own engineer, and my own carpenter, and my own plumber, and my own gardener, and my own Jack of all Trades," said Wemmick. "Well, it is a good thing you know. It brushes the Newgate cobwebs away, and pleases the Aged." That creature of all our consciences the aged parent added, "This is a fine place of my son's, sir . . . a pretty pleasure ground . . . it ought to be kept together by the Nation after my son's time, for the people's enjoyment.'"[48]

It is in the small gardens of Britain that traditional military neatness has been retained. In allotments with their miniature parade-ground proportions, everything in impeccable rows. In the immaculate trenching, ridging and earthing up of potatoes or celery, in the line of guardsmen-red salvias marching beside a path, in the tiny but precise forty-five degree angles and ditches where the well-kept lawn edges meet the weedless soil. This is not the stuff of present-day garden writing, nor of magazines, but it is the underground campaign of social history that lies in family photo albums, in the minutes of clubs and societies (when these are not more concerned with in-fighting and quarrels), unwritten in the literary sense, but slowly coming to light.

It is easily forgotten that Gertrude Jekyll was a soldier's daughter, and that her drawing of the batter of a dry wall has a military precision. In her second book, *Home & Garden* of 1900, she has a chapter on 'Gardening for Short Tenancies', in answer to queries which she feel come her way 'because I live within reach of Aldershot'. It turns out that 'all Aldershot tries to have a little garden', and it does (or did) as she soon points out, 'have a vast supply of stable manure'. Characteristically she is enthusiastic to have all Aldershot gardening in her own orderly manner: burn rubbish left behind by previous tenants, she advised, prune the good shrubs and dig and manure the soil, then look for swift results from poppies, sweet peas, larkspur, marigold, fast-growing shrubs, choisya, ceanothus Gloire de Versailles and cistus ('grand plants for Aldershot as they revel in light soil and sunshine'), lavender and rosemary.[49]

One of the army's favourite garrisons, Colchester, brought many military gardeners back to East Anglia in retirement: to Chris Falconer, the professional gardener in Akenfield, it was a source of amazement that about 70 per cent of gardens open to the public in the 1960s belonged to ex-army or ex-navy men. 'I think it must be something to

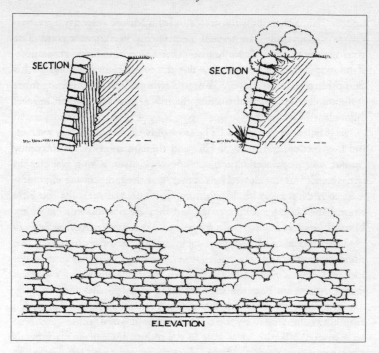

Gertrude Jekyll's construction drawing for a dry wall: section, showing the batter (slope) of the wall with the earth tightly rammed behind it represented by vertical lines: a second section shows how the wall should be planted and the elevation to present the effect. A Jekyll wall 'sprouted' white foxgloves, aubretias, thrift, cerastium and candytuft and was softened with overhanging rock roses, Jerusalem sage, lavender or roses. Here the soldier's daughter, which she was, met the gardener, which she became. From Jekyll & Weaver, *Gardens for Small Country Houses*, 1912.

do with time and order. They love complete order and nobody can stop them imposing it on a garden ... The things which they will do to make a garden is astounding. I've known them drive all the way to Wiltshire to pick up a stone sink. You see, gardening allows them to go on having routine, order, tidiness, straight edges, upright posts. You can be strict in a garden. They were fantastically strict in the RAC barracks. And tidy! "If it doesn't move, whitewash it", they used to say.'[50]

A soldierly bond between officers and men was preserved in the garden. This is beautifully illustrated in John Moore's emotive *Brensham Village*, a soapy post-war story of country folk in Worcestershire. The good-natured Colonel (who has no other name but clearly generations of military scouts in his lineage) 'felt the weather in his bones'. This has nothing to do with aches, pains and twinges, but is something more profound: 'he was aware of coming changes as the trees in their sap feel them'. It is May and the Colonel says: 'It's going to freeze smartish and I'm frightened for the plums.' The frost duly comes and is not too bad, and the next morning's sky is blue and the sun soon warms the chilly ground. But in the early afternoon the wind rises, a long black cloud brings a hail storm, followed by another, and the temperature plummets to sixteen degrees 'of black blighting frost'. In the orchards the little plums hang black upon their twigs, but they are not the only casualties. The village's star garden, open for teas and summer visitors, belongs to Joe Trentfield, a casual, happy-go-lucky, untidy personage in general life, but in his garden 'and only in his garden, the Regimental Serjeant-Major appeared'. His flower beds are laid out as immaculately as a barrack square, he cannot bear the slightest irregularity in the rows 'nor any sign of indiscipline among their occupants . . . the flowers in his garden must always be dressed by the right, numbered, sized, proved and properly covered off' with 'no talking in the rear rank'. But the black frost's sabre has mown them all down. 'A regiment of tulips had kept their dressing even as they fell; two companies of stocks, having formed square, had fallen in the same formation . . . a platoon of geraniums still held their ground . . . though the blackened head of each one drooped as if the scimitar had passed with precision along their unwavering line.'[51]

Chris Falconer at Akenfield was right about the flood of military and naval men to gardening after the war. It was a natural reaction: the retreat with honour to a new position. They re-polished the notions of neatness, and told the lower ranks what to do, though not always with the friendly charm that characterized Brigadier Lucas Phillips in *The Small Garden*. Military gardeners had a natural constituency at shows, where organization was needed, and medals and rosettes were awarded: a Field Marshal, Lord Grenfell, had seen the Royal Horticultural Society through the First World War, and Colonel Durham was secretary throughout the Second, to be succeeded in 1946 by Brigadier Lycett.

Many other army and navy men stalked the corridors of Vincent Square. Major-General Jeremy Rougier was appointed to mastermind the Society's new garden at Rosemoor in Devon. A professional soldier could slip easily into the role of garden designer: John Codrington found this when he was in his late fifties and his knowledge of plants mostly gathered on foreign postings was put to good use, especially in his own enchanting garden at Stone Cottage, Hambleton, in Rutland. His favourite joke to his visitors was to say how he had always longed for a garden lake, difficult on Hambleton's hilly site, but then the landscape architect Sylvia Crowe had designed Rutland Water to lap at his lawn. John Codrington was of a discreet company of designers, working for clients who did not think it done to employ such a person, and certainly did not wish to be photographed and written about in a gardening magazine. His best-known garden is in a courtyard at Emmanuel College, Cambridge, and this has cleverly controlled geometry, marshalled with herbs.

Which brings me to a final amusement for this chapter: the possibility of a whole garden planted with 'military' flowers. Things have moved on rather from Marvell's fantasies at Nunappleton House, with flowery garrisons, barred tulips and roses bearing arms and other puns, and generations of nurserymen and breeders have paid tribute to military tradition, and more particularly to the vanishing glory of military pageantry. Flowers have been named for great soldiers and sailors, for battles and for their ceasing, and for common heroes: the abundance of these connections endorses the importance of the military garden tradition, and also contributes to the lore of plants.

The garden might be a star fort, laid out in grass, with miniature embankments and tiny cannons set at the bastions. The place of honour on spring parade goes to *Cheiranthus* 'Old Bloody Warrior', a wallflower the colour of dried blood and certainly grown since the sixteenth century and possibly earlier. The Warriors' companions might include the black-ringed and mealy-edged auricula 'Lancashire Hero', auricula 'The Duke of Cumberland' (painted by Georg Ehret), *Crocus susianus* 'Cloth of Gold' and the silvery-blue *Crocus vernus* 'Vanguard.' Bearded iris hybrids, upright stalwarts, have been named 'Black Watch' (a deep, dark purple), 'Blue Ensign,' 'Red Torch', 'Chivalry', 'Rocket' and 'Fort Ticonderoga'. But it is the peony that most reflects spring soldierly glory. Single peonies include the maroon 'Lord Kitchener' named in 1907 by Kelways, and the deep rose pink and fringed 'Lady Wolseley' named in 1925 for Frances Wolseley (her father 'Sir Garnet Wolseley', later Lord Wolseley, chief of the British army, is an early Jackman clematis cultivar). Double peonies include the purplish-crimson 'Blaze of Glory', and the rosy red 'Bunker Hill' (named in 1906), 'Knighthood' is deep crimson, 'General Joffre' silvery rose-pink, 'Sir Galahad' is blush white and the 'Duc de Wellington' is creamy white and 'bomb shaped'. A Canadian hybrid lily is called 'Dunkirk' (with bowl-shaped red flowers) and there are Turk's cap Preston hybrid lilies 'Spitfire' and 'Mosquito'. Lupins have been on 'Royal Parade', there is an astilbe 'Red Sentinel', a red tulip 'Fusilier' and the vivid scarlet pink 'Rifleman' is one of the oldest of the florists' favourite carnations.

French rose breeders have frequently honoured their military history: the famous Bourbon 'Commandant Beaurepaire' and the noisette 'Maréchal Niel', the multiflora 'Souvenir de la Bataille de Marengo' – might flower against a backdrop of ivy 'Gloire de Marengo'. There would be a bare bed of hybrid teas, 'General McArthur' and 'President Eisenhower'.

Later summer perennials include the kniphofia 'Royal Standard', the anchusa 'Loddon Royalist', the salmon-scarlet phlox 'Brigadier' and the asters, 'Winston Churchill' (reddish-purple), 'Colonel Durham' (mauve), 'Peace' (lavender-blue) and 'Advance'. In the 1950s there was a splash of hybrid chrysanthemums, the rich browny 'Arnhem', orange 'Dauntless' and 'Golden Knight' and 'Crimson Champion'.

The military garden could be well enclosed in appropriate rhododendrons. Hybrids have been named for 'Lord Roberts' (an old dark crimson hybrid), the battle of 'Jutland' (geranium pink flecked darker red), 'General Sir John du Cane' (rose madder), red 'Fusilier', blood red 'Grenadier', a carmine-coloured 'General Eisenhower', there is a Waterer azalea named 'Ambush', and – finally – the scarlet rhododendron of 1930 named 'Armistice Day'.

CHAPTER FOUR

≻≻≻❖≺≺≺

Emancipated Gardeners

A garden is the perfect territory for planning and dreaming, and for realizing dreams. It is a friendly ground for proving personal worth, at first to oneself, and then to the watching world. Whether it is a rank five-acre field, a long thin rubbish tip, or a pint-sized terrace with a window box, the possibilities are, apparently, endless. This chapter explores the history of gardening as a means of self-expression, and perhaps even more powerfully as a means of fulfilment for those who in some way or other seem to have failed the great examination-board of life. Gardening allows happiness to the poor, ill-educated, the ugly, the weak, the guilty, the ungainly, the shy – and even to women.

Women are the silent gardeners of early history, shuffling down the medieval and Tudor years as the armies of 'weeding women' who maintained great gardens and are occasionally mentioned in account books. In a society which revolved entirely around the ownership of land those who merely worked that land were unimportant: but sometimes the ownership highlights a woman, such as the heiress Margaret Mauteby, born in Norfolk in the early 1420s and married to John Paston well before she was twenty. Margaret Paston managed her whole estate, farm, garden, orchard, dairy, still-room and larder, reared and educated six children, arranged their marriages, adjudicated in disputes, punished crimes and flattered officials, all while her husband was away on political or military campaigns. It is impossible to doubt that she took gardening knowledge in her stride, and that she was typical of a breed of super-women long before such a word was invented.[1] Others were perhaps of a gentler nature, and one would love to know more: such was Magdalen Herbert, born and brought up in a proud border family at Eyton-on-

Severn in Shropshire, married to Richard Herbert and mother of a family that included two poets, Edward (1st Baron Herbert of Cherbury, born 1583) and George (born 1593). The latter celebrates his mother in 'Memoria Matris Sacris', where he tells how her days began with prayers, a simple braiding of her hair and 'sparing aid of jewels',

> Then on her family forth she shone, and spent
> On kitchen, garden, house due management . . .[2]

Women of Magdalen Herbert's class and education kept their own notebooks on the use of plants for food and remedies. These handed-down 'receipts' were occasionally published – Bess of Hardwick's grand-daughter Elizabeth Talbot, Countess of Kent's *A Choice Manuall of Rare and Select Secrets in Physick and Chirugery* was printed in 1651. It was closely followed by *The Queen's Closet Opened*, in 1655, which purported to be the secrets of the medicine, preserving and cooking of Queen Henrietta Maria. As Antonia Fraser has observed in *The Weaker Vessel*, the 'desire to cash in on a famous name for commercial purposes' is no modern phenomenon (and the fact that the chief beneficiary of the Queen's potions, Charles I, had been so recently beheaded was no hindrance to popularity either).[3]

The secrecy of such notebooks, plant lore and knowledge passed from mother to daughters has undoubtedly prevented posterity from recognizing women's gardening achievements. Queens or courtiers could be careless of such knowledge, but to most women it was a matter of life or death – 'After all, how remarkable that if you eat a plant it keeps you alive! How remarkable that some plants do the opposite, and do it with despatch; that others affect the mind narcotically and strangely; that others have local effects on your body inside and out!' – thus Geoffrey Grigson in *The Englishman's Flora*, belying his title by praising the botanical knowledge of Tudor countrywomen.[4] Such women had to be discreet: on the one hand all the virtuous ideals once embodied in the Virgin had been transmuted into the 'good housewife', the 'crown to her husband'.[5] On the other, and the line was very finely drawn, using clary for backache, Solomon's Seal to bind broken bones and Opium poppies and feverfew for headaches, was the business of 'wise women', charmers, sorcerers and witches. Society wondered at the miracles of plants and, knowing no better, attributed these miracles to magic. All cultures had their myths: 'the Irish have a tale that the fairies were flung out of Heaven: then God threw the plants down after the fairies, instructing them to be good and useful – though matters were confused by the devil who duplicated many herbs to make them more difficult to recognize.'[6] In such a confusion of knowledge it is no wonder that the culture and use of plants was accompanied by prayers, bringing the desperate remedies to heal a sick child dangerously near to sorcery. In *Religion and the Decline of Magic* Keith Thomas has documented this shadowy world, where Catholic prayers in Latin 'long remained a common ingredient in the magical treatment of illness' and quoting the case of Goodwife Veazy, expert in the cure of ringworm and canker-worm, using honey and pepper and 'Thou canker-worm be gone from hence in the name of the Father, of the Son, and of the Holy Ghost' three times.[7]

Where a woman would have to guard her knowledge carefully, would forbear to publish (or not have the opportunity to publish), men could step in. All the early gardening books were written by men, the famous first being Thomas Hill's (or Hyll's) *Gardener's Labyrinth*, of 1577, which is full of common-sense tradition. William Lawson's *A New Orchard and Garden* – subtitled 'the best way for planting . . . with the Country Housewife's Garden' – of 1618 was steadily popular into the mid-seventeenth century, and may just be acknowledging the feminine skills of the past. John Parkinson dedicated his *Paradisi in Sole Paradisus Terrestris* of 1629 to the wise Queen Henrietta Maria, and he also acknowledged plants in his Long Acre garden collection from Mistress Tomazin Tunstall, a northern gentlewoman with an interest in hunting for rarities. But for the main part our knowledgeable and innovatory gardening sisters of the past remain nameless: the herb women from whom Sir Joseph Banks was to learn the names of flowers, the old women gathering herbs whom William Turner, the sixteenth-century physician, naturalist and reformer mentions in his *Herball*, and those nameless battalions of country housewives whom Geoffrey Grigson admires for knowing more of wild and cultivated plants 'than most country housewives know today'.[8]

Women in the more secure world of the nursery business were a little more visible. Patience Wise, the daughter of Royal Master Carpenter Matthew Banckes, was married to Henry Wise, Master Gardener to Queen Anne and a partner in the supreme Brompton Park Nursery.

Patience kept a receipt book, which survives, and she looks out from her portrait with dignity, dark eyes, a longish nose and determined chin, her white hair swept under her cap. Henry Wise was a steady bachelor-gardener of forty-two when he married her in 1695, but she saw him through the difficult years with Queen Anne and Sarah Churchill's tantrums at Blenheim, indeed for another forty years (he retired in 1728 and died in 1738); toasted rhubarb seemed to be a favourite remedy when he returned from long wet days at remote Chatsworth or Longleat. While Henry was away Patience played her part in the running of Brompton Park Nursery; she answered letters, directed work, placated customers and took decisions in the permanent state of emergency which must have marked the planting seasons. When Henry Wise died in 1738 he left substantial property at Brompton Park to Patience. George London's daughter, Henrietta Peachy, also worked at the nursery, illustrating the exotic flowers and fruits that were reared there; some of Henrietta's illustrations survive at Badminton House.[9]

John Harvey's *Early Nurserymen* (1974) reveals that nurseries were dynastic and family affairs, but though there are rich descriptions of personable nurserymen, the women are less easy to find. They include Eleanor Compton of Chiswick who married Henry Woodman of nearby Strand-on-the-Green in St Paul's Cathedral in 1728; when Henry died thirty years later Eleanor inherited six acres of nursery and the stock and continued to trade.[10] Elizabeth Clark was certainly right hand to her husband Henry Clark of Chipping Campden; the Clark correspondence of the 1750s reveals Henry travelling long hours as a land agent to make up for the nursery's bad debts, Elizabeth holding the fort, coping with missed appointments, bad weather holding up the work, unreliable carriers, Henry's gout and the state of the world ... 'the Wood Stealers, & other Theves, pesters me sadley, the World never was, for badness as Tis now'.[11] In Gloucester the women were an essential part of the Wheelers' business, with Elizabeth Wheeler listed as 'nursery and seedswoman' in Northgate Street, in 1814–20; and in London Elizabeth Bailey ran a seed business at the Rose & Crown in Bishopsgate from 1795–1813.[12] In Exeter Ann Ford took over from her husband, William Ford, who died about 1829; this distinguished nursery which introduced the Exeter elm (*Ulmus glabra* 'Exoniensis') carried on trading until it was built over in the 1850s.[13]

The eighteenth-century landscape style has traditionally been depicted as a dialogue between Capability Brown, the lesser landscapists (William Eames, Richard Woods and so on who slowly emerge from the shadow cast by the dazzling Brown) and the Whig landlords; acreages, however artistic or even picturesque, were a question of land management and a male preserve. Or were they? A number of women are now emerging from the shadows. The remarkable Eleanor Coade ran a business far larger than any modern equivalent, manufacturing vases and statues with her secret recipe for ceramic artificial stone for over forty years from King's Arms Stairs, Narrow Wall, Lambeth (near the site of the Royal Festival Hall). Mrs Coade's rescuer is Alison Kelly, who has found over 650 sites with surviving examples and knows of a further 500 places where Coade stone works have disappeared or have failed to be identified – indeed she thinks 'that its resemblance to natural fine-grained limestone is the reason why so few Coade stone pieces are recognized today, and why Mrs Coade's importance in the history of Georgian decorative art is so greatly underestimated'. Eleanor Coade conducted her business through a series of foremen sculptors (including Daniel Pincot, John Bacon, William and Thomas Croggon) and she dealt with the architects (Nash, Robert Adam, Sir John Soane – who used Coade stone for fifty years – the Wyatts, Charles Barry, Brown and Humphry Repton) as well as clients such as Warren Hastings, Mrs Thrale's family at Llewenny Hall, Clwyd, and the great houses of the landscape movement. Much of the Coade work was copied from classical originals (but stood the weather better than stone) though there were many modern touches, commentaries or coats of arms for specific clients, such as George III in Roman armour. Vases were good sellers, 'and their outstanding pieces were copies of the Medici and Borghese' (a Borghese will be found at Wrest Park, two Medici at Kew), and were intended to be paired, though now so often these have wandered apart. One pair survives at Cobham Hall in Kent where Repton put them. There were whole zoos of animals: a very perky couchant lion at Audley End, tigers, elephants, the Brahmin bulls at Sezincote, hawks and tortoises. Shakespeare, Milton and Michelangelo and sundry enormous fountains, small sundials and pineapples (a pineapple at Ham House) were also popular. A Coade hunt becomes addictive; the quality is superb (and has never been matched – Eleanor went to her grave with the secret) all evident in 'the finest Coade figure and certainly the most advanced technically' the River Thames God at Ham House, a nine foot reclining figure, designed by John Bacon, cast in a single mould, with much finishing to create deepened eye-sockets, sensual mouth, tangibly flowing beard and his elaborately exotic crowning wreath.

As Alison Kelly says, 'Mrs Coade could count herself lucky in living at a time when few questioned the basic importance of classical design' and also at a time when so much was going on in the construction of landscape gardens, formal and informal, which needed good ornament. She undoubtedly made the most of it: her product was as ubiquitous as the good Brown himself, and it is perhaps time her name was once more on everyone's lips.[14]

The other woman who should take her place among the eighteenth-century greats is Henrietta Knight, otherwise Lady Luxborough, the half-French, half-sister of Henry St John, Viscount Bolingbroke (impeached for Jacobite loyalties after the accession of George I but who had returned to his farm and garden at Dawley in Middlesex by the mid-1720s). Henrietta was married in 1727 but within a few years she and her husband had decided to live separate lives, and Henrietta's was at Barrells, apparently a run-down country house near Henley-in-Arden. From Barrells she conducted a lively social life with all her more interesting neighbours, but most importantly she took to gardening. 'The prospect is a very near one,' she wrote, 'being surrounded by hills, but is diversified and pretty enough, and I have made a garden which I am filling with all the flowering shrubs I can get.' She had all the regressive tastes of her time, and had made an aviary filled with singing birds, with a fountain in the middle and a grotto in which to sit and listen to the singing – but there is a much more attractive vision of her out in her woods 'from eleven to five each day, in the lower part of my long walk, planting and dis-planting, opening views, etc'. 'Dis-planting' – alone a term for which she deserves her place in history – invokes a vigorous attack on brambles, saplings and broken branches and an energy denied to us in the conventional portraits of the 1740s. Her tastes were catholic and encouraged by her brother: 'My brother Bolingbroke ... has sent me the most exquisite sorts of melon seeds and lettuce', and a host of garden friends who supplied seeds, 'a water engine made of lignum vitae, which will water my garden with much ease', a double snowdrop and seeds of Spanish broom.[15]

Lady Luxborough's liveliness in the face of social ostracization makes her the patroness of expressionist gardeners; she pioneered where Mary Delany[16] and Fanny Burney[17] followed. Mary Delany in her gardening paradise with the good doctor at Delville looking out over Dublin Bay, had eleven acres of walks, woods, meadows, a bowling green and flower borders. Fanny Burney, Mrs Delany's protégée and almost a prisoner at court, escaped to gardening with her marriage to Alexandre d'Arblay and their home Camilla Cottage, Westhumble, near Dorking in the 1790s.

Henrietta Luxborough is also admirable for her admiring and faithful friendship with one of the most curious figures in garden history; without her assistance he might never had made himself known to us at all. Her gardening correspondence with William Shenstone at The Leasowes near Halesowen was published in 1775, almost twenty years after her death in 1756. Shenstone's own *Works*, the prose including 'Unconnected Thoughts on Gardening' somewhat buried in the endless poetry that he habitually wrote, were published in 1764, the year after his death, but the *Letters* have always been the means of access to the *Works*. Shenstone is one of the true treasures of garden history, because – rather like Charles Hamilton at Painshill – he pursued his passion in spite of everything and to the point of poverty and despair. Shenstone was born in 1714[*] (he was fifteen years younger than Henrietta). His parents, modest Midlands gentry, died when he was young, and his only brother also died young, leaving William in revolt: painfully shy, despising fashion (he refused to wear a wig, sporting his own, lank hair), wary of people – especially more than one at a time – and prey to periods of lassitude and depression. Underneath, though it took a special person to unearth this, William was imaginative and kind – he came away from Pembroke College, Oxford, with one firm friend, Richard Graves, but without his degree, renouncing the Church for which he was intended when he became of age and inherited The Leasowes and £300 a year. He also apparently immediately fell in love with a lady of

---

[*] That Hanoverian moment, 1714, which perhaps foretells his future as the maker of a romantic landscape to compensate for the loss of the romantic Stuarts?

the Graves family at Mickleton in the Cotswolds, but indolence seemed to mark his approach to love as it did to life and, despite another passion for a Cheltenham lady of 'superior social rank' when he was twenty-nine, only reams of poetry materialized and he never married. What he did do was read Virgil, whose lines afforded him 'that Sort of Pleasure which one receives from melancholy music', write his own poetry and prose, and make his garden, though he let the house fall down around him.[18] He thought of The Leasowes as a *ferme ornée*, he made it an elegant grazing farm, a series of lawns which led the eye to wilder scenes, of splendid oaks 'in all respects the perfect image of the manly character', and of ornamental buildings. He wandered happily in his groves, along his own brook sides, feeding his wild ducks: really his favourite pastime was peopling his garden with epigrams and memorials to those he admired. 'I have an alcove, six elegies, a seat, two epitaphs (one upon myself), three ballads, four songs and a serpentine river to show you when you come,' he wrote to his friend Jago.[19] Henrietta Luxborough found Shenstone fascinating as only a fellow-gardener would; her letters, beginning in 1739 and ending only with her death in 1756, were bound up and labelled by him as 'of abundant Ease, Politeness and Vivacity', qualities in her in which he felt her unequalled. They are meandering rather in the same way as their romantic garden paths were; she writes of mutual ailments, the bad roads, ever-importuning hangers-on, of visits planned and cancelled largely because of these, and the gardening wonders she has seen both at The Leasowes and elsewhere. Shenstone designs ornaments for her, she asks him how best to use this design or urn, or that; these two distant rather isolated green rivers of life bubble on via Henrietta's vivacious pen and then, suddenly, she bridges the more than 200 years between us: 'Yesterday must be marked with the blackest ink in the kalendar of my life', she writes, mourning her departed friends and absent neighbours leaving her 'to solitude and regret'. She is in that mixture of enervation and gloom after partings, 'an image of death' from sleeplessness, and then 'Luckily a man came to fell some trees . . . and immediately looking upon him as upon a tutelar angel sent to my assistance, I never returned to the house, but walked, under his protection, all over my grounds . . .' A crooked row of scrub trees were to be felled, a straight row of elms to be planted and other views to be opened up, and suddenly she is carried away from all despair into succeeding possibilities – views around the summer house, the pool in the grove, showing the winding of the walk through the coppice, with several roots to be stocked up for future root-houses. The plans for the root house finally save the day.[20]

Some of Shenstone's characteristics would today undoubtedly be interpreted sexually; his unluckiness in love would soon mark him out a 'not the marrying kind'; Henrietta is herself recorded as having an 'intimate friendship' with Frances Hertford, Countess of Somerset.[21] In 1778 Eleanor Butler and Sarah Ponsonby fled from their unhappy homes in Ireland to Plas Newydd near Llangollen where they were lucky enough to spend the following fifty years in blissful enjoyment of their 'delicious solitude' making the romantic garden that reflected their relationship. The Picturesque lifestyle had few more appropriate exponents than the Ladies of Llangollen: they seemed born for each other. Rustic steps, root-twisted balustrade, a miniature ravine, a model dairy, the kitchen garden entered by a Gothic arch (gardeners who were made to work very hard and were frequently dismissed), a white lilac walk which suited the moonlight, a thicket of laburnum, weeping willow, white broom, 'seringas' in which to hide from unwanted visitors and a rustic summer-house complete with library. They read Gilpin and Uvedale Price on the picturesque (of which they had a copy each), with Celtic folkloric poetry and Hirschfeld's *De l'Art des Jardins* of 1779 which gave them patterns for rustic conceits and inscriptions to write on boards and hang in the trees.[22]

The Ladies, who were rather highly prized by society, exhibited the idea that the garden should represent a particular lifestyle, which lasted well into the nineteenth century. But this was essentially an inheritance from the gardening elite of a century earlier: the Scriblerus Club, of fleeting existence as a satirical clique in 1714, would probably have disappeared from our knowledge had not the associates included Pope, Jonathan Swift, John Gay and the newly lorded Bolingbroke and Bathurst. The club, once thought guilty of hatching Tory propaganda and who employed the *ferme ornée* as a symbol of anti-Hanoverian protest, has also been charged with a 'frequently homoerotic' tone in some of its correspondence. David Nokes' new assessment of John Gay concludes that Pope and Swift went to great ends to conceal something about Gay more serious than his 'mere background in trade' (in an age when, despite its excesses of all kinds, the Sodomy Acts of 1533 remained in force and demanded the death penalty).[23] As all the world knows Pope and Gay were splendidly equipped to use words as the best form of defence, and garden making became a powerful motif. In *Pursuing Innocent Pleasures*, Peter Martin has documented the virulent anarchy that accompanied circuitous expeditions from Pope's Twickenham to Dawley (Bolingbroke), to Chiswick (Lord Burlington), to Richings in Berkshire and Cirencester (Lord Bathurst), and Wimpole in Cambridgeshire (Lord Oxford). In the spring of 1726 Dean Swift arrived for a garden tour (fresh from his gardening friendship with Dr Delany at Delville) and after his thorough immersion in the frenetic world of Pope and Gay, he perhaps gave them away: much time had been spent at Marble Hill, where Pope was 'contriver' of the garden for Mrs Howard, which inspired Swift's 'A Pastoral Dialogue between Richmond-Lodge and Marble-Hill' and the following lines, spoken by Marble-Hill:

> No more the Dean, that grave Divine,
> Shall keep the Key of my (no) Wine;
> My Ice-house rob as heretofore,
> And steal my Artichokes no more;
> Poor Patty Blount no more be seen
> Bedraggled in my Walks so green:
> Plump Johnny Gay will now elope;
> And here no more will dangle Pope.[24]

Swift's *Pastoral Dialogue*, written on the precept 'That Walls have Tongues, and Hedges, Ears,'[25] only partly indicates the uproarious time that Pope and Gay had at Marble-Hill, making free with Mrs Howard's household during her absences at court. They twitted her in the manner of indulged house-mates – celebrating the birth of a calf 'I mean a female calf; she is as like her mother as she can stare' they wrote 'in their Scriblerian-like playfulness' – and staying to supper: 'Mrs Susan offer'd us wine upon the occasion, and upon such an occasion we could not refuse it. Our entertainment consisted of flesh and fish, and the lettice of a greek Island, called Cos.'[26] They had thoughts of dining the next day for the after-birthday, and the next day to celebrate the day after that and after that they were bringing Dean Swift 'because we think your hall the most delightful room in the world except that where you are'.[27]

John Harris's well-informed 'outing' of Lord Burlington and William Kent ('all his life Kent lived with Burlington; his place in the Burlington household was a very special one, and there is no reason not to presume a close homosexual relationship')[28] has now been followed by Timothy Mowl's incontrovertible evidence about Horace Walpole 'the first garden historian' and 'spiritual founder' of the Garden History Society.[29] Walpole was protected in his day by being the son of the prime minister and in that his grand passion was the 9th Earl of Lincoln (it being rather typical of Horace to choose a 9th Earl) later 2nd Duke of Newcastle. Walpole has been protected by posterity, too, and it was only with the death of the collector of almost all Walpoliana, the American Wilmarth Sheldon Lewis in 1979, that Mowl was allowed to take an objective reading of Walpole's correspondence. Horace Walpole, the progenitor of the Picturesque in Strawberry Hill gothick, inveterate scribbler and gossip-monger, the dispenser of *bon mots* that bolstered almost every discussion on architecture and landscape in the eighteenth century, is revealed as a gloriously fastidious, flamboyant figure, with a bitter tongue and generous heart. Walpole's fascination was always that he was incapable of being boring; even a walk in his garden delights: 'I have just come out from the garden in the most oriental of all evenings, and from breathing odours beyond those of Araby'. He talks of acacias 'which the Arabians had the sense to worship', festoons of honeysuckles, thickets of lilacs, new cut hay which 'tempers the balmy gale with simple freshness'.[30] If Pope invented garden snobbery, Walpole adorned it. He wrote *On Modern Gardening* in 1780, sneering at the formal as 'fit only for those born in and who never moved from Holborn';[31] his forty-five acres at Strawberry Hill were the last word in smartness with gloomy overtones, a chapel based on a chantry tomb at Salisbury, a gothic gate and bridge, spacious lawns with each tree allowed its space and moment of performance, trees and flowers chosen for their scent with conical pines phallically aspiring above the deciduous, and his ha-ha which separated the lawn terrace from the field of cows, the final gently bucolic touch. Walpole was in revolt against the beefier elements of England and in particular his own upbringing at Houghton Hall, a shrine of progressive farming, and it is perfectly possible to discern in eighteenth-century natural and picturesque gardening elements of camp disaffection. Walpole's intimate circle included Thomas Gray, the poet of epigrammatic gloom, his beloved 9th Earl, the owner of Oatlands and maker of the legendary Lane grotto there, and Thomas Wright of Durham 'the Wizard of Durham', intriguing polymath, astronomer and designer of 'a wild profusion of temples, kiosks, hermitages, and all sorts of garden buildings and follies'.[32]

Of course, whilst Walpole was circumspect, he was followed by a great gardener who was less so: William Beckford, whose Gothic fantasy at Fonthill enthrals us still. Both Walpole and Beckford were influenced by 'the rigorous blessings of the claustral life' of the Carthusian monks at the Grande Chartreuse in the mountainous Dauphiné[33] (and of course both wrote Gothic novels, *The Castle of Otranto* and *Vathek* respectively). Beckford was what we would call a keen artistic environmentalist: his Fonthill estate protected wildlife and he planted only native trees – a million of them – in the landscape, keeping his vast collections of American plants and exotic trees in the more secluded places. He regarded the creation of a flowering wilderness around Fonthill Abbey as his greatest achievement.

Beckford's fabulous life as the Caliph of Fonthill crashed around him and Fonthill was put up for sale with almost all his collections of furniture, paintings and books in 1822. The remainder of his life was spent in Lansdown Crescent in Bath (where he built his last folly, Beckford's Tower and a long narrow 'ride' between the two) until a fateful morning in April 1844 when an east wind and a drenching brought on a chill, and he died in early May.[34] He was an anachronism: the Victorian age was firmly under way, and it is time to return to the ladies.

Jane Loudon was an early heroine of the Victorian middle class: she stands in the flicker of gaslight in her crinoline and shawl, her hair in the inevitable bun, her face a white oval, with sombre dark eyes, a slim pointed nose and prim mouth, her fine long-fingered hands entwining long strings of unprecious beads. She appears a symbol of ordinariness, a stereotype of repressed Victorian womanhood, inadequate to the arrows of outrageous fortune that would inevitably come. And yet, she would do 'for the outdoor activities of the inexperienced mistress of a Victorian household' as much as Mrs Beeton did for indoor economy.[35] It is time Jane Loudon was a household name.

She was born Jane Webb and her mother died when she was twelve; she was an only child and her father, a Birmingham engineer, indulged her with books and continental travel until he too died, when she was seventeen. He had already helped her publish a volume of verse and prose and so when she discovered 'on the winding up of his affairs that it would be necessary for me to do something for my support' she decided to stick to writing.[36] She produced a melodrama, *The Mummy! A Tale of the Twenty-Second Century*, featuring the Pharaoh Cheops galvanized into a fantasy world of smokeless cities, air-conditioned houses, mechanical diggers, milking machines 'something very like an Expresso coffee machine' and radio; 'by St Wellington' was a popular oath, and there were terraced gardens along the banks of the Thames 'filled with clean and handsome British sculpture'.[37]

Jane knew herself to 'have naturally an independent spirit' but also that she could not push herself, or her books, forward, and that she was soon depressed 'and when anyone finds fault with any of my productions, instead of defending them, I throw them into the fire'.[38] Such candour never fails to attract a knight in shining armour, and William Jerdan, editor of the *Literary Gazette*, put himself forward. Jerdan sent a copy of *The Mummy!* to John Claudius Loudon, for his popular and scientific *Gardeners' Magazine* – Loudon liked futuristic ideas, and asked to meet the author. We know the barest facts of the outcome – Loudon may have been surprised to find that the author was a woman, but he was delighted to meet Miss Webb; that was in April 1830 and they were married the following September.

There was mutual affection in the Loudon marriage (a daughter Agnes was born in October 1832) but John Claudius was nearing fifty, a workaholic and 'dour, domineering and temperamental'. Jane responded with courage, devotion, good spirits and hard work; she re-invented herself, from a self-confessed complete ignorance of gardening to the editor of her own *Lady's Magazine of Gardening* and of *Botany for Ladies*, and for the rest of Loudon's life, though it was only thirteen years, they were a 'perfect partnership'. As well as her own responsibilities, Jane was editor-in-chief and perpetuator of the Loudon revolution: they were style gurus of the 1830s and an endless stream of encyclopaedias, magazines and the biblical *Suburban Gardener and Villa Companion* (1838) poured out of their home, office and experimental garden at 3 Porchester

Terrace in Bayswater (*Plate 27*). As a family they set forth on long tours to botanic gardens, to Wordsworth and Southey gardening in the Lake District, to head gardeners and innovators all over Britain and to Birmingham and Derby to oversee Loudon's great works, the Birmingham Botanic Gardens and Derby Arboretum.

John Claudius mellowed in Jane's company; he appreciated her, and she must have been happy enough, able to write, her intellect stimulated. She presided over celebrated Saturday evening dinners where one was 'sure to be gratified by persons of superior intelligence and information' including Charles Dickens, Thackeray, Mrs Gaskell, painters, journalists and younger writers. But this ceaseless activity was always rather driven, by Loudon's indifferent health and, most of all, his truly Dickensian horror of the debtor's prison; no matter how hard they worked the Loudons were never freed from debts. When John Claudius died, in Jane's arms, at about noon on 14 December 1843 (in the midst of dictating his *Self-Instruction for Young Gardeners*), there was fortunately immediate support from Sir Joseph Paxton and the Royal Horticultural Society's worthies to raise an appeal to pay his debts. Though Jane was never to be free of financial worries, she continued to write, revising and re-issuing Loudon's works, but also consolidating her own reputation. She was elected as a corresponding member of the Royal Horticultural Society of Paris in 1844. Jane died in the summer of 1858, she was buried with John Claudius in Kensal Green Cemetery.[39]

The Loudons' greatness lay in their ability to share their own gardening delights and knowledge with others, for whom gardening was an enlightenment and liberation. Jane recorded how 'a stranger stepped forward' as John Claudius was being lowered into his grave, who threw some pieces of ivy onto the coffin. This, it transpired, was an artificial flower maker who had once received tickets for the Horticultural Gardens from Loudon, and who wished finally to thank him.[40] But mid-nineteenth-century England was still not a place where the common touch, except that bestowed by lords upon their head gardeners, was appreciated. The Loudons' work was taken to America by Andrew Jackson Downing (he arranged for an American edition of *Gardening for Ladies* to be published) and it filtered into the liberal intelligentsia of New England, the milieu of Emerson and Thoreau, President Eliot of Harvard, the botanist Asa Gray, Charles Sprague Sargent of the

Arnold Arboretum, and the landscape architect Frederick Law Olmsted. Loudon's Scots radicalism was much appreciated in America – he in return thought George Washington and Thomas Jefferson 'the greatest men that ever lived'.[41] Though there was no official place for women in this world, there was an inclusiveness: Olmsted (whose wide-ranging social and environmental concerns ran parallel to Loudon's) was sympathetic to serious women. Mary Robeson Sargent painted exquisite botanical watercolours and her husband allowed women to attend courses at the Arnold Arboretum (which was a department of Harvard University) at Brookline outside Cambridge. Mariana van Rensselaer was very much part of this world; she used her privileged background, her opportunities for travel, to write perceptively on architecture and art criticism, and by the 1880s turned her attention to landscape gardening, especially for women, and was writing *Art out of Doors: Hints on Good Taste in Gardening*, which was published in 1893. This example led Beatrix Jones (who later married Max Farrand) to study at the Arnold, become a founding fellow of the American Association of Landscape Architects and – in a brilliant career which spanned over fifty years and 200 commissions[42] – take her place in a pioneering company who were steadily to confirm landscape gardening as an equal opportunities profession, at least on the eastern and western seaboards and around Chicago, in America.

Jane Loudon noted that John Claudius died on the anniversary of the death of his hero, George Washington, 14 December 1843: it is perhaps worth adding that on that day the baby Gertrude Jekyll was entering the second week of her life. The year that Jane Loudon died, 1858, saw the birth of a very different pioneer, Ellen Ann Willmott. On her seventh birthday, 19 August 1865, Ellen received on her breakfast plate the first of a series of £1000 cheques from her godmother, Helen Tasker. At that moment too, it can be confidently assumed that Miss Frances Hope of Wardie Lodge in Edinburgh, who has been called the Scottish disciple of Loudon, was contemplating her next piece for the *Gardeners' Chronicle* and perhaps the plants she would purchase from her few shillings' fees.

Where Jane Loudon was the advocate, these three, Miss Jekyll, Miss Willmott and Miss Hope, put articulate and intelligent gardening into practice; they were all very different from each other, both in temperament and circumstances, but equally all three asserted their distinction in male preserves. In 1897, Miss Jekyll and Miss Willmott were in the company of sixty men awarded the Royal Horticultural Society's Victoria Medal of Honour. Miss Hope was a Lady Associate of the Botanical Society of Edinburgh, if anything a loftier eminence.

Frances Jane Hope has left only a modest legacy, a small, rather obscure book of her writings from *The Garden* and *Gardeners' Chronicle*, collected after her untimely death in April 1880, *Notes & Thoughts on Garden and Woodland written chiefly for the amateur*.[43] Her prose is lucid, and seems easily to become her voice: quiet, educated, kindly, Scots: 'a love of Plants is a very different thing from a mere love of Flowers. Now that the extreme rage for Bedding-plants is on the wane, there is some chance of a wider range of plants becoming known to, and cultivated by, amateurs, and a deeper knowledge of gardening and plants in use – not merely a surface knowledge, such as is required for the ordinary style of bedding-out Florists' flowers. It is, perhaps, hardly fair to disparage a system that has satisfied so many for so long, without, at the same time, proposing a substitute.' Thus her opening to 'Effective Flower Beds' in *The Garden* of 7 February 1874; her ensuing stream of schemes for hardy and annual plants prompts a series of imaginary afternoon visit visions of Wardie Lodge, where she struggles knowingly with 'utterly dry and ash-like' soil, never enough rain and too much wind: in mid-January she has a pair of beds covered in the little white stars of *Aster ericoides*, with a golden holly at their centres, and edgings of variegated *Euonymus radicans* and the dark foliage of dwarf double red Sweet William. Her no. 4 bed is good for winter into spring – an outside edging of purple-leaved *Heuchera* and infilling of 'common double white pink', presumably 'Mrs Sinkins', with single red tulips amongst the silvery foliage, and blue *Scilla bifolia* amongst the *Heuchera*; bed no. 8 (these are all Wardie Lodge originals) has *Erica carnea*, violas and pansies in alternate rings, colours to suit individual taste – 'it is hardly possible to go wrong with this bed'; and no. 12 has a groundwork of low *Oenothera missouriensis* thinly dotted with purple lilac shades of viola or blue pansy; bed no. 13 has a centrepiece of *Yucca gloriosa* in a groundwork of dark blue-flowered *Ajuga reptans* 'atropurpurea', dotted with *Sedum spectabile*, 'fine large pink tassels of bloom which stands the first frosts', the whole edged with variegated ivy. Miss Hope is scrupulously honest: she has seen bed no. 19 in the damp and heavy soil of a Dumfriesshire garden – tall, scarlet *Lobelia fulgens* intermixed with variegated coltsfoot – 'a grand bed'; and bed no. 7 was seen in perfection at Jackman's nursery at Woking, unsurprisingly for it is massed Clematis Jackmanii hybrids edged with large and small and variegated vincas, the small vinca and euonymus being hardier for northern gardens.

Miss Hope is a philosophic garden visitor, especially to the Edin-burgh Botanics where she particularly covets Mr McNab's rock garden 'but one cannot have everything and we are well content with our Borders on the flat, and make the best of it'. The best turns out to be a refreshing insight into garden life before Jekyllian bouffance arrives to fill our garden horizons and block out the past: 'We have our Borders arranged in rows for convenience of hoeing, and to know exactly where each plant is' she writes. She is perfectly aware that 'some prefer to plant their borders in groups' but by the time that she has finished her readers will have dismissed such frippery. Her rows spring to life with her words: one magnificent row border, eighty-six feet long and a generous five feet eight inches deep, is completely edged with grey houseleeks, lined with purple crocus in spring and backed by scarlet *Sedum lydium*, which itself edges a carpet of common stonecrop, *Sedum acre*. The four corners of this bed are livened with blue and white lobelia in summer, and scilla and leucojum in winter; sixteen circles in a row are cut in the carpet of stonecrop, and filled alternately with rosemary, bright-leaved pelar-goniums or purple and lilac kale for winter, each set in ground cover of contrasting sedum or saxifrage. Sedums, asters and hellebores are the greatest favourites at Wardie Lodge, but there are a great variety of other collections – privets, pernettyas, old-fashioned roses, hollyhocks, helianthus, carnations, chrysanthemums and fuchsias, and a love of wild things, mistletoe, hops and brambles – or at least the white-stemmed *Rubus biflorus*, trained up the apple trees. Miss Hope has also learned the beauty of the 'healthy flowerless border' and stopped her daily inspec-tion in July to admire peony, iris, bergenia, *Anemone sulphurea* (in feath-ery seed), the non-climbing bitter vetch and *Waldsteinia*.

Frances Hope, in common with Gertrude Jekyll, saw the garden as the workshop for her writing, as well as a place for encounters and exchanges with a wide circle of botanical and horticultural fellows and friends, but perhaps Miss Hope was unique in the way she saw her garden as helping those less fortunate. She was clearly familiar with the 'ugly and utilitarian kale yards' with their bush of southernwood, of the Edinburgh poor, and she took sprigs of spearmint and rosemary to old women in cellars and garrets in Cowgate. A large part of the Wardie Lodge garden seems to have been devoted to supplying such philanthropic plants; sometimes hundreds of posies a day were delivered to the Royal Infirmary and to the Asylum for the Blind. As well as giving us a glimpse into the ordinary gardens of mid-nineteenth-century Britain, Miss Hope reveals to us the horrific realities of what it was to be ill and disabled: she started Flower Missions, and the blankets of houseleeks and sedums grown in the garden came into their own – a leaf of a houseleek being the surest of pain relievers for bad feet, the stonecrop, which would live on nothing except a little daylight, at least bringing another living thing into the Cowgate cellar. She dismissed hothouse plants for patients at the Infirmary, who had 'Sunday memories' of pimpernel and sweetbriar, and made them posies of sweet herbs, tied in worsted; but she is most revealing on flowers for the blind workers at the Asylum, where success took a great deal of forethought and initiative. The smell of balsam poplar was liked, but not its stickiness; bog myrtle was a success; lily of the valley 'an immense treat'; and willow catkins of various kinds 'a delight'. Blind women were excited to cultivate mint or musk, and one hyacinth or stock, to be tenderly felt over and trimmed of its dying flowers, gave hours of pleasure. Miss Hope told the blind workers that they could sort baskets of flowers for themselves, for it was 'not as if they were Infirmary patients with hardly strength to smell the flowers laid by their side'; baskets of fresh herbs and sweet leaves from plants lifted after the first frosts were sent in – the most popular favourites amongst the flowers were rosemary, lilac, Christmas roses, snowdrops, pinks, syringa, stocks and lily of the valley. We hardly have to ask why the Wardie Lodge baskets carried happy memories and touches of human dignity back into those dreary places, but we may be sad that one garden, however abundant, could not supply such overwhelming needs, and that Miss Hope seemingly wore herself out, perhaps to her early death, in trying.[44]

Gertrude Jekyll shared Frances Hope's opinions upon the benevolence of plants, and their potential benefits to people, especially in distress; her work for war graves and cemeteries is described in chapter two but one place in particular must come here. That is King Edward VII Hospital at Midhurst in Sussex, built as a sanatorium for the treatment of tuberculosis and consumptive diseases, with the patronage of the King and money from Sir Ernest Cassel, in 1906. It was designed by the most distinguished hospital architects of the day, H. Percy Adams and Charles Holden, with an integral garden layout, upon which Miss Jekyll was consulted from the first. The enormous building rests as two long parallel wings, an elongated butterfly layout, on its hilltop site; the approach from the north, through pines and rhododendrons is to the centre of the north-facing wing for administration and services. A spinal central corridor runs southward to connect the long, south-facing patients' wing, all the rooms facing south, with balconies, outdoor sitting alcoves at ground level, all basking in the sun, gazing out across the downs to the sea. In between the wings were open-air courts, and the south-facing terraces were laid out in a series of low-walled, sheltered garden spaces, some 2000 yards of walls, with beds and borders filled with the sandy spoil from building excavation. Miss Jekyll, who knew how to cope with mean, sandy soils, did the planting designs; the philosophy was to provide as many scented and sheltered sitting places as possible, along with easy plants that could give opportunities for raised-bed gardening therapy by the patients. To this end she drew over forty plans and supplied some plants. The rest of the plants and the gardening labour was supplied by Frances Wolseley's Glynde College for Lady Gardeners, from Ragged Lands, near Lewes. A photograph shows a dozen young ladies working, wearing the college uniform of khaki linen skirts and aprons, white blouses and soft felt sunhats; they tended the plants for at least two years, as part of their courses (though it seems likely that heavy work was done by men) and made a splendid job of it. In 1909 a *Country Life* contributor (most likely the eminent gardening editor, H. Avray Tipping) wrote lyrically of the wonderful result, and the illustrations with the article proved his point. Large beds show a grey, pink, lilac, purple and white scheme with catmint, dwarf lavenders, purple campanula and aubretia, white cerastium, pink rock pinks and thrift, purple and white iris, a taller lavender and *Geranium ibericum platyphyllum*, Miss Jekyll's favourite. White foxgloves sprout from the low rock walls, with Jerusalem sage and stonecrops; wall borders abound in pinks, bergamot, iris, rosemary and roses. In between the main wings were the enclosed courts, the East and West Rosemary Gardens, with rosemary hedges surrounding plantings of *Galega officinalis*, *Cistus cyprius*, *Magnolia conspicua*, fuchsias and 'Madame Plantier' roses.

King Edward VII Hospital has grown over the years; most of the inner gardens have been built over, though on my last visit a mature *Magnolia conspicua* lingered, filling a tiny inner court off the central corridor. But the terraces, many original trees and shrubs, the hedge of 'Madame Plantier' roses, with its scented leaves and curly petalled flowers, and dozens of indestructible white foxgloves, all survive, along with the healing spirit of this marvellous garden, which is loved and appreciated by generations of staff and patients and their families.[45]

Gertrude Jekyll[46] began gardening for her mother at Munstead House, near Godalming in Surrey, in the late 1870s and bought her own fifteen-acre plot across the road in 1883, where she experimented with planting, photographed the results and wrote articles. In 1889, when she was forty-five, she met the twenty-year-old Edwin Lutyens, educated him in garden design and they began their partnership, which resulted in almost one hundred gardens made before 1914. She had published her first book, *Wood and Garden*, in 1899, immediately followed by *Home and Garden*, which told of the building of her house, Munstead Wood, which Lutyens had designed; a dozen other major books followed, most published by *Country Life*, and by 1914 she was regarded as one of the most distinguished arbiters of good design in house and garden of her day. Many, even amongst those who knew her best, thought her eccentric, a workaholic and increasingly anti-social; the war aggravated her disinclination for sociability, but she maintained a friendship with Lutyens, a large correspondence and a large workload of garden and planting designing well into her late eighties; indeed she stopped working only shortly before her death in December 1932, a few days before her eighty-ninth birthday.

Hers was a secluded, even cloistered life; she regarded herself as a 'working amateur' at gardening and planting design, no money changed hands in her partnership with Lutyens and the bulk of the remainder of her design work, some 250 commissions large and small, came through correspondence, mostly from people who wrote to her as the result of an article in *Country Life* or a gardening paper. She designed into her planting schemes and articles the plants she grew at Munstead Wood.

This was firmly in line with her philosophy of never writing about what she had not practised, and it had the further advantage that some of her gardeners' wages were paid from the sale of plants. The system worked well – plans, detailing the number of plants in each bed, were accompanied by the equivalent plants, carefully packed in wet moss, bracken and straw and delivered by an efficient railway. About six of her fifteen acres at Munstead Wood were the nursery ground, and at her busiest time, from 1900 up until the war in 1914, she was employing as many as a dozen gardeners. She was, in fact, running a nursery. One catalogue survives: a sixteen-page paper-covered list, printed by Craddocks of Godalming – 'Some of the Best Hardy Plants for Border, Shrub and Rock Garden grown by Miss Jekyll'. It is a forerunner of favourite catalogues by Scotts of Merriott or Beth Chatto, in that the plant is described, plus its preferences and possible uses: '*Choisya ternata* (Mexican Orange Flower). The most beautiful wall shrub of recent introduction. Clusters of sweet scented flowers, closely resembling orange-blossom in May, 1/6d each; *Campanula persicifolia* "Chauderon" A fine variety, originally collected by Miss Jekyll in the Alps, and improved by garden culture. The stalk is slender and graceful, and the flowers larger than in the usual garden kind, 9d each, 8/- for 12'. Though she may have frugally refused to spend more on printing, it is more likely that the demands on her plants from design commissions used up her stock, and this catalogue was never superseded, though local people could stop and buy plants in the usual manner.[47]

However, all Miss Jekyll's industry and even her distinction in her day are cast into the shade by the glittering career of Ellen Willmott, the little girl with the £1000 cheque on her birthday breakfast plate, chronicled in Audrey le Lievre's biography (1980). The cheques continued to roll in, but they must have been pocket money, for the Willmott family were rich and apparently devoted: Ellen had two younger sisters, Rose and Ada, the latter sadly dying from diphtheria when aged eight. In 1876 they settled at Warley Place at Great Warley in Essex, where Ellen discovered her passion for gardening. The prominent firm of James Backhouse of York were called in to build her a rock garden, which probably cost most of one birthday cheque: her father proudly noted in his diary on 1 April 1882, 'Ellie began her new Alpine garden', and he bought another twenty-two acres of land in

SOME SWEET HERBS AND OLD PLANTS OF ENGLISH GARDENS.

The following are some of the sweet-scented or aromatic herbs and shrubs that are associated with the oldest of our English Gardens, and were there grown either for fragrance or medicinal virtues. Several of them were used for garden edgings.

	EACH.	DOZ.
Alecost or **Costmary** (*Tanacetum Balsamita*). Formerly used steeped in ale. The heads of yellow flowers were also tied up in tight bunches with lavender ...	9d.	
Balm Sweet herb for cooking and flavouring summer drinks ...	6d.	
Burnet Herb for flavouring salad	6d.	
Catmint (*Nepeta Mussini*) ...	6d.	
Hyssop A favourite edging plant in Tudor gardens; flowers in autumn ...	6d.	5/-
Lavender ...	9d. & 1/-	
,, dwarf variety, earlier and darker coloured ...	9d. & 1/-	
,, white ,, rare ...	1/6	
Lavender-Cotton (*Santolina Chamæcyparissus*) ...	9d.	
Marjoram Sweet herb ...	6d.	
Monk's Rhubarb Handsome leaves. Allied to Dock and Sorrel ...	6d.	
Rosemary ...	1/-	
Sage Grey foliage and handsome purple bloom. Kitchen herb but also good in flower-garden ...	6d.	
Sorrel The large-leaved kind. Culinary herb ...	9d.	
Sweet Cicely (*Myrrhis odorata*), sweet-scented foliage—an important plant of early summer ...	6d.	
Southernwood (*Artemisia Abrotanum*) ...	9d.	
Thyme, Bush Sweet herb ...	6d.	
,, **Golden Lemon** Sweet Herb. Both are used as edging ...	6d.	
Winter Savory Sweet Herb. Good as an edging ...	6d.	
Woodruff A lovely woodland plant, used to flavour Mai-trank	6d.	

Munstead Wood Potpourri.

This is offered at 20/- a gallon; one gallon will fill a large bowl and is equal to about four pounds weight, or per lb. 5/-. Postage extra.

The Munstead Wood catalogue, printed by Craddocks of Godalming in only one known edition, *c.*1895. In her large garden Gertrude Jekyll grew her favourite hardy perennials and scented herbs and shrubs which were the basis of her planting repertory: she would sell the plants with the plans she drew for her clients, but seems not to have charged for the drawings.

anticipation.[48] In early 1888 the benevolent godmother died, and Ellen and Rose became heiresses in their own right. To celebrate Ellen's thirtieth birthday the Willmotts went off on a grand tour which lasted until the summer of 1889; Ellen and Rose returned to Warley alone and then were off again, and the following year Ellen bought Le Château de Tresserve, near Aix-les-Bains, spending lavishly on restoration and making a garden. She was clearly in charge of the garden at Warley Place as well, and during the 1890s she bought plants enthusiastically, all over Europe; plants were her passion, alpines, narcissus of all kinds, rhododendrons, roses and trees. She bought both well and unwisely – Henry Correvon, whose nurseries at Geneva were famous in America and all over Europe, thought her stupidly extravagant for paying travelling costs for plants from him when she could have found them in England. In August 1891 Rose Willmott married Robert Berkeley and went to live at Spetchley Park in Worcestershire, where she made a spectacular garden, still famous for its drifts of daffodils. Ellen, perhaps making up for the loss of Rose's companionship, took to photography, working in fine woods on a German lathe, and joined the Royal Horticultural Society, where within three years she was on the Narcissus Committee. Her father had died in 1892, Mrs Willmott in 1898, and the remainder of the considerable family fortune fell to Ellen and Rose: Warley Place itself to Ellen. She was by now 'the greatest living woman gardener' or so Miss Jekyll said when they both received their Victoria Medal in 1897. For Ellen this was only the beginning; she became a fellow of the Linnaean Society, and won four consecutive RHS Gold Medals for her daffodils, her greatest passion and expertise. She bred them at Warley, naming exquisite *Narcissus triandrus* hybrids for her favourite people – 'Mrs Berkeley' and 'Ada' – as well as many of her friends. In 1905, she bought an Italian garden, La Boccanegra, near Ventimiglia, and barely two miles from the Hanburys' La Mortola. With three gardens, she told Professor Sargent from the Arnold Arboretum, 'my plants and my gardens come before anything in life for me, and all my time is given up to working in one garden or another'. At Warley Place in 1907, it was said, there were over 100 gardeners. The same year Tresserve was badly damaged by fire; it was uninsured, but Ellen spent lavishly to rebuild and restore. At the end of the year she had to take out her first mortgage from her father's old firm. Then another passion gripped her: to produce the most beautiful book on roses, the first in full colour, with 132 original illustrations commissioned from the artist Alfred Parsons. The first part of *The Genus Rosa* appeared in 1910, but it was a publishing disaster, and Ellen was forced into rapid retrenchment. She asked her head gardener James Preece at Warley to leave, let properties at Warley and La Boccanegra, sold family treasures (including Amati and Stradivarius violins – the Willmotts were a very musical family), and took out additional mortgages against the sale of Tresserve. Finally, her father's old partner, one of her ablest supporters, declared himself bankrupt. Then came the war.

Things only got worse: the army took over the Warley estate, Ellen's rose collection was destroyed, the banks were pressing, and her friends in horticulture, Sir Frank Crisp and Canon Ellacombe, as well as her beloved maid and companion Lalla Burge, who had been with her for more than twenty years, all died. For Ellen the worst blow came with Rose's death from cancer, on 21 August 1922 – for two years her writing paper carried black borders. In Ellen's last decade the continuing horticultural honours are paralleled by personal tragedies – she was awarded a medal by the National Rose Society and was arrested for shoplifting in Regent Street; she was elected to the RHS Flora Committee and had pneumonia; she sold all her precious belongings for cash and was elected to the RHS Lily Committee. Finally, she died in the early morning of 26 September 1934, probably from a heart attack, and alone.[49]

What remains is the awful vision of a callous committee life, in bleak rooms along those polished mahogany corridors at Vincent Square, where no one cared what happened before or after you had decided the fate of a lily and where, as Dawn Macleod records, they liked Miss Jekyll (who was frumpish, plain, rotund and hardly ever there) but where Miss Willmott, patently once so beautiful, with her fine clothes and persistent enthusiasms, justifiably upset by her misfortunes, was damned for the slightest misdemeanour.

After her death Warley Place and all her belongings were auctioned; her garden lies sleeping as I write, yet it is often beautiful.[50] *The Genus Rosa* has appeared in reprint, and she is remembered in all the *willmottiae* and *warleyensis* hybrids that still fill our gardens: *Narcissus* 'Ellen Willmott', *Primula willmottiae*, *Rosa willmottiae*, *Tulipa willmottiae*, *Ceratostigma willmottianum* ('that blue-eyed darling' Dawn Macleod called it)[51] and many others. And, one plant perhaps more aptly named than any other, *Eryngium giganteum* 'Miss Willmott's Ghost'.

Fortunes, especially feminine ones, went out of fashion with Miss Willmott. She was 'the greatest living woman gardener' as Miss Jekyll dubbed her, but who else was there? The nearest equivalent in style and flamboyance was undoubtedly 'Darling Daisy', the Prince of Wales's former mistress, the Countess of Warwick, who was genuinely a passionate gardener. Harold Peto made her a vast, romantic treillage garden at her own house, Easton Lodge near Dunmow, she was pursuing plans and schemes at Warwick Castle, and had founded Studley College to train women in horticulture. In 1897, Miss Jekyll might have included the redoubtable Mrs Theresa Earle, author of *Pot-Pourri from a Surrey Garden* and its sequels (including *Gardening for the Ignorant*, 1912), Lady Dorothy Nevill, a great expert on orchids, the rosarian Miss Rose Kingsley, also a contributor to Robinson's *The English Flower Garden* and, not to be forgotten, Miss Jekyll's elder sister, Caroline Eden, whose six-acre garden in Venice was much admired.[52]

The triumvirate of Earle, Jekyll and Willmott were patrons of Frances Wolseley's Glynde College for Lady Gardeners, which with Studley, Swanley in Kent, the Thatcham Fruit and Flower Farm School near Newbury and courses for women at Reading University School of Horticulture opened up careers in market gardening, horticulture and landscape architecture so as to make them almost fields of equal opportunity by the mid-twentieth century. A Thatcham graduate, Beatrix Havergal, with Avice Saunders, started their own school in the walled garden at Pusey House, Faringdon, in 1929, which moved to Waterperry House near Oxford in 1932, perhaps becoming the most famous school of all. Waterperry graduates have been prominent in modern gardening, with Valerie Finnis (later Lady Scott), Pamela Schwerdt and Sybille Kreutzberger, the head gardeners at Sissinghurst for over thirty years, just the first that come to mind.[53]

The first generations of students were often involved in suffragette politics, many were university women, and highly capable of living independent lives, though some might have married had it not been for the war. In the 1920s they spread out in all directions into interesting lives – Frances Wolseley was continuing her campaign to see her graduates as a means of reviving British rural life – but one of them has to represent the many here. Chrystabel and Joan Proctor were born in the 1890s in a comfortable, enlightened Quaker family, where they soon found individual interests: Joan, who had a pet crocodile named Rameses, in reptiles and invertebrates; Chrystabel in flowers – they were nicknamed Fauna and Flora. Both were severely handicapped by poor health: Joan, who became Curator of Reptiles at London Zoo and then Whipsnade, died in her early thirties. Chrystabel, poorly sighted and increasingly deaf, went to St Paul's Girls' School and then Lady Wolseley's college, and though she wanted most of all to be a gardener, she knew that her parents only allowed this because of her frail health. She went back to St Paul's to look after five acres growing produce for the school, then to Bingley College in Yorkshire as head gardener, and she wrote and lectured on gardening for schools. In 1933 Chrystabel (now bereft of all her immediate family) was the successful candidate as head gardener at Girton College Cambridge – virtually a country estate – in that fifty acres of pleasure gardens, sports grounds and woodlands, also supplied fruit, vegetables and flowers and eggs to the college. Chrystabel's reign is still remembered at Girton; her first five-year plan made the gardens one of the greatest sights of Cambridge, and through the war, with the help of her neighbour across the Huntingdon road, Professor Frank Engledow of the university's agricultural department, Girton's grounds fed the college and local community and supported the university farm. She left Girton after the war, having been head-hunted to manage the Bryanston Estate in Dorset, where she continued to write and lecture until she retired into a comfortable old age.[54]

Women artists will find a place in chapter nine, but in 1988 Patricia Jaffe opened her book, *Women Engravers*, with the jubilant, 'Women this century have adopted wood engraving', and in illustrating the work of Miriam McGregor (*Plate 38*), Joan Hassall, Clare Dalby, Agnes Miller Parker (and Pat Jaffe herself) it is good to see how wonderfully they express the character of gardens and plants.[55] One engraver stands supreme for this: Clare Leighton's *Four Hedges* (1935), is a physical, exuberant and enchanting description of becoming a gardener (*Plate 39*). It is the most encouraging book, full of the pitfalls, heartbreak and rejoicing of gardening, and also a rite of passage for the loss of her brother Roland in the First World War. Mention must also be made of a less exuberant soul, Eleanour Sinclair Rohde, who also lost her brother in the war, and this seemed to deprive her of the tougher part of herself. Eleanour Rohde, born in India, educated at Cheltenham Ladies' College and Oxford, was academically clever and politically minded; she became secretary to Lord Curzon but found she could not stand arguments, so took refuge in garden history. Her stream of books began with *The Scented Garden* (1931) and *Oxford College Gardens* (1932); she wrote sixteen more major books which were important for the beginnings of garden history and for the revival of herbs and herb gardening. She was a prolific contributor to *The Times* and the *Field* and president of the Society of Women Journalists. She was always quiet, rather fey and sad, she never married, and gardened unusual vegetables and old-fashioned flowers and sold them from her nursery at Cranham Lodge, Reigate, her family home where she lived until her sixty-ninth year, dying there in June 1960.[56]

A small place of honour must also be kept here for Constance Spry 'the woman who set flowers free from floristry', but who wrote of herself 'I was first, and hope to be last, a gardener'.[57] She began by not being allowed to study horticulture at Glasnevin because her father insisted upon a 'proper' career, which was as a lecturer in the Women's National Health Association for Ireland, set up by Lady Aberdeen in 1908. After a marriage which she knew was a terrible mistake, the birth of her son, the masterminding of the Red Cross through the Easter Rising of 1916, and then the loss of two of her brothers in the war, Constance fled to England. She met H. E. 'Shav' Spry and together they settled at the Old Rectory in Abinger Common in Surrey in 1926. Her parents were now so shocked that it hardly mattered that she took to gardening and flowers, so she did, and through the kindness of Norman Wilkinson, the theatrical and interior designer, made her debut with enormous vases of Abinger 'weeds', golden beech, trailing hops, old man's beard and berries, with rich green orchids, in the show windows of Atkinson's Perfumiers on the corner of Old Bond and Old Burlington Streets. Always on a shoe string, she opened her first shop in Pimlico, then one on South Audley Street, then the shop and flower school in Curzon Street, and finally her school at Winkfield after the war. In 1937 in *Flowers in House and Garden*, among many good things she lists the contents of a white border – *Achillea* 'The Pearl', asters, iris, delphinium, lupin, poppy, phlox, gypsophila and silver foliage, exactly as planted at Sissinghurst some eleven years later.[58] She writes of persuading everyone to grow old gallica, damask and centifolia roses; she had the most brilliant eye and intuition, noting the colouring and 'poise' of a plant like the giant fringed cyclamen, and the beauty of cyclamen leaves (which did much for its popularity as a house plant). But it was not enough to love, grow and arrange flowers, it was necessary to experiment, observe, criticize and be ever open to possibilities – thus not only old man's beard in Bond Street, but cow parsley (called Queen Anne's lace) and ox-eye daisies at society weddings and Claridge's balls. She could see that fireweed (willow-herb) added to a group of brilliant reds which 'seemed to resolve the clashing colours into harmony'. Constance Spry did everything she did with so much well-publicized panache and style that she made us see plants anew as well.

In post-war utility Britain there was a tremendous hunger for glamour, which cannot be underestimated, and slim resources for most people on which to achieve it: when Constance Spry set up Winkfield Place as a country-house school for home-making in 1946 it was done with patchwork curtains made from couturier offcuts from Victor Stiebel and bomber-felt dyed yellow 'like sunshine on the floor'. Doing the flowers for the wedding of Princess Elizabeth and the Duke of Edinburgh in 1947 was an overwhelming contribution to cheering up a whole Commonwealth; her bestselling, *Cordon Bleu Cookery School* books, written with her partner Rosemary Hume, and a stream of glitzy weddings and party flowers greatly enhanced Constance Spry's influence, which reached a heady crescendo with the flowers for the Coronation in 1953. Though others may have tramped more village halls, it is now often forgotten how in the grey post-war years the colour and variety of Constance Spry's flowers were liberating for many women. It was, after all, a flower arranger, Betty Massingham, who resurrected Gertrude Jekyll from complete obscurity with her biography in 1966. Also, the Spry perception did a great deal for the triumph of foliage and 'interesting' plants over horticultural garishness: Mrs Desmond Underwood's grey and silver specialization at Ramparts Nursery, Colchester, and the drawings and writings of the young Graham Stuart Thomas were the path which led to Andrew and Beth Chatto starting their garden in 1960 (with added inspiration from Sir Cedric Morris).

Constance Spry's achievements were the result of her tremendous energy and humour, and she was greatly mourned when she died in 1960 aged seventy-three. After a decent interval Shav Spry married Val Pirie, Constance's old friend and business partner. They had been lovers for years, but their loyalty to the Spry reputation and to Constance herself, had kept the *status quo*: that was the way things were done.

By the end of the decade all such façades were cracking, and things and people who had been taken for granted were questioned. The old joke that the British 'discovered sex' in the 1960s has more than a grain of truth and, stimulated by the liberalizing 1967 Sexual Offences Act (which legalized homosexual acts between consenting adults in private), they started talking about it. Gardening was not immune, and there were many jokes about women in breeches and pansy-loving men. The wall of silence crumbled with Nigel Nicolson's publication of his mother's locked-away diary of her affair with Violet Trefusis, *Portrait of a Marriage*, in 1973, a betrayal in the eyes of his own generation for which they never forgave him. But for those that were younger it was a liberation, and gardening won the accolade of being 'sexy', 'better than sex' – or, as Beverley Nichols wrote at the end of his long, bachelor, gardening life 'the only mistress who never fades, who never fails'.[59] A garden is perhaps more demanding than a mistress, constantly demanding sweated exertions and a tender touch, constantly offering sensual arousal, virtually pornographic fantasy pictures (explicit in the paintings of Georgia O'Keeffe) and attentions at all hours. A shared garden might hold a shaky relationship together, as it did with Vita and Harold Nicolson, but it is more likely to be a battleground, as it was with Walter and Margery Fish. Noticeably Mrs Fish really blossomed after Walter's death in 1947; she was a big, strong woman and 'dealt with the hard stuff of garden toil in a manner few men could outdo', wrote Dawn MacLeod. It was Mrs Fish who opined: 'Clearing bindweed is far more exciting than golf or fishing. Tracing this tenacious creeping Judas of a weed to its source and getting it out without leaving any small broken pieces behind requires skill and patience. The reward is a barrow-load of obscene twisting white roots and the joy of burning them.'[60] Surely there is something medieval about such glee, but we know what she means.

The Judas hunt brooks no break for meals or family demands, and a garden inspires jealousy. In fact recent history proves – at least for most of the twentieth century when women have had some self-determination – that the majority of committed gardeners have lived alone, or at least alone as far as outward appearances are concerned. Sir Frederick Gibberd is the only gardener I know to have admitted this 'selfish pleasure' of making a garden: but then he had two independently talented and loving wives. If people stay together for reasons other than love, then a garden can be one of them; a garden can mask the (now) old-fashioned *'mariage blanc'* as I understand it did with Alvilde and James Lees-Milne, and it has long been a symbol, part of the code, perhaps instinctively, inherited from Burlington and Kent of a gay partnership: lesbian couples have certainly taken it as such since the outing of Vita Sackville-West. For homosexuals it has always been more difficult (the world did not change overnight in 1967) and what Stephen Fry has called the code (flamboyance, the south of France, worshipping Barbra Streisand) has long held gardening as a powerful message, a celebration of home together, a private joy in a hostile world. This too has been liberating, for if Cedric Morris and Lett Haines had been dashing around teaching art instead of confined to Benton End and the locality, there would have been no milky-mauve iris 'Benton Cordelia' (*Plate 25*), or all those marvellous paintings of flowers and vegetables.

My final point and garden concern the way of the world. There has recently been a firestorm concerning Eric Gill's *Stations of the Cross*, supposedly removed from Westminster Cathedral at the request of an abused children support group who cast Gill as the devil incarnate for his belief in incestuous sex within his family. Such judgements would clearly empty the galleries and concert halls of the world. There has equally been a lot of attention given to Benjamin Britten on the fiftieth anniversary of the founding of the Aldeburgh Festival, which included a play, *The Ceremony of Innocence* by Martyn Wade, broadcast on Radio Three on 7 June 1998, with Simon Russell Beale as Britten. I asked a marvellously dignified old lady who had known Britten well if she had heard it, and she said no, she was told it would be upsetting. This was such a pity, for what she meant by 'upsetting' was that the play dealt frankly with Britten's yearning for young boys, a tender yearning without violence as befitted his nature, but whenever the dialogue reached the point of agony, they played his music. The sound of the violins ('Sea

Interludes' from *Peter Grimes*) was so sublimely lovely as to wash away all pain, as the sea cleans the seashore. What has all this to do with expressionist gardens? Well, on a more southerly shore, the shingly vastness of Dungeness, not unlike Britten's Suffolk strand, and both with looming grave hulks of nuclear power stations on their horizons, a tiny unfenced spot has become a place of pilgrimage as the garden made by the *enfant terrible* film director Derek Jarman before he died of an AIDS-related illness. Jarman was a persistently outspoken, outrageous, purveyor of creative extremes of violence and colour, but here is the window to his soul: circles and stones, witty and childish, flotsam and jetsam, sea lavenders, thorns and grasses, symbols and games, unarguably made into a garden. It is, in many weathers, a garden of haunting beauty, lovingly maintained. The most unlikely place for a garden, and yet here, at the end of the land, at the end of his life, as with Britten's music, is redemptive peace.

CHAPTER FIVE

> ✦ <

The Rise of the Small Garden

From the earliest *chahar bagh* known in Persia two thousand years before Christ, we have created gardens as jewelled miniatures. Even large gardens that we love are invariably collections of small garden spaces. However, the small garden *per se*, the only one that is possessed, has an elusive past which has to be cherry-picked from other aspects of social history. It had a first flutter of attention with the Loudons and their villa gardens, but truly pervades universal consciousness with the twentieth-century suburbs, captured amongst other icons in John Betjeman's 'Middlesex':

> Well cut Windsmoor flapping lightly,
>   Jacqmar scarf of mauve and green
> Hiding hair which, Friday nightly,
>   Delicately drowns in Drene;
> Fair Elaine the bobby-soxer,
> Fresh complexioned with Innoxa,
> Gains the garden – father's hobby –
> Hangs her Windsmoor in the lobby,
> Settles down to sandwich supper and the television screen.[1]

Elaine's father was a likely reader of one of the most popular and well-thumbed of gardening books, C. E. Lucas Phillips's *The Small Garden*, first published in 1952 because there was nothing to meet the needs of 'those of us who have only small gardens, as most of us understand the term'. Brigadier Lucas Phillips, a war hero with an MC and Croix de Guerre, brought a brisk military fellowship to his readers. He wanted to save them 'from back-aches and disappointments' and he exhorted them to 'adventure forward on your own' probably in a tone similar to that with which he had addressed his men. *The Small Garden* has sold hundreds of thousands of copies through fifty years and it must be one of the most popular books of the century: the Brigadier defined the small garden with 'a limit of about an acre, but with special consideration for the suburban garden of less than half that size'.[2] This is the definition adopted for this chapter, which sets out to construct a pedigree for this most familiar garden.

Until quite recently archaeologists had seemed to ignore gardens. Even the great pioneer of landscape history, W. G. Hoskins, gave them little mention in *The Making of the English Landscape* first published in 1955. All this changed in the late summer of 1965 when Barry Cunliffe and his team excavating at Fishbourne Roman palace (only found by accident five years earlier) stumbled upon the layout for the garden. Fishbourne, of Chatsworth magnificence, has no place here, but the excitement of the discovery turned archaeologists' eyes to the possibilities of gardens. Mick Aston, then Reader in Archaeology at Bristol University, did extensive survey and fieldwork on the earthworks at Hardington and Low Ham in Somerset in the 1970s; he verified the mysterious patterns in the grass as garden features, terraces and layouts of seventeenth-century gardens which had been abandoned.[3] Suddenly, garden historians looked with new eyes at every hump and bump outlying an ancient site. Christopher Taylor, re-assessing sites in the Midlands for the Royal Commission on Historic Monuments, systematically used aerial photographs to clarify patterns on the ground, and cultivated a perception of gardens which made sense of banks, ditches and overgrown mounds. Sites identified included Sir Thomas Tresham's abandoned gardens at Lyveden[4] and a moated herbarium at Linton, outside Cambridge, exactly like Abbot Godfrey de Crowland's vanished medieval herbarium at Peterborough.[5] With such encouragements the Council for British Archaeology formally recognized garden archaeology in 1986.[6]

Thus launched, garden archaeology could work backwards, and down the social scale. Hand cultivation with digging sticks and stone hoes pre-dated the arrival of the plough, and so in looking for a 'garden' it is possible to see that 'the small, perhaps temporary plots of the earliest nomadic groups may be considered the first gardens of Britain'.[7] In the earliest settlements the ploughed land can be identified from cut marks in the subsoil, leaving aside the spade-dug plots; paleobotanists can identify seeds and pollen of Fat Hen, black bindweed, Good King Henry and onion couch. Numberless generations were raised on the beneficent Fat Hen (*Chenopodium album*) which has been found in Neolithic sites in Switzerland and Sussex, and was part of the last meal of Tollund Man, who lived somewhere between 400 BC and AD 400. Fat Hen's oily virtues persisted down the centuries in other names – 'Bacon Weed', 'Lambs Quarters' and – 'its habitats were clear' – Dungweed.[8] Good Henry (the King is a modern fancy), a spinach-like green, had to be differentiated from Bad Henry, the poisonous *Mercurialis perennis*.

Whether they were scratching in patches of peaty soil around the stone and turf courtyard houses at Chysauster[9] or digging in the sand between the round houses at Fengate, it is perfectly possible to imagine our distant gardening ancestors growing not only Fat Hen but celery, carrots, brassicas and parsnips; chickweed was also a food plant but assuredly grew of its own accord. Seeds of all these, as well as herbs such as dill, henbane, calamint, hop, horehound, marjoram and opium poppies, have been identified in the Nene valley archaeological sites.[10] The people of Fengate and Flag Fen kept Soay-type sheep and Dexter cattle, they farmed a complex landscape of round houses, droveways and fields along the flood-free Fengate, and migrated to summer pastures and garden plots in the fen, at Flag Fen. They were surrounded by spring blossoms and dog roses, and summer flowers, cranesbill, meadowsweet, centaury, saxifrages and purple loosestrife: they were skilled enough to erect a great timbered palisade and platform (covering a hectare or slightly more) to maintain and defend the summer pastures as the waters began to rise. This structure was maintained for hundreds of years, so that it must have become a legend, and a ceremonial burial site. The rich ornaments and tools dredged from these sites – including an exquisite pair of bronze shears with their own fitting wooden case – reveal a people we should be proud to acknowledge as early gardeners.

Much later we encounter the story of the finding of Wharram Percy, a deserted village in the Yorkshire Wolds, south-east of Malton. In the late 1940s there was a revived interest in medieval archaeology, and while most scholars had persistently aristocratic tastes in castles and monasteries, Maurice Beresford and John Hirst spent their spare time exploring around the ruined church of Wharram Percy, and started excavating in 1950. Beresford pioneered 'lost' villages – he published *The Lost Villages of England* in 1954 – but now prefers to call them 'deserted' villages, as they were not lost, merely had not been found. Wharram Percy has now been investigated, excavated and documented through forty years and can be appreciated: a street of cruck-built thatched houses, with gardens and strip fields, culminating in the manorial complex with barns, dovecote and gardens, all abandoned to make a sheep run by 1520.[11] In the artist's reconstruction Wharram Percy has the look of a well-regulated model community, with the thatched houses ranged in their regular plots close to the street, some with a pig pen, some with vegetable plots, all with private space fenced from their neighbours, and all with their ploughed strips hedged and tailing across the valley or up the hillsides.

A very similar peasant's house, thatched and with flint walls, built in the thirteenth century and abandoned some two hundred years later, has been re-erected at the Weald and Downland Open Air Museum at Singleton in Sussex. The museum started as a collection of rescued buildings (this one from the deserted village of Hangleton was in the line of a railway cutting near Hove) but expertly researched gardens are being added as appropriate. Sylvia Landsberg, author of *The Medieval Garden*, based Hangleton's garden on a retirement contract for a peasant able to do light work in return for his hovel and a fenced plot 40 × 48 feet in which to grow vegetables and keep a pig. This was a fortunate peasant: he has a square plot edged with flints to allow the soil to be built up for a simple rotation of roots and brassicas, with space for perennial onion clumps and herbs. Part of a grass bank has been levelled for a turf seat in the sun, with honeysuckles and sweetbriar wreathing the wattle fence and a skep for bees. Both cottage and garden are realistically untidy, they are sensitively sited farthest from modern contamination, at the edge of a wood and invariably wreathed in smoke from the charcoal burner's camp; the impression is of a primitive earthiness, the cottage seems to grow out of the ground like a burrow, and though more than a thousand years separates Hangleton from the round houses, it seems 'prehistoric'.[12] (Conversely, only two hundred years or so separate Hangleton from my thatched stone cottage, now full of electronic gadgets.)

The star of the Weald and Downland Museum's recreations in garden terms is Sylvia Landsberg's careful evocation of Merrie England around Bayleaf, a Wealden farmhouse rescued from drowning in Bough

Beech reservoir in Kent (*Plate 31*). A barn from Cowfold, built of timbers ring-dated to 1536, has been added to complete a yeoman's steading of garden, yards, orchard and shaw – a shelterbelt of oaks and hazels for coppicing. In this way Kent cob nuts were planted in rows making a Nuttery, typical of the gardens of England.

Sylvia Landsberg has explained in *The Medieval Garden* that the recreation of Bayleaf's garden was 'laid out more accurately than would have been likely' to demonstrate how the yeoman would have been familiar with a perch-length stick, 16ft 6in long, as a basic unit of measurement. The vegetable plots and surrounding paths, a 2 × 1 perch unit, are grouped in two lots of three, for a threefold rotation system to feed a household of six adults. The rotation is made up of a miniature field-system, with root crops sown from spring to summer and kept through the winter, followed by fallow weeds which could be grazed, and in the third year a spring sowing of beans, peas, salads, annual herbs and edible flowers, harvested by late autumn. In practice, the paths, made by scraping down to the flinty sub-soil and putting the topsoil on the beds, worked well, but the careful geometry of the layout was soon askew 'when the wattler's rectangular boundary became a trapezium due to the inherent nature of wattling'.[13] (Also the wattle had to be wired against rabbits, a problem the yeoman would not have had as, though rabbits were recorded here by 1100 – Oliver Rackham calls them 'a delicious and commercial animal' from the Mediterranean – they found it chilly and were kept in warrens. They did not naturalize and become a pest until the eighteenth century.)[14]

Bayleaf's comfortable yeoman status is most evident in the beginnings of a scented border, the beds of aromatic sweet herbs, raised beds for extra fertility, and grown immediately at the front of the house; here are lavender, hyssop, sage, savory and wild marjoram. Another collection is of precious medicinal germander, betony, horehound, pennyroyal, wormwood and camomile, for infusions and broths, also grown close to the house where the good housewife or her mother could keep a close eye on them. By the gate into the side lane is a clump of Madonna lilies (*Lilium candidum*) six feet tall; they are grown in a deep pit of rich chalky loam, the bulbs planted just below the surface and treated annually with a dressing of manure and ground charcoal. These are the symbol of pre-Reformation England,

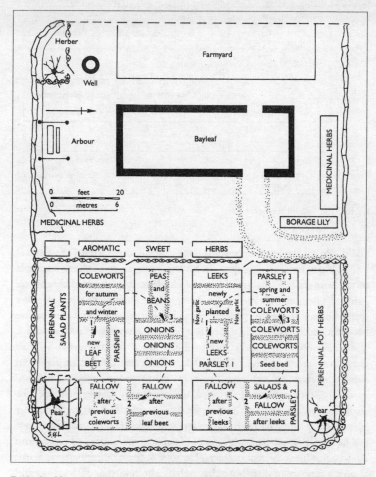

Bayleaf, a Yeoman's garden showing the three-fold rotation whereby crops in plots 1 are replaced by crops in plots 2, and crops in plots 2 are followed by those in plots 3, and so on. This system, to keep soil and crops healthy, unites gardeners who grow vegetables across more than five hundred years. Drawings from Sylvia Landsberg's *The Medieval Garden*, 1996.

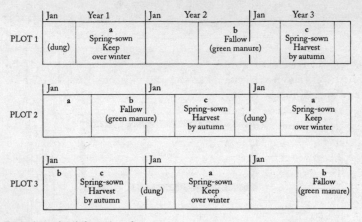

Bayleaf: the detailed rotation plan.

and doubtless Bayleaf's important contribution to the Virgin's festivals.[15]

So, can Bayleaf's garden to be regarded as the earliest example of the holy grail of small gardens, the English, and Elizabethan, cottage garden? The buildings and the plantings are accurately restored: pluck it from the museum setting and imagine it by a Wealden lane somewhere between Penshurst and Groombridge, indulge it with a little honeysuckle and a sweetbriar rose, perhaps dirty the limewash a little, and it will suit the picture. It would have to be well back from the lane, for the garden in front is seventy-five feet long; two generations on from the Reformation in, say, 1588, the year of the Armada, the house may have been divided, so there are two gardens, fifty feet wide, side by side. The left-hand cottage is reached by a long path, the lavenders and sages have moved to the path edge, and perhaps there is a clump of rosemary (*Rosmarinus officinalis*) and a tall purple lilac (*Syringa vulgaris*) for both of these immigrants have had almost a century to distribute themselves; the right-hand cottage is still entered from the side lane leading to the barn yard, but the Madonna lilies have disappeared. Long front gardens of vegetables, fruit and flowers, backed by picturesque timbered buildings, are a familiar sight in fertile, lowland Britain, but can they be substantiated as our Elizabethan idyll?

The first hurdle to clear away is that of the nostalgically recreated imagery, the nineteenth-century paintings of Birket Foster and Helen

Allingham, the foundation for the ubiquitous commercial cottage garden of our mass-market culture. Next we have to cross a ravine between the woods and the bedroom, into which Elizabethan poets seem to have dropped any familiar gardens. The pastoralists were mostly away to the sheep-runs and forests with milkmaids and shepherds named Mellifleur or Colin, or they were enigmatically serenading their Queen or patron, who only wished to hear about fashionable gardening, knots and emblems, alleys or labyrinths in the continental style. The literary and painted gardens are almost exclusively versions of Hatfield or Burghley, far, far removed from any native reality. The smallest garden Dr Donne has left us belonged to a highly fashionable Countess, his adored Lucy Harington, whose 'Twicknam Garden'[16] was sketched by Robert Smythson in 1609 (and is thought to have been designed by Francis Bacon) and is a formal wilderness planted with circles of birch and lime trees around a central pool, where the lovelorn Donne waits:

> Love let mee Some senslesse peece of this place bee;
> Make me a mandrake, so I may groane here,
> Or a stone fountaine weeping out my yeare.[17]

This is a real and tangible connection with Elizabethan England, but it is too grand a garden. These fragments of delicious chatter between Doron and Carmela, from the poet Robert Greene in 1589 are more apt:[18] after 'Sit downe Carmela let me kisse thy toes', she urges him to 'leave my toes and kisse my lippes my love'. 'At foote ball sport thou shalt my champion be,' she declares: for Doron her 'breath is like the steeme of apple pies' and her 'lippes resemble two Cowcumbers faire' – these blandishments before he crowns her with 'this garland made of Holly-hocks'. Can we doubt that they are in a garden, or fail to understand them? Shakespeare has masses of flowers, and his gardens are invariably grand: however, *The Winter's Tale* (Act IV, scene 4) has Perdita still innocent of any background other than being brought up by the kind shepherd, who has taught her to garden. When the awesome Polixenes and his entourage arrive she welcomes them –

> Reverend sirs,
> For you there's rosemary and rue; these keep
> Seeming and savour all the winter long.
> When Polixenes criticises the 'flowers of Winter', Perdita replies (this
>   being late summer):

> ... the fairest flow'rs o'th' season
> Are our carnations and streak'd gillyvors,
> Which some call nature's bastards. Of that kind
> Our rustic garden's barren; and I care not
> To get slips of them.[19]

Perdita seems to possess a rural distrust of florist's hybrids, which she does not bother to propagate from slips bought or begged from a neighbour. Perhaps here we can intimate the essence of cottage gardening in a world of hard agricultural labours; Shakespeare allows us an insight into the rustic temperament, its conservatism and conservation of both hard-won energy and new fashions (Perdita understood the hybrid carnations to be a threat to her own breeding) and reliance on the old and trusty in both plants and people. The cottager's garden thrived in a well-peopled countryside, in a society that revolved around the home. Even if the men went off to plough, market or tend the sheep, the old, the young and the women were at home. Community life was made up of share, barter, borrow and exchange – any village street would reveal who was friends with whom, or related, by the display of the same flowers, the same highly-prized red rose or peony. Competition in 'cowcumbers' and the gardener's traditional cantankerous temper were part of it all.

In his wonderfully detailed evocation of life in Foxton, Cambridgeshire, Rowland Parker[20] lists thirty-two transgressions brought to the manor court against John Rayner from 1541 to 1586, and though many related to his ploughed land some were for lopping his neighbours' trees, failing to repair his fences or encroaching on his neighbours' garden – he was both churchwarden and ale-taster, pillar of the community and typical of a certain kind of Englishman. Also in Foxton, where cottage rents were unchanged until the early seventeenth-century, it cost about £100 to build a house with a chimney, two rooms and one loft; a surviving record shows the purchase of a plot six perches and six feet long (i.e. 105 ft) by three perches and one foot (approx fifty foot) wide, with a small outbuilding, for £11 12s 4d in Elizabethan money. On the same terms, a skilled gardener could earn six to eight pence per day, while leek seed cost one shilling per pound, with onion seed a little more.[21]

Elizabethan England saw the slow rise of the professional gardener.

John Gerard was the greatest living gardener, adviser to Lord Burghley, he published a list of plants in his Holborn garden in 1596 which included the novelty potato, and his famous *Herball* the following year. Gerard (1545–1612) and Thomas Hill (born in 1529) also known as Didymus Mountaine, author of the first known gardening book in English in 1563, which was extended into *The Gardener's Labyrinth* of 1577, were clearly the forerunners of a familiar entrepreneurial type who marches down the centuries[22]. The London Gardeners' Company was founded in 1605, and the Company of Barber-Surgeons, of which Gerard became Master, was older; undoubtedly the knowledge of gardening spread by influence and contact from the great houses and lesser patrons, but this process was painfully slow. From these late Elizabethan years it is almost two centuries before the whole British gardening establishment can be assessed as a thousand 'principal practitioners' in 1760, which include some 150 great-house gardeners, 400 for the gentry, 100 nurserymen and 200 market gardeners.[23] The first priced catalogues appear in 1775 and the recognizable 'modern' nursery system can be dated to rapid improvements in transport systems in 1790.[24] For some three centuries the English cottage gardener was on his or her own, pursuing a native art in a fellowship of equals, probably less advanced than contemporaries in France, Italy or the Netherlands, but powerfully symbolizing an aspect of our national character nonetheless.

The history of town planning begins in ancient cities like Bishop Richard le Poore's New Sarum (Salisbury) which purposely adopted a continental-style grid in the 1220s: straight streets with streams down the centre to channel the springs and tributaries of the Avon, divided the city into chequers or bastides. The market place, important buildings, and even some allotments and a 'green croft' which remained 'common' occupied a whole chequer, and the house and garden plots in a standard size of seven by three perches (49ft 6 wide by 115ft 6 long gardens – 12d ground rent paid annually to the Bishop) filled the rest. Salisbury retained its grid because subsequent development grew east and west of the old core, and despite modern development and swirling one-way traffic it is still possible to imagine the garden plots. But such regimentation suited neither the English landscape nor temper, and the classic example of nature and natives in combined revolt is Winchelsea in Sussex, laid out as a commercial venture as a wine-trading base with

Bordeaux in 1283, with the advice of an expert on bastides, one Itier Bochard of Angoulême.[25] New Winchelsea's chequers were filled with churches, friaries and hospitals but French raids, storms and finally the silting of the harbour discouraged houses and gardens. Today the Cinque Port is a charming skeleton (a word both Defoe and John Wesley used) conserved in grass plots and larger than intended gardens.

Local history sources are sometimes so rich that it is easy to identify a specific small garden as Elizabethan. Land surveying with theodolite and drawing to scale (the latter from continental treatises, including Dürer's of 1527 on plans 'measured by the little foot' i.e. his foot on the ground) were mastered in England 'from about 1540'.[26] Part of the first-known map of London of the late 1550s makes an accurate comparison with the modern street map for the area where Bishopsgate meets London Wall: ornamental gardens and the drying-enclosures of tenter frames, with bosky hedges and action-figures gives a vivid picture of life in the far-off green garden city and the equally green suburb that is now Liverpool Street Station and Finsbury Circus (*Plate 28*).[27]

Maps soon became the technological toys of powerful Elizabethans; Lord Burghley was as enthusiastic about maps as he was about gardens; he drew them as an *aide mémoire* of landowners (especially recusant Catholics) and is said to have kept the first 'modern' map of Britain, Lawrence Nowell's of 1564, always with him (it measures 212 × 309 mm, or about 8½ × 12½ inches, between A4 and foolscap, and is in the British Library with the fold marks still visible).[28] One of the two earliest large-scale maps was drawn for him by John Norden the elder in 1591, as a sample to convince Burghley that a county by county survey of England was useful and possible.[29] Norden's sample was of Higham Ferrers in Northamptonshire, a medieval town typical of the stone belt, the glorious oolites, that England wears like a sash of honour from East Yorkshire to Dorset, and where, if anywhere, the Elizabethan cottage garden will have been encased for posterity (*Plate 32*).

Over four hundred years later Norden would recognize Higham perfectly easily, the stony faces that front the old A6 'the way to Bedforde' are those that he saw: Chichele College, founded by a local yeoman's son Henry Chichele, who became Archbishop of Canterbury in 1414 (and founded All Souls College, Oxford) is now a noble ruin but still fills the whole block between College Street (A6) and the back way, now Saffron Road. Norden marked 'a new enclosure of Mr Hughes' on the forfeited College meadows, with their medieval fish ponds; these remain, but the meadows, now Saffron Meadows, have become public recreation and games grounds. Perhaps Mr Hughes fared badly; it was a widely held superstition that it was unlucky to take over church lands. Or perhaps he grew saffron there? This was a crop for gardens and closes in this part of the country in the sixteenth century (an acre of crocus corms would yield about twenty-five pounds of the powder-covered stamens which were dried and pressed into a cake six pounds in weight, selling for about £6 for colouring cakes and biscuits as well as wool dyes) and the 1789 Duchy of Lancaster estate map of Higham shows orchards, closes and long gardens along Saffron Road (*Plate 33*). The market place, with its medieval market cross (erected about 1280) is intact and, interestingly, Norden has mis-drawn its shape, apparently confused by the temporary buildings on the north side which had, and have, become permanent. The present Hind Stile is a lovely Chinese whisper originating with 'Behind-the-sty',[30] i.e. the livestock market pens. The church and its attendant buildings, the chantry and bede house, are also as Norden saw them. Wharf Road – 'the way to Attle-borro' (Wellingborough) – remains a public right of way with a foot-bridge over the river Nene, which was navigable here, between Peterborough and Northampton. Norden is surprisingly apt in some details; he shows 'Mr Rudde's' – Thomas Rudd, who died in 1656 and was author of his own epitaphs, lies in the church – and the rectory dovecote and that of the College are differentiated from other buildings. But, we may assume, Norden did not examine every back garden; he does show where some long plots were being halved and built on, or how corner plots were sacrificed, as were yards, to stables, sheds and workshops. The triumph of little Higham Ferrers is, that in three stages, we can see the rise of the small townhouse and garden, ideally on a three-perch wide plot (3 × 16 ft 6 in = 49 6 – the surveyor had too much to drink, the lawyer lost patience, and the fifty-foot frontage was born) and equally ideally stretching as far back as possible, 100 feet or more, to the Back Lane or Way or to the common fields. Enough of the town has been set in stone, still bearing dates – like College House of 1633 – and Archbishop Chichele's holy hand seems to have stayed spoliation, to confirm that the townspeople of 400 years ago were enjoying their long thin gardens (*Plate 34*).

The reason for searching so hard for these Elizabethan and early seventeenth-century gardens is to confirm their presence in the glorious world that Professor Hoskins assures us existed from about 1570 to 1770 – 'seven human generations (when) rural England flowered'. Towns and villages benefited from the Elizabethan building spree, the landscape was settled, the population was enough for an agricultural country, there was time for rest and play. 'The Stuart or the Georgian yeoman reached for a book in the evenings, rather than for the axe or mattock of his forebears'[31] . . . or perhaps he just enjoyed his garden?

The essential allure of the small seventeenth-century garden is that it glows with a sturdily independent glory, for use and pleasure untouched by any commercial or professional hierarchies – no batterings from seed companies, magazines or experts. What bliss was in that freedom of expression, that revelled in a healthy competitiveness, a glut of beans or self-sown poppies, throwing rotten eggs at the local gardening know-all if one felt like it, and unashamedly showing off a bright red rose over the front porch, because it was the most precious plant owned.

Small gardens were to become the playthings of the vast social changes of the eighteenth century, perhaps the victims, in ways that have hardly been considered by historians of either town or countryside. In some ways decline was inevitable, as anyone who has tried to dig the dead grey dust and abundant bony, stony and iron artifacts of a hundred-year-old plot will know, but this earthy failure was subsumed by great waves of changing circumstances that were irresistible, and are assumed to have been progress. New men with new money and systems came into the countryside: 'It is with infinite pain I see Lord T,' says the heroine of Frances Brookes's *History of Lady Julia Mandeville* of 1761, 'pursuing a plan which has drawn on him the curse of thousands, and made his estate a scene of desolation; his farms are in the hands of a few men, to whom the sons of the old tenants are either forced to be servants, or to leave the country to get their bread elsewhere. The village, large and once populous, is reduced to about eight families; a dreary silence reigns on their deserted fields . . .'[32] These new landowners wanted privacy and seclusion, the chief stock in trade of Capability

Brown: the creation of landscaped parks often meant the removal of unsightly cottages and gardens or, in the classic case of Milton Abbas in Dorset, of a sizeable market town, with a grammar school, almshouses, shops, four inns and a brewery. Persecution mania seized the landowner, Joseph Damer MP, later Earl of Dorchester, who felt that pillaging schoolboys and even the church bells were a personal insult, and William Chambers and Brown between them re-sited and built the model village, a sloping street of thatched cottages, with frontages of smooth, bare green grass and occupants who were required to dress-up for important visitors.[33] The 'model' villages may have been landmarks in housing design, but they exploited gardens, and introduced impositions and coercions, which became accepted in the name of philanthropic virtue. In 1806 the architect George Dance laid out a row of semi-detached brick cottages on the East Stratton estate of Francis Baring MP; he sketched the desired layout of rectangular beds for the plots which were 45 feet wide and 225 feet long – this may have been generous, but it was also onerous, an enormous area to cultivate by spade and fork after a hard day's work. Whether to the credit of a landowner or for art's sake, gardening became contrived – conceited, in the original meaning of the word: John Nash's famous Blaise Hamlet of 1811, for instance, had rustic cottages so picturesque they become a parody of themselves, with thatched roundels and dovecotes in the eaves and gardens that were obligatorily decorative. A veritable nineteenth-century Disneyland, in other words.

The fate of the country cottage garden is essentially a matter of local circumstance: in the estate village of Elton in Cambridgeshire where I am writing this, the evidence is outside my door. Elton has been encased in stone and in the same family ownership for hundreds of years, and the cottages and houses have been carefully researched by the local historian, A. G. Clark.[34] John Clare would have known my cottage, and the Crown Inn next door, and he would also have known David Laurance, foreman gardener at Burghley before he came to Elton Hall in 1792. Clare was eyewitness to Elton's decline, along with the rest of this agricultural countryside, to the point where there were only two cottage gardens of any merit in the village: the pride of Laurance's successors as head gardener at the Hall at the gardener's cottage, and the cottage belonging to the Hankins family (John Hankins was the estate bailiff responsible for the park and village, its trees, greens and gravel roads). Hankins's cottage was wreathed in ivy, and called Ivy Cottage, and he maintained neat lawns and flower beds of asters, antirrhinums, rudbeckias and a topiary bird and picket fence, the absolute image of cottage gardens, but the exception rather than the rule. The family at the Hall were nothing if not caring of their tenants, and with troubles and ills of their own, found the distress of decline especially painful: Lady Claud Hamilton found the continual complaints exhausting but was content to minister to a sick cottager – 'What she really did seem to like was a couple of roses which I took her. I do believe flowers are an intense enjoyment in illness especially to those who have them not.'[35] My cottage, a double cottage of twenty-five foot frontage, lived in by the village engineer (who ministered to traction engines and carts), two rooms down and up, was home to a family of fourteen in the early years of this century. The walled back garden, with its surviving privies, trampled by tiny feet, repository of washing water and general rubbish, and of dead, dead soil, could not have been gardened (fortunately there is an allotment at the side) – it was simply worn out of existence, as were so many cottage yards.[36] And yet this is Rose Cottage, and sported a rose across its front: Rose Cottage was also quoted in John Burnett's *Social History of Housing 1815–1970*, in a hamlet near Minehead, the home of a carter earning ten shillings a week, with five children and a bedridden mother of ninety-three (the eldest boy, aged nine and a half, already supplementing the family income by 5d a day), paying a rent raised to over £3 a year by the new squire, plus rates, school rate and gas rate – though there was no gas within a mile of them.[37]

The small garden had become a virtuous endeavour – 'good for you' – in the eyes of a conscientious gentry and middle class: even Gilbert White (usually so sensible) loftily asserts in a letter to Daines Barrington of 8 January 1778 that 'fresh meat had replaced salted, linen shirts were worn next to the skin and there was plenty of good wheaten bread', that the locals were eating their green vegetables and 'every decent labourer also has his garden, which is half his support, as well as his delight' – not only sounding like a nanny, but an obsequious nanny, as the credit goes to the gentry who have been so graciously interested in horticulture as to forward its progress.[38] The gentry had often commercial hearts and were interested in selling plants imported from their overseas properties, but they were emulated by an aspiring middle class as far as smaller gardens were concerned. The steady creation of a class of professional gardeners and nurserymen through the eighteenth century was paralleled by the growth of provincial florists' societies (*Plates 14 & 15*); the weekly newspapers of Worcester, Gloucester, Ipswich, Newcastle, Canterbury, York and Norwich regularly advertised 'feasts' in celebration of the eight classic flowers – carnation, tulip, anemone, ranunculus, hyacinth, polyanthus, pink, and auricula (with pansy and dahlia added in the 1830s).[39] We can imagine the villa gardens on the leafier fringes of these towns, with their greenhouses and frames for cultivation. Just such a garden is pictured at the front of *Every Man His Own Gardener*, the sixteenth edition of a month-by-month instruction book of 1800, which included a portrait of the author John Abercrombie, aged seventy-two, resplendent in tail coat, light waistcoat and shoes that looked fit for dancing rather than gardening. The gentrified image was fostered by the gardening solicitor Thomas Attree, who founded Ditchling Horticultural Society in the early 1820s; the society drew 'men of substance', wealthy farmers and tradesmen from all over Sussex, it fostered fruit growing and well-kept cottagers' gardens in the village, with the classes for the show carefully adjusted to social niceties. Copper kettles were the top prize to cottagers for 'the heaviest pint of Red Rouge Gooseberries' or the best baskets of vegetables, fruits or bunches of wild flowers. In July 1843 nineteen cottages were inspected, and judged for cleanliness of cottage and garden, circumstances of the owners, number of children, pigs etc., as well as cropping; fifteen were 'well cropped', almost all kept a pig.[40]

It is incredible but apparently true that city dwellers of all classes were equally deprived of gardens; though Georgian London may look like a city of garden spaces, it was not, and these were in the main drab yards for privies and clotheslines, invariably inaccessible from the 'front' part of the house. A rare, if not unique, exception is the plan for Francis Douce's garden at 13 Upper Gower Street dated 28 November 1791 which has been found in the Bodleian Library.[41] The garden is a 25 ft × 50 ft rectangle, edged with Lombardy poplars underplanted with perennials; a central rectangular bed is filled with carefully graduated trees – the tallest a Liriodendron (tulip tree) in the centre, with almonds, flowering cherry, and cistus, hibiscus, robinia and roses. Mr Douce seems to have been a keen collector – or was he trying hard to exclude the noxious airs of the city from his home?

The absence of private London gardens seems to have been responsible for the great demand for flowers: James Cochran was a florist and plant contractor to Regency London society and his trade prospered simply because flowers and plants were so difficult to keep alive because of the 'pernicious blacks'.[42] Cochran specialized in tons of mignonette, stocks, violas, verbena, geranium, heathers and myrtles crowded into boxes and placed to catch the air, to scent the stairways and rooms opened for balls, routs and conversazioni throughout summer nights. Cochran worked for the very rich, but more modest florists' businesses served middle-class villas in Pimlico and Bayswater, where it was impossible to keep plants because of the gas fumes, unless they were cramped in a Wardian glass case. The difficulties of city life and gardening only increased the love of flowers, encouraging ready acceptance of the painted myth of the country cottage garden. It would not seem an exaggeration to say that with the smoke-ridden cities and depressed countryside of early Victorian England, the small garden was an endangered species.[43]

The saviour at hand was the unsung hero of the small garden, John Claudius Loudon. His story has the ring of Victorian melodrama: he was born at Cambuslang in Lanarkshire on 8 April 1783, the eldest child of a farming family, whose father gave him a garden of his own and an 'avaricious desire for self improvement'. He studied languages, botany, chemistry, drawing, agriculture, hothouse management and nursery practice and arrived in London in 1803 with an introduction to Sir Joseph Banks, Jeremy Bentham and the Linnaean Society. He published madly; papers on forestry practice, colour schemes for flowers, and plans for river embanking, and though he planned some estates for gentry, his heart was stoutly middle class; he adored Bentham, who was approaching sixty when Loudon met him, and adopted his creed of seeking his own happiness in the promotion of the greatest happiness for the greatest number of others. Loudon questioned everything and approached it anew, but he was accident-prone. In the autumn of 1806 he caught a chill riding on the outside of a coach on a wet night, which developed into rheumatic fever: 'Alas, How I have neglected the important task of improving myself!' he moaned to his diary from his sick bed. 'I am now twenty-three years of age, and perhaps one third of my life has passed away, and yet what have I done to benefit my fellowmen?'[44] He was depressed by the state of farming, tried it and failed, wrote about it (and the design of public houses) and then set off overland to Moscow (where he was struck by the lack of a common garden heritage and the fact that more pineapples were grown in hothouses around St Petersburg than in the rest of Europe). Loudon made several continental tours as fuel for his writings, then decided to settle down and produce books and magazines that the public at large could afford; these included encyclopaedias – of gardening (1822), of plants (1829) – *The Green House Companion* (1824), a catalogue of native plants and *A Manual of Cottage Gardening*, these last two in 1830, the year he married Jane Webb. Settled in Porchester Terrace, Bayswater, in his own villa and garden (*Plate 27*), he produced his *Suburban Gardener and Villa Companion* in monthly parts in 1836–8. He had started a quarterly popular magazine *The Gardener's Magazine*, in 1826, but this became a monthly and ran until 1844.

Loudon wrote so much that only a fraction of it all can have been assessed or appreciated. To Loudon everything was garden-worthy. He educated the genteel villa owners of Herne Hill, St John's Wood and Clapham when they were new to gardening, he advocated gardening schools, garden libraries and gardens for public houses, he designed parks and arboreta, garden cemeteries and much, much more. He was plain-speaking, blunt, dour, and a workaholic, but his worst crime was to be middle class; he sank without trace in the backlash to all things Victorian, and is only tardily being resurrected because the English prefer their garden heroes to be aristocratic.

Loudon was also so far in advance of his time that some of his dearest endeavours did not become reality until long after his death, and invariably to someone else's credit. The 'villa' garden which displayed novelties in little circles spotted over the lawn, for a magnolia, or standard rose edged with mignonette, could not have reached the small gardens of the Victorian suburbs until the last quarter of the century. They were enshrined in the earliest photographs, small and personal achievements that were miniatures of the amazing bedding schemes of the public parks. But perfection in bedding was very hard to maintain, and this gave the opportunity for criticism in the 1890s: Gertrude Jekyll was to write repeatedly that it was not the plants – the begonias, calceolarias, pelargoniums and aubretias – which were at fault, merely the way they were used. Perhaps it was just because they were so difficult to maintain to perfection that these mounds and lozenges of colour embedded themselves so deeply in the small gardener's desiring heart?*

As early as 1829, and perhaps prompted by Jane's futuristic vision of London in her novel *The Mummy*, Loudon had published *Hints for Breathing Places in the Metropolis*. His plan showed greater London covered by five concentric circles, alternately built and green; the inner green circle linked, anti-clockwise, Bethnal Green, Islington, Somers Town, Regent's Park, Hyde Park, Lambeth, Kennington and Camberwell; an outer country circle linked Stratford and West Ham to Highgate and Hampstead, and round to Fulham and Greenwich. His scheme does not feature in the history of town planning, but seventy years later the man who was in the right place at the right time, Ebenezer Howard, founded the garden city movement with his famous town-country magnets diagram and similar reasoning.[46] The small garden, now so exceedingly worthy and desirable as almost to be sacred, reaches its apotheosis at Letchworth, First Garden City Limited, designed for thirty thousand small gardeners at about five houses or twenty-four people to the acre, and set out by the surveyors and engineers in the autumn of 1903. The road to Letchworth had been the triumphant advance of architect-designed houses in gardens from the dozens of 'villages of vision', to Bedford Park in Chiswick in 1875 (small gardens for the 'arty'), to William Lever's Port Sunlight (where every house had an allotment) and to the Quaker chocolate preserves, George Cadbury's Bourneville and Joseph and Seebohm Rowntree's New Earswick. Bourneville especially favoured gardens, as Cadbury believed gardening the perfect antidote to repetitive work, and his employees were given lessons on special teaching plots. New Earswick, designed like Letchworth, by Barry Parker and Raymond Unwin, has been called by Gillian Darley 'the most successful of all industrial villages – perhaps of all model villages': it demonstrated Parker and Unwin's innovatory desires for the high

---

* *The Diary of a Nobody* features Charles Pooter's enthusiasm for his little garden running down to the railway in Holloway in the late 1880s. Between smog and smuts gardening would have been virtually impossible except for dust-proof laurel and privet (the house is called The Laurels) – villa gardens could only survive in Bromley, Cricklewood or Surbiton, the outer suburbs. *The Diary* steadfastly ignores the realities of social change.[45]

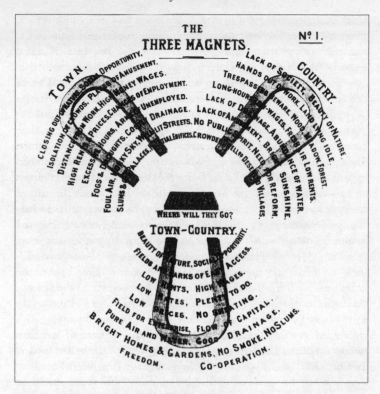

Ebenezer Howard's celebrated Three Magnets diagram from *Garden Cities of Tomorrow*, 1898: the co-existing disadvantages of both town and country life are turned to the economic and environmental pleasures of the town-country hybrid, the garden city.

quality of the simple life, with houses twelve to the acre, set to catch the sun, tiny front gardens and lawns beside wide footways and cul-de-sacs (the first planning to consider where children might play), well-treed and with green commons and generous back gardens.[47]

Parker and Unwin, thrice-bound as cousins, brothers-in-law and partners, were deservedly admired as prophets in their own day, on both sides of the Atlantic, and they were to influence Anglo-American town planning for the first half of the twentieth century. They were also tweedy and perhaps 'cranky' devotees of the Morrisian belief 'that art, which is the expression of beauty as conceived and created by man, is primarily concerned with the making of the useful garments of life beautiful, not with the trimming of them'.[48] Because they were influential planners (and Hampstead Garden Suburb followed Letchworth) they gave many architects of similar beliefs – a veritable Who's Who of Edwardian domestic architecture including M. H. Baillie Scott, Edwin Lutyens, Guy Dawber, Geoffry Lucas, Harrison Townsend and W. Curtis Green[49] – the chance to build small houses of great quality. Parker and Unwin also 'gave' thousands of people gardens, often for the first time, and they certainly did not dictate how these gardens should be used. But when M. H. Baillie Scott, the designer and theorist closest to their taste, considers the use and beauty of the outdoor garment of life in *Houses and Gardens* of 1906,[50] he inevitably resorts to the homely beauty of the cottager's ideal 'including in its borders roses, lilies and perennial flowers, with a background of cabbages, potatoes and other vegetables'. However, 'under the specialising influence of modern civilisation' he finds that the new small garden owners have neither the knowledge nor the inclination to grow their own vegetables and flowers. Baillie Scott (who had a first degree in agriculture) begins at the beginning: beauty for minimum expenditure of labour requires working with nature and growing the natives of the soil, a wild garden, and then perhaps an orchard underplanted with spring bulbs. Shrubs and borders may be added in the orchard if the gardening bug bites. For those already bitten he warns of the labour of lawns, that paths should be direct and to the point, and paved if at all possible to save weeding gravel. Keen gardeners can arrange 'outdoor apartments' with straight paths and vistas, a square rose garden centred on a sundial, long perennial borders of delphiniums, phlox, hollyhocks and day lilies in large clumps, not repeated, but in a 'well-studied arrangement' for colour and summer-long bloom, a pergola and trellis for enclosure and mystery, tubs and pots at entrances, a seat 'of good design and solid structure' placed to view the vista down to the vegetable and orchard plots. This ideal garden became a reality up and down the land, the happiest solution to the long, narrow plot.

Letchworth was, however, the small gardener's Utopia, 'a community of gardeners' with winning ways, astutely described by C. B. Purdom in 1913:

However various our occupations and tastes, however conflicting our opinions, in the garden we are united. There we find a common interest . . . There we have the same enemies, and join in one battle, and aim after a single perfection. A community brought together by such means . . . will, in the development of its social consciousness, acquire the strong qualities of mind and body which will fit it to undertake experiment and adventure, without which our common life becomes stagnant. The occupations of the garden provide excellent training for the world and the government of affairs. They add to dignity and self-confidence, and cause men to think well of themselves. A gardener has the caution that reformers lack . . . He knows that while great things come from small beginnings, a goodly tree does not spring up in one night; that what quickly grows as quickly perishes. He knows how complex and variable is nature and how utterly we are in her hands. He will know, if others forget it, that the building of a Garden City will not be the work of one day.[51]

With the Arts and Crafts architects, assisted by the magnificent William Robinson and his sympathetic advocacy of hardy and native plants and wild gardening, the small garden attained the zenith of its popularity during the 1890s and the Edwardian years. Even the *Gardeners' Chronicle* of 18 August 1894 carried a holiday-season leader 'A Suburban Garden', on a fifty-feet square plot – which must have seemed an oddity to its horticulturally aristocratic readership of head gardeners and nurserymen. 'Looking out from the upper windows of my house I catch glimpses of a score or two precisely similar in size and shape', wrote small gardener Chas. T. Druery; some were grassed for children and dogs, some filled with maples, poplars or fruit trees, and some monotonously bedded with calceolarias and pelargoniums. He describes proudly his raised beds with alpines, his spring scillas, tulips and fritillaries, with lily of the valley and Solomon's Seal in the shady corners, his peonies, lilies, phlox, iris, delphiniums and Japanese anemones and his prize collection of ferns in glass frames. Ferns were popular for they survived the smoke-laden air from east London, though the garden is just over the Essex border; his roses, his Queen of Flowers, however, only held their own and were not good representatives of 'her floral Majesty'.[52] Our hearts fly out to him across a century of suburban gardens, for his plot was where the mortar had been mixed for all the surrounding houses; the landscape contractor had merely spread the carefully specified imported topsoil over the concrete. Being a resourceful gardener, Mr Druery broke up the lime mortar and incorporated it into his gravelly soil, thereby snatching victory out of the jaws of disaster.

Mr Druery was also, as is the nature of small gardeners, especially cottage ones, a believer in straight lines, straight paths and borders, softened with planting. Designers were thought unnecessary evils in the Arts and Crafts small garden, but that did not stop designers trying, or magazines staging design competitions. The 'ideal' was illustrated in *Country Life* for a smallish house by Edwin Lutyens on a plot 75 feet wide × 350 feet long, of which the house and its front garden (lawn with evergreen borders) occupied about a third. The remainder was designed by Gertrude Jekyll as three shallow terracings, the first with four rose beds around a sundial, the second with a central path through perennial borders, and the longest, lowest level with a central path through grass, spring flowers, wild borders and fruit trees. There is a side path for a barrow route, and a tiny sitting area on a final fourth, and lowest level at the end, as the garden overlooked Miss Jekyll's childhood home, Bramley Park in Surrey, and she fondly remembered its contemplative corner. Other influential British architects, including Charles Voysey, Charles Mallows, Gerald C. Horsley, Oliver Hill as well as Baillie Scott designed small gardens, whereas professional garden designers could not afford to be bothered with such trifles. These architectural gardens were rigidly formal and geometric, but softened with Jekyll-style planting, they elevated the tradition to a work of art in miniature.[53] Both Jekyll and the Arts and Crafts ideals were an enormous influence in the development of American commuter suburbs; in 1910 *Country Life* in America and the Architectural League ran a competition for an Ideal Suburban Place. The young landscape gardener Beatrix Jones (later Farrand) designed for the plot 75 feet × 125 feet, with the house set back by twenty feet, and a central path to the front door flanked with clumps of philadelphus, lilac and quince and small lawns. The whole plot is wicket fenced and neatly hedged – spruce, hemlock, arborvitae, beech, thorn or privet or a mixture might be used; the back lot is mostly lawn with borders around the edges for annuals – heliotrope, verbena, scarlet salvias or for those 'of our Grandmother's gardens', columbines, day lilies, moss pinks, campanulas and Japanese anemones.[54]

The small garden was thus established across a wide spectrum of society and amongst the higher echelons of artistic taste when the First World War started. When the men came home in 1918 there was little doubt about what they wanted, and 'a garden' summed up the space, air and privacy for living that they felt they had earned. Richard Reiss of the North Lancashire Regiment wrote a remarkable small book *The Home I Want*, with the slogan on the cover 'You cannot expect to get an A1 population out of C3 homes'. The industrial back to backs were contrasted with the garden suburbs, and New Earswick was admired, with its front gardens, picket fences and back gardens. It was well known that garden-city-style low density, picturesque housing had been built by the government for the munitions workers of Woolwich arsenal on the Well Hall estate in 1915, similar housing at Roe Green, Hendon, for aircraft workers, and a pioneer estate of elegant brick boxes, in the sub-Lutyens Wrennaissance style of Hampstead Garden suburb at Gretna in Dumfries. Why should the men who won the war, including the rest of the munitions workers, about 10 million people, deserve any less? This sentiment forced Lloyd George famously to pledge 'habitations fit for the heroes who have won the war', as reported in *The Times* of 13 November 1918, and popularized as 'homes fit for heroes'.[55] Daylight saving, British Summer Time had been introduced in 1916 to help the war effort, and now remained to help the amateur gardener; working hours were also reduced to 9 to 5 or 5.30 pm., with finishing on Saturday at 12 or 12.30. But, despite endless reports and committees and the best of wills, in 1921 'homes fit for heroes' fell foul of the 'grave' financial state of the nation, opening the flood gates for the developers who were to build semi-detached Britain in the 1920s.

The three-bedroomed 'semi' of the inter-war years is now regarded as a triumph of housing design, and it certainly gave the most enormous boost to the small garden; indeed it was the beginning of popular gardening as one of the great marketing success stories of this century. 'Well-groomed gardens were seen everywhere in the new suburbs', writes Alan A. Jackson in *Semi-Detached London*,[56] 'an outlet for creative drives suppressed in the routines of office life; many of the new house owners devoted almost all their leisure daylight hours to them, growing vegetables and fruits as well as mounting a floral display for nine months of the year. Prowess was encouraged by office gardening societies, which organized shows and competitions, obtaining seeds and other goods at wholesale prices.'

From the long front gardens of the countryside to the street-bound façades of town houses, the suburbs had settled on a happy medium: the small front garden and long rectangle at the rear. Developers and builders did nothing with gardens, except provide the space and sometimes the fence, and not a jot of imagination was allowed to interfere with the blanket set-square uniformity of the layouts. Corner treatments and the cul-de-sac, which Raymond Unwin had proved an economy in road costs, were the only variations, except that is for price. Alan Jackson again: 'At Tadworth in 1934, Costains provided a 300-foot garden with their £1,180 detached houses, and Morrells offered similar length gardens with their 1935 semis at Coneyhall, Hayes, Kent. At Bookham in 1939 there were £1,150 houses in 250-foot gardens. Sites of half an acre, with gardens up to 400 feet in length, were on sale at Pinner Hall in 1923, and in the same year, gardens of equal length came with £900 houses at Taplow . . . at Hillingdon Court in 1923, every garden was said to be large enough for a tennis court and the brochure included hints on gardening, bee and poultry-keeping, with the comforting assurance that "Our Resident Gardener will give advice".'[57]

Was it the bleakness of the new estates or the reactionary nature of gardening advice that encouraged so much nostalgia, or simply the native urge to return to the land? For the popular semi-detached garden of the early twentieth century became not of the twentieth century at all, but of the seventeenth, an evocation of middle-class paradise in Tudor England. The great Richard Norman Shaw had much to do with this, for he revived 'old English' timbered building and bequeathed it to the Arts and Crafts architects, who in turn displayed it in the garden suburbs, so it was little wonder if in imitating Letchworth and Hampstead a rash of timbering appeared. The amount and quality of timber was in direct relationship to the cost and size of the houses, but it was always there, a little touch of Tudorbethan that made the newness and bleakness of the surroundings less strange, an instantly evoked link with

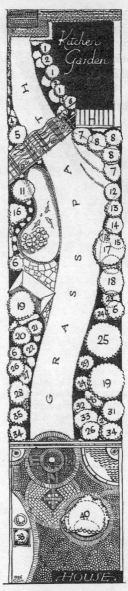

1. Standard roses.
2. Lilium auratum.
3. Ceanothus dentatus (on E fence).
4. Choisya ternata.
5. Judas tree (Cercis).
6. Poplars (black Italian)
7. Berberis stenophylla.
8. Pyrus Malus Niedzwetzkyana.
9. On pergola. Wistaria.
10. „ Clematis (blue and white).
11. Salix babylonica (Weeping Willow).
12. Berberis Wilsonae.
13. Pyrus Malus atropurpurea.
14. Viburnum plicatum.
15. Berberis Aquifolium.
16. Bambusa japonica.
17. Aesculus Pavia (red buckeye), June-July.
18. „ parviflora (Aug.).
19. „ Hippocastanum scarlet.
20. Arbutus Unedo.
21. Spiraea Margaritae.
22. Paeonia Moutan
23. Robinia hispida.
24. Flowering currant (Ribes).

25. Catalpa bignonioides.
26. Magnolia Soulangeana.
27. Ceanothus azureus.
28. Stewartia or white rhododendron.
29. Brier, Lady Penzance.
30. Foxgloves.
31. Diervilla, Abel Carrière Weigelia).
32. Daphne Mezereum.
33. Cistus obtusa.
34. Irish yew.
35. Crataegus pendula.
36. Iris sibirica.
37. Iris Kaempferi.
38. Sun roses.
39. Camellia in tub.
40. Juniperus Sabina prostrata.

The dotted line represents the original slope of the garden.

The small views are of cross-sections of the garden at about the positions that they occupy on the plan.

C. Geoffrey Holme, design for a sloping garden 30 feet by 150 feet, 1936: the natural slope was from right to left, partially corrected by hollowing the wide grass path and building up the side beds. The intention in using the whole length of the garden is to give a sense of space.

C. Geoffrey Holme, design for a garden
30 feet by 150 feet, 1936: The garden
is flat. The sitting and eating area is
shaded by lattice and horse chestnut trees
(somewhat surprisingly for a small garden
but these were very fashionable in the 1930s
and the designer notes 'the property of the
horse chestnut for keeping insects at bay will be
appreciated'). Otherwise the garden has a good
selection of smaller trees notable for their foliage,
blossom or bark, a fair-sized lawn, topiary to screen
the kitchen garden, and all this foliage protects the
lawn from the surrounding windows and gardens. The
wavy line in the kitchen garden is 'a well-constructed
runnel' which holds rainwater collected from the roofs of
the shed and greenhouse. A shady garden, but a private
one. From *The Studio Gardens* and *Gardening*, 1937.

1 Sweet Bay
2 Standard roses
3 Wall fruit
4 Greenhouse
5 Toolshed
6 Wooden seat screened by clipped yew
7 Low hedge of Dutch lavender
8 Silver birches
9 *Magnolia soulangeana*
10 *Magnolia parviflora*
11 Plane trees
12 Pink Camellia
13 *Magnolia stellata*
14 *Cytisus praecox albus*
15 White tree paeony
16 Pernettya
17 *Ceanothus azureus*
18 *Menziesia alba*
19 *Kalmia latifolia*
20 *Myrica gale*
21 *Catalpa bignonioides* (Indian bean tree)
22 *Aesculus parviflora*
23 *Aesculus hippocastanum* (common)

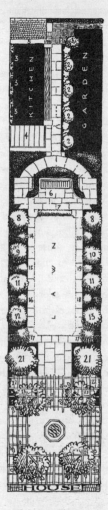

PLAN

the security of the past. Post and chain fences all of one-foot high carried 'associations of drawbridges and symbolically helped to define the right of passage of the visitor', storks in pairs were features ('fecundity and faithfulness'), as were squirrels ('thrift, industry and foresight') and dogs (the hunter's friend). Along with the candytuft around the sundial, the lawn, the rustic pergola with rose 'Dorothy Perkins' in her shocking pink masses, phlox, sweet peas, alyssum and lobelia edgings and the neat Austin 10 outside the garage, together with the coloured-glass galleon in full sail on the front door, thus was glorious 'Dunroamin' in its prime.[58]

And then the Dunroaminers went to war again.

This time Britain emerged from war with a socially engineered Planning machine (with a capital P) which has ruled the development of houses and gardens for the last fifty years. At the urban extreme were high-rise blocks of flats with no gardens at all, set in a parkland of open space, while the rural dream (especially from 1950 when restrictions on private builders were lifted) spread bungalows at a leafy two or four per acre. A house with a garden was still the national ideal but planners learned to engineer their way around this; the childless and the elderly in flats could have allotments if they so wished, the majority of new house-dwellers who were in redevelopments and new towns would be in terraces and three-storey blocks with small plots for washing and children's play. Front gardens became socially incorrect, giving way to bland green frontages on the American open-plan principle, a bleakness emphasized by the regulation overly wide tarmac roads and pavements, enormous bell-mouths and turning bays that were the realm of the motor car. Increasingly, compensation for tiny gardens and motorized deserts came by way of richly landscaped footpaths linking neighbour-hoods and cul-de-sacs, which were matched by landscaped and leafy pedestrian squares and shopping precincts.

There seems to have been a lull in post-war enthusiasm that allowed gardens to slip very low in planners' priorities. Redevelopment of fac-tories, hospitals and schools put tremendous pressures on land use which squeezed gardens out: Beeching's railway cuts compounded the losses of thousands of allotments in the 1950s and early 1960s, a tale told by David Crouch and Colin Ward in their 1988 history.[59] To quote just one figure, in Leeds between 1948 and 1963, 5000 plots declined to 500, from 400 acres to forty-three. Then came the baby boom and the lurch skywards in the post-war birthrate of the 1961 census: families now needed schools, hospitals, parks and public playgrounds but they had no time for gardening, and leisure was car borne to beyond the green belts, to the outstandingly naturally beautiful countryside or National Parks, themselves the product of the planning engineers.

Here was the terrible vacuum into which a new generation of designers stepped: three great books hauled British gardening out of post-war gloom. I love them all, and they all three deserve examination.

Lanning Roper's *Successful Town Gardening* was published in 1957 with a painting by his wife Primrose Harley on the cover, showing their garden, attached to a Georgian cottage behind Onslow Square, which had cheered hundreds of Sunday afternoon visitors in the drab 1950s. It was a patch of countryside in the heart of the city, a town dweller's dream, which was harnessed by Lanning's breezy American charm – even if all his readers had was a rubble-strewn yard, it was a delusion to think a weekend's onslaught would clear it, fill it with flowers and keep it perfect. He makes friends with these deluded mortals with a sunniness and optimism that was far from the gloomy pessimism of professional gardeners of the old school. Lanning admitted the problems: lack of space, sun, air, the atmospheric pollution, too much water or not enough and too little, and cats. He warned that basic decisions must be made: one could have children's activities or peace and plants, but not both. Gently, at his reader's elbow, he considers design – viewpoints, access, changes of level, hard surfaces, walls and fences, and colours: 'flowers in strong rich colours like bright reds, scarlets, purples and yellows look best on lighter walls'. Walls were better tinted pale yellow, soft grey, a dusky pink or pale orange. There were endless possibilities of trellis, floodlights, pools, ornaments, trough gardens, raised beds, with all these ideas he generated the enthusiasm to get started. He suggested eliminating grass when it had no chance, and ingenious adaptations – surplus ammunition cases painted green made excellent planters. Lanning had an elegant talent; he had studied fine arts and a little architecture at home before the war, and learned his gardening at Kew and Edinburgh Botanics. More than anything he wanted to make gardens in Britain and so his writing carried happy conviction. *Successful Town Gardening* was a tonic.[60]

Interestingly, Lanning Roper had been discouraged from studying landscape design in America because it was too difficult to earn a living.

As designers of new parks and new town landscapes, a few British landscape architects were to step into the limelight in the post-war years: Sylvia Crowe was already well known for dealing with power stations and planning 'blight' problems in the large scale, she was President of the Institute of Landscape Architects and in 1958 she published *Garden Design*, because she profoundly believed that 'Gardens are the link between men and the world in which they live'.[61] *Garden Design* philosophically disposes of history, but is most superb on the principles of design, giving the layman an insight into the professional mystique which had been squirrelled away since the founding of the Institute in 1929. As these principles came mostly from Repton they were gardener's territory, but had been forgotten or concealed, and perhaps with reason, for scale, time, space division, light and shade, texture, tone and colour are difficult to handle. In *Garden Design* they are in the hands of an expert: on Unity, the first and greatest principle, Sylvia Crowe wrote, 'most lacking in the average garden today is a sense of unity. It is a quality found in all great landscapes, based on the rhythm of natural land-form, the domination of one type of vegetation and the fact that human use and buildings have kept in sympathy with their surroundings. When we say that a landscape has been spoilt we mean that it has lost its unity.'[62] *Garden Design* teaches us our place in the landscape, with our gardens as the intermediary; unity requires either the acceptance of limiting factors, such as chalk soil or the way in which the wind sculpts trees and large shrubs, or the imposition of some unifying feature, such as Villa d'Este's water or Lutyens's geometry. The lack of unity in gardens was a social disease, the same that caused chaos in the post-war landscape: 'too many new things, ill-digested; new plants which we have not yet learnt to use; materials, such as Westmoreland rock and crazy paving, which are transported to all parts of the country and used in positions for which they are unsuited; foreign influences, copied without being assimilated or understood. But, above all, there is a lack of decision as to what each man really wants in his garden'.[63]

Sylvia Crowe is not for the squeamish, but for the garden adventurer with time to think. *Garden Design* is undoubtedly the most intelligent book that has ever been written on the subject.

At the outset of the 1960s gardeners had caught the scent of consumerism, and restraint went on the rubbish heap. One young designer, who had worked with Sylvia Crowe and Brenda Colvin at their 182 Gloucester Place office, and had seen the Californian gardens of Thomas Church and Lawrence Halprin, decided to go for gardens as a career. His name was John Brookes. In *Room Outside*, 'a new approach to garden design' first published in 1969, the debt to Sylvia Crowe's book is evident, but the approach is stripped down, jazzed up and aimed at people in a hurry – What do you want? What have you got? *Room Outside* introduced the small garden as just that, an extra room or series of rooms outdoors, with the emphasis on texture and pattern in fences and pavings and a rise in the percentage of hard surfacing, all using mass produced and inexpensive materials and making the best of 'found' objects. Almost all the illustrations came from American or continental modernist sources. Brookes was a pioneer, but he was also the modern designer *par excellence*, encouraging many new professionals. He completely re-vamped the idea in 1985, calling his bigger, lavishly-coloured book full of British examples *The Small Garden*.[64]

In *Garden Design* Sylvia Crowe had noted how allotments were out of favour in the 1950s because they were usually so neglected and untidy; there had undoubtedly been some digging fatigue after the great war effort. The consumerist affluence and pop culture of the 1960s (busily converting gardens to outdoor dining-rooms and playgrounds) wanted nothing to do with such symbols of poverty, charity and wartime needs as the allotments, now that there were frozen peas and fish fingers. Prime Minister Harold Wilson commissioned Harry Thorpe's committee of inquiry into allotments in 1964. 'The intention must have been', say Crouch and Ward,[65] 'to straighten out an antiquated, backward-looking activity, selfishly squatting on valuable urban land.' What Thorpe actually suggested was the import of the idea of leisure gardens from Holland and America, whereby the plots were let to garden-less city dwellers who could choose to have vegetables, flowers or lawn, with a small summerhouse on each site, and a central meeting room with kitchen and toilets. Leisure gardens were developed in Birmingham (under the wing of a research unit at the university)* and an International Leisure Gardeners' Federation congress was held there in 1976. What no one

---

* Had we known it, the concept had been here all the time; some late-nineteenth-century leisure gardens with Victorian and Arts & Crafts style brick summer-houses and high privet hedges around each one are now being restored in Hill Close, Warwick.[66]

foresaw was the green revolution, and by the mid-1970s waiting lists for allotments in all the great conurbations began to soar. The word allotment is now happily back in favour, and it is doubtful that anyone will try and dispossess it again: allotments bestow pride and honour, and in an increasingly frenetic world of food scares and pesticide-drenched or genetically altered vegetables, they, as the organic alternative, will remain both useful and beautiful.

The small garden has one last, important role to fill in the closing decades of the twentieth century. Along with the return of the allotments, city farms and the wildlife gardens of the late 1970s, an involved landscape architect who lived in the West Midlands, Chris Baines, discovered that rich habitats for wildlife began at home. He deconstructed his own garden, which featured in a BBC 2 film *Bluetits and Bumblebees*, first shown in 1984, and followed it with his small book, *How To Make a Wildlife Garden*, which immediately became a bestseller. To a nation already spending enormous sums on bird food, encouraged by their children who were the quickest to catch on, the back garden wildlife sanctuary became a popular reality. It had a serious message that the over-use of pesticides and herbicides was as bad for humans as it was for the birds, and that everyone should try to contribute rich habitat to the greening of cities and towns. It was also an informed response to the endless staggering perfection of films from the Serengeti or on the social habits of Galapagos lizards being presented to a public totally ignorant of the residents of their own back gardens.

The small garden has become great in stature: it can be part of a ribbon nature reserve with like-minded neighbours, it can collect plant rarities as part of the NCCPG, it can be 'open' to visitors for the National Gardens Scheme and other charities, even if the visitors have to look over the wall, it can win prizes and prizes mean television appearances, or it can be for bouncy castles on summer afternoons. Chris Baines's message is that the small garden is a first lesson in global housekeeping, it leads out to community gardens and woodlands, to the discovery that the most exciting of wild creatures and plants have moved into urban and suburban life along with the rest of us. From being a tiny enclosure brought in from the wild, the small garden, by existing in such enormous numbers, has become the key to a much improved quality of life in these small islands, on this small planet.

CHAPTER SIX

⊱⊰ ❀ ⊱⊰

Acquiring Eden

B y now it has become clear that the English garden is nothing of the sort, neither 'English' nor even British: gardens cannot be confined by nationalistic notions, and the story of the past is again and again of the discovery of a good idea or beautiful plant, which is immediately coveted by everyone else. Gardens are an international currency, the exchange of which can be seen either as a two-thousand-year-old exercise in diplomacy that has contributed enormously to the sum of human health and pleasure, or as a commercially motivated greedy scramble. All the old empires, especially the Spanish, French and Dutch, are the villains, but equally so are the British: and it is not only the plant-hunting villainry, so rightly accused by environmental movements, and which institutions like the Royal Horticultural Society and Kew are working so hard to re-write and redress, but the trade in garden fashions and styles that needs re-examination.

It is the British climate that encourages gardens, rather than any native tendency to green fingers or nonsense about 'love of plants' – at which the Dutch beat us hands down. Outside, as I begin this chapter, it is a mild and gently damp November afternoon; in my small garden the soil is dark chocolatey crumble – friable, that desirable state, just as soil should be – mounded with black hummocks of compost awaiting the frost. This is perfect weather for planting roses and for breaking up herbaceous clumps, knowing that plants young and old are settling in for the winter, luxuriating in the misty droplets, their leaves shiny and clean, with the promises for next year nestling at their hearts. King Charles II, with the heightened appreciation of the returning exile, expressed his love for this climate which allowed him to spend part of almost every day out of doors; in *The Englishness of English Art*, Nikolaus

Pevsner has observed that this same climate fostered sports, pastimes and art, because it was also cool enough to encourage outdoor activity, 'the Englishman digging his own bathing pool or building his own garden wall'.[1] If our beloved Gulf Stream, the patron of this climate, is threatened by melting ice-floes, if we are to be become subject to hurricanes and Mediterranean hot and dry summers, with deeply penetrating New England-like frosts in winter, then it will be farewell to the 'English' garden. The combination of a cool temperate zone, warm wet summers and cool wet winters is the overwhelming reason why plants and ideas from all over the world have found a second home in these islands.

First, with the sandal on the other foot, the Roman invasion. In the advances and reverses of 400 years of occupation there must be a Roman legacy, but the vast and efficient trading system of the empire is only recently becoming appreciated. If Whitby jet and Whitstable oysters could get to Rome and a contractor based in Lincoln could operate a regular service to Bordeaux for fruits and wine, then plants could clearly travel freely. Box clippings and weeds left by a Roman gardener have been found in Silchester and vinestocks at Boxmoor villa in Hertfordshire. It would be nice to think that the herb shop at Colchester, burned during Boudicca's rebellion, where dill, coriander, aniseed, celery and poppy seed were found, was selling home-grown produce.[2]

Gardens at Pompeii now being evaluated related little to chilly Britain:[3] in John Harvey's opinion, after he had examined the written evidence and the treatises of Cato, Varro, Columella and Palladius, it 'remains doubtful' that any of these applied to British gardens. In the eighth century the Venerable Bede had a copy of the *Naturalis Historia* of Pliny the Elder, but Dr Harvey concludes that this was also unlikely to have been generally used, and continues: 'it is unquestionable that the garden flora of Britain has been enriched by the living descendants of certain kinds of plants introduced by the Romans from the South'. Plant names derived from Latin suggest these naturalized sorts: 'fruits such as sweet chestnut, cherry, mulberry, peach and the grapevine; almonds and figs; beet, cabbages (kale, coleworts), lettuce and radish; and in the flower garden the rose, lily and violet'.[4]

For *Food & Cooking in Roman Britain* Jane Renfrew has researched the letters at Vindolanda which, incredible as it may seem, soldiers on the wall fort wrote to their families at home – one lists foods such as 'spice, goats' milk, salt, young pig, ham, corn, venison and flour', and another 'vintage wine, Celtic beer, ordinary wine, fish sauce and pork fat'. All Roman soldiers it seems had a passion for fish sauce (there was a factory for producing it in Londinium) and it appears in the following recipe. Feeding the occupying forces brought out the entrepreneurial talents of the Romano-British, and I like to think of lettuces, onions and herbs being delivered for this appetizer to some general's dinner of milk-fed snails, stuffed dormouse and venison in plum sauce:

PUREE OF LETTUCE LEAVES WITH ONIONS

Take: 6 small lettuce; a pinch of pepper, lovage, celery seeds, mint, oregano; ½ teasp bicarb. of soda; 1 finely chopped onion; 1 tblsp (15 ml) wine; 1 tblsp (15 ml) olive oil and 1 teasp. (5 ml) of anchovy essence.
Plunge the lettuces into a pan of boiling water with the bicarb. of soda, and simmer for 2 mins. Drain, chop finely; pound the pepper, herbs and onions in a mortar. Add the wine, oil and anchovy essence. Cook gently for 30 mins, pour over the lettuce and serve.[5]

Constance Spry has a similar recipe and Sophie Grigson adds chopped bacon and mushrooms instead of the wine; food effectively makes the point that those distant Romans were not so different from us.

For interested garden historians, the Roman villa sites of Britain still retain their secret pasts and much remains to be discovered. The only major excavation and restoration has been done at Fishbourne Palace, near Chichester: this has revealed a rectangular formal garden (83 m × 100 m) enclosed by colonnades (as in a cloister) with a wide central path dividing it from east to west, linking the doors of the entrance hall to the audience chamber. A secondary path ran around the four sides. A great deal of work had been necessary to level the area of the garden, and long trenches had been dug and filled with loam for planting; each side of the main path these parallel trenches were indented with alternately semi-circular and square niches for a decorative hedging, with perhaps pots or statues in them. Trenches also flank the perimeter path, and on the east side of the garden the post holes for an upright structure, presumably a pergola, were found with planting pits for shrubs. The garden was completely underlaid with pressurized water pipes for fountains and fragments of marble basins were found. Fishbourne also has another formal garden of similar size, a kitchen garden and five small peristyle gardens; its excavator Barry Cunliffe thought that it was 'totally alien to anything hitherto seen in the country and must imply immigrant designers and craftsmen, brought possibly from the Mediterranean'.[6]

The latest archaeological thinking is that the Romans left with great reluctance, and their culture survived, gradually slipping westwards; the citizens of Exeter still thought themselves Roman at the end of the sixth century, and still hoped the Empire would return. It seems unlikely that the Saxons had any use for Roman gardens, though they did re-use building materials and sites, but it is intriguing to suppose that the image, or smell, of a box-hedged courtyard and a plashing fountain might have survived in folk memory, to spark a gleam of recognition perhaps from a Crusader knight or even a Grand Tourist?

The spread of Christianity and monasticism recreated the Roman Empire in another name, and though the dispensation of medicinal knowledge and herbal lore was a force for the good, it was strictly controlled. The monks drew on classical sources to which they had privileged (and sole) access, and this applies not only to plant knowledge but also to design. Roman logic pervades the Benedictine ideal plan for St Gall (see page 53), which was translated to sites all over Britain, and it is worth repeating that the ghostly form of the great fort at Chesters on Hadrian's Wall has more than passing resemblance to the plan of Cardinal Gambara's Villa Lante.

The monks also drew on the knowledge of their sworn enemies, the infidel hordes of the East, without – naturally – giving credit. The Arabs were much better at gardens than any Europeans, and curiosity may not have been the least motive for some Crusaders. Eleanor of Aquitaine was brave, educated and curious, and she went on Crusade as Queen of France to Constantinople and Antioch in 1148, bringing back Islamic ideas to her sunny courts at Poitiers. It would be surprising if she had not brought these ideas northwards when she became Queen of England. The fact that the Plantagenet kings ruled as far as Bordeaux and married Spanish princesses was also a boon to gardens, for Islamic or Moorish gardens were 'a fully developed tradition' throughout the Iberian peninsula in the tenth century. Eleanor of Castile, married to Edward I, is now revealed as 'an enthusiastic gardener' by researchers in Wales, and accounts of the making of gardens for her at Rhuddlan (Clwyd) and Conwy (Gwynedd) castles survive. At Rhuddlan in 1282 the courtyard was laid with 6000 turves; water meadow turf was used for a temporary garden at Conwy the following year and another at Caernarfon. At Conwy the small formal garden overlooking the river estuary survived to appear in paintings of the castle in 1600. Roger Bigod III, 5th Earl of Norfolk, inherited Chepstow Castle in 1270 and set about civilizing it; surviving accounts mention a 'gloriette' which was, perhaps, a Moorish pavilion on the castle walls.[7] These early, fragile evidences soften the grim images of medieval fortresses and perhaps support the idea of the bowers of courtly love. Some of our most favourite plants have these associations – *Phlomis* (Jerusalem sage), Spanish and Portuguese iris (*Iris xiphium, Iris lusitanica*), Southernwood (*Artemesia abrotanum*), Spanish broom and Turk's cap lilies.

These, along with *Ballota*, the cistus, the white tree heath, yellow jasmine, santolina, *Yucca gloriosa*, Crown Imperials, *Hemerocallis flava*, some campanulas, centaureas, the original hollyhock, *Althea rosea*, and tulips – are all among the first known wave of Mediterranean exotics recorded by the plantsmen of curiosity, notably John Gerard and John Parkinson, who had emerged from the mêlée following the dissolution of the monasteries to become the first herbalists and apothecaries. They were not yet deemed scientists, for science was yet to come. John Parkinson was an apothecary and a founder of the Society of Apothecaries in 1617, but he was able to 'retire' to his garden in Long Acre by about 1622 to concentrate on his plants and his books, *Paradisus Terrestris* (1629) and *Theatrum Botanicum* (1640). Parkinson's seeds were collected by English doctors studying in Italy, expeditions to Spain and Portugal and travellers in Turkey.

But the ambitious were already looking farther afield: John Tradescant the Elder, gardener for Robert Cecil, 1st Earl of Salisbury, at Hatfield, went collecting in Russia and Virginia (though we may regret him bringing back the Stag's Horn sumach and spiderwort (*Tradescantia virginiana*) and not everyone feels the Virginia creeper an unmixed blessing. John Tradescant the Younger continued going to Virginia in 1637, 1642 and 1654 – while Britain was immersed in Civil War and the Commonwealth experiment, he was still exploring – and the tulip tree, *Liriodendron tulipifera*, and swamp cypress, both beloved in gardens, are among his hauls. The Tradescants are rather special because they were collectors in the widest sense and great keepers of lists. While cultivating their exotic plants they curated their Ark museum of stuffed alligators and other curiosities, being great practitioners of the English fascination with the curious in the name of scientific enquiry. John the Younger happened to be friends with one Elias Ashmole, who carefully preserved the Tradescant legacy in his new museum in Oxford, founded in 1683.[8]

At Fulham Palace, Henry Compton, Bishop of London, with John Rose as his gardener, had more than a thousand tender exotics from America; Bishop Compton traded in souls and plants with the colonists, sending out priests who were also collectors – the beginning of a duality of role which was always to be seen as the conveniently disguised (and cheap) way of acquisition. Compton's most famous priest, the Revd John Bannister, is credited with sending home the first *Magnolia virginiana*, but Bannister was to 'go native' and become a pioneer of American botany – the first in a line of martyr collectors, he was shot accidentally while botanizing along the Roanoake River in 1692.[9]

It is tempting to imagine that at least he died a happy man, knowing that he had found an Eden in the beautiful landscape of Virginia. For Eden, paradise on earth, was to be found several times during the exploration of our planet, though never recognized, or at least acknowledged, for various political reasons. That the Americas were so bountiful, and so carefully cultivated in parts by native Americans, was appreciated by many travellers who spoke with quiet voices, but these voices were drowned in the scramble for territories and trade, and are only recently being resurrected. In his book *Enduring Seeds*, Dr Gary Nabhan has brought to light the sixteenth-century descriptions of arboreta in the valleys of Central Mexico – one in the forest of Tetzcotzinco 'was like falling into a garden raining with aromatic tropical flowers' – gardens of medicinal and aromatic herbs, native roses and trees with fragrant blossoms.[10] Twenty-five years ago Michael Foss (in *Undreamed Shores: England's Wasted Empire in America*) revived Governor John

White's diaries and drawings of the gardens and cultural wisdom of the Indians of the Virginia shore. White, a persevering but unassertive man, sent out on a several expeditions masterminded by Sir Walter Raleigh, had his sensitive approach trampled and obliterated from history by his more piratical colleagues.[11] And one truly great book, Leo Marx's *The Machine in the Garden*, revived Robert Beverley's 1705 *History and Present State of Virginia* in which he lauds 'the Fruitfullest, and Pleasantest of all Clymates . . . reckon'd the Gardens of the World', of his new-found home.[12] Leo Marx's chapter 'The Garden', published in 1964, inspired American historians to look at their pre-colonial landscape for the first time, and they realized how Eden had been lost: 'the Garden' is now applied as a general name to the period before the arrival of white Europeans.

That this is no misnomer is supported by a description of the coastal landscape and native flora of Maine: forests of pine, spruce and larch, giving way to natural meadows and rocky screes, with trillium, wild iris and lilies, ferns, violets, roses, asters, dwarf cornel, various viburnums, rhodora and clintonia, all wreathed in spring blossom of *Amelanchier canadensis*. A flora known well, though by other names, to the Micmac Indians, who spent summers on Maine beaches, living on seafood and blackberries, redcurrants, blueberries, wild strawberries and nuts from the woodlands. Against this vision of paradise must be set that of the portly London horticulturist with pride in his glasshouses, his pockets jingling with money for new plants.

This American Eden was trampled in the first wave of popularity of American plants in Britain in the 1730s and 1740s, plants often supplied by the Quaker cloth merchant Peter Collinson, who gardened in Peckham, then at Mill Hill (now the site of Mill Hill School) and traded with John Bartram in Quaker Pennsylvania, the greatest pioneer figure in American gardening.[13] Charles Hamilton at Painshill bought American shrubs in this first wave (there were to be revivals in succeeding centuries) and research and restoration there allows us to see them in authentic eighteenth-century use. Hamilton used evergreens, box, hollies (these in many varieties, more than we now have) and laurels in masses to create a layered look to hide the trunks of trees and larger shrubs, so that the foliage appeared to hang, unsuspended. He massed pines, tulip trees (*Liriodendron*), magnolias, liquidambar, kalmias and scarlet oaks to resemble the frothy foliage of a painting by Claude.

However, the real haul of plants from both North and South America, brought as the booty of various empires, can only be conveyed by a roll-call of names, most of which will be very familiar: the Revd Adam Buddle, a mosses and grasses man, died in 1715 but is immortalized by *Buddleia globosa*, named for him by Linnaeus and introduced from Peru in 1774; Père David and the Revd Buddle combine in *Buddleia davidii* in 1896; Dr John Fothergill was a Quaker physician, friend of Collinson, after whom *Fothergilla major* is named; he in turn patronized the painter and collector William Bartram, who found *Franklinia alatamaha* on the river of that name in Georgia, and named it after Benjamin Franklin. Antonio José Escalon y Flores, a Spanish botanist and sometime page to the Viceroy of New Granada (Colombia) found *Escallonia*; the Viceroy himself, the Marquis de la Vega Armigo, had been a pupil and patron of José Celestino Mutis (*Mutisia*); Colonel John Fremont (*Fremontodendron*) found *Carpentaria californica* which he named after Professor William Carpenter, the botanist of the Louisiana swamplands; the Irish horticulturist Bernard MacMahon went to Philadelphia, and became *Mahonia*; as did Peter Kalm from Sweden (*Kalmia*), Dr Gaulthier, physician to the Governor of Quebec, travelled with Kalm, and found *Gaultheria procumbens*, a Maine native known as creeping wintergreen. *Garrya* was named by David Douglas in gratitude for his support from Nicholas Garry, deputy governor of the Hudson Bay Company (the Indians knew Garrya as the quinine or silk tassel bush). Dr Thomas Coulter, an Irish botanist, went to Mexico in 1824 as physician to a mining company, and over the non-existent border in California, he found *Romneya coulteri*, named after Dr T. Romney Robinson (as there was already a genus *Robinsonia* found on Robinson Crusoe's island, Juan Fernandez). We owe *Pernettya* to Dom Antoine Joseph Pernetty who took part in the de Bougainville expedition to the Falklands and Magellan Straits in 1763 and, of course, de Bougainville himself wreaths the Mediterranean garden and northern conservatory. Having lost a colony the British had found a planting scheme, and interest turned elsewhere.[14]

The Far East was the most intriguing. Aesthetic speculation on Chinese gardens began with the travellers' tales of Dutch and Flemish traders recorded by the diplomat and keen gardener Sir William Temple in the 1680s. Sir William had used a wonderful 'Chinese whisper-word'

Sharawadjii, which has puzzled scholars ever since (see glossary), for the creative spontaneity, the 'artificial rudeness' and irregularity that they loved in their garden landscapes. The first real accounts of Chinese gardens came in Father Attiret's famous letter home from his little studio inside the sacred walls of Ch'ien-lung, the Emperor's favourite summer retreat – The Garden of Perfect Brightness – which was published in Paris in 1749 and translated into English in 1752. All things Chinese became fashionable, to the advantage of the young architect William Chambers, who had been to India and China with the Swedish East India Company and who was enterprising enough to publish a book of designs for Chinese buildings and net himself the design of the gardens at Kew for Princess Augusta. The Pagoda, inspired by engravings of the Porcelain Tower of Nanking and a Chinese Tea Pagoda, nine storeys and 163 feet high, with glittering glazed canopies and dragons and red lacquered balconies was the most daring and marvellous of Chambers's buildings, and it remains firmly fixed in the popular imagination as one of the most famous garden buildings in the world. For once gardens were at the height of fashion instead of lagging behind; China tea, chinoiserie in wallpapers and fabrics and Mr Chippendale's furniture, porcelain and garden buildings all carried the smartest labels of the 1760s and following decades. One of the most evocative relics from that craze, because it is so fragile and has been so tenderly enjoyed and maintained, is the Chinese Pavilion now kept indoors at Boughton House. It is twelve sided, with twelve wooden posts supporting the tip-tilted roof which is topped with a gilded dragon. It is really a framed and collapsible tent, made of oil cloth, with the fine oil-cloth ceiling lining painted with writhing dragons, and oil-cloth side panels that could be raised as required. The Pavilion now rests in honourable retirement, having served for over 200 summers in four different gardens, and been carefully dismantled and packed away for over 200 winters – one can only imagine the tea parties, trysts, deals, fan flutterings, meetings and partings it has witnessed.[15]

Chinoiserie was a court fashion throughout Europe; China itself sank into an opium-clouded insularity. Any curiosity about China's garden heritage was suspended for over fifty years, until the Treaty of Nanking at the end of the First Opium War in 1842 gained Hong Kong and other ports of access and safeguards for travellers. Robert Fortune's

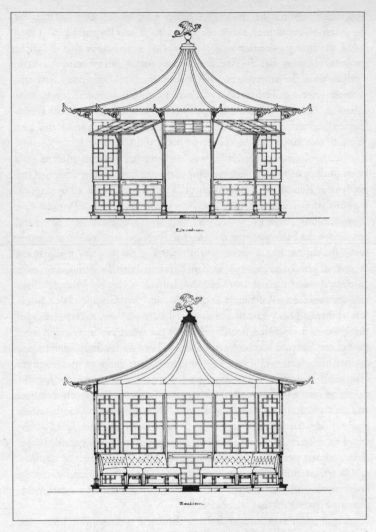

The Chinese Pavilion, Boughton House, Northamptonshire: section and elevation of
this delightful monument to chinoiserie, made of oil-cloth and timber, with painted
dragons for decoration, which has served for two hundred summers in four gardens.
Now on display at Boughton House. Measured drawings by William A. Thompson,
from *The Chinese Pavilion* by Rosemary Bowden-Smith, 1988.

expeditions during the 1840s and 1850s were to tightly detailed agendas from the Horticultural Society in London, chiefly dictated by the East India Company's former inspector of tea, to find teas that could be grown in Assam and Sikkim: gardeners bless Robert Fortune for also finding time for other plants, the winter jasmine, 'Japanese' anemone, weigela, winter-flowering honeysuckles and *Mahonia bealei* among them. Economic botany ruled the day, though, and the subtleties of China's garden heritage were ignored, until they eventually came to the west secondhand, via Japan.

Economic botanist and pirate king, Sir Joseph Banks was the kind of wealthy, well-connected and superbly self-confident character who enjoyed horticultural empire building. Banks paid and persuaded his way on to the *Endeavour* for the trip to lay claim to Australia with Captain Cook, believing that the South Seas were a kind of floral El Dorado – Banks and Cook are said to have 'viewed their destination as a secret garden whose fruits might be harvested to Britain's advantage'[16]. We now know that here was Eden, disregarded yet another time: in *The Fatal Shore*, Australian-born Robert Hughes writes lovingly of the magical innocence of the Iora peoples who had tended 'New South Wales' for 30,000 years, treasuring their 'locus of myth, their dreaming' until Banks barged in, shooting albatross (the reluctance of men to sail with Cook's future trips might have had something to do with this), wallaby and kangaroo, and deciding that their land would solve the problem of prison overcrowding at home.[17]

Sir Joseph Banks was given charge of Kew by George III when he returned from Australia and he was to be one of the founder members of the Horticultural Society, that met in Hatchard's Bookshop in 1804. He was a man of his time, eager to impress his dinner guests rather than steward the earth, loving to parade in his Maori trophy cloak, in which his portrait was painted by Benjamin West, as a chairman of the board, enjoying the telling of his traveller's tales for their effect. He does not deserve to be the icon of the gardening world that he has long been, and is much more appropriately regarded as an economic botanist, his name now perpetuated in the Sir Joseph Banks Centre for Economic Botany, an environmentally sensitive building sited among the trees and off the beaten track at Kew Gardens. The Banks memorial in his native city of Lincoln, at the city's visitor centre, The Lawn, reveals him to be the patron of office and atrium gardeners: the immaculately maintained Sir Joseph Banks Conservatory has a splendid collection of philodendrons, begonias, dracaenas, fittonias, cordyline, vriesias, marantas and monsteras, plants of obscure purpose in surroundings hostile to them, until they were marketed as house plants by Thomas Rochford in the 1950s and 1960s.[18]

In contrast to the powerful myth of Indian and Mogul gardens already discussed, the actuality of gardens in India was not appreciated until Edward Lear and other sensitive travellers saw them: Edwin Lutyens was encouraged to study Mogul architecture and especially its garden tradition by Lady Hardinge, the former Winifred Sturt, when he first went there with the commission for New Delhi in 1912. Her tragic death in 1914 and Charles Hardinge's subsequent collapse as Viceroy threatened the whole project, and it was in part Lutyens's characteristic loyalty that meant the garden was eventually completed in the late 1920s and is carefully tended and much admired today. But for this, the British in India have an appalling record: in the eighteenth century the chief ambitions of the more important employees of the East India Company were to make a fortune to finance 'Indian' gardens at home. An example, though briefly known, is the convoluted financial history of the agency house of Paxton, Cockerell, Traill and Company, which led to the funding of two well-known gardens, Sezincote in Gloucestershire and Middleton Hall in Carmarthenshire. Middleton, where William Paxton lived like a nabob 'eclipses the proudest Cambrian mansions in Asiatic pomp and splendour', with formal gardens, engineered lakes and a gazebo tower with 'one of the best views of south Wales over the beautiful Towy valley'. The same architect, Samuel Pepys Cockerell, worked for both Paxton and his own brother, Sir Charles Cockerell, at Sezincote, the most famous oriental house in Britain, with Indian features in the garden built exactly to replicate the drawings of Thomas and William Daniell, made on a tour of India between 1786 and late 1793. The Daniells' sketching trip took in temples, tombs, forts and landscapes; 261 of their originals are in the British Architectural Library's drawings collection, including the special commissions from Sir Charles Cockerell for his Sezincote garden: the temple of Surya, the wall of mossy recesses (of funerary origin but used for ornaments) and the Indian Bridge, guarded by Nandi, the Happy One, a Brahmin white bull made from Coade stone. Middleton Hall is being made into a national botanic garden for Wales and Sezincote, beloved of John Betjeman, remains a fantasy curiosity in deepest Gloucestershire (*Plates 8 & 9*): the most magical effect is being able to see the Daniell drawings made so far away, and then the faithfully constructed realities in the garden.[19]

The most exciting garden to embrace all these oriental fashions and the plants that match them is Biddulph Grange in Staffordshire, which languished in decay for many decades but has recently been acquired and restored by the National Trust. The maker of Biddulph, James Bateman, was born in 1811 to a rich and dandified precocity, which seemed to improve upon marriage to Maria Warburton, when he was twenty-seven. Prior to this Bateman's passion was for orchids, and he was subjected to much horticultural ridicule when he published his tome on those from Mexico and Guatemala with its famous vital statistics – 2 6 high × 1 9 wide × 3 thick, weighing 38 lbs, with forty superb double crown plates by Mrs Withers and Miss Drake – lampooned by George Cruickshank as 'the librarian's nightmare'.[20] James and Maria decided to take over a farm which James's father had bought for its coal-mining potential, not far from the Bateman home, Knypersley Hall, and with their generous resources and the help of friends, notably a marine artist called Edward Cooke, they set out to proclaim what Geoffrey Jellicoe was to call 'a new era of British internationalism'.[21]

This is an interesting accolade, but a fair one, for the Batemans possessed all the exotica that Charles Hamilton at Painshill exactly a century earlier could only imagine. With both Painshill and Biddulph restored, it is immensely rewarding to see them within a short interval of each other. Painshill is much the larger (158 acres), as befits an eighteenth-century pleasure landscape, but they are both setting out to present a kaleidoscopic series of views and experiences, pictures that compose and dissolve as we, the viewers, are in motion between them, lured on by skilfully laid paths to find out what is around the next corner. Hamilton's fantastical tour introduces the Romans, a mausoleum and Robert Adam's Temple of Bacchus, as well as the vineyard now restored on the sloping bank of the lake (Hamilton believed his vines were the first grown on a large scale since the Romans left and he produced a sparkling, champagne-like wine), American plants, including the first rhododendrons, a Gothic temple, a Chinese bridge, a Turkish tent, a Scottish medieval castle and the regulation Picturesque hermitage. A century later the world had become Britannia's oyster, and the Batemans' circuit at Biddulph, tightened into fifteen intense acres divided into rocky glens and miniature mountain ranges, encompasses the Italianate, Egypt, the Chile Pine or Monkey Puzzle (first introduced by Archibald Menzies in 1795, re-introduced by William Lobb in 1844), some of the first of Lobb's Wellingtonias from California via Veitch's nursery, American maples and liquidambar, a pinetum of David Douglas's conifers from the Rocky Mountains, and the grand finale, China, along with many of Joseph Hooker's rhododendrons from his expeditions to Sikkim, Bhutan and Nepal in 1849–51.[22] The Egyptian 'mysteries' include sphinxes, a pyramid and the ape of Thoth, 'a sub-human associate of the Egyptian god of botany'; things Egyptian had been popularized by Sir John Soane and the opening of Edward Bullock's Egyptian Hall in Piccadilly. Thomas Cook's first tours to the Nile started in the 1860s.

Biddulph's riches are more than a collection of curiosities, though; they are a reminder that so many of Bateman's plants were procured at a very high price. David Douglas was sent out in Menzies' footsteps and in 1824 he began his dangerous journeyings in the Pacific north-west, through British Columbia and Oregon; apart from the first commercial spruces he brought our gardens *Garrya elliptica*, *Ribes* (flowering currant), the Californian poppy and *Lupinus polyphyllus*, the parent of most garden lupins. Douglas met a terrible death in Hawaii in 1834 (aged only thirty-six) where he went to recover from exhausting white-water navigation of the Fraser River; he fell into a pit in which an enraged bull was already trapped. We also owe a great deal to men who were not plant hunters at all, but Jesuit priests, who were allowed the first privileged access to China's mountain flowers, and who became knowledgeable botanists. Pierre Nicolas D'Incarville went to China as early as 1740 and sent back large quantities of seeds and specimens; he is in our gardens with a successor, Jean Maria Delavay, who went out in 1874, as *Incarvillea delavayi*. Other Jesuits too are familiar: Armand David, Paul Farges and Jean André Soulié (after whom the pale pinky-white, round leaved *Rhododendron souliei*, which prefers the eastern counties, was named), who was tortured and killed by Tibetan monks as a frenzied reprisal for

Francis Younghusband's expedition which opened their fortress country to western eyes.

The last expeditions were by the most famous: the tough and industrious George Forrest (1873–1932) who died on his last expedition; Reginald Farrer (1880–1920) who overcame immense personal difficulties and wrote beautifully of his Alpine expeditions (some with E. A. Bowles) and who died in Upper Burma of pneumonia aged forty; Frank Kingdon Ward (1885–1958) who has the largest number of primula and rhododendron finds to his name, and (my favourite, whom I share with E. H. M. Cox), Ernest 'Chinese' Wilson. These are the names forever connected with the revolution in gardens, the natural or rock garden, from rhododendron valleys of the Cornish ravines to the smallest stone sink of miniature specialities.

A tribute to E. H. Wilson exists in the form of a small garden in the shadow of the church tower in Chipping Campden in Gloucestershire, where he was born in 1876. Wilson left the town as a child and was to do his greatest work for the Arnold Arboretum in Boston and its autocratic, 'but the kindliest of autocrats' Charles Sprague Sargent.[23] This little garden (designed by Peter Shepheard) is an effective thanks for the paperbark maple, *Acer griseum, Arundinaria murieliae* (named after Wilson's daughter), *Hydrangea sargentiana, Berberis wilsoniae, Kolkwitzia amabilis*, the Beauty Bush, and *Ceratostigma willmottianum* (for the contribution Ellen Willmott made to one of his trips). Wilson was not blameless; infamously, he collected over 18,000 bulbs of *Lilium regale*, most of which perished on the way to America; the next year his native collectors amassed another 25,000 (clearing whole valleys) which were packed in wet clay and reached the Arnold safely – 'something that fills us with horror' says modern collector Peter Cox.[24] Wilson is, however, frequently blessed for *Lilium regale* and for the Chinese gooseberry, *Actinidia deliciosa*, and most of all, for the great *Davidia involucrata* treasure-hunt.

Wilson was late coming to China, and by the end of the nineteenth century it was the opinion of 'some knowledgeable plantsmen' that every worthwhile plant from China had already been brought to Europe.[25] However Sir Harry Veitch of the Royal Exotic Nursery in Chelsea, part of the vast Veitch empire, had seen a specimen of desiccated *Davidia* at Kew, and he was determined to have one more expedition. By this time plant hunting was not a popular pastime: the *Davidia* had been sent to Kew with other wonderful material by the Irish Augustine Henry, a medical officer of the Chinese Imperial Maritime Customs Service, who, to stem his isolation and loneliness, had started a botanic correspondence. 'Letters are the only stimulus of a healthy kind an exile has to cheer him in moments of depression,' he wrote, 'and to remind him that there is a fair world on the other side of the globe, where men and women live . . . In such a place as this (Mengste in Yunnan) letters are esteemed more than gold, more than tobacco . . . they are the only little joys we have.' He had heard of Russian officers in similar conditions in Siberia who committed suicide at the rate of 5 per cent a year.[26] It was to counter his depression that Henry began collecting (very convenient for Kew, so poor as to need cheap and desperate plant hunters) and Henry had found the flowering *Davidia*, named after the Jesuit Abbé David who had found it first in 1869. Professor Sargent at the Arnold Arboretum was very keen to locate this *Davidia*, but Henry urged that a younger man was needed and as a result of this worldwide correspondence, from London, Boston and remote Yunnan, it was finally agreed to send Wilson, a star student from Kew who was working for Sir Harry Veitch. Augustine Henry stuck to his post long enough to welcome Ernest Wilson and give him a rough sketch map (of an area roughly the size of Newfoundland) of the upper reaches of the Yangtse where the *Davidia* had been seen and Wilson set out in the New Year of 1900 in a picturesque river boat, with a sedan chair, his bearers and guides. It was a journey full of threats and ambushes, but ten days later he arrived in a hamlet where Henry was remembered and was directed towards the tree: after walking for about two miles he came upon a rather new house . . . and the stump of the *Davidia*, which had been felled for the beams and posts of the house: 'I did not sleep during the night of April 25 1900' he wrote.[27] Three weeks and many miles later Wilson found a fifty-foot tree in flower with the famous 'pocket handkerchiefs' and then located ten more. He arrived home in April 1902 to great joy, James H. Veitch gave him a gold watch engraved 'Well done!' The seeds were germinated at the Coombe Wood Nursery at Kingston Hill in Surrey and Wilson and his assistant potted up thirteen thousand young plants; in May 1922 the first one flowered in the nursery. This magnificent and marvellous tree is now in so many of our gardens, treated with the awe and wonder that it deserves; Augustine Henry retired home to Ireland, where he pursued forestry development to help his country's economy. According to Stephen Spongberg (who has chronicled the Arnold Arboretum's story in *A Reunion of Trees*) most Chinese botanists see their first *Davidia* flowering either at the Arnold or Kew – and presumably they do not call it *Davidia* at all?

Wilson, who was the most tactful of plant hunters, made a second trip for Veitch, returning in March 1905. He had married in 1902 and he and his wife Helen had put off a family because of this trip: Muriel Primrose Wilson was born in May 1906, and Wilson went off once more at Sargent's pleading in the winter following, and on his final trip in 1910 – Sargent was difficult to refuse. The prize was masses of *Lilium regale*, the *Hydrangea sargentiana* with the large velvety leaves, the *Ceratostigma* which nods its blue flowers to Miss Willmott, *Spiraea veitchii*, for the supporters at home (Wilson was now living in America), and *Viburnum davidii* the elegant mound of ridged leaves with turquoise berries, and several magnolias including *Magnolia dawsoniana* after the Arnold's Chief Propagator, Jackson Dawson. The Wilson family went to Japan, for *Kurume* azaleas, and were happily famous and settled in America, so that Wilson took over as Director of the Arnold when Sargent died in 1927.[28] Tragically they were killed in a car crash in 1930 after visiting their daughter; it was the end of the old order at the Arnold, and an unfortunate omen for a new society.

The nature of rock gardens as miniature landscapes of China and Japan has already been touched upon, but the history of the alpine garden is, as far as I know, unwritten. An interest in alpines dates from the mid-eighteenth century (von Haller published his *Alpine Flora* in 1741), an enthusiasm for mountaineering and the founding of the Alpine Club, the elitist sporting society, in 1857. A particular kind of mind, predominantly male at least to start with, seemed to prize the Chinese philosophy of intensifying pleasurable experience by miniaturization; and, of course, practically speaking the exquisite flowers of the mountain heights had to be housed in sympathetic habitats. William Robinson wrote of the delights of thrifts, saxifrages and ferns which lodged themselves in walls in *The Wild Garden* (1870), a natural phenomenon of cottage gardens in stone country, and in *The English Flower Garden* there was an expert article on alpine gardening. Sir Charles Isham's rockery at Lamport Hall in Northamptonshire was the first British garden to feature gnomes, imported from Nuremburg (where they were used as good luck tokens by miners) as a workforce for rockery maintenance.

It was Reginald Farrer, who had started his rock gardening in childhood at Ingleborough in Yorkshire, who really awakened interest with *My Rock Garden* (1907) in which he identified the classic howlers – the Almond Pudding (the spikiest pinnacles of limestone stuck into a pile of earth with the appearance 'of a tipsy-cake stuck with almonds'), the Dog's Grave and the Devil's Lapful, a large load of bald, square-faced boulders just tipped, with 'things' planted amongst them.[29] None of these, said Farrer, would grow anything of worth or interest: the detailed study of stratification and scree structure, and the ineffable challenge of finding the right plants to fit – as Miles Hadfield said 'the joy of the alpine gardener is that within a few square yards he may encompass the plants not only of different continents but of the two hemispheres'.[30] Alpines, in sinks, on screes and rocks, and under glass or in the smallest back yard were at a peak of popularity between the wars, the best way for an owner of a small garden to explore the highest reaches of horticultural achievement. Walter Ingwersen's nursery, started on a patch of William Robinson's Gravetye estate in 1927 (Robinson left the estate to the nation when he died in 1925), is one of the greatest treasure houses for alpinists – I have Ingwersens' Golden Jubilee Catalogue of 1977 with its miniature crowds of dianthus, lewisias, sedums, saxifrage, tiny cyclamen and campanulas, all priced at around 40 pence per plant.

One of the last plant collectors (in the old sense) was E. H. M. Cox from Glendoick in Perthshire, who travelled with Farrer on his last expedition to China. Cox was to write about Farrer and plant hunting for an inter-war audience, effectively documenting the end of the age of adventure, which closed down completely in 1939. But E. H. M. Cox also wrote an interesting little book, *Wild Gardening*, in 1927, which filled the gap between alpine miniatures and rhododendron-frilled Cornish combes, and gave an insight into the real professionalism of a rising crowd of amateur gardeners. Cox's no-nonsense approach opens up the world of wild gardening which begins with a life-changing decision on finding a site: 'Look for an area where the contours are as broken as possible, so that you may have the choice of positions that face every point of the compass . . . An old quarry is excellent, not only for the variety it gives but also for the shelter, and the probability of first-class drainage, the latter with the possible exception of chalk.'[31] These quarry sites were more generally available than we might think now, for the Arts and Crafts revival of stone building had, with no restrictions on such things, opened up hundreds of one-house quarries, or holes in the ground, and these miniature estates of anything between five to fifty acres were now being broken up for development. Quarries were also fashionable; Miss Jekyll's plan for a sheltered garden for Lady Ridley in the quarry at Blagdon in Northumberland dates from this time, as does the beginning of Sir Frederick Stern's famous chalk quarry garden at Highdown near Worthing in Sussex. To return to Cox, 'A wood or broken ground would be my next choice, preferably with a gully, whether it contained water or not. If there are outcrops of rock, so much the better, but in all cases I should choose an area that for want of a better term I shall call knobbly. Knobbles present an infinite variety of situations, and they allow for definite areas being set aside for one group of plants ... the natural features of the ground make their best effect.'[32]

In his *Wild Gardening* Cox has identified the core ideal of a new kind of twentieth-century garden – that habitat, scientifically examined, is all, that differing habitats can be constructed, that they change and mature, and endless opportunities are opened up. Perhaps his most revolutionary phrase is, 'One of the features of the natural wild garden is that it is not meant to be filled at once; it is a playground to last for years.'[33] Here is Britain on the verge of the 1930s, a hundred years on from Biddulph Grange, two hundred on from Painshill, about to enter the last age of internationalism, to indulge in the creation of habitats in miniature for foreign plants, most especially rhododendrons, azaleas, Asiatic primulas and meconopsis, Mediterranean shrubs and alpines.

For many who would not take Mr Cox's amount of trouble, there were habitat manufacturers, capable of turning a suburban plot into the Himalaya – rather in the way that Sir Joseph Paxton had re-created the Strid from Bolton Abbey into the rockery at Chatsworth, and 'by some supernatural means, cut out a slice of one of the Derbyshire hills and transferred it to the spot'.[34] George G. Whitelegg was supreme among 1930s rockery builders, in the best tradition of Backhouse of York, Veitch's and the famous Pulhams (James Pulham was a decorative modeller in cement who invented Pulhamite, i.e. cemented brick rubble formed into blocks, very durable, lighter to use, and now beloved of rockery connoisseurs), winning Chelsea awards year after year (*Plate 44*). His exhibition rock gardens were sold and transported rock by rock to their new owners. Some owners were so enthusiastic that they bought rockeries year after year and added them one to another. In 1932 Mr Whitelegg described the making of a garden, preferably on a south-westerly facing slope, with background trees and good drainage, and his outline plan shows the highest portion in the centre. On the much-debated question of choosing stone (which had in those days nothing to do with environmental concerns), he wrote, 'Some say use the local stone; but if this is an ugly stone, why use it? Is it not permissible to improve on the product of the county – to take the beautiful product of one county to another ... I personally prefer the beautiful restful-coloured limestone from Cheddar ... another ... at the same time wonderfully laminated limestone is that which is found in North York-shire and in Westmoreland.'[35] When the rock had arrived the most interesting part was setting it out, keystones first, seeing the stratification right, connecting up the lines in the rocks, arranging turf at the approach, filling pockets with soil, grit, leaf-mould and lime where needed, and finally, the planting. One of Whitelegg's rock gardens was made in flat woodland at Sevenoaks, taking out about sixty trees to insert rocks in their place

Rockeries for alpines and azaleas were imported to thousands of suburban gardens in both professional (another famous alpinist and rock-garden maker was Clarence Elliott at Six Hills Nursery near Stevenage) and amateur hands, and this groundswell of popular enthusiasm for the exotic rose to match the private groves and combes of rhododendrons that had been established in grander circumstances.

Ever since the distribution of Joseph Hooker's rhododendrons from Kew in the 1850s, these gorgeous immigrants had been nestling into their new homes. Successes and failures, deaths and revivals of the species, the sublime giant *R. falconeri* or *R. griffithianum*, became a saga of greater than human importances, breeding turbulent rivalries and friendships as these wonders grew to great heights and flowered in hundreds of magnificent blooms. The passion funded expeditions for more; as the Veitches supported Wilson, A. K. Bulley of Ness in

Cheshire (now the Ness Botanic) 'sent out' George Forrest, and Sir John Ramsden of Muncaster in Cumbria subscribed to Kingdon Ward's trips. Collections were sold (Tregothan bought Canon Boscawen's from Lamorran,)[36] given (as Muncaster sent plants to Brodick to start the garden there) and fought over – rhododendron societies formed and foundered on argument and mistrust.[37] The lords of the rhododendron buried their rivalries and emerged into the limelight in the early 1930s in support of King George VI's and Queen Elizabeth's great project, to make a garden in Windsor Great Park. That royal bond, formed by Queen Victoria when the Prince Consort died so soon after planting the Wellingtonia at Kensington in 1861, flowered as the gardening monarchs and their friends, Lord Aberconway, Lionel de Rothschild, J. B. Stevenson of Tower Court, Ascot, Sir John Ramsden, George Johnstone of Trewithen and the Earl of Stair of Lochinch, formed a great fellowship to make first the Savill Garden, then after the war, the great sweeps of the rhododendron-filled Valley Gardens and the Kurume azalea 'Punchbowl'. This was more than gardening, it was social engineering, in part publicly funded, and thus the gardens have always been open for the public to enjoy. More than this it was a modern royal entertainment, or court masque, with serious purpose to cheer a nation when it needed it most.[38]

Old-style plant hunting ceased in the 1950s. Perhaps with Everest conquered in 1953 the bargaining ground for permits was monopolized by the expeditions to the mountains: on the lower slopes botany was complicated by tourism, regulations and local officialdom. Not that young men did not still have the urge to tread in giant's footsteps, often taking keen amateurs with them, and in the cases of Roy Lancaster, Peter Cox, Ron McBeath, Tony Schilling and Chris Grey-Wilson, doing useful work as well. But, along with some of the 'civilized' minds they left behind, the modern plant hunters developed a concern for the consequences of their actions, and with some mountaineers, have become the voices of conservation. Tony Schilling has written magnificently of '*Abies spectabilis* and *Betula utilis* wreathed in huge tattered strings of grey-green lichen' and the roses, rhododendrons, berberis and gentians of the mountain valleys around Thang-boche Monastery, of the stabilized moraine – coloured with polygonums, potentillas and dwarf rhododendrons – at the foot of the Khumbu glacier. At the end of the day he is left with the majesty of sterile rock and ice and 'an almost unreal silence . . . broken only by the periodic groan of over-burdened stone'. Schilling allowed himself a moment alone with 'the birth of a Himalayan night . . . I turned and looked back at Pumori's summit; a last pallor had taken its snows and the first of the moonlight was filtering along the ridges leading up to its summit cone',[39] and the inevitable conclusion that we, in a quest for knowledge (or in raiding the treasures) of these great wild places have threatened the pattern of their existence, producing problems that we now must solve.

The corrective is the reasoning behind the founding of the NCCPG, who have national collections of rhododendrons and azaleas (protecting and propagating what we have got) at Brodick, Bodnant, Sheffield Park, the Savill and Valley Gardens, Wentworth Castle, Heaselands and Inverewe, as well as in public gardens in Swansea and Richmond Park. The NCCPG also publicize plants by their countries of origin, particularly the Americas, New Zealand and South African genera, which have historic value as the older varieties fall foul of a vigorous commercial interchange which has operated for the last fifty years. The entrée to this new style of collecting is via the NCCPG's annual directory of opening times and visitor information regarding national collections, which includes the 'pink sheet' of rare and endangered garden plants. The exciting work is now to be done 'at home'.

CHAPTER SEVEN

>》-》-❄-く-くく

Science Lends a Hand

Apart from exploiting the great wildernesses of the world for plants, the other accusation levelled at gardeners concerns their close associations with botany and chemistry. This chapter was envisaged as a kind of 'Search for the Silent Spring', that is, a description of the garden history that led to Rachel Carson's book of 1962 and its indictment of the use of pesticides and herbicides, which implicated gardeners by association. This has proved to be a difficult story to find.

The chapter takes its title from a friendly book of 1939, *Science Lends a Hand in the Garden*, written by a retired Ministry of Agriculture scientist and ex-director of Wisley garden, Sir Frederick Keeble, in what it soon becomes clear was a falsely cheerful tone. Like so many eminent scientists Sir Frederick treats us like children. There will be more of *Science Lends a Hand* in a few pages, but now I think its title, even if it duped us all, is more than ever apt.

Before science there were old wives' remedies and, most important of all, lots of people. People were employed as slug pickers, rat catchers, garden boys, gamekeepers and weeding women, all doing their part in keeping pests at bay. King among them was the molecatcher, whose centuries-long duel with the little gentleman in the brown velvet waistcoat has found him a place in poetry and legend: the Molecatcher was the first to address Queen Elizabeth in a garden masque at Theobalds in 1591: 'I cannot discourse of knots and mazes, sure I am that the ground was so knotty that the gardener was amazed to see it, and as easy had it been, if I had not been, to make a shaft of a cammock (a crooked tree) as a garden of that croft.'[1] Molecatchers were well paid and full of curious knowledge: using red herrings cut up and burnt or smoking out with a brimstone mixture, stuffing the mole's entrance with onions and leeks, or training the cat or weasel to wait at the 'strait passage'. A last resort was to burn one victim alive so that its screams would frighten the others away – if only next door. Olive oil, a rarity, was hated by ants, who equally disliked burnt snail shells – as presumably did the snails – and much store was laid by the efficacy of red ochre and white chalk circles on the ground to protect precious plants and trees. Red ochre, butter and pitch made a deterrent as bark dressing, and it was known that mice objected to wild cucumber or bitter almonds made into balls with meal and oil, or that equally the ashes of a cremated weasel added to rows of seed would frighten them off. When all else failed there was a spell or prayer; the abbey of Bury St Edmunds was stocked with 'relics for rain and certain other superstitious uses for avoiding of weeds growing in corn'.[2] Science crept in gently: John Evelyn suggested pouring brandy into holes bored in tree roots for 'lousiness', or washing the bark with urine and vinegar twice a week for a month. Richard Bradley, first botany professor at Cambridge, advocated burning fires on the east sides of orchards and that mercury in a gimlet hole in fruit tree trunks would rid them of 'little white worms' – this at a time when mercury was used as a cure for worms in human beings. Thomas Hogg, a Paddington florist, suggested keeping a pheasant to eat the wireworms and, in 1830, a Mr Spence was offering three halfpence for every hundred of them caught by boys. An alternative was sowing mustard, which the wireworms did not like. The old shoe to attract earwigs was a favourite and long-lasting remedy, but a dried-out hoof hung on a stick was better. Tobacco water was bad for spider mite and thrips, and bruised laurel leaves, used to kill specimen butterflies for collectors without damaging them, also did for red spider mite and, as a powerful hallucinogenic and depressant, only too often for the gardeners who used this remedy.[3]

These excruciating delights have not faded yet: we still hang up dead crows to warn the others off and plastic windmills are seen everywhere on lawns. From William Cobbett to my mother, and to me until comparatively recently, the instant response to a plague of ants was a kettle of boiling water. These are the age-old practices of people in our benign cool temperate climate, which breeds no truly terrible pests, the natural interaction of people in garden and landscape. There is a strong argu-

Advertisements from *The Garden* and *Gardeners' Chronicle* of the late nineteenth and early twentieth century for proprietary garden chemicals.

ment, well represented in the most modern (and especially organic) gardening books, that most ills can be cured by good methods and management. In *An Essay on the Weeds of Agriculture* by Benjamin Holdich published in the early nineteenth century, with a frontispiece of great thistles, the dominant argument was that noxious weeds came from bad soil conditions and bad management, and most would succumb to good drainage, the addition of nutrients and hard work. The garden remains the ideal experimental ground for this philosophy, because the input of labour is still high and cleanliness and healthiness through strength of plants and well-fed soil can be maintained, especially with pavings and nettings and such wiles as companion planting.

If good practice was an old remedy, so has the chain of cause and effect long been understood: Daniel Defoe stressed the importance of keeping fertile and healthy pasture and fields, because every element of crop and beast made its way back into our lives and homes, down to horn for cutlery handles and soaps and glue. But equally there was always ambiguity, and different points of view: the *Complete Vermin-Killer*, a popular handbook in eighteenth-century towns, offered safe and quick methods for destroying almost every living small beastie, though did allow that a mix of arsenic and honey for ants should be kept away from children in a box, with holes pierced in it that were too small for bees. It also had remedies to kill bees; as weeds are flowers in the wrong place, so pests are unwanted honey-makers. The situation might have changed little, or much more slowly, had it not been for the need to develop commercially chemicals for the great mono-cultures, vines and cotton, and for malaria.

The background to the development of chemicals (which is very hard to find and certainly does not appear in gardening books) invariably begins with the Romans using sulphur as an insecticide and helleborine as a rat poison: nicotine, pyrethrum and veratrines also 'have been used since antiquity'.[4] Paris green (so prettily named) was the first deadly mix: copper aceto-arsenite, developed in the mid-1860s as a stomach poison for chewing insects, including Colorado beetles in potato crops. It was used in gardens, for leatherjackets and slugs, and 'improved' arsenicals, lead arsenate and calcium arsenate, were developed to kill cotton crop pests in America, though fully understood to be highly toxic to humans and animals and to persist in the soil. In France, Bordeaux Mixture, copper sulphate and lime, was used originally to prevent people stealing grapes from roadside vineyards, but demonstrated by Millardet in the 1880s to act as a fungicide against downy mildew on vines and against potato blight and fruit tree scab. Though it is harmful to fish, copper sulphate in strong solution is still recommended to gardeners as a weedkiller and to clear blanket weed and algae from the fishpond.[5]

Biological control is also not new: the first well-documented case dates from 1762 when a Mynah bird was taken from India to Mauritius to eat up locusts and, remarkable as it may seem, there is evidence from the 1770s of a bamboo runway laid between rows of orange and lemon trees to enable the ants to move more quickly to control the caterpillars. The first serious success came in the 1880s when ladybirds were used to control scale insect on Californian fruit trees: after this there was a heightened interest in biological controls, and also the use of pathogens, the spraying of insect diseases on to crops. This was tried in Russia and developed in Paris, the disadvantages being that the pathogens were difficult to manufacture, and the crops – cabbages or whatever – were full of insects' corpses. All these developments lost their momentum with the arrival of DDT.[6]

After the First World War, it is easy to forget, malaria was asserting itself as the most monstrous enemy of mankind.[7] It was endemic in many countries around the Mediterranean, including Italy (and the English Fens where babes in arms were given opium to counteract the fever) as well as throughout Africa and the tropics. Paris green was spread over mosquito swamps from aircraft in the 1920s, and a biological remedy, gambusia, a tiny fish which ate mosquito larvae, was introduced. These were only patchily effective, and it was in response to political determination, especially by Mussolini in Italy, that the Swiss chemists at J. R. Geigy were driven to the announcement that they had found 'the perfect insecticide', evaluated from hundreds of thousands of synthetic organic chemicals. This was dichlorodiphenyltrichloroethane, a house spray with 'staying power' which necessitated only infrequent use. It brought the cases of malaria in Italy down to an all-time low, but the disease's hold was re-established during the Second World War.

That war brought further political complications that were inevitably in the national interest. The government's involvement in the synthetic manufacture of nitrogen – by techniques largely wrested from the vanquished Germans after the First World War – was privatized into Imperial Chemical Industries in 1926. A company history, written by Julian Phillips, ascribes 'the inspiration for Britain's modern nitrogen industry' to Sir William Crookes' presidential address to the British Association in 1896 when he warned that 'starvation was inevitable' simply because the amount of land for agricultural production was insufficient for the rising population.[8] In 1939 this prophecy of doom resounded even more loudly: the supplies of Chilean guano for fertilizer would once again be cut off, the nitrogen-producing plants at home had to find capacity for explosive manufacture as well as fertilizers, and yet somehow Britain had to feed herself. The desirability of nitrogenous fertilizer became plainly obvious to all but the most reactionary farmers and gardeners: at Girton College, Cambridge, the highly professional Chrystabel Proctor was proud of her bright-green grass, clearly won as part of her cooperation with the neighbouring University Farm, which was in the front-line of the agricultural war.[9] But fertilizers alone were not enough and, in desperate measures that approached panic in scientific advisory quarters, DDT and its related synthetic chemicals, dieldrin and aldrin, were brought into the war effort. Many eminent scientists were sceptical and fearful, but the Ministry of Agriculture refused any controls, or to provide protective clothing, or even adequate information, in case it hampered the task of the British farmer and gardener in feeding the nation. DDT-based mixes were marketed for gardeners in the Dig for Victory campaign: the September 1943 *Farm Journal and Farmer's Wife* noted the arrival of a new word in the language – 'pesticide' (the old term had been pestology) – and it was universally imagined that a longed-for panacea had arrived.

It was into this context that *Science Lends a Hand in the Garden* was published, with Sir Frederick Keeble writing as if from his fireside at Fowey in Cornwall, to other gardeners by their firesides. He was partly saying 'look, how clever we are', and partly lulling them into a smiling acquiescence. He hopes his readers will glance at a chapter each evening, and that his words will produce a somnolent smile until bedtime 'is announced'. 'Gardens have brought me peace of mind when most I needed it', his preface concludes, 'may a little of it pass with this book into the hearts of others who need it too: and in these days are there any who do not?'[10]

Sir Frederick's background was distinguished: he was drafted in from Reading University to the RHS and to become director at Wisley in 1914, as the result of a memorandum he had in part produced supporting the scientific lobby within the Society (whose Scientific Committee had been formed in 1868 at the instigation of the Revd M. J. Berkeley). Wisley was already testing and trialing plants, dealing with nomenclature and educating students, but the new regime wanted a mycologist, chemist and entomologist as part of the garden's establishment. With some irony, science was to be housed in the most romantic of garden buildings, the Laboratory, a Surrey vernacular timber and tiled 'house' – so much in the Lutyens style that everyone thinks Lutyens designed it – by Pine-Coffin, Imrie and Angell, completed in 1916. Trials of sundries, especially those relating to pests and diseases, had been started in 1913 at the request of the Society's Fellows, and though some evaluation of knapsack sprayers had been done, these were soon discontinued as impractical.[11] In 1917 Sir Frederick Keeble was seconded to the Ministry of Agriculture's Food Production department: he resigned from the Society at the end of the war to become Sheridian Professor of Botany at Oxford.

Sir Frederick was therefore a scientist full of wisdom, and the perfect voice to lull simple gardening souls into the unquestioning acceptance of 'benefits' they did not understand. He begins by making the crime-ridden world of the virus sound amusing: 'Consider for example the innocent Violet . . . the Violet grows in tranquil purity until it chances, through no fault of its own to have Cucumbers for neighbours. The evil communications of the Cucumber corrupt the good, modest manners of the Violet, aphids act as go-betweens and inoculate the plants so that their petals are no longer pure in colour, but raddled mauve and white.'[12] That violets and cucumbers could never meet in their natural habitats has been 'overcome' by the ingenuity of science in the course of identifying the culprit aphids. (Quite why this was necessary remains a mystery, for this phenomenon was the 'breaking' of tulips, which William Hanbury had announced as a 'disease' in 1770.) Science continues to lend a hand in this way, with Sir Frederick's jolly introductions to organic and chemical fertilizers, vitamins and hormones, plant genetics and 'vernalization' – the forcing of early growth – and all the implications of the scientific frontier brought to the gardener's fireside. At such a time of trial as the opening of the 1940s, every gardener who read this book, or part of it, or one of its constituent articles in the *Gardeners' Chronicle*, must have only too readily accepted the chemist and geneticist as an ally and friend.

Another dimension of the scientist's well intentioned but disastrous role as a friendly gardener-uncle is personified in Professor Geoffrey Blackman, lecturer in Ecology at Imperial College, London, from 1935 to 1945, and sometime associate editor of the *Chronicle*. In an article in 1937 he identified the difference between horticulture and ecology, the first the study of plants in a man-made environment, the second the study of life untouched by man. Though scientists were working on wildernesses at continental scale, he wrote, there were lessons for gardeners.

Blackman's own war work was at the forefront of government policies with research on plant nutrition, introducing sunflowers as an oilseed crop and the development of selective weedkillers. He was to regret that it was his work that destroyed the traditional poppies in cornfields (and in post-war road schemes he insisted they should be part of the mixture for verges). Blackman also developed the rubber industry in Malaya, using hormones to increase the flow of latex from the trees, and after the war in Vietnam he advised on the aftermath of the military use of defoliants. He personifies the scientist as both patriarch and destroyer: he was also proud of his garden on Boar's Hill, outside Oxford, where he grew rhododendrons and had wild woods full of bluebells. Neither Keeble nor Blackman were evil geniuses, in fact they were the opposite, wise servants in a time of national need and emergency. If only they had refrained from opening their Pandora's boxes in front of their fellow gardeners. If only they could have foreseen that the necessary evils of war contingencies worked upon continental scales could not be harmlessly applied in the miniature plot. But they were gardeners, as well as scientists, and it seems that the fellowship of gardening overcame their – and many of their colleagues' – doubts, and prompted them to introduce their friends to the devil.

The assimilation of complex pesticides into garden use over the last fifty years has proved to be dangerous simply because the garden is the green, private space of home in which any level of skill is acceptable, even the lowest. There is an analogy with all the well-aired arguments over the presence of the television in the living-room: the technological invader might be a source of enlightenment, but its worldliness can be a threat, too, to the securities of 'home'. With pesticides, even in weakened solution, introduction into the minutely interactive garden realm is often like sledge-hammering a hazelnut: gardens are where children and pet animals play, they are closest to the domestic sewage system and consequently the water supply, and they are the primary feeding ground of

"As sure as God's in Gloucestershire"

This lovely old saying recalls the days when there were twice as many religious houses in Gloucestershire as in any other county in England. "It's as long coming as Cotswold barley" is another ancient Gloucestershire proverb which, says Francis Grose ("Collection of Local Proverbs", 1787) "is applied to such things as are slow but sure. The corn in this cold country on the Woulds," he says, "exposed to the winds, bleak and shelterless, is very backward at the first and afterwards overtakes the forwardest in the county, if not in the barn, in the bushel, both for the quantity and the goodness thereof".

Words and phrases change with time. But "Fisons" means the same thing always — and to everybody, everywhere. Fisons, with its 20 factories and their auxiliary distributing centres, covers the whole country. The factory at Avonmouth, one of the main producing units, supplies the requirements of South Wales and the South Western Counties.

It's Fisons for Fertilizers

The Times, 19 August 1945, next to the cricket reports and an advertisement for Jaguar cars is the attractive 'Fisons for Fertilizers', equating the use of chemicals with all that is most traditional and fondly regarded in the countryside.

urban birds, insects and wild animals. Over time amateur gardeners, learning from the professional gardeners of the past, have brought chemicals into garden use with habitual disregard for the dangers. In January 1946 the most popular guru of the day, the *Sunday Express*'s Adam the Gardener, a strip cartoon, was spreading the arsenical Paris green, one part to twenty-four parts coarse bran ('wash hands after mixing') to kill the 'millipedes' in his soil; an indiscrimate slaughter of the good and the bad, but also evidence that the expectation of chemical aids in the garden was endemic. Post-war gardeners, worn out with digging for victory, needing to grow food in a dismally rationed society, demanded and deserved, at least as far as the Ministry of Food was concerned, the helpful chemicals developed for agriculture and wartime necessity. The popular 1950s Penguin handbook on roses advocated dusting and spraying with DDT as the accepted practice of the day. DDT was followed into the garden by organo-phosphate insecticides, including malathion and fenitrothion, and (although we cared not to differentiate between good and bad insects, we were confident that there were good and bad plants) the selective phenoxyacetic herbicides such as 24-D and MCPA. The fact that the nettles and thistles that we might despise were so necessary for butterflies did not enter into our heads. There was a post-war concern that the spraying of roadside verges, enthusiastically adopted by local authorities to cut down labour costs, was a major threat to wildlife, and controls were instigated. But gardens were too small to enter into the minds of conservationists, who were beginning to coordinate campaigns on habitat conservation (creating the Nature Conservancy in 1949) and combine fears about soil erosion, failure of fertility, pollution and chemically based agriculture (which led to the founding of The Soil Association in 1945).

Rachel Carson's *The Silent Spring* was first published in America in 1962: its principle impact was to ring the alarm bells among the public over the use of DDT in agriculture. But in chapter eleven, 'Beyond the dreams of the Borgias', she addresses the garden: 'Gardening is now firmly linked with the super poisons. Every hardware, garden supply store ... has rows of insecticides for every conceivable horticultural situation. Those who fail to make wide use of this array of lethal sprays and dusts are by implication remiss, for almost every newspaper's garden page and the majority of garden magazines take their use for granted

... little is done to warn the gardener that he is handling extremely dangerous materials' and a constant stream of gadgets made it ever 'easier'. Carson quotes a doctor whom she knew who used DDT and malathion in weekly applications with a hand spray or hose attachment, until one day he collapsed: he was subsequently diagnosed with permanent nerve damage and muscular weakness due to the accretive effect of the malathion.[13]

Largely because of the furore over *The Silent Spring*, followed by evidence of contaminated water supplies and proof of havoc caused in the food chains of tropical lizards, DDT was banned in America in 1971. It was subject to a voluntary ban here from 1974 to 1984 and removed from the market in line with the Control of Pesticides Regulations of 1986: dieldrin and aldrin were banned in 1989. The desire of gardeners for success at all costs, however, ensured that there would be alternatives, and garden chemicals flowered as big business. The chemical manufacturers quite understandably saw themselves as the gardeners' friends, and the intense cultivation of a 'low maintenance' fashion and philosophy, which implied that only fools laboured in their gardens, allied to the desirability of 'leisure' as well as an iridescently green-striped lawn, supported this view. From the chemical companies' point of view the long and expensive development programmes that were necessary prior to the debut of any product, now further lengthened and increasingly complicated by the testings and monitorings that the law demanded, gave them a place of honour in the garden world. It was a position further justified when they let it be known that only about one-tenth of the 'novel compounds' identified by research entered commercial use, and by the publication of such books as *Pesticides: Boon or Bane*, by a former ICI man M. B. Green in 1976. This opened the argument by unrestrained illustration of the horrible scabbings, swellings and eruptions of diseased humans, animals and plants[14]: there was little one could object to after hearing how pesticides had rescued us from a similar fate.[15]

The question remains – should chemicals with a killing power of epidemic proportions, that can defoliate whole jungles, even in their toxicity-reduced forms that are supposed to make them unskilled-user-friendly, be in our gardens at all? This was a question that history has overlooked, and it now seems impossible that it will be answered. The chemical industry has been completely reorganized and re-packaged in the last twenty years or so, since the early 1980s and the rise of environmental consciousness. Media-friendly names like Miracle or Gem or Solaris, all meaningless and amorphously harmless, now front the manufacture of over 200 different garden chemicals, names shorn of any pasts by takeovers and re-groupings, so that no one has to answer for the nasty old connections any more. The manufacturers' trade association, the British Agrochemicals Association, issues an excellent booklet of which the first twenty-seven pages – almost one-third of the whole – are devoted to explanations of good practice and safe procedures. If the safety procedures are this complex (and clearly twenty-seven pages' worth does not get on to every packet) should we really be playing with them in gardens? Every gardener should have this booklet* and every gardener should also notice that amongst the 'over two hundred' products listed there are 'sheep dip' and 'Gulf War' organo-phosphates 24-D and MCPA. It is also worrying that this is still an evolving maelstrom: my copy came with an extra leaflet on the withdrawal of Roseclear as no longer approved for use by amateur gardeners. 'A regulatory reclassification following a recent routine review of data on potential eye irritation' has now brought Roseclear's ten years of wide use in our gardens to an end. The withdrawal notice has a regretful tone towards the 'blackening' of the reputation of 'the leading product', on which the pack labels have always warned of such dangers when the liquid was undiluted: some '40 million applications of Roseclear have shown a maximum of 4 reports of such problems' since 1982, is the manufacturer's rather hurt statement.[16] One is left more concerned than ever, for where is the sense of a ban on such flimsy evidence? Are the '4 reports' just the tip of an iceberg? How can the simple gardener believe anyone?

No doubt there are hundreds of thousands of half-bottles of Roseclear still in garden sheds: we no longer pour them down the drain with abandon, but neither do we deposit them into the safe keeping of the local environmental centre. They await a doomsday scenario that is clearly so widely accepted that it has found its way into a comic strip: the *Beano*'s Calamity James was recently sent out to cut the back lawn

---

* Free upon request from BAA, 4 Lincoln Court, Lincoln Road, Peterborough, PE1 2RP.

– deprived of the motor-mower, defeated by the scythe, he dashed into the garden shed to where the Weedo killer was next to the Jungle grower. In haste he grabbed the wrong bottle and was soon swinging, Tarzan-style, amongst his garden jungle.[17]

Such fears about the effects of chemicals in our lives are nothing new: in the early years of the eighteenth century Richard Bradley and William Derham had identified what we call the food chain, what Derham called 'a curious Harmony and just Proportion between the increase of all Animals, and the length of their Lives', and Linnaeus elaborated the trajectories of predators and their prey to express a balance in nature kept by the natural reproductive capacities of each species.[18] Unfortunately the implication of divine intervention in such chains and balances meant that they fell foul of evolutionary thinking: it was rather as if creation had to be blown asunder and put together again in neat academic disciplines, which slowly and with painstaking deliberations emerged from their several dark tunnels to pronounce 'ecology' as the science of interactive nature, officially invented in 1893. Dr J. T. Wrench's book, *The Wheel of Health*, focused attention in 1938 on researches into human, plant and animal nutrition and the links between them and 'also gave an account of certain human communities which all possessed a full measure of sound health, the only common factor between them being a diet of indigenous natural whole food grown from naturally treated soil, or culled from the sea'. This book, and Dr Wrench himself, eventually became part of Lady Eve Balfour's experiments at Haughley in Suffolk which developed what we know as organic farming and the founding of the Soil Association. Lady Eve's philosophy of 'living in harmony not only with our own species but with all others' determined her attitude to the soil, which was a universe within itself, dependent upon a food chain of decay and renewal and a resulting balance. 'Soil is a mixture of disintegrating mineral rock and humus, with its population of micro-organisms', she wrote in *The Living Soil*:

> The two are inter-mingled, and growth and reproduction cannot long be maintained under natural conditions in the absence of humus. Besides growth-promoting substances which it contains, humus gives soil its texture, its stability and much of its water-retaining capacity. A product of the decomposition of animals

and vegetable residues brought about through the agency of micro-organisms, humus is far from dead in the sense of having returned to the inorganic world. It is still organic matter, in the transition stage between one form of life and another.

This is why Lady Eve's experimental farming at Haughley was called 'organic': the word also applies to any chemical compound which contains carbon, which is why so many agricultural chemicals have the similar prefix, causing unlimited confusion and misunderstanding. With the present increased profile of organic farming and produce, and the magic O sprinkled ever more widely over the supermarket shelves, it seems hopeful that Lady Eve Balfour's meaning will win the day.[19]

Though many gardeners were early members of the Soil Association, a parallel cause in compost was pioneered by Dr W. E. Shewell-Cooper and The Good Gardeners' Association at Arkley Manor near Barnet. Dr Shewell-Cooper gardened at Arkley from the early 1950s, without chemicals and without digging, hoeing or forking: like Lady Eve he believed in the power of humus for a healthy soil, and that composting of garden and household rubbish produced the necessary ingredients. He had studied ancient methods of minimal cultivation and believed that modern gardeners would appreciate not having to deep and double dig, which was itself a harmful process. Cultivation to little more than an inch depth was necessary for seed sowing, and a mulch of compost one-inch thick over flower beds and borders suppressed weeds, was the delight of worms and other good citizens of the region, and relieved the gardener of hoeing. The worms did all the soil engineering, and the gardener merely repeated the layerings of compost. An important factor was avoiding soil compression, with as little walking on the soil as possible, encouraging the design of reachable beds and plots divided by pavings.[20] The No Dig Garden, run on Dr Shewell-Cooper's lines, has many loyal adherents, and it is one of the methods demonstrated at the Ryton Organic Gardens at Ryton-on-Dunsmore, near Coventry (*Plate 13*). These educational and display gardens were opened in 1986 by the Henry Doubleday Research Association, the largest organic organization in Europe, which also more recently developed the Yalding Organic Gardens near Maidstone in Kent. Organic gardening demands, and inspires, a forensic interest in details of climate, micro-climate and the soil which is wholly infectious: the challenge of good compost making soon matches any sporting or artistic goal. The home garden becomes its own recycling centre; there is little that cannot be composted – except plastic, glass and metal – and cardboard, old clothes, newspapers and perennial weeds can all be assimilated with caution and judicious amounts of 'activators' i.e. fresh manures or herbal commercial products. Ryton's display is composter's heaven, with all the techniques to be examined and results assessed, and a shop for supplies. The Organic Display Gardens have been endorsed by the late and much-lamented Geoff Hamilton of BBC TV *Gardener's World* and the Ryton restaurant, serving organic produce, praised by Derek Cooper, of Radio Four's radical, campaigning *Food Programme*, with 'If organic food tastes this good, let's make the future organic.'[21]

An organic future seems to bring the fun back into gardening, not the least because each of us can feel we count, and can make a difference. (You can apparently, even pee on the compost, and use activator immediately, to save flushing the lavatory.) Composting helps alleviate another gardening crime in environmental terms, the commercial digging of peat on a large scale. Sedge peat and sphagnum moss were increasingly marketed to gardeners for soil improving and mulching as farmyard manures, 'shoddy' woollen waste, sewage sludge and hop waste became less available or less to the liking of town gardeners, who used their weekly-washed cars as transport. Peat was 'perfect', clean, light to carry, and safe to use. The environmentalists protested against the result-ant uncontrolled digging, first in Holland, and then in Ireland, where eventually a halt was called and the National Peatlands Conservation Council is now an influential voice. Sometimes gardeners can be stead-fastly stubborn, and though it seems these protests have been going on for a long time, only very recently has Wisley carried out trials into the alternatives, published in the June 1997 issue of the *Garden*.[22] Using sphagnum moss peat as a control, the alternatives of coconut fibre and various mixes of compost were all found to be 'capable of supporting satisfactory plant growth' as long as allowances were made for the dif-fering character (texture and drainage characteristics) of the mixes. The trials were done because 'Gardeners continue to be concerned about the use of peat in horticulture' (as if those concerns might or perhaps should conveniently de-materialize) which confirms my prejudice that there is more environmentally friendly gardening among the lower than the higher echelons of the establishment.[23]

A rather more cheerful aspect of science in the garden concerns herbalism, and the wider flourishing interest in the cultivation and use of herbs, extending into aromatherapy, herbal medicine, natural therapies and cookery which informs present-day herb gardening. The Herb Society, which celebrated its seventieth anniversary in 1997, was founded by Hilda Leyel, born Hilda Wauton, the daughter of a master at Uppingham, who was taught botany during her childhood by Uppingham's pioneering head, Dr Edward Thring. Hilda Wauton married the Swiss theatrical manager, Carl Frederick Leyel, had two sons and did a great deal for hospital charities, before she was widowed in 1926. Looking for a consoling interest she found old herbals, a subject then being revived by Eleanour Sinclair Rohde, and with the practical help of Maude Grieve of The Whins Medicinal and Commercial Herb School and Farm at Chalfont St Peter, Mrs Leyel produced *A Modern Herbal* and formed The Society of Herbalists, with a shop at Culpeper House, No. 10 Baker Street, officially opened on St Valentine's Day 1927. 'Success was instantaneous,' wrote Mrs Leyel, 'the sight of an attractive herbalist's shop in the centre of London seems to revive memories of childhood colds cured by blackcurrant tea, of the healing properties of many herbs, and of walks in old physic gardens.'[24] This success lasted until the Pharmacy Act of 1941 regulated the counter sales of medicines and effectively outlawed herbal medicine and the practice of consulting herbalists: Mrs Leyel reorganized the Society so that prospective patients could become members and receive treatment, and she kept things going in this way until she became ill in 1953. She died in 1957.

Mrs Leyel's story explains the rises and falls in the popularity of herb gardening. The renewed interest sprang from Alicia Amherst's researches into medieval gardening for her *History* of 1895, which were expanded by Gertrude Jekyll's lavish and consistent use of rosemary, lavender, rue, sages, anchusa, mullein, monarda (bergamot) and valerian in scented plantings. When asked, as at Knebworth House and Barrington Court, Miss Jekyll designed old-style formal herb gardens; many of her small gardens for King Edward VII Hospital at Midhurst were scented, therapeutic gardens, and she grew a selection of herbs for sale from her nursery at Munstead Wood.

Margaret Boden's plan for a Herb Garden originally drawn for *The Times* and reproduced here from *The Studio Gardens & Gardening Annual*, 1940.

Eleanour Sinclair Rohde's herb garden at Lullingstone Castle in Kent for Lady Hart-Dyke was very celebrated, and provided the inspiration, along with her love of Shakespeare and all the plants he mentioned, for Vita Sackville-West's yew enclosed small herb collection at

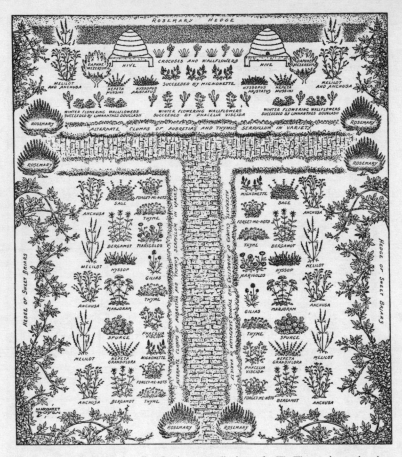

Margaret Boden's plan for a Bee Garden originally drawn for *The Times* and reproduced here from *The Studio Gardens & Gardening Annual*, 1940. Both plans are self-explanatory, but their appearance in such prominent places symbolizes the 1930s revival of herbs and herb gardening, as well as wartime remembrance of old remedies and comforts.

Sissinghurst, made in the 1930s. With the Pharmacy Act and banning of herbalism, herbs not only went out of general fashion, but became faintly disreputable, a notion which would have spurred Vita to greater efforts when her herb garden was restored after the war. But cooking, too, was reviving with Constance Spry (*Come Into the Garden, Cook* of 1942) and Rosemary Hume en route to *Cordon Bleu*, Mrs Leyel's own *The Gentle Art of Cookery*, with Miss Olga Hartley (1947), and Elizabeth David's *Book of Mediterranean Food* of 1950. Almost the only specialist herb farm was at Seal in Kent, where an energetic, down-to-earth member of the Plymouth Brethren, Dorothy Hewer (who had done great things for the recognition and respectability of herbs before the war, only to have them 'outlawed'), was still growing, accompanied by Margaret Brownlow. The latter led the post-war revival of herbs, with exhibits at Chelsea, her own books, including *Herbs and the Fragrant Garden* of 1957, and her making and planting of a large ornamental herb garden and a thyme lawn at Knole.[25] The Medicines Act of 1968 lifted the veil from herbalism, and allowed the emergence of the related remedial practices using herbs and oils: Mrs Leyel's Culpeper shops, although no longer in the Herb Society's ownership, were re-vitalized and expanded to provincial towns and cities. The products and information that issued forth from Claire Loewenfeld and Phillipa Back at the Chiltern Herb Farms all contributed to a wide and enthusiastic revival of the use of herbs in cookery and home remedies.

Growing herbs appealed even to non-gardeners as a useful and minimalist kind of gardening, which could perfectly well be carried on in window boxes or in pots on a balcony or beside the back door. The gradual revival of Gertrude Jekyll's planting ideas, steeped in her profound love for the Mediterranean countries she travelled in her youth, brought her favourite plants back to the nurseries and garden centres, and thus into gardens. Miss Jekyll is most lyrical on her favourites in 'the aromatic class, where they seem to have a wholesome resinous or balsamic base, with a delicate perfume added. When I pick and crush in my hand a twig of Bay, or brush against a bush of Rosemary, or tread upon a tuft of Thyme, or pass through incense-laden brakes of Cistus, I feel that here is all that is best and purest and most refined, and nearest to poetry, in the range of faculty of the sense of smell.'[26] The popularity of Mediterranean holidays transformed the idea of herb growing into a sensual reality, and what better way to embalm happy memories than in scented plants?

One of the deeper satisfactions of herbs, as the botanist and sometime Curator of Chelsea Physic Garden, Allen Paterson, pointed out, was their ecological neatness. He writes of the 'classic' rosemary and her relatives:

> This family is the Labiatae, in turn a classic herb family. It includes all the herbs which, with rosemary, immediately come to mind – lavenders, mints, savories, marjorams, thymes, sages. All, it will be noticed, are referred to in the plural: all are Mediterraneans, evocative of their home with their scented leaves, and their tight narrow-foliaged greyness. They are evocative too of old-fashioned English gardens which perfectly provide the conditions – as far as northern gardens can – which make such plants feel at home. These are essentially protection from cold winds for the top growth, perfect drainage at the root and full sun for both. Only mints are moisture lovers. All these conditions are exactly what Philip Miller (then in charge of the Chelsea Botanic Garden) was recommending 250 years ago.[27]

Allen Paterson pursues the Labiates which include almost forty out of around 300 garden herbs, a proportion only approached by the Umbelliferae: parsley, caraway, coriander and chervil. The Labiatae are centred upon the Mediterranean: 'of the forty labiate herbs only three (lemon verbena and bergamot native to South and North America respectively, and basil, originally from India) do not grow wild in some or all of the countries with a Mediterranean coastline', though half of them are in the British flora by adoption. 'How convenient for the plants that, as the Dissolution deprived the (Beaulieu) Abbey herb garden of its monkish gardeners, so too was the fabric of the great building deprived of its masons, thus providing in its decay perfect homes for these sun-loving subshrubs.' The Labiates' range of tolerance is also convenient for the herb garden, with southerners like white horehound and catmint needing sun, while the mints, self-heal and bugle 'really are northerners and become plants of wooded uplands as they go south' and will therefore flourish in the shadier parts of the herb plot.[28] The Umbellifers are also happy in the shade. Thus science meets culture and the sunny enchantment that the Mediterranean has long held for us chilly northerners: the notions of the scented gardens of the Middle East and the healing refuges of the monastic gardens, all come tumbling forward in time to combine into the goodnesses of growing herbs.

The final fillip to herb revival came in the marvellously coincidental timing of Rosemary Verey's emergence as a gardener at Barnsley House in Gloucestershire, where the design of her herb beds of box-hedged triangles and diamonds and her scented knot garden of box and germander 'threadings' surrounded by a rosemary hedge was informed by her collection of herbals and antique gardening books. Through her many bestselling books, her television programmes and her much-visited garden, Rosemary Verey has become a most influential gardening voice of the late twentieth century, perhaps even more influential in America and Australia than here at home. She, her husband David Verey and their young family had come to Barnsley House in 1951 with no time for gardening: ten years later 'he reminded me that I had grassed over most of his parents' borders to make wide open spaces for cricket, croquet and even ponies' she wrote, admitting that she had always intended one day to reinstate the plants and, now 'suddenly that day had come'.[29] Barnsley, a lovely late seventeenth-century house of honey-coloured stone, had the bones of a dignified garden: Rosemary Verey had an enquiring mind, ever prompted by David Verey's gentle architectural historian's expertise which guided her explorations. She cultivated a fine eye for plantings which she viewed with a covetousness, tinged with wonder in other gardens – 'mounds of purple sage with dark red tulips . . . with velvety-red Tuscany roses . . . apple green hart's tongue ferns between grey hostas . . . Those circular pools of grey and gold carpeting under old apple trees at Powis Castle, rue and golden marjoram, lamium and creeping jenny – one day they would be adopted in our garden.'[30] This mouth-watering sense of wonder has inspired her gardening and her garden writing, and her ability to both trawl the limitless wonders of things seen in the present and use them in the secure context of the past has been the essence of her appeal to a nostalgic gardening public. Through her knowledge of Parkinson and Gerard and early botanical books her plantsman's knowledge has a sound base in that distant time of treasures which allows her to cull and choose wisely from present plenty: her famous decorative vegetable garden at Barnsley, which has inspired the popular revival of rosy cabbages and ruby chard and thousands of imitations, was made in the early 1980s from a seventeenth-century layout in William Lawson's *Country Housewife's Garden*.

Rosemary Verey's historicist approach, the revival of herb growing as well as the general rise of conservation and 'green' thinking, have brought about the present appreciation of the 'physick' and 'herball' approach of early scientific gardeners, which adds a sense of curiosity to gardening. To satisfy this many of the old botanic gardens now find themselves with a new popularity: no continental garden tour is complete without a visit to Pisa or Padua (which vie to be the oldest, both founded in the 1540s) or Leiden (1587) or the Jardin des Plantes in Paris (1635). In Britain it is Oxford that holds the palm; founded in 1621 and still the epitome of a learned garden, it is funded exclusively by the university, still aids teaching and research and is still visibly loyal to its ordered plan: entered by its Inigo Jones gateway, walled, secure in sight of Magdalen's Tower, and open to the public. Oxford's Botanic Garden is a living textbook, the kind much sought after by gardeners bewildered by mis-labellings in nurseries and garden centres: it possesses an academic certainty ever more precious in a world where names change with confusing frequency, and has been described as possessing 'a lyrical spirituality, somehow removed from time . . . one can walk and contemplate the plants with serenity, secure in the knowledge that the wilderness is excluded, and experience "the subtle psychological nexus between the Garden Spirit and the soul of Universities and Academies – the classic and sacred Groves of Thought, Learning".'[31]

Much of the same precious sense of botanical retreat reigns at Chelsea Physic Garden, where one walks in the sacred footsteps of John Evelyn, Sir Hans Sloane and his appointee, the great transforming curator Philip Miller, Peter Kalm, William Forsyth and William Curtis, founder of *The Botanical Magazine* in 1787, which still goes strong. Chelsea Physic is still essentially 'the Apothecaries' Garden of simples' that Evelyn saw, it is small and has only restricted opening: because of where it is, and the residence of Rosemary Alexander's English Gardening School in the old laboratories since 1983, it has become a fashionable haven, a return to sanity from the mayhem of the Chelsea Flower Show just along the Royal Hospital Road. More astute London gardeners know also of the tiny retreat of Hume's South London Botanical Institute at 323 Norwood Road, SE24, founded by Allan Octavian Hume in 1910, with its extensive library, herbarium, Edwardian atmosphere and tiny ordered garden. Hume specialized in polygonums, a small plant generating great recent taxonomic debate concerning their re-grouping into *Persicaria, Fallopia, Fagopyrum* and only a rump named *Polygonum*, with most garden desirables being *Persicaria* (the former *Polygonum persicaria* being regarded as a weed). Prettier name though it might be, the internecine hostilities between those who name and those who grow have not abated!

The term 'botanical garden' has also expanded since the seventeenth century as enquiring science (or commercial exploits) discovered ever more and larger specimens that needed more spacious and varied habitats. Rectangular order beds gave way to borders and shrubberies, and especially to rockeries and glasshouses. The Royal 'Botanics' in Edinburgh, the second oldest after Oxford, moved out of the city to Inverleith in the early 1820s. Whole trees, the largest a forty-foot weeping birch, were dug up and trailed through the streets on William McNab's transplanting machine. (Transplanting ever larger trees has been an obsession since the invention of the wheel – from ancient Egypt and Queen Hatshepsut's vain attempt to bring incense trees from Somalia to adorn her temple to a concerted stream of nurserymen and head gardeners' patent inventions.) The Edinburgh Botanic claims the largest and most comprehensive of rock gardens, a miniature Himalaya constructed in the rockery heyday of the early 1900s, endorsing rather than pioneering scientific habitat creation which was – as we have seen – vastly popular in the gardening world. Arguably the earliest habitats were created indoors, in the great glasshouses such as the Palm House at Kew built in the 1840s. This kind of habitat display remains one of the greatest attractions of botanic gardens, not the least because the Victorian plant houses have become valued and invariably listed buildings in their own right, sometimes in disregard of their environmental efficiency. Decimus Burton's Palm and Temperate Houses and the exquisite Water Lily House, all magnificently restored at Kew, can induce an addictive passion for plants in such settings – which can be indulged via some equally marvellous but less known buildings throughout Britain, to the Kibble Palace, no less, at Glasgow Botanic, and beyond. Glasshouses as vegetable zoos, homes to ancient palms and personable dicksonias, as well as ever-changing displays to fire window-sill ambitions as at Cambridge University's more modest but endearing stove and tropical houses, are the very temples of garden passion. And scientific dissatisfaction with the old temples has given modern glass-loving architects a field day with technological innovation in tensile steel, beginning with the Princess of Wales Conservatory at Kew and the vast new glasshouses at Edinburgh.

The wonders of scientific collections are even greater when they are not protected by glass: Tresco in the Scilly Isles is perhaps expectedly exotic, but Edinburgh Botanic's Logan garden on the Rhinns of Galloway is more so – here seen through the wondering eyes of the Lanning Roper in the 1950s – a full-blown miracle of a garden, warmed by the moist airs across the Gulf Stream and protected from major gales. Avenues of dracaenas, of *Chamaerops excelsa* palms, with cordylines and embothriums, New Zealand flax (then a stranger here) and *Strelitzia reginae* all at home. Familiar plants grew to giant size, shoulder-high candelabra primulas, tree-like hydrangeas and giant olearias, and then with all these unbelievable sights and more 'one of the most delightful combinations of flowers' he had ever seen: 'In June there was a mass of *Calceolaria violacea*, which was at least 5ft tall, and completely smothered with little bells, mauve without and spotted with violet within . . . against this mauve background there were fine blue *Meconopsis betonicifolia*, candelabra primulas, in all the shades of pink and mauve, a particularly fine, rich wine-coloured one known as Logan's Purple, a film of mauve thalictrum, *Polemonium alba* and the clear apricot and strong wine-purple of violas.'[32]

At the other extreme are the arboreta – John Claudius Loudon's Derby Arboretum designed in 1839 as the first public park for both educational and recreational purposes, the cathedral-like groves of Bedgebury in Kent for conifer-lovers, Wilfred Fox's Winkworth in Surrey and Sir William Holford's autumn colours at Westonbirt, the last two now belonging to the National Trust.

The final phase of scientific gardens started with Victorian philanthropy – the site for Derby Arboretum was given by Joseph Strutt – and has continued well into the twentieth century with donations, public–private partnerships and civic societies. Bristol's Bracken Hill belonged to the Wills tobacco family, Liverpool's Ness Botanic on the Wirral was given by the daughter of A. K. Bulley, the Liverpool cotton broker who financed Forrest and Kingdon Ward and founded Bees Seeds especially to supply working-class gardeners. Leicester University has an accumulation of fabulous Arts & Crafts gardens, including a most splendid rocky ravine, which were formerly the private gardens of

an extraordinary society of successful industrialists including the God-
dards, of silver-polish fame. Aberdeen's was started in 1898 by Miss
Anne Cruickshank and Birmingham University's School of Continuing
Studies has Winterbourne, originally the home of John Nettlefold and
his wife Margaret (who was a Chamberlain) which was given to the
university in 1941 by the then owner J. M. Nicholson. (Birmingham
also has the Botanical Society garden; the two are near neighbours in
Edgbaston.) There are many more gardens, tightly or loosely connected
with scientific research (Hull University's is a working garden, Durham's
is eighteen low-maintenance acres which seem little different from a
park) up and down Britain. It is difficult not to conclude that they are,
when reviewed like this, a vast and under-rated treasure, mostly visited
by people who treat them as parks. Upon closer inspection most have
– from my immediate experience of Ness and Leicester, Cambridge and
Winterbourne – devoted Friends and volunteers, many of them keen
gardeners who value botanical and horticultural heritage, and social
heritage, too, rather more than the university authorities. Endless cuts
in university funding, the bio-diversification of botany so that it hardly
exists and the post-environmental revolution decades have brought many
botanic gardens to a sad state, excluded from the general gardening
bonanza.[33] Looking across at America, where British botanists and their
fellows have toured in rather open-eyed wonder for the last fifteen
years, they see great glittering enterprises like the New York or Chicago
Botanic Gardens who have mounted mega-campaigns and attracted
millions of dollars from prestigious sponsors for restoring glasshouses
and garden features and running public education programmes. The
nineteenth-century New York Botanic Garden has marketed its historical settings as the smart venue for all kinds of events, which draws an
affluent crowd to its unfashionable location in the Bronx, north of
Manhattan across the Harlem river. But it has also promoted an imaginative interpretation of 'applied botany', from aromatherapy and alternative medicine, through all the horticultural and floral arts, to soil science
and 'beasties' and almost to zoology, to a complete cross-section of New
York's teeming population, young and old. The Chicago Botanic Garden
is extensive and comparatively new, laid out in the last fifty years, but
it has developed an enormous popularity as a centre for everyone interested in almost any aspect of plant life, which results in its profile as

an upbeat and wholly pleasurable community service. Chicago is especially noted for authentic Japanese, Italian and even English gardens made as cultural history experiences for the multi-racial community. Most recently it has been in the forefront of recalling the prairie grasslands of the mid-west, a natural heritage which has all but disappeared.

American botanic gardens have also been through their Disneyland phase, they have re-invented dinosaurs, erected Climatrons (a high-tech name for a plastic greenhouse) to recreate exotic jungles and ice deserts, but these soon go out of fashion. There has been a long heart-searching as to whether botanic gardens that go so far to reach public appreciation remain scientific institutions at all, even though they are teaching science rather than initiating it. The high-minded foundations, such as Harvard's Arnold Arboretum, which are still involved in major research projects on medicinal extracts or crop technologies on the international scale, can afford to look askance at more provincial gardens which serve a local rather than global need.

In Britain this crisis of identity seems to have numbed most gardens into merely being, rather than growing. It would be logical to assume they had an important role in National Collections, but only a few appear as holders: Leicester has the aubretias and some lawsonia (a comical mix in terms of scale), Harlow Car, the Northern Horticultural Society's successful garden (with no identity crisis at all), has the callunas, and Cambridge and Kew have several collections each.[34] National Collection enthusiasts seem to be attached more to horticultural colleges than botanical gardens: and here the display gardens and public education role seems fulfilled by Wisley and Rosemoor, or the Ryton Organic Gardens, or the commercial exuberance of Bridgemere Garden World in Cheshire, to the satisfaction of thousands.

In these times of such openly aired concerns about the uses of plants and the origins of our food crops surely the independently academic research role of the botanic gardens has more importance than ever? How can we afford to let them slip away? This subject has been addressed most recently by the Royal Botanic Gardens at Kew, which has been highlighting its vital scientific role and turning out its attics. Kew now explains itself,[35] a first step to appreciation, and its listed buildings, including three of the world's greatest glasshouses (which it mostly neglected for years), its living and preserved collections and its specimen habitats. Of tremendous satisfaction to me and other visitors on what was apparently only the day after the opening by the Princess Royal was the restored Decimus Burton Museum in which Sir William Hooker's economic botany collection is returned to public view, with appropriate push-button interactivities and back lighting. Here is the stuff of life – the paraphernalia of tea, cocoa and coffee growing and making, of Chinese opium smoking, of medicines and loofahs and Panama hats (really made from the Panama hat plant, *Carludovica palmata*), of rattan baskets (sold in every market and high street) and coir matting, of paper-making and sugar-sweeting, of rubber, linen and silk, and on and on. Is it that I was nostalgic for my geography lessons of long ago returned to life? If so, I was not the only one: there is real magic in this exhibition, and it lies in seeing Hooker's old cricket bat, made from cricket bat willow, and the beans and boxes and Panama hat, and knowing that we have relied on these recognizable systems for so long. It is very good, especially for the young, to know that someone has this store of past knowledge – so much more healthy than growing up believing that food grows on the supermarket shelf, and that is all one needs to know. Even more reassuring is that Kew's scientists are re-addressing via new technologies how plants can help people and vice versa.

Nothing is perhaps more redolent of Kew's revaluation of assets than the hesitant acknowledgement of Marianne North's work on postcards, playing cards, posters and in books. I suspect there were suspicions about Marianne's indefatigable journeyings and 'lack of sensibility' even before Wilfrid Blunt damned her with faint praise: 'The disagreeable impression made by her pictures is enhanced by her determination to display 832 paintings in a gallery barely capable of showing fifty to advantage.'[36] Professor William Stearn's edition of Blunt's 1950 classic *The Art of Botanical Illustration*, fortunately has a footnote, 'Personally I enjoy both the gorgeous luxuriance of her massed paintings and the scrupulous detail in individual pictures'[37] (which is exactly how I feel). Marianne had the misfortune, like Ellen Willmott, to be rich and successful on her own – if she had been a man she would have been another Sir Joseph Banks, and thought a hero. She was born in Hastings in 1830 and grew up loving to travel and to paint. After her mother's death when she was twenty-five, she and her father travelled all around the Mediterranean, and when he died in 1869 Marianne set off on intrepid expeditions to North and South America and the West Indies, then to South Africa, Borneo, Sarawak, India, Ceylon and Australasia.[38] Everywhere she pursued her plants into the wild, up mountain paths and through jungle valleys, and that is the first wonder of her paintings: they are so definitely of plants in their natural habitats. The white datura trumpets hang daringly close to the water (she includes the humming birds and their nest) and their leaves have a bug-eaten realism; her morning glory, its blue bells turning this way and that is convincingly growing on a verandah in Durban, where she apparently found it. Some of her big landscape views are paint-heavy, but she portrays blue distances out to sea or over mountain tops with a breath of fresh air and she revels in the luxuriance of rhododendron flowers and foliage, as well as in all trumpet flowers which she seemed especially to like. She presented her paintings to Kew and paid for her gallery, designed by James Fergusson, which was opened in 1882.

The magnificent revival of botanical painting since Blunt's 1950 book (he ends with Alfred Parsons, E. A. Bowles, John Nash, Henry Moon, George Maw and the American Charles Faxon) has been a triumph that gardeners like to share. Raymond Booth, Lilian Snelling, Mary Emily Eaton and Helen Garside are famous names, even before we arrive at Professor Stearn's nineteen modern British botanists, celebrated in *Flower Artists of Kew* of 1990.

This much happier scientific tour ends in a garden and a gallery. The garden is the Fairhaven Trust Garden, a beautiful wild and natural garden of rich habitat in some 230 acres of mixed woodland and wetland on South Walsham Inner Broad. Here the paths in spring are edged with candelabra primulas, and there are azaleas and water-loving plants mixed as garden surprises amongst the carefully tended wilderness: the woodland is rich in bird life and wild flowers; it is all a carefully balanced little paradise.[39] This garden was made and left in trust by Henry Broughton, the 2nd Lord Fairhaven, who also collected botanical paintings. In 1966 he gave thirty-seven paintings, mainly Dutch, Flemish and French of the seventeenth and eighteenth centuries, to the Fitzwilliam Museum, with the promise of more. Lord Fairhaven died in 1973, and the museum received a further eighty-two paintings, and 'quite unexpectedly' the many little boxes and miniatures with floral decorations that he had also treasured. Promised drawings also revealed surprises – 'the sheer quality and quantity of the drawings, thirty-eight albums of them, and about nine hundred mounted and boxed'. The paintings are one of the supreme flower treasures of the world, of delicate amaryllis, lady's slipper and roses captured by Redouté, Georg Ehret, Ferdinand and Francis Bauer, the Dietsche family, Jan van Huysum and Philip Reinagle and any number of less known but wonderful artists. There are glorious sprays of auriculas and parrot tulips, bowls of tumbling garden flowers, refined and delicate botanical studies of trillium and orchis, the strange and the exotic, *Selenicereus grandiflorus*, the Queen of the Night, and *Hura crepitans*, the West Indian sandbox tree.[40] The Fitzwilliam Museum keeps a generous number of these paintings on rotating permanent display. But perhaps this is the very basis of our problems with science in the garden. These depictions of belladonna or a broken tulip were in their time at the frontiers of scientific discovery, and now they are in a museum. Sometimes, in fact very often, the gardener's enthusiasm for plants seems entirely misplaced, founded on prettiness, innocent wonder, familiar associations or mouth-watering anticipation. The fact is that the plants of the world are just as inventive and adaptable, as resourceful and full of potential as we are. They are serious living entities, our knowledge of which has lessened to a dangerous degree of ignorance and, often, contempt. Surely this is a poor relationship which we tolerate at our peril?

CHAPTER EIGHT

✦✦✦✦ ✦✦✦✦

'It's Clever, but is it Art?'[1]

There is much use of the word art in relation to gardens: the art of the garden, art and the garden, garden art, the art of design, the artist-gardener; the phrases are many, the plethora of painted gardens is self-evidently pretty, and there is an unspoken ruling that to combine three or four plants together satisfactorily demands artistry. Is this merely an extension of the art of living, or does it mean more? Have artists made a serious contribution to gardens, or vice versa? Both flowers and fields have a glorious and important painted history: the concoctions of the Dutch still-life painters have continually inspired gardeners as well as flower decorators, and they have played a part in the modern fashion for a jungle of flowers. Fields are sacred in landscape painting, but in flying out to discover their bucolic roots did the great painters leap over the garden: Constable hated contrivance, 'I do not regret not seeing Fonthill' he wrote in 1822, when all were agog over Beckford's creation, 'it is not beauty because it is not nature'.[2] Leaping the garden transformed Constable from 'an eclectic amateur to a great painter', in Graham Reynolds' opinion,[3] but out of affection Constable did paint his father Golding Constable's garden, from an upstairs window of East Bergholt House in the late summer of 1815. The landscapes, one with the Flower Garden, one with the Kitchen Garden, remain as a tribute, painted after the death of his mother and in what was to be Golding Constable's last summer (*Plate 18*). Turner did not linger in gardens either; he painted Pope's Twickenham riverside in 1808 in protest at the decline of the poet's garden, and dashed off a delicious watercolour of lilies and dahlias one afternoon at Petworth. But these examples only show that gardens, once painted at the Virgin's feet or behind the shoulders of Georgian status-portraits, seem to have

fallen to low esteem, just as landscape painting reached its early nineteenth-century prime. At Petworth it was Brown's landscape park that
was sublime and paintable art, and the source of the dahlias, the domestic
establishment, was sunk to a kind of vegetable unworthiness. Turner's
own spell of garden ownership at the house he designed and had built,
Sandycombe Lodge, Twickenham, from 1814 to 1826, was also professionally demanding, and his garden was a rare relaxation or relegated
to an amusement for his elderly father – though his complaint 'poor
Daddy seems as much plagued with weeds as I am with disappointments'[4] indicates it was also an irksome burden.

Victorian painters, in pursuing the past or the picturesque corners
of reality, place the garden into the fey realms of fantasy. Pre-Raphaelite-
style set pieces – such as J. W. Waterhouse's *The Enchanted Garden*,
crowded with doe-eyed damsels dressed for medieval Florence and
wreathed in roses and poppies – were not taking gardens anywhere
except into the land of nostalgia. This was the land the Victorian painters
and illustrators were to discover, the land of fairy gardens and rushy
glens, of kittens on the lawn and ladies under parasols, of prettiness
that demanded to be painted, and could be painted by the growing
crowd of gifted amateurs. Myles Birket Foster and Helen Allingham
painted rural Surrey with great and professional skill, and they were
emulated by the king of the nursery Randolph Caldecott and his 'consort'
Kate Greenaway, who ushered an old English vision of a garden into
children's myths and minds. This was in tribute to the countryside image
disappearing from view for town children, and was an important part
of the revival of 'cottage' gardens. Towards the end of the nineteenth
century two names made great careers out of painting gardens, George
Samuel Elgood and Alfred Parsons; Elgood specialized in exquisitely
soft images of the old gardens of England and Italy, Parsons had the
greater botanical skill, and his paintings of Ellen Willmott's Warley
Place are dazzling. Yet it has to be said that this whole rich haul of
genre painting, the nostalgic Victorian garden, can constantly be called
charming, enchanting, delightful, attractive, delicate – all these flattering
adjectives – until the end of time, and they will remain just that. Perhaps
the most damning thing that can be said is that they are useful for
historical research. For all these reasons they are also popular in the
saleroom – a fragment of Jekyll border in watercolour by Helen Alling-

ham recently sold for over £30,000 – but even that does not make them into transforming art.

For that we have to turn to the French Impressionists who saw things differently: the young Monet wrote excitedly to Frédéric Bazille in the summer of 1864 about the 'really beautiful flowers about at this time' and the 'gorgeous daisies' he wished he had time to paint, 'Why don't you do some yourself, since they are, I think an excellent thing to paint.'[5] Bazille, Renoir and Gustave Caillebotte followed Monet's enthusiasm and enlisted flowers into their repertories – roses, dahlias, gladioli and chrysanthemums painted with such passion that they 'induce a fresh outburst of wonder that still leaves us breathless'.[6] Part of their power was to paint gardens that they loved: Caillebotte painted the shady walks and flower beds and kitchen garden of his family home at Yerres in the Ile de France* and Monet and Bazille both enjoyed family summer homes. When they became gardeners on their own accounts they became enmeshed: Pissarro at Eragny had fruit, vegetables and flowers mixed in abundance, Caillebotte lovingly painted his roses at Petit-Gennevilliers and Monet, especially in his third and final garden at Giverny, pursued in painting after painting the shifting lights and kaleidoscopic colours of his splendid flowery vistas. Monet and Caillebotte were gardening correspondents and friends, exchanging plants and visits – 'Don't forget to come on Monday as arranged, all my irises will be in flower, later they will have faded',[7] Monet wrote on 12 May 1890. Caillebotte died four years later, aged only forty-six. Monet, who lived to be eighty-six, invented the persona of the artist-gardener, entirely through his perennial striving: in 1926, three months before he died, he assessed his own achievement. 'In the end, the only merit that I have is to have painted directly from nature with the aim of conveying my impressions in front of the most fugitive effects.'[8]

Monet and the Impressionists (including Manet, Renoir, Sisley, Berthe Morisot and Van Gogh in one blithe breath!) were a company of such artistic force as to raise gardens from the merely pretty. They saw gardens clearly through love and involvement, so that with them 'we step into light and air as if for the first time'; of equal importance

---

* Parc Caillebotte, 6 rue de Concy, 91330 Yerres (23 km SE of Paris), where Gustave Caillebotte lived for nearly twenty years, is open to visitors.

they saw them in small-scale or even fragmentary compositions, so that small becomes beautiful in painting, which is an advantage for small or 'ordinary' gardens as opposed to the ancient and aristocratic. Monet's 'fugitive' or fleeting effects of light and colour introduce hallucinatory (or what will be called psychedelic) notions into our way of seeing.

Thus gardens enter the twentieth century as legitimate grounds for visual and sensual exploration, their straight paths, dominant vistas and even boundaries melting away.

A dream exhibition for the first half of the century might be introduced with three paintings of a day in the 1890s by the members of the New English Art Club: Dame Ethel Walker's beautiful plein-airist simply titled *The Garden*, seems like morning, with a young woman in a white dress dappled in sunlight beneath a blossoming tree; James Henry Charles' *The Swing*, is of his daughters Ida and Marion, black-stockinged, with aprons over their pink dresses, playing on the swing, watched over from the tea table by their mother; for evening, John Singer Sargent's *Carnation Lily, Lily Rose*, the carefully staged vision of Polly and Molly Barnard in a Broadway garden with Liberty paper lanterns – there is just the hint of darker things to come in this famous painting.[9] The century proper opens in Stanley Spencer-land, where Christ is so often in Cookham front gardens, or there are the bosky cottage gardens of Burghclere viewed as from the top of a crooked ladder; *The Resurrection* itself, rose and lily wreathed, makes the churchyard a holy garden, and for contrast there is the immaculate *Greenhouse*. The Bloomsbury pacifists cannot be omitted; there is a flowery open-door view of Charleston Farmhouse garden by Duncan Grant, and Vanessa Bell's life there was so enmeshed between gardening and painting it is scarcely possible to separate the two. There are so many painted and embroidered images, and Vanessa's garden, too, could be included, sensitively restored by Peter Shepheard so that the ghosts may feel able to return; the garden survives to be worshipped along with the paintings and footstools. Carrington also painted, like she did most things 'with a touch of genius' according to Frances Partridge:[10] her offerings might include a vase of dahlias, grown and painted at Ham Spray, then Lytton Strachey in the garden at Tidmarsh Mill, the spirited painting of the red-roofed mill, and perhaps her outward looking and 'wonderfully Cezanne views' of the trees reflected in the river Pang. Paul Nash's

Thatched Cottage of 1926 has an untidy front garden, real countryside; and there are many views of town gardens – Gilbert Spencer's wintry tree and wicket gate, Douglas Percy Bliss's equally wintry but complex meeting of fences, sheds, trees, paths and flower beds in London back gardens.[11] Also David Jones' *Brockley Gardens*, with the cat prowling the wall's top, his characteristically ferny trees, and his vaguely sinister stolen kiss in *The Garden Enclosed* – his work more than any other perhaps explores the darker mythology of gardens.[12] Above all, the garden meant home: Edward Bawden and Eric Ravilious and their wives shared Brick House at Great Bardfield in Essex in the 1930s and they painted similar bird's eye views – Bawden's cheerfully full of action, a woman walking up the front path, the fence being painted, a bicycle half in the porch and the village police sergeant snooping around the big barn. Ravilious's was 'an experiment in colours and geometric shapes with the usual mysterious emptiness' (*Plates 35 & 36*). *Tennis* was painted on door panels as a commission for Sir Geoffrey Fry's Portman Court flat in 1930 – red courts, green lawns, bright young things clad in white. There would have to be an exhibition case for Ravilious' china for Tom Wedgwood, designed on the brink of war: the Queen's Ware was introduced in 1939 but curtailed by the war and (despite some limited bone china production in the 1950s) remains the unique and supremely enchanting ideal for a gardener's table – the 1938 tureens, teapots, plates and jugs were decorated with vignettes of down to earth activities, logging for winter, a spring scene with a swing, a tent and a tree in bud, high summer and the swimming pool and striped awning and an autumn book and a deckchair in which to rest from leaf sweeping (*Plate 37*). Most delicious of all are Garden Implements: trophy sprays of hoe, scythe, shears, fork, rake, broom and a water butt wreathed in ivy, rhubarb forcing pots, a bee skep and barrow, cloche and greenhouse.[13]

Wedgwood was too late with this very sophisticated china and the few pieces produced are now rare and for the museum. Eric Ravilious was killed on war service in 1942, and there has been no one since with such a fine eye for design to please the gardening fraternity: or, perhaps, the appeal was far wider, and the painters and designers of the 1930s particularly, who were contending with the prospect of war and loss, conveyed the most powerful symbolism of home with the soft grasses and sheltering trees of the garden. Wood engravings played an important role – Clare Leighton's *Four Hedges*,[14] her gardener's chronicle of happiness found after the misery of the First World War, and Nancy Nicholson's lino-block *Bunch* of wild and garden flowers carefully noted and named, represent the garden flowering in the applied arts.[15] Rex Whistler worked for a society that adored gardens. His illustrations and murals – the striped Tent Room at Port Lympne with faux-scrolled plan of the gardens for Philip Sassoon – raised garden imagery to new heights of fashion, with serious undertones.[16] John Piper, always aware of gardens, worked at Stourhead and Hafod as the war started, and then was summoned to Windsor to paint buildings, gardens and grottoes in the footsteps of Paul Sandby because it was feared that all would be bombed.[17] The ultimate images are perhaps Cecil Beaton's garden portraits – of the elderly Sickerts, Walter and Therese Lessore, of Lady Diana Cooper 'gathering daisies' – and literally, at the top of the tree, his greatest photographic moment, the Faerie Queen, Queen Elizabeth all diaphanous tulle and diamonds in the garden of Buckingham Palace.[18]

This flowering of domestic garden art – some of it of international reputation – continued for a while after the war, when in some state or another, artists seem to fly back to their gardens. Cedric Morris at Benton End is proudly represented by his icon painting *Iris Seedlings*, but let us not forget the vigour and amusement of his still-life cabbages, marrows, peppers and mushrooms, the produce of his garden, or *Benton End Wartime Gardening (Plate 19)* and the glorious *Heralding* of 1959 with the flowers of summer set against the Brett valley which nourished them.[19] Sir Cedric's long-time friend and neighbour John Aldridge resumed painting at Place House, Great Bardfield, with his own neat kitchen garden, but he gloried in a new 1950s and 1960s taste for wildness – shoulder-high swathes of cow parsley, borage *en masse* and the biggest and baddest, giant hogweed, adored by artists, grown and painted in the wood at the end of the orchard.[20] This trio of gardening friends was completed by John Nash, who wrote his gardening autobiography *The Artist's Plantsman*, in 1976, the year before his death – telling how he won botany prizes at school, redesigned his father's garden and corresponded with Clarence Elliott at Six Hills Nursery, leading to his illustrations for the 1926 catalogue, his first 'book'. Nash confesses to his long struggle – 'not without some success, to be both professional painter and an amateur gardener', how he actually wrote for *Gardens Illustrated* for a while, and produced his famous illustrations for *Poisonous Plants* (1927), *Plants With Personality* (1938) and for Robert Gathorne-Hardy's garden books and Jason Hill's *The Curious Gardener*. As well as being the definitive artist-plantsman, Nash perfected aesthetic wildness at his garden at Bottengoms, near Wormingford, where Essex meets Suffolk. The writer Ronald Blythe inherited the garden, and in 1985 he wrote of the unspoken rules: 'a certain weed tolerance, severe exclusion of some plants, retaining of some seed heads for aesthetic reasons, a dead tree might also be thought a pleasure ... the garden was expected to merge imperceptibly with the wildwood ... Tidiness must *never* get anywhere near suburbanness, the ultimate damned state.'[21]

Here we must forgo the amassing of garden images, for we have come well into the second half of the twentieth century with the artist-gardener, especially the painter-gardener, living with succulent home-grown, chemically free fruit and vegetables, cultivating the curious and even dangerous as well as the prettiest of plants and administering their gardens with a distrait-ness, a soon-to-be-fashionable untidiness. How have things come this far, this happily, without any mention of design?

Design? From a painterly point of view, to the best of my understanding, this must be an intrinsic process that resolves masses and voids, lights and darks, colours and margins via internal conversations and visions as a preliminary to work and during the painting process. History tells us that painters have come to gardening in various ways – witness Monet's desire to capture the colours of flowers, John Nash's fascination with botany and the curiosities of the plant world, and Cedric Morris's tender and discerning eye for the rainbow shades of his iris seedlings. It also seems to tell us that painters, if they are so moved, make wonderful gardens simply by being painters; that they not only make their own gardens but give quiet 'design' advice to their friends. Does history also tell us that garden designers are failed, or second-rate painters? Leonardo da Vinci clearly was not a failed painter, and yet he could not resist some garden design directives: 'the herbage of the little brooks ought to be cut frequently so that the clearness of the water may be seen upon its shingly bed' holds good. More interesting is this observation on foliage: 'The lights on such leaves as are darkest in colour will most closely resemble the colour of the atmosphere reflected in them . . .'[22] Compare this to Gertrude Jekyll in the pinewood in April: 'Where the sun catches the edge of the nearer trunks it lights them in a sharp line, leaving the rest warmly dark; but where the trees stand in shade the trunks are of a cool grey that is almost blue, borrowing their colour, through the opening of the track behind me, from the hard blue cloudless sky.'[23] Across 400 years these are painterly perceptions of the highest order. For Gertrude Jekyll painting was the holiest calling, though she was better at applied arts of silverwork and embroidery, and she came to be the great garden artist. She was a failed painter, a fact she blamed all her life long on her myopic and weak eyes (though myopia was an essential tool for Impressionists and she continued to draw planting plans in finest detail through her eighties) but was probably a result of her inability to allow her mind to sink into pools of colour dissolved in light, the necessary immersion of Impressionism. She was tactlessly criticized by Christopher Tunnard shortly after her death for failing to paint her garden visions, as Monet had done, but this was just what she could not do. Her perception outstripped her painting talent. She was not alone; W. A. Nesfield and Repton are just the beginning of a long line of talented artists who turned to garden and landscape design. This may suggest that garden designers are failed painters, but it also shows that the level of perception required for both occupations is equally high, as Leonardo and Jekyll convincingly demonstrate.

The more practical problem is that of scale. The communal triumph of the artists of gardens listed above is that they unerringly moved out of the landscape-painting tradition to master garden scale. If only it had proved so certain on the ground.

Garden design was conceived as landscape design, a large-scale art. We know that the first designers were soldiers, architects, masons or surveyors who worked for kings and cardinals on vast projects. The young hopefuls in exile or on the Grand Tour saw everything on the grand scale, a widening of youthful horizons: great swathes of *campagne* transformed on to great canvases by Poussin and Claude. The lure was the distance, the lauded 'prospect'. The sober perception of John Evelyn was stirred to superlatives for the views from stairways and terraces that he took in on his tour to Rome in 1644, and he was even inspired to sketch. For the following two centuries, travellers wondered at these continental prospects and returned to try to imitate them at home. The ambition of the landscape style was to be fulfilled by embracing as many beloved English acres into the prospect as possible, judiciously protecting them with perimeter plantations and enhancing the beauties of nature, the valleys and hills. The influential pioneer of the movement, Batty Langley, sought to save the gentlemen of England from 'some of our Theorical [sic] Engineers, who, in their aspiring Garrets ... frame Designs for Situations they never saw', from the nurseryman who 'advises the Gentleman to such Forms and Trees as will make the greatest Draught out of his Nursery, without Regard to any Thing more', as well as the Cox-comb 'who takes upon himself to be an excellent Draughtsman, as well as an incomparable Gardener'.[24] Langley follows these comforts with a list of thirty-seven rules (almost the thirty-nine articles of landscape design), wholly concerned with rejecting the near, the geometric, the certainties of old-style formal design in favour of the new vistas and prospects. His pioneering fellows Shenstone and Switzer published variations on these rules, and between them they carved out the artistic philosophy of landscape design.

The profession of landscape gardening thus entailed an ability quickly to become familiar with acres and prospects and to identify their 'capabilities' – at which Lancelot Brown excelled – as well as to keep the nurserymen and labourers in order. With the second generation – and Sylvia Crowe credited Humphry Repton as the man who had 'codified' her profession[25] – the long struggle to reduce the scale of operations from thousands of acres, a seeming quarter of Hertfordshire or any other county, to something more manageable, was initiated.

As the 'codifier', the father of landscape designers, who adeptly turned his amateurish talent for watercolours to good professional uses, Repton deserves our affection. He also epitomizes an experience common to the profession he unwittingly launched in his ability to learn from 'the university of life': he was born, close to Shakespeare and St George, on 21 April 1752 in Bury St Edmunds, into that well-known station in life: comfortable enough to discourage effort, but not with enough landed connections to make it unnecessary. He wished that he might be a Repton 'of the snug and silvery Trent'[26] but was not, so after a taste of the high-life in Holland he settled down to the niceties of

Mecklenburgs, worsted satins and calimancoes in the Norwich textile trade. He married for love – Mary Clarke, in May 1773, a month after his twenty-first birthday – but he could not settle to business. His parents both died in 1776, releasing him from the duty to persist, and with his inheritance he moved the family to Sustead Old Hall (his brother John was farming at Oxnead Hall and his sister and her lawyer husband John Adey were in Aylsham) where he assumed a squirish role. This is the time-honoured occupation of country gentry with too little to do (and has a noble place in the pedigree of landscape gardeners): he was churchwarden, surveyor of the roads and general counsellor to the community, and his sitting room constantly echoed to 'Old Poppet is lame, Lord, our apples won't keep, Sir . . . and the tatoes are fruz'n and the post has declared that he can't come nomore, for the road isn't cleared.'[27] With a spell as a political secretary and election agent, Repton lived in arcadia for ten years before his family and financial worries forced him to move to a cottage at Hare Street in Essex. And then, on a hot sleepless night a decision 'entered his imagination with almost the vague uncertainty of a dream' and the next day, 26 August 1788, he spent the morning writing letters, announcing to everyone he thought might have use for it, that it was his intention to become a landscape gardener. He bought ledgers, set up accounts, visited Brown's son who gave him some drawings as a kind of passing on of the flame and had 500 trade cards printed.[28]

Repton became the second most famous landscape gardener in history. Apart from his experience with road-mending Repton was not a technical man: he traded on his 'faculty of foreknowing effects', his good eye and fertility of invention, and most of all his timely use of the fashionable art of aquatint in his reports to his clients. These reports, in copperplate text, full of warm appreciations of his clients' tastes and virtues and the beauties of their grounds, were illustrated with 'before' and 'after' views by means of ingenious slides and flaps and bound in brown calf or red morocco. (Repton charged for his 'red books' but posterity has repaid their owners a thousand fold by turning them into saleroom treasures.) His humanity ensured a warm relationship with many of his clients: he appreciated their pretensions, could whisk away the washing lines and replace them with rosy trellis. He worked on some large landscaped parks but his list of about 250 commissions are for the most part on the more modest scale (if not ambitions) of houses and villas in the country rather than the traditional country house. Repton saw his red books and his books on theory and practice, beginning with *Sketches and Hints on Landscape Gardening* in 1795,[29] as the principal justification of his professionalism and he saw himself as an artist. He published, with all the agony and expenditure of tints and engravings, to rescue 'the art I profess from the imputation of the effect of caprice or fancy and not the result of fixed principles',[30] these being the charges of his critics.

Repton's reliance on enchanting (but second-rate) watercolours spurred on the nineteenth-century development of his profession, especially in the design of public parks. Professional gardeners, who laid out beds, borders, walks, orchards and kitchen grounds from two to fifty acres as part of their work, and with cheerful derision of art, had little to say to the 'landscapists'. A rift, if not an actual antagonism, developed over sharing the title 'gardener' so the landscapists looked around for an alternative and lighted on Loudon's 1840 edition of Repton's complete works, *The Landscape Gardening and Landscape Architecture of the late Humphry Repton Esq*. The 'landscape architecture' was presumably intended by Loudon to describe Repton's ornamental buildings, of which there were many, but it had just the longed-for connotations of a sister art, especially in America where the profession came of age. In debating what they would call themselves Calvert Vaux wrote to Olmsted on how essential it was to be thought of as artists: 'I think it is the art title we want to set our art ahead ... and make it command its position – administration, management, funds ... and everything else.' Olmsted was less sure, 'I love beautiful landscapes ... better than anybody else I know ... But I don't feel strong on the art side. I don't feel myself an artist ... and it would be rather sacrilegious to post myself at the portals of art'.[31] So it was rather for the negative reasons that they could not agree on anything else that landscape architects came to be mis-named; the American Society of Landscape Architects was founded in 1899, but in Britain the debate continued, with terms encompassing 'garden architect', 'parks and gardens designer' or 'landscape gardener'. The first professional alliance was called the British Association of Garden Architects in 1928, but a year later was changed to the Institute of Landscape Architects. The history and art of large-scale designs, of vast royal gardens and landscape parks had found both home and future; their 'spatial experiences', their styles and details could be analysed and transformed into industrial landscapes, motorways, new towns, parks, parkways and playgrounds. But who would be left to care for the garden?

Gertrude Jekyll died towards the end of 1932 and the words 'ARTIST, GARDENER, CRAFTSWOMAN' were carved upon her tomb, in that order. The garden-artist, the persona she had invented by applying her painter's eye for colours and lights to her planting died with her. The world had moved on while she had been old, and her wonderfully luxuriant planting in Lutyens's geometrical gardens was so emphatically Edwardian that it was now *passé*. Lutyens's dictum that there was 'no such thing as a free curve' had imprisoned her later struggles with naturalistic planting and her paths and margins – full of foresight when viewed against the Edwardian sunset – now had a morning-after nervousness, that same hesitancy that had imprisoned her painting style. The abstract and constructivist artists of the 1930s would completely re-order the scale and perception of gardens, but this would not influence practical design until the 1950s.

Meanwhile, the inter-war boom in new gardens, invariably patches of field adorned with builders' rubbish, found its saviour in the expansion of the big contracting nurseries, who must have moved millions of lorry loads of paving and rockery about the land. In launching the first of *The Studio Garden Annuals* in 1932, the editor F. A. Mercer wished to appeal to town and country gardeners with all sizes of plots. Rock gardens and sweet peas were the favourites for everyone, and the illustrations have a generality of tone, of lawns fringed with thick flower borders, perhaps fading to rockery and rhododendrons, and of crazy paving with bird path or pool, rose-bedded terraces and baby conifers. Vernon Brothers, headed by their designer J. Bowater Vernon, and the Mawson family's Lakeland Nurseries Ltd, were the major businesses in the south and north respectively: there is a whole rash of rockeries by George Whitelegg of Chislehurst, with one of more exceptional interest by Clarence Elliott of Six Hills Nursery at Stevenage. The most interesting designer was Percy Cane,[32] but even he could not give these self-satisfied and pretentious gardens the status of art. And if comfort and convenience were what was important, who was interested in art anyway?

Against this suburban background the young and the clever, in their shorts and shingled hair, discovered gardens to be entertainingly funny, and the 1930s' greatest contribution to garden arts is in the comic novel and the poetic parody. Gardens taking themselves too seriously had invited ridicule, ever since Pope's topiary catalogue mentioned 'A Lavender Pig with Sage growing in his Belly', and 'St George in box; his arm scarce long enough, but will be in a Condition to stick the Dragon by next April',[33] and since Payne Knight purposely misquoted Repton's 'mere stone' as 'mile-stone' (to ridicule the vanity of private acreages) and gave Thomas Love Peacock a name for the pompous and taste-ridden landscape improver in Headlong Hall.[34] Elders and betters were inclined to get carried away – Sir George Sitwell, after his nervous breakdown, called Isola Bella 'Not a garden, but a mirage in a lake of dreams . . . a great galleon with flower-laden terraces', and described Caprarola's giant guard of sylvan deities 'playing, quarrelling, laughing the long centuries away', in *On the Making of Gardens* (1905). This kind of enthusiasm turned the garden into a vehicle for laughter, in E. F. Benson's Mapp and Lucia novels or Wodehouse's Blandings Castle, and the mood was raised to fever pitch by Ronald Firbank and Amanda Ros. Firbank's *Flower Beneath the Foot* is peopled all-too-clearly with gardeners – 'the Countess decided on presenting the fallen senator with a pannier of well-grown, early pears, a small "heath" and the Erotic Poems, bound in calf with tasteful tooling, of a Schoolboy Poet'. In his exotic settings of hedges of towering red geraniums, roses from the Land of Punt renamed 'Mrs Lloyd George' and gardeners silently raking paths and tying chrysanthemums to little sticks, we find the future of English Letters, Victoria Gellybore-Frinton, the Hon. Mrs Chilleywater (Vita Sackville-West): 'I've such a darling description of a cornfield. I make you feel England'.[35] Unintentionally, Amanda M. Ros became 'something of an hilarious in-joke' for what Mark Twain called 'hogwash' literature, with characters in her Helen Huddleson melodrama named Raspberry, Cherry, Sir Peter Plum, Mrs Strawberry (a fallen wife), Sir Christopher Currant and Lentil (the maid).[36]

In January 1934 Theo Stephens published the first volume of *My Garden: An Intimate Magazine for Garden Lovers*, bedside reading with regular contributions from Reginald Arkell, the gardeners' favourite laureate:

A garden is a lovesome thing –
When it starts blooming in the Spring.
The daffodil, the snowdrop white, The dainty Winter Aconite . . .
And just as it is going strong, The Woolly Aphis comes along.
Wire Worms and Weevils think it fun To eat your annuals one by one.
Until the Caterpillars start To break your horticultural heart.
Go, take a flat or buy a yacht, A garden is a lovesome thing – God wot![37]

My Garden was born of a sleepless night, like Repton's career. Arkell set the tone for eminent barristers and surgeons lovingly to ponder their gardens in a hearty kind of way, with jovial snippets from A. T. Johnson, Eleanour Sinclair Rohde and B. H. B. Symons-Jeune (apart from Miss Rohde, a very prominent journalist and author, the women were rather scarce). *My Garden* – welcomed by Courtney Page, Hon Secretary of the National Rose Society, as being 'not a book about Gardening, but Gardens' – started the vogue for garden writing, rather than reportage or instruction, which featured a little humour, a little reminiscence, some history, a plant or two in detail, some practical hints like patterns for brick paths and garden descriptions. There were also lovely advertisements – the Vauxhall Big Six 'As modern as the minute – as steadfast as the Hills', Lloyd Loom chairs for garden or for lounge, Carter's seeds, Cuprinol, garden sheds, cigarettes and Kolynos tooth paste – a varied world, a 1930s world and fascinating to us, but a comforting haven for middle-class philistinism that could ignore any tendencies to art.[38]

Garden literature made a hybrid of the Hon. Victoria Chilleywater and the little lady who ruled at home: *Elizabeth and Her German Garden* had much to do with this; Elizabeth von Arnim's account of her garden life at Nassenheide which opens with the words 'I love my garden' had been enduringly popular, and was revived with her autobiography *All The Dogs in My Life* published in 1936. Her 'German Garden' had been wittily discreet but now everyone knew of her amorous Count, The Man of Wrath, and her subsequent adventures, and the garden – blowing wildly and not gardened at all in the view of (male) experts – became the symbol of a woman's space, somewhere to think, and write, to escape housekeeping and contemplate life and love. E. M. Forster had been a tutor to the von Arnim children in 1904 and the romance of this feminine domain informs all his novels, especially *Howard's End*; we know that there was a duality in Forster's tenderness and that the garden was also a refuge for homosexual love. This gave garden writing an invariable double entendre that was especially attractive – and had something to do with the attention paid to Vita Sackville-West's Sissinghurst garden, constructed during the 1930s and open to visitors immediately before the war, and with the popularity of the writings of the wittily unmarried Beverley Nichols whose cosmopolitan garden adventures sold in hundreds of thousands from the 1930s until the early 1970s. By this time the sheer sexiness of the garden was out in the open with John Hadfield's *Love on a Branch Line* and its unbeatable mix of steam trains, cricket and gardens, and Lady Flamborough who always seems to be in the middle of a bed, trowel in one hand, trug in the other, in a tattered tweed skirt and 'very ancient sun-browned straw hat with a brilliant peacock's feather stuck into it'. The garden was even sexier than Lady F. or her rampageous daughters: 'All was stillness and seclusion. Great bearded irises stood motionless in flaring grandeur, their veined and velvet petals almost lasciviously reflexed to the touch of the sun. Behind them, in high relief against the green-and-gold of the yew hedge, rose stately groups of tall, sophisticated delphiniums. The air was soft with the fragrance of damask roses and the musky scent of sun-baked lichen on the walls.'[39] Only a happy garden historian and gardener like Hadfield could have written that. And it made everyone snigger, if they had not done so before, at 'Come into the garden, Maud!' or the bouncing jollity of Percy Grainger's 'English Country Garden'. English gardens echoed to English music of the bucolic school, neither of which could be taken wholly seriously ever again.

The backlash consisted of taking gardens into levity-free and distant realms of the mind and modernism. Modern design surfaced at the Festival of Britain in 1951 and entered gardens via three landscape architects, Geoffrey Jellicoe, Frederick Gibberd and Russell Page, and one brilliant maverick, John Brookes, who woke up the garden world with his design based on a geometric abstract by Piet Mondrian for Penguin Books at Harmondsworth. Sir Geoffrey always told a story of how he and Gibberd both prepared new town plans, for Hemel Hempstead and Harlow respectively, in 1947, and how his plan being 'a comparative failure and Frederick's being so successful as a modern concept, I questioned why this should be so . . . I then took note of the pictures on his walls, peculiar prints by an artist called Paul Klee, an incomprehensible drawing or two by a Ben Nicholson . . . and I asked him if they meant anything to him in his work and I shall always remember his reply – that "they flow electricity into me", so I broke into this world and have been electrified ever since.'[40] Electrification brought gardens back on to the artistic plane: Klee and Nicholson threw geometry to the wind, Moore and Hepworth hi-jacked conventional scale, Jellicoe and Gibberd felt they were working in the same context as the many distinguished artists and sculptors who were their friends. Design problem-solving came about by contemplation of the problems solved by both landscape architects' collections of Nicholson, Moore, Hepworth, Frink, Sutherland, Victor Pasmore, David Jones, Edward Burra and other artists. Jellicoe designed an abstract rose garden for Cliveden adapted from Paul Klee's *The Fruit*, expressing enclosure and fecundity in a womb-like way. Gibberd, the architect of unpopular modern icons including the first buildings of Heathrow Airport, the InterContinental Hotel at Hyde Park Corner and the Roman Catholic Cathedral at Liverpool ('Paddy's Wigwam'), made only one garden, his own at Marsh Lane, Harlow – a magical weaving of groves, soft vistas and spaces, of contrasts with clipped or free screens of holly, yew, laurel or box and filigree delicacy of blossom trees, of witty groups of seven trees or nine potted plants, a garden made on a shoestring with recycled features (one waterfall is made of old fridges, well disguised) and ingenious use of concrete and pebbles for pavings (*Plate 20*). Gibberd's garden became a setting for a collection of modern sculpture and he became the guru: 'The sculpture is static; the sensibility in siting lies in changing factors of light, weather, plant growth and the moving viewpoint of the spectator.' His example is Mary Gorrara's *Swan* with half-spread wings, on a plinth and placed at the end of a Gothic nave of lime trees, planted much too close together by the previous owner of his garden; the Swan rises against a tangled backdrop of cornus and bamboo, and the dappled light encourages moss and lichen to soften its concrete surface.'[41]

Freedom, both in design and planting maintenance, an ease of living, love of modern art and use of contemporary materials, and a greenness with an oriental tinge, these were the tenets of modernist gardens. The minimalist idea and occult symmetry, even the philosophy of Zen, arrived by way of Bernard Leach the potter and his interest in Japanese craft traditions: Leach and Shoji Hamada set up their pottery in St Ives in 1920 and soon became part of the close-knit world of Cornish artists and London galleries. Their painter friends were fascinated by Shoji's Zen beliefs; he lived simply above the pottery workshop (while Leach and his family were in the house next door) and thought that living and working in the same place 'achieved a higher dimension' of both work and self. Much of this filtered into Leach's philosophy of the artist-potter, and the idea that 'the pot is the man' grew in attractiveness as his fame grew during the 1920s and 1930s, in parallel with the reputations of his artist friends, Ben Nicholson and Barbara Hepworth. Leach's career culminated with *A Potter's Book*, published in 1940, the result of his experiences of a burgeoning Japanese craft revival movement seen on a visit to Hamada's friends in Tokyo and Osaka.[42]

Clearly the identification of workplace and self, the inspiration of the artist-craftsmen, had direct relevance to the artist-gardener, and these Zen overtones fell on well-prepared soil, inviting very widespread interest in Japanese culture. Arthur Waley's translation of the *Tale of Genji* was published between 1925–33 and was fashionably popular: it told of the court life of Murasaki Shikibu, a Japanese Scheherazade, whose intricate sagas of love, death and family pride (told to amuse the Empress Akiko in the eleventh century) were wreathed in gardens. Through the tales Japanese gardens were found to be full of enchanting subtleties echoing the state of triumph or disaster, where young men plucked single exquisite blooms in the hope of winning womanly equivalents, where wild gardens meant tangled carnations and blossoms, where the Lady Murasaki lists her likes and dislikes amongst blossoms and where it was customary for a court lady to receive a letter and a single splendid flower each morning from the gentleman with whom she had spent the night. Such delicate traditions fascinated the clumsy westerners, who clamoured for Japanese flower paintings expressing the 'natural pose' of an azalea or branch of plum blossom, the dignity of a miniature pine or tall, leaning fronds of bamboo.[43] There was a tremendous interest in Japanese plants – the Yano Nurseries in West Hampstead and Yokohama nurseries at St Albans supplied miniature trees and gardens called 'Bonkai gardening' (was this a printing error?) and instructions for growing them by means of a series of pinchings, knottings and starvation – cruel processes that were the improving tasks of Japanese girls (and not unlike the bindings of breasts and feet in geisha traditions). As well as E. H. Wilson's Kurume azalea hybrids, which poured on to the market, there were chrysanthemums, large, shaggy, curled, and prized: western journalists were lost in admiration of these flowers on display at the Imperial Palace at Yeddo – a russet-bronze like a large curled cabbage, a dazzling yellow with hundreds of long thin shaggy petals 'falling over like a sheath of golden thread, with names like "ten-thousand-times-dipped-in-gold", Mountain Vapours, "Kissed-by-the-Sunset".' The fascination of the flowers was enhanced by 'the little fairy-like creatures in their long humming-bird-like gowns' who accompanied the visitors with 'a look of pre-occupied condescension' and agitated and opened and shut their large court fans as the heat became more intense – each fan with 'a very large, tinselled tassel . . . fastened to the base of the fan with long threads of shaded silk hanging down to the ground, and sweeping the fine gravel as the wearer fans herself.'[44]

All the fascination of Japanese garden tradition seems to emanate from this report: these traditions were thoroughly absorbed into inter-war British art and garden culture, so much so that in 1940 Charles Holme, the editor of *The Studio*, declared the Japanese the best gardeners in the world.

The interplay between politics and the acceptability of cultural ideas is necessarily present throughout much of this book, but clearly at this point, with the Second World War one of the moments of conflict has arrived. Both German architectural modernism and Japanese garden philosophy were unceremoniously dropped, and the British middle classes refused to countenance modern architecture or garden design for the next fifty years. Artists and landscape architects were different though, and a determined internationalism in the 1950s – the Leach family were united with their Japanese friends at an international gathering of craftsmen and women at Dartington in 1952 – meant that the exchange of ideas was renewed and revived on a personal basis. The International Federation of Landscape Architects, led by Geoffrey and Susan Jellicoe, was instrumental in a British appreciation for the work of the Brazilian landscape artist Roberto Burle Marx and his dramatic abstract designs with their colourful sweeps of native plantings, and for the powerful impact of the raked sand gardens, with their sublime patterns and symbolic groupings of rocks, of the Zen temples of Kyoto. After the interval of war, the 'international modern' influences on garden design had re-grouped by the early 1960s: the *Studio Gardens & Gardening* editor of 1936, F. A. Mercer, had looked forward to the 'interesting' influence of modernism – was this belatedly about to flower?

Garden modernism was exclusively in the hands of the 'landscape' brigade, who were then the only professionals involved in garden design. Percy Cane, who understood serene groves and smooth pavings perfectly, had chosen not to join the Institute of Landscape Architects, preferring to keep his rich clients discreetly to himself.[45] Russell Page had found a niche in France with André de Vilmorin's ancient and distinguished nursery, and his clients were to be on the continent and in America.[46] Sylvia Crowe and Brenda Colvin were to design some expertly serene gardens, in the manner of Gibberd's Marsh Lane: Crowe's book *Garden Design* of 1958 was in one respect a means of getting gardens out of the system, for she dispensed the highest design theory. She wrote about the question of scale that:

> There is a school of thought which contends that man's mind has an infinite capacity for expansion or contraction; that he can, like Graham Sutherland, see the vast complexity of the Alps in one small stone, or bring down the immensity of the universe to that of his own stature. This is true, but it is only valid while man is alone. If other human figures appear in his giant or pigmy landscape the true human scale is revealed. For this reason, the garden, at least of the average man, must still keep man as its measuring rod.[47]

There is an element of capitulation about this, as if design could scale the heights with modern art, but that gardens were for more earthly people, and perhaps should be designed with appropriate restraint. It was impossible for a professional landscape architect, like Crowe or Colvin or Peter Shepheard, to earn a worthwhile fee on a garden, charging a small percentage on a few hundred pounds, and so the professionals turned to local authority work on parks and housing or consultancy for roads, reservoirs or forestry undertakings. It was not until he was eighty and in distinguished 'retirement' that Geoffrey Jellicoe could dare to play with scale in the Sutherland manner, with his introduction of the gigantic ex-Mentmore vases at Sutton Place. With exceptions that can be numbered on two hands and are only now coming to light, landscape architects did not design modern gardens to set the style of the post-1960s decades. Lanning Roper, with his fine arts background and self-financed horticultural training at Kew and Edinburgh Botanics, had to work immensely hard to build a networking of clients, for whom he designed 'on the ground' and actually gardened on a regular consultancy basis, but his clients in the main wanted the traditional English garden, not modernist fancies.[48]

If modernism was rejected because of native conservatism it was also to be flushed out in the coming horticultural bonanza and simply over-run with jungles of flowers. At the same moment a new generation of city-reared painters took the stage, responding to American consumerist culture and tempted by the 'art boom' and Pop Art: gardens were despised and rejected, flowers were 'the ultimate taboo', as David Hockney recently admitted, when thirty years on he exhibited flower drawings to celebrate his sixtieth birthday – 'shocking really, for a boy from the sixties'.[49]

However, if Hockney and his Hollywood swimming pools were to be the cultural icons, then there was bound to be an underground counter-movement, and ironically it was this that was to move gardens further back into the past. To a generation born and brought up in the shadow of war there was – in the teeth of agri-business and the development boom – a longing for rural peace, a green-tinged and environmentally aware longing in part, but not dominantly so. These were feelings encapsulated by Ken Russell's film on Elgar's life, with the *Serenade for Strings* rippling along the Malvern Hills, and by the young Jacqueline du Pré's playing of the Cello Concerto: this was a generational consciousness which became particular to a group of students at the Royal Academy Schools who were taught by Graham Arnold. Arnold and his wife Ann felt 'that Elgar expressed in music what we were longing to express in our paintings'[50] – they lived in the West Sussex countryside near Fittleworth, also near Brinkwells where the Elgars had lived for a while, and were making a garden inspired by Levens Hall topiary and Sissinghurst Castle, where they had chanced upon a meeting with Vita Sackville-West in her garden one afternoon in the autumn of 1960. The Arnolds and Graham's students, David Inshaw, Diana Howard and John Morley, with their affinity to Samuel Palmer and the Brotherhood of Ancients, and the Pre-Raphaelites, knowing themselves to be deeply unfashionable, formed the Broadheath Brotherhood, named after Elgar's birthplace, in the early 1970s.

John Morley was an enthusiastic gardener and knowledgeable plantsman: he painted the layered and umbrella'd topiary of Beckley Park in Oxfordshire, and his *Old Florists' Auriculas and Flowerpots* first appeared in 1972, the first of many famous and delightful images which did an immense amount for the fashionable revival of auriculas. With the work of Diana Howard the garden attains a mystical aura; the critic Nicholas Usherwood described her work in 1981:[51] 'Painted in sombre blues and greens, sometimes with a solitary figure of a beekeeper, dancer or clown, her landscapes possess a ghostly, mysterious atmosphere, a medieval quality, in which the enclosures seem somehow to retain the not quite forgotten passions of the people who once inhabited them.' Her *Dancer in the Garden* (1975–7) has the splayed perspective of a fifteenth-century painting, with dark topiary-topped walls sheltering a dancing floor for a lone figure in a party dress, the sky lit by a shooting star. But it was David Inshaw who produced the 'garden' painting which caused most stir then, and which remains a familiar image: he called it *The Badminton Game*: two girls, one in purple and green, the other in glowing red velvet, flip a shuttlecock over a net. They play on a lawn overlooked by a gathering of topiary images, enormous, perhaps protective, rather menacing also and very personable, looking as if they are about to get up and walk away. The house in the background is tall and prim, built of bricks of as fierce a red as only the West Midlands can produce, and half-covered in a pointillist veil of ivy.

Soon after *The Badminton Game*, the 'brotherhood' reformed, Diana Howard married John Morley and they moved to Suffolk (where they now grow North Green Plants and are treasured amongst gardeners for their snowdrop rarities) – and they were joined by the previously pop-artist Peter Blake with some others, becoming The Brotherhood of Ruralists in 1975. Blake and Graham Ovenden led them into the realms of darker sexual fantasy, inspired by Tenniel's Alice, Richard Dadd, Arthur Rackham and Maxfield Parrish, and also to Victorian medieval-ists, Morris and Pugin. In the late 1970s and 1980s they painted *Ophelia* as a group project, and their cover designs for Methuen's new editions of the Arden Shakespeare multiplied their garden images. Inshaw's *The River Bank (Ophelia)* is both sinister and enchanting: a girl in party dress runs away from the discovery of the figure floating in the stream in the foreground, a stream adorned in water-iris of botanical-like detail, with a bee-skep nearby. The background is the enclosed garden, empty and still, hedged and walled, and trellised with Virginia creeper, which contains a monkey puzzle tree, Inshaw's favourite creamy-plates of flowers on a bush that is elder-like, and a treillage pyramid. As he now lived in Devizes it is likely that he had seen this last rarity in Rosemary Verey's garden at Barnsley House, where she was reviving this French fashion. Inshaw's cover for *Love's Labour's Lost* has a cheerfully sunlit garden of topiary umbrellas, with the Princess, Maria, Katharine and Rosaline adjusting their veils before their courtly lovers enter. Annie Ovenden's cover for *Measure for Measure* captures the intrigue of a scene that is not actually in the play but is crucial to the plot, the Duke in his friar's disguise hiding from Mariana and Angelo in 'a garden circummur'd with brick' with the 'planched gate' that leads to the vineyard beyond. Other covers – especially for the English history plays – are generously wreathed in roses and oak leaves, and the Ruralists' paintings continued to repeat this quality of veiled menace (also used to effect in Peter Greenaway's film *The Draughtsman's Contract*), ending with Inshaw's sinister *Presentiment* – a lady in white with a parasol wanders in the shadows of giant topiary, and her stalker, albeit with a posy, lurks in the shade: a cat pounces and the flag of St George flies over the garden.[52]

These garden images were not only sinister, they were overwhelmingly formal, as if in the profoundly wished-for belief that order and formality might keep the chaos at bay. These painted notions coincided with a rise in historic garden visiting – Graham Stuart Thomas's *Gardens of the National Trust* was published in 1979, and it was becoming clear that visitors found the gardens more relaxing and interesting than the over-protected houses. Sissinghurst Castle and Hidcote Manor were two of the most popular gardens, beloved for their small compartments which were of contrasting character but somehow contrived to be endearingly similar and of familiar appeal. The historical appeal of formalism, so beautifully illustrated by Rosemary Verey's planting, itself soon to be sharing the limelight with Penelope Hobhouse's magical interpretations of the formal spaces around Tintinhull House, was significantly further popularized by the Gertrude Jekyll revival.

Miss Jekyll stepped on to the stage, with her young architect friend

Edwin Lutyens, at the South Bank Hayward Gallery's Lutyens exhibition, which opened in November 1980 and ran through to the following spring, and was seen by almost 100,000 pairs of eyes. In May 1981 at the Chelsea Flower Show, John Brookes and the Inchbald School won a Gold Medal for their recreation of Lutyens's garden at 100 Cheyne Walk, Chelsea, a formal garden with a central lawn, surrounding borders and a central circular pool, originally designed in 1910 and now reinterpreted as a white garden. Gertrude Jekyll, artist-gardener and plantswoman, was to be patroness-extraordinary for the next fifteen years, and she may yet guide gardeners through the millennium. She has launched more than a Jekyll industry of books, exhibitions and restored and imitated gardens, she has suited everyone: her love of old roses has done wonders for the shrub rose revival and her name adorns a new English rose; herbaceous borders, silver and grey-leaved plants, older varieties of perennials, herbs, wall shrubs, spring and winter flowers – all have been given a Jekyll fillip. Her colour-graded borders and monochromatic gardens in blue, gold, green, red and even others she did not try (including white) have filled thousands of column-inches, and her 'naturalism' in wilderness, wild gardens and under-planted orchards has fitted conveniently into newer ecological priorities. Her formal garden rooms, planted to Lutyens's geometrically perfect detailings, have blossomed in a hundred thousand pocket-handkerchief back gardens, to the delight of growers of box and yew and the makers of pavings, pots and pergolas. The Lutyens design for a wave-backed seat has proved an industry in itself. Most importantly, from the perspective of art, architectural formalism allied to luxuriant planting has been possible to teach effectively (whereas abstract modernism was almost impossibly difficult) and garden designers have emerged from diploma schools into a new and vibrant (though some say already overcrowded) profession. In a neatly cyclical ending, a new Society of Garden Designers now flourishes, with John Brookes as its Chairman, and has recently (in the spring of 1998) merged its journal into the high quality *Garden Design* magazine, published in the professional landscape design stable. Garden design, now offered as a degree subject, is still uncertain as to whether it is an art, a science or even a craft, but it has certainly come of age.

CHAPTER NINE

✦✦✦ ✦✦ ✦✦✦

Labour of Love

Along with hundreds of thousands of others I visited the garden at Heligan in Cornwall in 1997 in the aftermath of the first television series about the garden's discovery and revival: the spring day was dreary, flecked with rain and muddy underfoot, but the garden was crowded with smiling faces (the widest smiles on those of us who were surprised and delighted to be able to take our dogs – garden-trained dogs all). From a long enjoyable morning I find there remains one ineradicable memorial moment, that brought me almost to my knees in awe, bending down to press my nose against the murky glass to peer into the steamy bed where the enceinte Queen pineapples were fructifying. The Heligan pineapples, triumphantly harvested the following autumn, were the first culinary pineapples to be grown in Britain for decades, possibly the first in the twentieth century. There is something far more miraculous about this juicy yellow orb, with all its chin-dribbling lusciousness, emerging from the chill of a bleak Cornish frameyard and piles of dung, than about all the sun-drenched fruits jetted from afar daily to our supermarket shelves. Pineapples, not cast by Mrs Coade to adorn the grandest gate piers and roofscapes for nothing, are the golden orbs of horticultural achievement, the ultimate challenge in growing what all nature says cannot be grown in cool temperate climates. As an object of desire the pineapple takes centre stage in that curious painting, attributed to Danckerts, with royal gardener John Rose on bended knee offering one to Charles II. (Pineapples were first grown in Europe at Leiden in the 1650s where Charles may have first tasted them.) Tim Smit, the saviour of Heligan, takes the place of Rose in a version of the painting in *Country Life*, 4 December 1997.[1]

That a gardener may look at a king, that the gardener holds the golden orb, and may amaze and please a monarch (Heligan pineapples were sent to the Queen and Prince of Wales) says a great deal about the lure of gardening in professional guise. The pineapples, however, say even more, for the downside of pineapple culture is hard work: real back-breaking barrowing of hundreds of tons of dung and other noisesome mixes, repeated pottings and earthings up, daily ministrations for months on end, nightmares about dropping temperatures, noonday panics about scorching ... and then, after harvesting and celebration, beginning all over again. These were the toils, sweats and devotions that elevated gardening to a religious observance, especially in Victorian Britain. Work, the ability to work, and then to rise to the position to command armies of journeyman and garden boys to work, and finally to advise the gardening world in general, amateur and professional, on how to work, this is the legacy of the great head gardeners. Like the pineapple, they and their creed matured in the shade of the eighteenth-century landscape style, emerging into the sunlit glory of the High Victorian gardening empire – in the pineapple heyday stocks of as many as 1500 plants, as at Cyfartha Castle in Merthyr Tydfil, occupied the pits and pine-stoves. And like the pineapple, the twentieth century brought decline to professional gardeners in number and status: in 1911 C. R. L. Fletcher and Rudyard Kipling collaborated on the anthem to decline, to work reduced to 'grubbing-weeds from gravel-paths with broken dinner-knives', to gardening as fit only for pathetic loons:

> And some can pot begonias and some can bud a rose,
> And some are hardly fit to trust with anything that grows;
> But they can roll and trim the lawns and sift the sand and loam,
> For the Glory of the Garden occupieth all who come.[2]

Gardeners were fit enough for war though, and more than half the staff of Heligan were lost in Flanders fields. The dying profession was for only the lame and the old, antedeluvian but wily rustics parodied by Wodehouse, Hadfield and Tom Sharpe. Adam the Gardener, with string around his trousers and horny hands, droning the lore of his ancestors became an antique. The mid-twentieth century preferred sunbathing to working outdoors, and after the Second World War gardening without work, i.e. the labour-saving garden, was invented. But, as with the pineapples, there is now something of a revival, not only of the shrines of work such as the kitchen garden establishments, together with a reawakened interest in their techniques, but of the respectability of labour, with mud-spattered trousers and soil beneath the finger-nails worn as badges of honour in the smarter society.

The labours of gardening are historically elusive, the temple being well guarded by a legendarily fearsome and secretive band of head gardeners, and are so also because history has been written by classically educated minds who have inherited a Greek disdain for menial labour. Cyrus the Great is a garden hero because he was unique in liking to get his hands dirty in his own gardens: Francis Bacon rattles on for pages about the flowers springing, the grass 'kept finely shorn', the ordered hedges and a fountain or two without slime and mud, and in the third line from the end of his famous essay *On Gardens* mentions taking advice with workmen – by which he means giving orders to men, without whom all would be entirely in his imagination. The 3rd Earl of Burlington has long been credited with encouraging William Kent to leap the fence and invent the landscape style, but only comparatively recently have we learned, through Blanche Henrey's painstaking researches, of the stalwart Thomas Knowlton, his head gardener at Londesborough in Yorkshire, who upheld his Lordship's horticultural reputation and provided pineapples, fruits, flowers, vegetables and exotic plants for Chiswick House's glory. That Lord Burlington designed the principal gateway into the walled garden from the house at Londesborough, was seen as an honour but actually marked the stamp of ownership, on gardens that his Lordship rarely visited.[3] Owners were always only too happy to dabble and take all the credit, a perennial battle, since history is most conventionally represented by Gilbert White's observation to Daines Barrington in 1778 that the rise of horticulture stemmed from the interest of gentlemen.

In great part the gentry were ignorant of what their gardeners actually did, for this was an unwritten knowledge, largely passed on by apostolic succession, handed down through the apprentice system. The real 'secrets' of some new begonia or giant tomato were jealously guarded, which gave rise to all the old wives' tales, presumably the tips of weeding women 'spies' or informers, and the protestations of authors from *The Gardener's Labyrinth* (1577) onwards as to authenticity and genuine

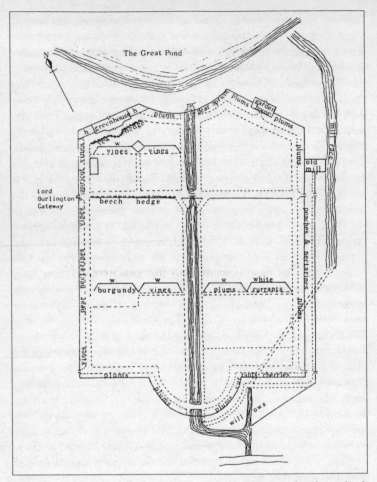

Lord Burlington's Kitchen Garden, Londesborough, Yorkshire, 1792, based on a sketch by the head gardener Thomas Knowlton. A walled garden built at great expense, channelling a natural water supply through the garden, with an overflow to the mill race, and divided with internal walls (w) giving extra space for fruit and vines. His Lordship's Gate, designed by himself, and convenient to the house, allows him and his visitors to inspect the hot beds and glasshouse at the north end of the garden, with any vegetable untidiness screened by the beech hedge. Drawn by D. Neave (1977) and reproduced from Blanche Henrey, *No Ordinary Gardener, Thomas Knowlton's Life and Letters 1691–1781*, 1986.

methods. Work was an indoctrination, from the earliest years, when the son of a gardener or agricultural worker was taken on as a garden boy at twelve years old. It was also something of a conversion, for that same smaller boy shared with cats a reputation as the garden's greatest pest: Mrs Beeton's *Book of Garden Management* of the 1890s suggested smearing garden walls with a mix of red ochre and grease because it would mark the culprit's clothes or fur with an immovable stain. Cats were sometimes redeemed, as in a letter to the *Garden* of 13 May 1905, responding to an anti-cat article with a glowing description from Mr Swanwick of Knutsford on his lamented puss (shot by the gamekeeper) who had kept fruit, spring flowers, carnations and columbines protected from birds, mice and rats. Boys were cured by apprenticeships, a twelve-hour day that started at 6 a.m. bird and cat scaring with clappers, then on to slug picking and washing pots. After a year of such menial tasks his nimble fingers were employed pricking out seedlings and tying wall plants in one of the departments, kitchen garden, greenhouses or flower gardens. With hindsight it seems a pity that girls were not given such apprenticeships. Hannah Clarke was the youngest of ten children of the head gardener at Clyro Court (Kilvert's village) on the Welsh borders; she was born in 1893 and when the First World War started she was needed in the garden with her brothers and the other gardeners gone away. After she had seen to her invalid mother she went on happily to washing pots and picking fruit and graduated to fruit work and the finicky tying of every single bunch of grapes, but she loved it and knew she would not have had the opportunity but for the war.[4]

At sixteen or so, though the seniors might persist in calling him 'boy', the apprentice became an under-gardener, with perhaps a change of establishment, and then a journeyman, with another move. As a foreman in one of the departments he had his own set of tools, and by the time he was thirty he could look out for a headship. As a system gardening worked on a grapevine of opportunity which was a cross between the old-boy network and philanthropic promotion, like boxing for city boys: if you were good looking, hard working and surrounded by well-meaning people the sky was undoubtedly the limit, but equally many fell aside through exploitation, abuse, cruelty and a breakdown in health. We can only guess at the histories of the lowliest in Kipling's glorious garden:

> There's not a pair of legs so thin, there's not a head so thick,
> There's not a hand so weak and white, nor yet a heart so sick,
> But that can find some needful job that's crying to be done,
> For the Glory of the Garden glorifieth every one.[5]

Possibly it was the Presbyterian work ethic, but Scotland produced the greatest head gardeners, determined and brilliant men who poured out of the grand estates of Dalkeith, Drumlanrig, Scone Palace and the Edinburgh Botanic Garden, and much of nineteenth-century gardening world conversed in a Scots burr. Loudon, a kind of Moses of the potting shed, proud of his own Scots birth (at Cambuslang in 1783) and his training at the nursery and experimental hothouses of John Mawer, where he started aged twelve, published an ethical code in his *Encyclopaedia of Gardening* of 1822. Loudon deeply believed in gardening as the great improver of the conditions of men, and etiquette for young ladies pales into insignificance beside his strictures for the decorous behaviour of young gardeners: 'refinement' is the first commandment. While it may be proper to barrow stable-dung for hot beds when it is needed, it is *decorous* to do this early in the morning so that the putrescent vapours and dropping litter may not be offensive to the owner or his casual visitors. *Neatness* is the second rule – 'having everything where it ought to be' confirms the regimentation of the tool shed; finish one job before beginning another, leave your work in an orderly manner, and when walking to and from the work area keep an eye open for weeds and remove them 'as you pass along'. Personal habits are vital: never do anything without gloves that can be done with gloves on, even weeding – 'no gardener need have hands like bear's paws' – be clean, neat and harmonious in dressing, maintain an erect posture and an easy and free gait and motion. 'Elevate, meliorate and otherwise improve any raw, crude, harsh or inharmonious features in your physiognomy, by looking often at the faces of agreeable people, by occupying your mind with agreeable and useful ideas, and by continually instructing yourself by reading. This will also give you features if you have none. Remember you are paid and maintained by and for the use and pleasure of your employer, who may no more wish to see a dirty, ragged, uncouth-looking, grinning or conceited biped in his garden, than a starved, haggard, untutored horse in his stable.'[6]

Whether Loudon's ideal young man became a statuesque Mellors awaiting the attentions of a bored countess, history does not record; otherwise virtues went long unrewarded for marriage was out of the question until the gardener had achieved a headship and house to go with it. Wives who were discreet treasures must have been abundant, but the garden establishment seems to have an ingrained prejudice against women. John Evelyn's translation of La Quintinie's *Compleat Gard'ner* (1693) describes a wife as a debateable asset – either she might 'love and be capable of working about her Husband's Trade' as an unpaid apprentice with the worn-out dinner knife, or she might go off and be a housekeeper, this last often the solution. In 1704 George London apologized for his mistake in sending Lord Weymouth a married gardener, hoping that as he and Henry Wise thought so highly of the man his lordship 'may overlook that drawback'.[7]

As the secret ogres of history they have much to answer for: Emily Davies, the pioneer of women's education and foundress of Girton College, Cambridge, endured a strange childhood, keeping out of the sight of her father, a good Christian reverend gentleman, who banished girls from his school and generally from his sight because they lowered the tone of everything.[8] Emily, bright and intelligent, was left to the society of Lister, the gardener, a man of extreme views and workaholic obsessions which undoubtedly coloured her trenchant style and fostered a judgemental sarcasm. In her *Country Notes*, Vita Sackville-West immortalized the 'terror' of her childhood, the great black-bearded head gardener 'his majestic appearance' enhanced by his green baize apron which set him apart from other men, his pride and power, but 'charming little habits' of putting the first pear or apple, complete with name label, on the lunch table for her father, or the breakfast notes on the temperature range of the night and day.[9] Some of the best head-gardener stories come from America, where they have been preserved in amazement: Jackson Thornton Dawson, born in Yorkshire and taken to America by his widowed mother as a child about 1850, rose to become chief propagator and superintendent at the Arnold Arboretum of Harvard University. Passionate about his plants and their daily care, Dawson was also a devoted family man and rose breeder – his famed trademark (in the best Loudon tradition) was a shirt freshly boiled white for every morning, the gift of his doting wife. To clean his plant labels he would wipe them on the lily-white shirtsleeve, secretly enjoying hearing his visitors gasp and shudder.[10] In the flashy upstate New York estates the million-aire owners vied with each other to employ English butlers and Scots gardeners, who became a kind of mafia of domestic employment orchestrated by the expatriate grapevine and through letters home; the New York state census records the number of seedsmen, nurserymen and gardeners rising by 275 per cent between 1870 and 1930.[11] In their vast tome, *The Golden Age of American Gardens*, Griswold and Weller have documented the secret history of the British gardener abroad; one story concerns Marshall Field III, department store and publishing tycoon, who bought a New York estate, Caumsett, in the 1920s, and despite every lavishment had not got it right – 'Mr Field, I must tell you that you won't get anywhere at all until you have a good gardener' was the advice of his English butler. Did the butler know anyone? Of course he did – George Gillies, from Devon, went to Caumsett in 1923 and outlasted his master. He stayed until 1965, handing over the keys to the NY State Park Commission (and died in 1987).[12]

The temples of garden labour, the walled kitchen gardens, lie like beached barques in crumbling ruin across the face of Britain, thousands of them, at least one or the remnants of one near every community in the land. They are a neglected phenomenon, perhaps as important in the landscape as churches and yet, in the race to conserve the country house and document the ornamental gardens, they have slipped into limbo. Walled gardens were the first gardens to be sited for the good of the soil and aspect (now known as the micro-climate, then well understood if not so named). The great ages of kitchen garden building seem in retrospect to coincide with the great building sprees – that of Tudor to Restoration England, and the nineteenth century, from the Victorians to the Edwardians. The eighteenth century – fast becoming the bête noire of this book – cared enough for the expertise of the kitchen garden (witness Stephen Switzer's *The Practical Kitchen Gardiner* of 1727 and Batty Langley's *New Principles of Gardening* of 1728) but then turned to its obsessions with the ornamental landscape. The old kitchen gardens, many of them with rich, red walls of narrow Tudor bricks, were subjected to seismic shiftings of taste: sometimes they were so well-sited as to be immovable, as at Erlestoke in Wiltshire, where they were ranged along elongated south-facing terraces between the river and the park road. The designer William Eames, one of Brown's

successors, wisely left them, screening them with plantations so that
from the house they appeared as a hanging wood. At Clyro Court,
Hannah Clarke found she had a three-mile walk from the old walled
garden to the newer big house: sometimes the gardens stayed with the
village, and the big house moved off to isolated splendour.

Whatever the status of kitchen gardens, their style and function
seemed to change little; William Cobbett felt he had 'seen and observed
upon as many fine gardens as any man in England' but that nowhere
compared to that of the medieval Cistercian monks of Waverley Abbey.
This, he wrote in *The English Gardener* of 1829, was 'the finest situation
for a kitchen garden that I ever saw'; it was terraced into a south-facing
slope, sheltered from the north by a tree-covered hill, with walls three
feet thick and twelve to fourteen feet high: the upper part, which would
have been sandy, had been terraced with loam, and the lower part sloped
to the moist meadow soil beside the river Wey. In typical manner
Cobbett curses the new owner who has demolished this garden in order
to leave the abbey ruin in solitary, artistic grace, but then he excuses
his bitterness, for this was where, as a boy in the 1770s he had learned
to work 'or rather, where I first began to eat fine fruit'.[13]

This of course was the perk of the working gardener, and one of
the attractions of the profession was to share the quality and variety of
the gentry's food. Cobbett was a champion of this entire system, and
he gives an ideal and detailed design for a brick-walled enclosure 247
feet 6 inches long by 165 feet wide with walls which would be 2 feet
thick, of brick and 12 feet high, round topped, with 'jams' or buttresses
every 8 or 10 feet and on the outside. This left the maximum area of
precious interior wall space for fruit. The garden should be fully south
facing, longways, with shelter from trees north and east, though the
trees would be at a respectful distance, both because of shading, leaf
drop and taking too much out of the soil but also so as not to provide
an easy way in for schoolboys. Inside, a slight slope was desirable –
strawberries were Cobbett's favourites (one can hear him smacking his
lips at the memory of the 'bushels of haut-boy strawberries' tasted at
Waverley in his youth) and strawberries liked a slope, as did early
broccoli, cabbages, peas and beans. It all depended upon whether the
soil needed the slope for drainage, or whether – as with Cobbett's native
Farnham sand – it needed every drop of moisture to soak in on level

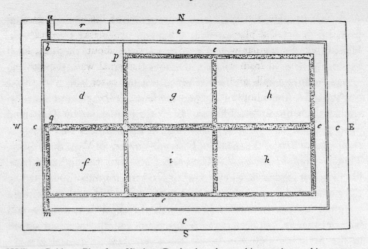

William Cobbett, Plan for a Kitchen Garden based upon his experience: this measures 247 ft 6 ins from east to west, by 165 ft from north to south (giving long south-facing walls) but the outer enclosure is a hedge of thorn or beech, making an outer garden (c) so that apples and pears can be grown on the outer faces of the walls but are still protected from plunder. The narrow double line is the wall, with 10 ft wide beds (e) and the shaded divisions are the paths. (d) is the hot-bed ground, nearest the tool-house (r) and doorways through the wall (b) and the hedge (a). (f), (g), (h), (i) and (k) are the plats for vegetables which are about 50 ft wide.

ground. The bed inside the walls was to be 10 feet deep, with a wide, well-founded gravel path 6 feet wide all round; the low box hedges edged the gravel path to protect it from soil and rubbish when the beds were cultivated. Cobbett's garden had only one gate, at the north-west corner next to the tool house and the hot-bed ground, which needed to be convenient for the barrowing in of manure etc. The hot-bed ground was one-sixth of the total area inside the gravel path; the other five 'plats', roughly 50 feet square, were for vegetables.

Cobbett's garden was for modest country families, managed by one gardener, perhaps a pensioner and a garden boy – the kind of garden that had been worked in the countryside for 500 years. With the accession of Queen Victoria, the kitchen garden was due for a second grand age. Great architects were drafted in to design the gardens for the new estates. At Worsley Hall near Manchester, Edward Blore (who designed the ceremonial east front of Buckingham Palace) built a vast establishment between 1839 and 1845, with every detail of the kitchen garden described in detailed plans, which survive in two massive bound volumes.[14] The rectangular walled garden enclosed about 3½ acres, four square, but divided from east to west by an internal wall, thus giving two south facing walls and borders. Against the outer wall were three vineries and a peach house (though peaches might be grown on a bare south wall in the south of England). With great economy of design, the bothies on the outer, north side of the garden, hard on the estate road, were divided into potting sheds, mushroom house and the (sometimes firewarmed) dining and sleeping quarters for the under-gardeners who were on twenty-four-hour duty to tend the pineapples and melon pits and asparagus beds in their enclosures on the other side of the road.

Inventions and innovations gave the head gardeners scope for achievement: Edwin Budding's lawn mower, patented in 1830, was licensed for production by Ransome's of Ipswich three years later, though horse-drawn mowing was still thought best by the grander gardeners and the sale of leather lawn boots for horses kept up until the Great War (which was to be the last reveillé for hundreds of thousands of working horses). Sheet glass and concrete were both garden innovations; there were pond-concreting competitions, frames and greenhouses became widely available. Heating also advanced, first by steam but most satisfactorily by hot-water piped systems. Head gardeners loved gadgets; Charles M'Intosh perfected a verge cutter and Alexander Forsyth invented a combination of plumb line and level, but the basic garden tools hardly changed at all (and with the exception of stainless steel have not changed in form and use to this day). Iron hoes, rakes, picks and spades have been excavated from Celtic settlements of 1000 B C which are immediately recognizable, and strikingly similar to the illustrations in John Evelyn's *Elysium Britannicum* of 1660.[15] Evelyn's well-stocked tool and potting sheds contained long-handled shears, a wheeled platform with ladder attached for clipping topiary and high hedges, a garden line wound on a square frame, dibbers, plant markers, frost matting, besoms and a many-drawered seed chest. Tender seedlings were covered in glass bells and jars, and a neat little house made of glass squares with a pointed roof and carrying ring looks very like a Wardian case, supposedly not invented until a hundred years later. Larger seedlings in trays were transported in what looks like a curtained four-poster on wheels.

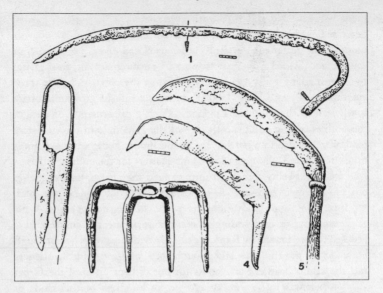

Tools for gardening also unite us across the centuries: scythes, shears and a rake from excavations of prehistoric settlements in northern Europe. (From Audouze and Buchsenschutz, *Towns, Villages and Countryside of Celtic Europe*, 1991, trans. H. Cleere, drawing G. Tosello after M. Beranova, 1980).

(OPPOSITE) As the Celtic tools would have been familiar to John Evelyn, so those he drew for *Elysium Britannicum*, c.1660, are mostly familiar to us: he includes, nos. 10 to 19, surveying and drawing equipment, no. 23 is a 'planting lattice' for regularly setting out bulbs or flowers, no. 31 a stone roller, no. 32 a roller and tamper for banks of earth, and no. 35 is a long pruner with pulley device.

It is easy to appreciate how the young foreman gardener acquiring his own set of tools felt accepted into a fellowship of the ages, or how mournful a row of well-worn initialled handles might seem on the morning the oldest pensioner failed to turn up for work. The pride in polishing them, in sharpening spade edges with the carborundum stone, in cleaning them in an oily-sand mix – the worst crime being to put away dirty tools – in discussing their efficiency and age, afforded a convivial, bantering end to the day's work. Hoes were an art in themselves – as precious to the Victorian gardener as a golf club is to a player, and needed in the same variety for all sorts and conditions of soil,

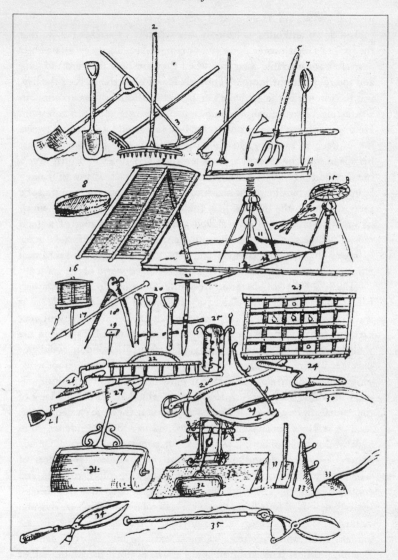

weather and season. Hoes needed to be as bright as a golf club, handles rubbed down and oiled as lovingly as a schoolboy's cricket bat, so that the splinters didn't come up in sun or rain. Rakes, like hoes 'attain their best after considerable wear, for when they are new they are too long and too rough in the tooth'.[16] Tool talk like this, in the dusk of the day, was the essence of the gardener's craft, and a measure of his isolation, in a thrusting Victorian world of industry, engineering and mechanization. Here was still hard, hand labour; the best man could dig an acre twelve inches deep in twenty eight-hour days, and in doing so would thrust his spade into the ground around ten thousand times and turn over a hundred tons of soil. The art, which came with practice, was in making light of this – 'not merely a knack of muscular action, the tool must be proportioned to the muscles that guide it and to the material in which it works'. The rhythm of a skilled spadesman, the swing of a good mower, whose scythe moves through the swathe with an effortless grace – it was this melding of man and tool that approached mechanical efficiency and beauty. All in the quiet, unobserved world of the garden.[17]

Endless hours of rhythmic trenching, pottings up, plantings out, hoeing and watering were the basic drudgery of a gardener's life, so it was little wonder that as a race professionals exhibited flamboyant *alter egos*, and became impresarios of the gaudy and absurd. Escape from the walled confines was every young gardener's goal. Loudon could not have been more right when he advocated gardening as the 'improving' profession, and the glory of Victorian gardening was in the multifarious ways in which gardeners made sure they would be noticed. Many of the annuals from warmer climates were too puny for large gardens unless used *en masse*, a conclusion usually credited to a Scots gardener, John Cale working in London in the 1830s, but popularized by more famous names. George Fleming used the patterned, stone-edged acres of Charles Barry's terrace at Trentham for showing off harmonies and contrasts in colours and subtleties in blending trailing and erect species, with thousands of little lobelia, petunia, calceolaria, nemophila, alyssum, clarkia, salvia, snapdragons and candytuft. Somehow Barry's Italianate garden architecture invited the most extravagant displays: Donald Beaton, head gardener at Shrubland Park in Suffolk, used hundreds of potted scarlet pelargoniums along the balustrades of the great stone staircase, which swept down to a round terrace with wreaths and scrolls outlined in yew and turf, filled with more pelargoniums set in silver sand. The whole creation was held together by a 'serpent' of variegated box, which twisted itself around and through the yew outlines. It was Beaton's development of red pelargoniums which made them a cottage-window tradition by the beginning of the twentieth century. 'Ribbon bedding' was another conceit, using bands of blue nemophila, yellow calceolaria, and a red pelargonium 'Frogmore' in the manner of twisted ribbons beside a path or, at Cliveden, around a great circular bed which, seen from a distance from the terrace, was magically transformed into silky twists. The highest art was to make plants look like something else: the *Gardeners' Chronicle* coined the term 'carpet bedding' for John Fleming's *tour de force* at Cliveden, the Duchess of Sutherland's mono-gram in succulent rosettes of sempervivums and echevarias which were clipped (by some wizardry that avoided bruising) to look as soft and even as the finest Turkish carpet. The competition engendered by such sleights of trowel and clippers rose to a crescendo of 'phyllomania', a leaf-craze, in the 1870s with arms and insignias in all grand gardens and public parks (*Plate 12*). The first floral clock is recorded in 1903.[18]

The head gardeners' professional passions were for the greenhouse exotics, with orchids, gloxinias and begonias as the queens of the show stands. Orchids seem to have exerted an obsessional sway, in all their curious varieties, the large-as-life seductiveness of flowery goddesses, their soft lips and dusky deeps of trumpets, curvaceous and many-lobed generosities, pendunculate perfections illustrated week after week in the engravings of the *Gardeners' Chronicle*. To the eyes of a mere woman, this curious passion for orchids seemed to exert an enormous power in the age of repressed Victorians, which went beyond any knowledge or skill required in propagating them. A country gardener who raised an unusually good specimen of *Cattleya* or *Odontoglossum* might send it to compete with the Veitch Exotic nursery in Chelsea or Lord Rothschild from Tring Park at the RHS show: the status of a potential star plant was such that, carefully packed in a specially constructed crate, it could reach the Horticultural Hall by rail and carter and be unpacked by a careful steward without spoiling the chance of success. A general benev-olence respected effort, the gardener was given his chance (though as Harry Veitch was Chairman of the Orchid Committee it was a slim one) but of course the credit went to the owner, and it needed substantial success at shows before the gardener himself was allowed a trip to London.

Once he himself had become a 'garden escape', he might write for the *Gardeners' Chronicle*, where weekly pages had to be filled with the repeated rounds of jobs to be done in flower garden, kitchen garden, under glass and with hardy fruit, the information drawn from head gardeners all over Britain. The *Chronicle* was the gardener's lifeline, reporting shows and successes in minute detail, with useful advertisements, weather summaries, market notes, question and answer sessions, book reviews and a tremendous widening of horizons with articles from outposts of the empire. Specialization, making yourself an expert on something, whether carnations and picotees or broccoli, was often the way to be noticed. But the highest flyers were the decorators, the head gardeners and their assistants who were so admired for their decorations in country and then town houses, that they were able to set up in business on their own account. Nothing we do today can approach the sheer lavishness of Victorian floral art and the priceless treasures kept in glasshouses of varying temperatures by the head gardeners: a thousand pots of amaryllis at Westonbirt, at Dalkeith whole ranges crammed with foliage of what we still call 'house plants' and use in ones or twos, hundreds of marantas, anthuriums, dracaenas, caladiums and palms, and a cooler range of glass, 300 feet long for cinerarias, heliotrope, primulas and mignonette. Mignonette for scent was greatly in demand, cultivated as a standard in a nine-inch pot, and used to fill the seasonal gap between the lily-of-the-valley and the roses, but all could disappear in a day if a careless housemaid left the window open. The damage done to pot plants by their stay in the smoke-filled and gaslit houses for very brief periods was often fatal, or took endless care to repair, and one night at a ball meant instant death. The balls were the biggest occasions, and tons of foliage and flowers were carried to London for banking stairways and draping ballrooms. The time and labour entailed can be deduced from William Taylor's method for packing roses: cut them early with the dew on them, half open, hang upside down in special trays, their stems wedged with soft wood, the top space in the boxes between the stems filled with other loose flowers, lay them gently, protected with asparagus green or young spinach leaves.[19]

Country-house flowers were a never-ending, scented labour from dawn till evening: the flower room, where the gardeners worked with mystical paraphernalia of knives, string, wire and gum arabic (which was dissolved in water and dropped into azaleas and pelargoniums to stop their petals falling) was a jealously guarded shrine which must have been irresistible temptation to mischievous housemaids. Charcoal was used to keep flower water sweet; the flowers themselves were supported in wet sand, with masses of moss collected and used to conceal underlying structures. The day started with breakfast-tray posies of violets or primroses, then perhaps buttonholes for the twelve o'clock meet of the hunt; flowers for the lunch table, for the drawing room, and corsages of gardenias, stephanotis and roses for the ladies in the evening, as well as the dining table to be wreathed in ivy and roses and set with silver bowls of the scented noisettes 'Maréchal Niel' and 'Gloire de Dijon', grown in glasshouses for faultless blooms. There was a mute invisibility about all this. 'We had to creep in early in the morning before breakfast and replace the flowers,' says gardener Christopher Falconer at Akenfield, 'Lordship and Ladyship must never hear or see you doing it; fresh flowers had to be just there, that was all there was to it. There was never a dead flower. It was as if flowers, for them, lived for ever. It was part of the magic of their lives.'[20]

Robert Felton, the son of a nurseryman, became a court florist, the summit of horticultural ambition: for him Rochfords grew *Rosa wichurana* hybrids trained to represent windmills, elephants, their Majesties in coronation robes (this was for George V and Queen Mary) and Prince of Wales's feathers, 'although a yacht in full sail was considered to be the most spectacular' for the sailor king. Later in 1911 Felton arranged rose spectaculars, baskets twelve feet across and eight feet tall, in golds, coppers and bronze, for the Queen and Queen Alexandra, the gift of the rose breeders of Britain, with hundreds of blooms left over and sent to 'leading London hospitals'.[21]

The increasing popularity of flowers for decoration spilled out of the smart houses and into public life, largely by means of the development of the Covent Garden flower market, which was explained in a leading article in the *Chronicle* on 7 July 1894. The market was licensed for vegetables and fruit by Act of Parliament in 1828, with the last and smallest section H for flowers, but demand rose steadily with Victorian prosperity and the RHS shows so that in 1886 the Floral Hall was opened. Trade was in two sections, potted plants and cut flowers, and made up of two types, regular growers and seasonal suppliers, these often being the head gardeners. The *Chronicles*' contributor, probably a market dealer, was proud of the perfection of the pot plants, mignonette with six to eight giant trusses in a small pot, the heads of bloom on hydrangeas, lilies and even 'common flowers' like Marguerites, ivy-leaved pelargoniums and calceolarias of which there were great banks every morning. (He quickly dismissed 'the sentimental' who might look for wild flowers, and find them on the outer areas, proffered by 'rough-looking gipsy chaps' or dirty flower girls – Eliza Doolittles were objects of despair to the superior marketeers.) There was nothing 'more spectacular and certainly nothing more profitable' than the growing demand for cut-flowers, and the point of the article was to make the head gardeners aware of this: they certainly responded, and great hampers of delphiniums, agapanthus, tuberoses, peonies and eryngiums with lush foliages supplied a growing country-house trade to the market throughout the Edwardian years and into the 1930s.

Selling flowers, and surplus vegetables, was however the first sign of a crack in the foundations of the head gardener's absolutism in his world: the economy of the great house alone no longer sustained him. By the turn of the century the profession was in trouble, accused of arrogance and of taking the credit which rightly belonged to owners (especially at shows) and turned on by a former under-gardener William Robinson, who was the loudest critic of the waste of labour and plants that the bedding system entailed. It had become an overcrowded profession, with too many calling themselves gardeners who were not properly trained, worst of all being the 'jobbing gardeners' who were a worthless disgrace. And a new generation of owners who had grown up with the Victorian head gardeners were in revolt, their feelings well expressed by Charles Wade at his family home at Yoxford in Suffolk where the gardener 'had become such an autocrat, it ceased to be our garden any more, it became his garden in which we were allowed to walk. If asked to move a plant, we were told it was always the wrong time of year, or the plant was too old or too young, or the moon was not old enough . . . he ordered all the seeds and plants and put them where he wished, our only part was to pay.'[22] Wade was typical of the younger and newer kinds of owners who wanted pleasure from their own gardens rather than running battles with a tyrant; indeed they may not even want a man at all and perhaps the gardener's world was on the brink of the unthinkable. In 1908 Frances Wolseley published her first book, *Gardening for Women*, explaining the purpose of her college for lady gardeners: 'Why employ a woman?' she asked, 'well, would you not rather have a nice cheerful bright girl about the place if she really knew her job?' There was a new future for women gardeners, especially where women were on their own at home all day, and a rash of women's training colleges (including Swanley in Kent, Studley in Warwickshire and horticulture courses for women at Reading University)[23] were opening.

The isolation of gardeners in their thousands of scattered, independent kingdoms meant that though they met over their show benches of auriculas, it was not in their nature to band together and march for better conditions. A union or guild was often suggested but the suggestion just as often quashed. Ordinary gardeners felt the Royal Horticultural Society was unsympathetic, an inward-looking clique of gentlemen and grander gardeners absorbed in their special committees for orchids or iris, perhaps on good terms with their own head gardeners but unaware of the wider world. And there was a subtler difficulty: whereas agricultural workers spoke up for themselves, the gardeners were regarded as too close to the big house, part of the establishment and yet not. Gardeners were, like butlers and housekeepers, notoriously conservative and seen as loyal, their loyalty 'bought' by fruit and vegetables and fuel, and daily contact with their employer. Gardeners are notably absent from involvement in politics. They grumbled discontentedly but ineffectively, and in their thousands they were, in the end, only too ready for the adventure of war.

During the war at Clyro Court, the young Hannah Clarke worked seven days a week – 'we tried to carry on the vineries and the lawns, and all that sort of thing, but some of the less important had to go'[24] – Clyro, like everywhere else, was the haunt of the very young, the sick and very old. Tremendous crumblings and decay began in gardens all over Britain during those four years, so gradual that perhaps they were not noticed among so many larger tragedies, but when it was over there were so many changes, so many let houses and new owners, a quickening of the pace of life and lack of patience to wait for slow regimes to be reinstated, that it was much easier to order fruit and vegetables from local suppliers. At Clyro Court, the tenants were a Greek gentleman and his English wife, who was her own housekeeper – 'sort of', sniffed Hannah, who gives the impression that there was a lot of money but very little expertise. It was to be a painful revolution for gardeners trained in the old ways. In *Akenfield*, Ronald Blythe writes of the 'good deal of worship' and 'forgotten mystery' that had managed 'to interpose themselves in the ritual toil of the manor or "big house".'[25] For gardeners this was a puzzling loss: it brought alien behaviour as well as an amateurish enthusiasm, which they despised, into their private world. When the National Gardens Scheme to open gardens as a way of raising funds for district nurses started in 1927, Betty Hussey at Scotney Castle persuaded all the 'best' gardens to open, but gardeners of the old school, like Chris Falconer at Akenfield were horrified: 'I know a colonel near here who, when he opens his garden . . . has all his machines and tools on display. All the mowers, barrows, spades – everything – are polished and oiled and lined up! You wouldn't have got Lordship doing a daft thing like that – but then you wouldn't have got Lordship letting Tom, Dick and Harry into the park, let alone the gardens.'[26]

Another *arriviste* tenant, Cecil Beaton at Ashcombe in Wiltshire, did a great deal for the transformation of dispossessed gardeners into national treasures: Old Dove, the spirit of England incarnate, a sprightly eighty-plus wearing leggings and clothes which were 'by their elaborate cut and fashion, obviously made in Queen Victoria's reign, and had grown by now as lichen becomes part of a stone . . . to become part of his trim body', had wandered up from the village with his son Dove, Beaton's proper gardener. Together they re-made the worn out kitchen garden, revived the fruit trees into production and turned their rather fey, romantic employer (with his overblown notions of rapturous disarray and stucco cherubs) into a respected prizewinner at the local flower show. In his turn[27] Cecil Beaton lovingly portrayed Old Dove, and the gleams of gardening lore shine through: 'He spoke in a simple, yet graphic way that had a poetic effect . . . He related how in the service of some of the Rothschild family he learnt to show off flowers "artistically", and came to know that, in the spring, a border of forget-me-nots is incomplete unless backed with yellow wallflowers, which in turn must be seen against a row of crimson tulips. [Ribbon bedding] . . . He knew to which "classes" various flowers belonged and which "go" with another. Roses, being a different "class" of flower, in no circumstances should be mixed with carnations. Carnations must be arranged in a silver trumpet-shaped vase to look like a sunburst, a few sprigs of asparagus or maidenhair fern to supply the finishing glory. Certain rules must never be broken.'[28]

By this time the Second World War had started, and the unruffled and quietly assured old gardener, who was verger, bell-ringer, and a gardener-general, deputing old cronies and young lads to help in half-a-dozen gardens and allotments, had become for Beaton a symbol of England's stalwart stand. And then he died, quietly and alone of a stroke, in the greenhouse on a sunny morning, and young Dove said quietly, 'I wouldn't have had him go any other way'. Young Dove resisted Beaton's offerings of roses and Canterbury bells – 'good enough for the Chelsea Flower Show' – knowing his father would want 'artistic' restraint and taste, just pinks and maidenhair, with carnations from Mr Rankin at the Manor. The whole village turned out for the funeral. Beaton wrote: 'So the old gardener had gone back to the earth. The aeroplanes, which had brought the proximity of war to the churchyard ... had flown away. By none could this passing of Dove be considered a tragedy of major importance at a time when each day young men were flying off to die in battle, when slaughter was on such a vast scale and the fate of the world was still in the balance. Yet even during the great upheaval of war, one wondered if by the loss of a man of such grace, intuitive knowledge and simplicity of purpose, another valuable link had not been broken with a vanishing England.'[29]

However, old Dove's remaining comrades had a national service to perform. The campaign for feeding the nation by replacing flowers with vegetables had been patchily efficient in the First World War (George V had decreed cabbages around the Victoria Memorial and the Archbishop of Canterbury sanctioned Sunday work)[30] and the Ministry of Agriculture were determined to be hotter off the mark in 1939. Ministerial broadcasts were followed by a 1940 play *Digging for Victory* and the first version of *Gardener's Question Time* was broadcast. The message to the home front was that 'potatoes and onions were munitions of war as surely as shells and bullets'. Land use stipulations and cropping orders were strict, and were expected to be enforced in the national interest.

With hindsight the waste was appalling – Harry Wheatcroft apparently destroyed 100,000 roses, Cornish growers sacrificed their bulbfields, and 90 per cent of the nation's glasshouses had to be given over to tomatoes, with their flowery treasures turned out to die. Head gardeners were to run their establishments as market gardens, selling vegetables to the local community at the garden gate or, quite often, to the military occupants of the requisitioned houses. They were expected to turn their careful traditions upside down, destroying the hedges that created the precious micro-climates inside and around the walled gardens, turning turf paths and lawns into compost, ploughing out the flower beds, letting the hedges go and leaving trees and shrubs untended after weather damage. Of course they did it with splendid efficiency, but when they 'handed back' their gardens at the end of the war, much was gone, forever beyond repair.[31]

The main thrust of digging for victory was, however, directed at the gardening public in general, who were to turn their lawns into potato plots, grow lettuces and tomatoes in window boxes and marrows across the roofs of their Anderson shelters (and perhaps mushrooms inside!). For this effort a great deal of professional guidance was needed, something more than the Ministry leaflets and head gardener's talks to Women's Institutes, somebody who could reach the heart of the nation, advising them of jobs to be done in such a modest way that they would quietly carry them out: the home front needed just such a person as old Dove, the 'treasure' that smart weekenders like Cecil Beaton had discovered in their country retreats, just as Vita Sackville-West had at Sissinghurst, where she fought her private war:

> And in the gloom, with his slow gesture, moves
> The leathern demiurge of this domain,
> Like an old minor god in corduroy
> Setting and picking up the things he needs.
> Deliberate as though all Time were his.[32]

'Honour the gardener! that patient man' she continues, knowing that honour and exasperation were about equal: but it was this image – more than likely ushered into being by Harold Nicolson at the Ministry of Information and his friends at the BBC, who was to be deified as 'Adam the Gardener'. As drawn for the *Sunday Express*, the old head gardener in battered trilby had kindly brown eyes and a square jaw haloed by a cotton-woolly fringe, he wore a cast-off but clearly once Savile Row black waistcoat, white shirt, stout boots and serviceable-looking trousers, which were upon close examination not tied with straw below his knees – it was just that the artist's crease-lines made them look that way. 'Adam', alongside the good-humoured legends C. H. Middleton ('Mr Middleton') and Fred Streeter on the radio, established the public image of the head gardener, which passed into national acceptance (and helped to win the war).

There were fewer and fewer of the genuine article around, but one was Ted Humphris at Aynhoe, who fortunately wrote his memories in *Garden Glory*, published in 1969.[33] He was born in 1901, started work when he was fifteen and was to remain for fifty years through four generations of the Cartwright family at Aynhoe Park. From his earliest memory of hunt days and being stationed to head off the fox from refuge in the garden to his final triumph with his orchids on Percy Thrower's BBC television *Gardening Club*, he gives a thorough account of his progress, the way he worked in various departments and why, and especially of his loving care of his orchids and other flowers. But there is an undercurrent of larger events, of wars, of deaths and death duties, of revivals and celebratory balls, of horticultural honours and garden openings, of tragedies (Richard Cartwright and his only son were both killed in a car crash in 1954) and recoveries, that somehow symbolize – in this quiet corner on the Oxfordshire–Northamptonshire borders – the fate of the country house garden.

To some extent Ted Humphris and his beloved 'orchid called Portia' typify what was happening to gardeners. The *Cattleya* Portia had been bought at Harrods sometime in the 1920s, and with Ted's interest and care, brought to show standard to win a Lindley Medal at the RHS in 1938. War restrictions allowed precious collections to be kept, so 'Portia' had her 10 per cent of allowable greenhouse space at Aynhoe, and in 1948 she took another trip to the Horticultural Hall, in the back of a van with Ted, to win a Lindley Silver Medal. Hundreds of her blooms – she was now a giant – were sold at Covent Garden for enormous sums. By this time she was bringing in fan mail, questions and pleas for assistance from other orchid owners, and quite naturally Ted and his 'Portia' graduated to television. In many ways it was to be television and magazines who took over the professional gardeners' knowledge, and in the characters like 'Adam', the old treasures, would broadcast it to our amateur world.

Television gardening had emerged from the wartime campaigning, from the gathering of expertise and the patient demonstration of how it should be done, and the pots of plants were simply transferred to the studio when *Gardening Club* started in 1954. A derelict allotment in Birmingham was actually the first TV garden but with the advent of BBC 2 and Percy Thrower's *Gardener's World*, the producers found a retired Boots research chemist named Arthur Billitt, happily making a garden in deepest Worcestershire, at Clack's Farm near Ombersley.[34] The name was perfect; Arthur Billitt, pursuing his retirement dream and having set out his ornamental garden in the summer of 1968, found his life transformed and the television cameras moving in on his 600 square yards of vegetable garden and small greenhouse. The rest is television history, as through the 1970s the weekly adventures of Clack's Farm featured in the nation's sitting rooms. Through producers Bill Duncalf, then Barrie Edgar, and presenters Percy Thrower and Peter Seabrook, gardening became entertainment: the greenhouse had removable windows for good views, the garden paths were pavement smooth to allow cameras to move about freely, the Royal National Rose Society, the Dahlia Society, and all the other flower societies had to show off their specialities, every specimen was stage-ready and what was not did not appear on camera that week. For the very best of reasons – that television was first and foremost entertainment, and that the founding (wartime) tradition had been to promote the biggest and most perfect vegetables and fruit – the modern view of stage-set gardens and glossy, unreal perfection was born. There was emphasis, too, on making best use of fertilizers and other chemicals, which must have been related to Arthur Billitt's connection to Boots, who at their Lenton Research Station were examining plant nutrition and trace elements. In a way the worst side of the old head gardener's traditions, the contrivance and distortion of the show table, had emerged triumphantly as the dominant image of gardening excellence.

In its way Clack's Farm was seeking to restore something that had been lost. A famous Mass Observation survey immediately after the war revealed that 80 per cent of Britons, when asked how they wanted to live, wanted a house and a garden. In reality relatively few of these proved to be active gardeners; the garden was more of a symbol of space, and the right to do what one liked with it (including concreting it over). Across all classes there was either a plain dislike or distaste for the work involved or an inability to cope: as the gardens of the nation must have resembled a moonscape of bombed rubble, crumbling air-raid shelters, piles of rubbish and worn-out vegetable plots, a stage of despair was understandable. The *Studio Gardening Annual* returned in smaller, utility format in 1950 (after a ten-year absence) devoted to 'Remaking and Rehabilitation'; at least that sub-title was listed five years later, though the words do not appear in the actual issue. Neither do any pictures of less than perfect lawns or borders or less than sunnily serene gardens and spring woodlands, and the whole tone of the issue is suspiciously optimistic.

Such optimism was the way of the magazines and undoubtedly of the nurseries who wished to boost business; yet normal service was not resumed. The traditional joy of gardening as the reward for intense labour was gone for good. Post-war gardeners wanted none of it; they wanted 'low maintenance' gardens of year-round beauty: if there were some who enjoyed painstakingly tieing up chrysanthemums and sweet peas that was well and good – many gardeners wanted the chance of a challenge or adventure, to grow Bartley primulas in the damp patch, to cut an occasional dash with a cactus dahlia at the village show – but the relentless routine, the boredom of repeated efforts was out of fashion. The *Studio Annual*, co-edited by Roy Hay who was on the staff of the *Gardener's Chronicle* and a gardening broadcaster, gave space in 1952 to the young landscape architect Brenda Colvin to write a piece called 'Gardens to Enjoy'. She expounded radical, modernist ideas: 'a garden can be thought of as an extension to the house', one should have 'a small plot for herbs and vegetables near the kitchen, the rest for recreation', 'working in the garden is in itself a relaxation to many of us, but the ideal is to have as little essential work as possible'. There was more: 'flowers, in most cases, last but a short time. Foliage is more enduring'. She advocated plenty of shade-giving trees, good groupings of flowering shrubs, a comparatively small area of sunlit lawn, and a few flowers near the house, if necessary. A designer's eye could appreciate minimalist pleasures, 'the deeply fissured and twisted bark' of a sweet chestnut, the peeling-bark maples, the twisting stems of *Arbutus* and a

The Pursuit of Paradise

trim box hedge contrasted to bouffant lavender. For non-gardeners, the
new race of potterers, she suggested mown grass paths through orchard
trees with bulbs, bluebells and forget-me-nots, or if grass refused to
grow beneath the trees, then a carpet of woodruff, ivy and violets enlivened with foxgloves, Solomon's Seal and late Japanese anemones.[35]

Ted Humphris encountered Brenda Colvin at the end of *Garden
Glory*, when in 1960 she re-designed a garden for his final employer; he
is characteristically polite, but clearly did not appreciate her approach –
which was designing his labour of love out of existence – and he retired
to his greenhouse and his pots of lilies. But the new breed of designer-
gardeners were to win the day over the old school. Work was desperately
out of fashion: from under the very roof of the RHS Roy Hay enthused
about, 'Gardening the modern way saving time and labour'.[36] No right-
minded gardener could refuse mechanization (a portable power-pack
long grass cutter, chain saw, a Bantam rotovator with attachments, the
Webb battery lawn mower, the 4-stroke Suffolk Punch) or new gadgets
(polythene pipes, pop-up and oscillating sprinklers, the Wolf Dutch
weeder and three-tined cultivator, the Wilkinson Swoe, a knapsack
sprayer and butane blowlamp) or trouble-free plants, those that did not
need staking and especially those that covered the ground so closely as
to shade out any small seedlings. Graham Stuart Thomas elaborated on
ground-cover plants, of whom the highest praise uttered was 'no annual
maintenance required'. These (unfortunately) materialized as sheets of
clashing ericas and callunas (as in the Heath garden at Wisley), the
ground-gobbling *Lamium galeobdolon variegatum*, surface-running *Hed-
era colchica*, big leaved hostas (as long as there were no snails) and hardy
Geranium macrorrhizum, these two keeping each other at bay, and 'high
ground-cover' *Gunnera manicata*.

Low maintenance ground-covers were the ugliest and most drab
kind of planting ever invented: they were an understandable response
to a declining labour force, but even more significant was the advent of
the new container marketing. In 1953 the managing director of John
Waterer, Sons and Crisp, Gerald Pinkney, had visited America and
seen what were called 'garden centres'. Waterers' Nurseries enjoyed the
highest reputation of the day and when they exhibited a 'garden centre'
at the Chelsea Flower Show, with plants in tin containers ready to take
away, it was certain that everyone else would follow. They took over

James Russell's Sunningdale Nurseries in 1968: instant plants had come to stay.

No one did more for the development of mechanical gardening, garden-making by dozer and bucket excavator and dragline, than Alan Bloom at Bressingham. He has written at length and energetically about his tremendous efforts to carve out Bressingham's success from unyielding and wet acres in the years since the war.[37] One of the current horticultural innovations is his – the island bed – which he first tried in the early 1950s: digging up the old lawn at Bressingham and pondering the boredom of working long borders, with all their attendant staking, it struck him that perennials would do better with light and air in beds with all round access. His first half-dozen island beds were made as an experiment, for holding reserve nursery stock, and the more he followed up the notion 'the more rational and sensible it appeared'. When Bressingham's steam railway and gardens opened to an amazed public in the 1960s the island beds were an established part of the layout, their philosophy thoroughly explained in *Island Beds for Perennials* in 1975.

If the legacy of the old head gardeners lingered anywhere it was in the backrooms of the National Trust's gardens; at Bodnant Charles Puddle had taken over from his father in 1947, and taking as many as 135,000 visitors a year in his stride had remained until he handed over to his son, Martin, in 1982; and at Anglesey Abbey Richard Ayres took over from his father, and is now coming up to his own retirement age. These are remarkable people, devoted to their gardens, for they have found themselves stranded a little like dinosaurs left from another age. The National Trust retained a loftily autocratic attitude to its gardeners for many years, which Graham Stuart Thomas as gardens adviser had to work hard to mollify. In 1979 he dedicated *The Gardens of the National Trust* to the head gardeners, and ruefully remarked that he had perhaps progressed from working for the Trust to working with it, but he was optimistic. His successor as chief gardens adviser, John Sales, has just retired having brought about a revolution, in that through the improved status, and visibility, of the head gardeners, the whole professional structure has been boosted and revived. In 1976 Brian Hutchinson from Castle Howard and others set up the Professional Gardeners' Guild, because so many felt they worked in isolation, and this too has had an important influence.[38]

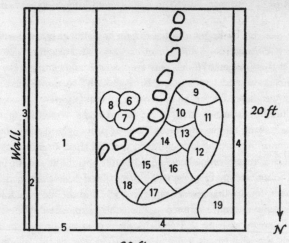

1. Drive for car
2. Border of spring bulbs and candelabra primulas
3. Rose 'Mme Alfred Carrière' (white) on wall with *Clematis* 'Jackmannii'
4. Hedge of *Berberis thunbergii* 'Atropurpurea'. (purple). Ruby foliage
5. Gates
6. *Azalea mucronatum* White. May
7. *Azalea mucronatum* 'Ripense'. Lilac. May
8. *Rhododendron* 'Sapphire'. Blue. Apr.
9. *Potentilla mandschurica*. White. Grey leaves. Summer
10. *Erica mediterranea* 'W. T. Rackliff'. White. Feb.–Apr.
11. *Potentilla* 'Moonlight'. Sulphur. Summer
12. *Erica stricta*. Pink. Autumn
13. *Hypericum* 'Hidcote'. Gold. Summer
14. *Erica vagans* 'Mrs Maxwell'. Raspberry pink. Aug.
15. *Rhododendron* 'Arthur Osborne' (very late flowering). Crimson
16. *Hydrangea* 'Vicomtesse de Vibraye'. Blue on acid soil. Pink on lime
17. *Erica carnea* 'Winter Beauty'. Pink. Dec.–Mar.
18. *Erica carnea* 'Springwood Pink'. Jan.–Mar. (Salmon bells. June. Autumn colour)
19. *Enkianthus chinensis* or Japanese maple. Foliage interest

Judith Berrisford, plan for the front garden of a semi-detached house or bungalow facing north on acid soil, *c.*1965, using plants that need little maintenance and yet give colour at all seasons. From *The Very Small Garden, Unlimited Ideas for Limited Space*, 1968.

The head gardeners' kingdoms, the walled kitchen garden, has not fared so well. Ever since the late 1940s, the philosophy of conservation has been driven by keeping the roofs on the stately homes, and then dressing the dining rooms and bedrooms up in true aristocratic splendour for proletarian delectation. Visitors would also enjoy the pleasure gardens, the lawns and terraces and lakes, but the working areas of the garden were disposable. Walled gardens became convenient car parks, and as nothing struck horror into administrative hearts more than a range of rotting greenhouses and glass frames, these were speedily demolished. Our appreciation of garden history seems to have been a series of sleeps and reawakenings: a cookery writer, 'fed up with recipe books', Susan Campbell awakened in 1981, finding herself 'as if it was conceived with the aid of some external force' offering to write a history of kitchen gardening. 'Nowhere, in the early 1980s', she recalls, 'with the exception of a modest but lovely garden at Deans Court in Wimborne and a handful of similar gardens in Scotland, did I find a kitchen garden in full production.' Susan Campbell's finds were rather walled gardens being garden centres, grassed over, abandoned, filled with a swimming pool or tennis court, but usually the answer to her enquiry was 'You've seen it already – it's the car park'.[39] She persisted and made her contacts, she became deeply involved with her gardens, travelling the length of Britain with her camera and notebook, and she published a book of 'snippets' so becoming known for her subject. It was infectious: the BBC asked her if she knew of a garden within reasonable distance of the Natural History Film Unit at Bristol which they could use as a television project. The only one she knew was insistently private, so she declined to help.

The BBC and Jennifer Davies found the walled garden on the Chilton Foliat estate and the head gardener, Harry Dodson, who was a superb representative of his breed: the *Victorian Kitchen Garden* series was a triumph when it was first shown in the autumn of 1987, revealing a public fascination with behind-the-scenes at the country house (where, after all, the majority of us will find our forebears). The spell was broken. Susan Campbell published her 'private' garden as *Cottesbrooke, An English Kitchen Garden* (1987) and Heligan's elaborate vegetable and fruit gardens also came into public view. Joan Morgan and Alison Richards scripted a series of Radio Three talks on their researches at Linton in

Kent, 'A Paradise Out of a Common Field', which was published in book form in 1990. Susan Campbell's idealized *Charleston Kedding* (1997) has only confirmed the riches of this area of research, and now everyone is scrambling around to find a kitchen garden to restore. Or it seems like it, though the restorations will only emphasize the complete spectrum of social history that has been largely abandoned and lost. Heligan's kitchen quarters are working again, but perhaps the most poignant pleasures are those of a less high profile, which can be found by happy accident. In north Lincolnshire, Sir Robert Sheffield's Normanby Hall was acquired by the county council after his death, and the resulting country park includes the kitchen garden establishment. This was inherited intact and in working order, the walled garden and stores and potting sheds were caught and perpetuated and are now lovingly maintained. There is much magic, a lump in the throat indeed, in the rows of tools and assemblies of pots, in the carefully brushed floors and the coal fire in the bothy, which welcomes the gardeners in for their tea.

CHAPTER TEN

>⊹> ⊹⊹✸⊹⊹ <⊹<

The Formative Garden

The combination of children and gardens invites extremes of reaction, either a soft indulgent sigh or an immediate dash for the nearest offensive weapon. The history of children and gardens is equally polarized; they were strictly excluded as pests for a long time, but then taken in and put to work, and finally in modern times cajoled, encouraged, given small wheelbarrows and allowed educational play.

The pretty image of the darling little gardener has sold books and tiny tools for 200 years: the famous painted images include Martha Rhodes in grey satin, her podgy hand on an auricula in its pot, painted by Christopher Steele about 1750, the angel-faced Sir William Clayton, 4th baronet at ten years old, by Joseph Wright of Derby, in spotless shirt and knickerbockers with his miniature barrow and spade, and John Singleton Copley's *The Little Gardener* of around 1790, a five- or six-year-old of indeterminate sex in a long skirt with a painted barrow full of flowers. In 1789 Richard and Maria Edgeworth's *Essays on Practical Education* advocated practical play, with sturdy carts and small gardening tools, as well as printing presses, weaving looms and furniture construction kits. Adults, especially the world weary, obviously thought fondly of such images: old Lord Albemarle 'happened to look over the hedge into the gardens of Kensington Palace' and smiled over the enchanting picture of the young Princess Victoria watering her flowers.[1] The rather younger Leigh Hunt had the same vision, with the princess loomed over by a hovering footman looking like a giant fairy. The Princess had a sprig of holly pinned to her dress to make her keep her chin up, and did not grow up to be a gardener; but of course Prince Albert was keen, and the tools and barrows for the use of their children in their garden plots can still be seen at Osborne House. The best manufacturers, such as Wilkinson, Brades, Thornhill and later Webb lawnmowers, fell over themselves to make miniatures, finding them to be powerful advertising tools.

Young and royal gardeners captivated the nation when the young Princesses Elizabeth and Margaret Rose took gardening and tree-planting photo calls at Windsor: the thirteen-year-old Princess Elizabeth grew vegetables and fruit in her own plot for the war effort, and when Rex Whistler sketched the royal family on the terrace at Royal Lodge he gave Princess Elizabeth a rake to hold rather in the manner she would one day hold the sceptre, with a toppled-over watering can at Queen Elizabeth's feet (*Plate 26*).

Such images clearly had their uses, and in the 1930s the doings of the Princesses were enthusiastically copied by the many fortunate children of the Empire. However we should not forget that they were paralleled by centuries of child labour in gardens, to which there was a harsher side. Children with their nimble fingers always worked in gardens as cheap labour, but the particular intensity of the nineteenth century establishments must have seen cruelty and forced labour that should have earned them their own chronicle to match that of the chimney sweep boys in *The Water Babies*. Bad establishments, in the way of the world more numerous than good, sent boys weeding gravel paths in the frosty dawn then withdrew them out of sight to hump coal, manure or bark for the boilers and hotbeds, often in semi-underground conditions little better than a mine. They became stokers and flue cleaners, their tasks going on all night in the coldest weather, and they watered and cleaned in the greenhouses in summer heats, before going out to shake poisonous powders over growing crops, and themselves. Mealtimes were missed or shortened, they were kept working into the evenings, perhaps retiring to a freezing bothy if the fire had been let out; their sleeping lofts were often thatched or filled with straw and close to erratic boilers and flying sparks – many must have been burnt in their beds.[2]

No sensible Victorian child would wish to work in a garden, but it could be converted into a play-place by choice. In the 1820s, almost thirty years on from the Edgeworths' advocacy of garden play, the extremely happy home of Samuel Reynolds Hole, the future great gardening Dean of Rochester, and his sisters was only the nursery out of doors. The dolls' house faced down their plot and the 'gardener' was a toy soldier who 'spent most of his time lying on his stomach, his form being fragile and the situation windy': the children made fishponds out of metal pans and a grotto out of an oyster-barrel on its side, 'tastefully ornamented' with evergreens, and animals from their indoor Noah's Ark. Real gardening was hampered because the head gardener had several differences of opinion with the children and would not help them, especially as they liked to 'transfer specimens in full beauty from his garden into our own'.[3]

Jane Loudon had the good sense to see that it was a question of ownership. She wrote a little book of child-friendly appearance and character called *My Own Garden* or *The Young Gardener's Yearbook* in 1855, with good advice and much emphasis on the Victorian virtues of patience and perseverance as the lessons of the garden. From then onwards writing for children, including apprentice boys, seemed to take off, with a magazine, *Gardening for Children*, edited by the Revd C. A. Johns (author of *Flowers of the Field*) as well as Robert Louis Stevenson's anthems to garden adventures, *The Child's Garden of Verses* first published in 1885. *The Garden* magazine ran a column 'The Child's Garden' as one of the territories of its regular contributor Augusta de Lacy Lacy: this was not written for the 'little chap who will insist on having a flower pinned to its frock' but for mothers, governesses and nurses to learn the value of a daily hour outdoors, made fun, and especially for delicate children. Miss Lacy knew of a ten-year-old with chronic asthma who could not go to school but was a born gardener 'now quite a good Carnation specialist' and another small boy who could walk his mother along the herbaceous border and name all the plants. Miss Lacy suggested children grew mustard and cress an old wet flannel, sow aconites and snowdrops to learn that the growing year started early, patiently transplant, not leaving a single seedling to die, watering after, and learn to pot, 'the little hands growing conversant' with bulbs and tubers, the crocking, pressing of the earth, the turning and tapping, the settling of roots in new quarters, staking and tying, cutting the raffia, twice round the stake and once round the plant, knotting on the stake *not* the stem and cutting all off neatly 'with his little gardening scissors'.[4] Gertrude Jekyll could not have missed this in *The Garden* and wrote her own *Children and Gardens*, published in 1908. She worked hard on the photographs of her nieces Barbara and Pamela, with Barbara and Robert

Lutyens and other friends and neighbours – one of her most evocative images is of black stockings and shiny boots discarded on a seat, the wearer playing in the water. Miss Jekyll was team leader in activities that were more science than horticulture, constructing sand castles, seed hunting and sorting, the study of leaf shapes and bark patterns – and perhaps art – making daisy chains and cowslip balls: the children were led into the things she did in her own childhood. However much it spoke to the children as young adults, the book was really for well-meaning grown-ups. It was quickly followed in 1911 by Frances H. Burnett's *The Secret Garden* which had three important elements: (i) the children actually gardened, (ii) they found friendship and help in the boy Dickon, and (iii) it illustrated the benefits for sickly children, just as Miss Lacy had expounded.

Possession of the garden was so important. Vita Sackville-West was an unruly child in turn-of-the-century summers (she was eight in 1900) whose favourite game was soldiers, she in command of all the servants' children she could muster, accused of robbing peach trees and destroying borders by Knole's head gardener, whom she regarded as an ogre and spoil-sport.[5] The trouble was that her garden plot was in too prominent a place, and 'weeds grew too fast and flowers too slowly' so when it became untidy the gardeners descended and tidied it up, so that she did not feel it was hers at all. Almost as soon as she was married and had a garden of her own, which happened to be in Constantinople, she became interested.[6] One more picture illuminates this period: Edwin Lutyens liked children, often in preference to their parents, his clients, and in July 1904, on a glorious evening 'the great Downs bathed in reflected light' he arrived at one of his favourite happy family houses, Little Thakeham in Sussex, which he had built for Ernest Blackburn and his family. Blackburn (with a little help from his architect but *none* from Miss Jekyll) made a magnificent garden, and as a fond and liberally inclined parent had given his four eldest children their plots. 'The children's gardens are very amusing', Lutyens wrote to his wife, Emily, 'Aileen's garden was dull but tidy and fairly full. Sylvia's garden was rather wayward, Barbara's absolutely neglected, Aubrey's garden, aged four, is really wonderful, he watches things grow, knows the names of all his plants and is thrilled and thrilling over it, so wise and sensible, picks off dead things, weeds, waters, propagates with sense and care.

He has a row of sweet peas and roared with laughter of the idea of their climbing sticks, he put them in under protest, now in transport of delight, they climb!'[7] The Blackburn children obviously had both ownership and freedom of expression.

It was not the least of Gertrude Jekyll's influences that her values were carried into women's education through her friendships with pioneers of Oxford and Cambridge colleges, especially with Barbara Bodichon and Barbara Stephen at Girton and Nora Sidgwick and Blanche Athena Clough at Newnham in Cambridge. Their grounds and gardens were vital to college life, for privacy, relaxation, recreation and produce (that being the order of priorities at least before the First World War) and this rubbed off on the students. Frances Dove (later Dame) was one of the earliest students at Girton and she became the first headmistress of Wycombe Abbey School for Girls in 1896. There she introduced gardening into the curriculum on the basis of current educational researches which showed that intellectual development could only match the development 'of muscular skill of some kind', and she supported the landscape gardener Madeline Agar in producing *A Primer of School Gardening*, an early book on the subject in 1909. In her introduction Miss Dove remarks that the Primer's readers could not but be 'braced and refreshed by the quiet, simple, breezy activity' of the chapters on setting up the system of six by ten feet plots, care of tools, arrangement of classes ('weather difficulties'), cropping ideas, costs, and holding of competitions and shows. Advice on suitable flowers, especially for pots in the girls' rooms, pests and diseases and propagation methods was included but the emphasis was upon gardening rather than horticultural science.[8]

The Primer understood school gardening to be at least partially about muscular development, but also the making of a nation of amateur gardeners to boost home food production as well as a pleasurable pastime, which if understood by the age of fourteen would last for life. The progressive educators went for rather more: the melding of the green environment into spiritual and moral development, diet and health; progressive schools depended upon being in beautiful places. Bedales was founded by John Haden Badley in 1893 in a beautiful Elizabethan house near Haywards Heath but moved to the even more dramatically enchanting landscape of Steep, near Petersfield, in 1900. The adventure of helping to level and lay out games pitches, dig the swimming pool and carry out drainage projects was an integral part of school life: gardening parties meant teamworks led by the second master, Oswald Byrom Powell – 'Osbos' to forty years of Bedalians – constructing cold frames, surveying, working the allotments or picking fruit, whatever the timely task. Osbos was a keen beekeeper and taught book-binding, along with all the usual lectures and lessons and games, yet he was never too busy to cure the new boy who stammered or be hauled out at dawn to see the bee orchid found by the excited boy who might grow up to be a great naturalist. Marjory Gill, a rather wild, open-air child, whose father Georgie was Eric Gill's cousin, with a temperamental resemblance, went to Bedales in 1910 after an unhappy experience at an 'arty' school run by two ladies in Westerham. Marjory discovered she was good at sports and games, but also worked hard at book-binding and gardening. She found Osbos 'a man after my own heart, a craftsman and beekeeper, with a large-hearted and transparent nature and a weatherbeaten face like a russet apple' and he encouraged her first experiments in garden design so that she planned and planted the herbaceous border round the hall and library, built by Ernest Gimson in 1911.[9]

Private progressive schools which burgeoned during the 1920s all valued gardens in one way or another. Bertrand and Dora Russell set up their school at Beacon Hill in Sussex in order to fulfil their exacting requirements for their own children and those of friends: Beacon Hill was secluded inside 200 acres of gardens and grounds on the South Downs, with an emphasis on the provision of Tuberculin Tested milk and fresh fruit and vegetables (but no meat). Open-air free gymnastics, dancing and running wild were the uses for the safe grounds as the necessary balance to the stimulation of minds and hands – Beacon Hill was for the children of highly gifted parents and it was thus assumed that they would be similarly gifted. Everything was achieved by discussion and agreement between the children and grown-ups, gardens and pets were allowed as it was to be a home from home, but one senses that these were not wholly approved of, in this commonwealth of higher things.[10]

At Dartington Hall in Devon, looked on rather bitterly by the British in general and Dora Russell in particular, as 'splendidly equipped and endowed with American money', the emphasis was more on the arts and traditional crafts. The money came from Dorothy Elmhirst's

Whitney family fortune, and she and Leonard Elmhirst were brought together by their shared desire for an educational utopia that would bring new life to the historic Dartington Hall and its estate. They brought in the best consultants in architectural restoration and garden design – H. Avray Tipping, the autocratic *Country Life* contributor, Dorothy's American friend Beatrix Farrand, and the talented but diffident Percy Cane.[11] For the school the garden was an outdoor great hall, used for theatricals and musical events, and as a backdrop to all great occasions: undoubtedly the Elmhirsts saw their splendid garden as a passport to acceptance (which they never achieved) in a rather reserved West Country society but for generations of pupils it became a beloved and beautiful remembrance. More importantly it never disappeared into a childhood ether, for Dartington Hall's garden has remained permanently open, free of charge, to all local residents and visitors for almost eighty years.[12]

The British reluctance to see beyond envied American money, and suspect radical motives, has meant that the use of Dartington's garden as an educational asset has not been emulated by the mainstream of private education. This despite an enormous takeover of formerly magnificent gardens, a largely unremarked phenomenon of twentieth-century Britain. From the 1920s, and Stowe School settling into its sublimely beautiful landscape garden[13] – arguably a work of art of international value – a large proportion of the boys and girls of Britain have been educated in rhododendron-girt piles, have kicked metaphoric footballs in the Elysian fields, and learned adult vices in Temples of Virtue. Many parents sacrificed themselves to private education for the sake of the beautiful surroundings, and the hoped-for elevation of young minds: now, after eighty years of schools in Victorian shrubberies and on manicured lawns, which were invariably viewed as a maintenance problem rather than an environmental opportunity, it is certain that hundreds of nineteenth-century gardens have been sacrificed to the pressures of twentieth-century education. Up and down the land the trees that sheltered the rhododendrons have been felled, the lawns put down to hard tennis courts, and whilst the rose garden may have been maintained for the sake of the headmasters' tea parties, garden buildings and greenhouses have become ruins, haunted by the ghosts of homesick children. The gardening plots for pupils were invariably in obscure, sunless corners, the designed terraces and relics of yew-walled rooms usually out-of-bounds, the daily slog of cross-country running across the park marked by a single muddy track. Thousands of former pupils have memories tainted by the *laissez-faire* attitude of private educators who saw these gardens and grounds as a burden or as a fringe of valuable building plots. Whole generations, now empowered by adulthood, have a fondness – or disdain – for gardens in decay, a desire to rescue – or obliterate – a vast heritage of garden and grove environments.

In national education, the province of Church and State, the legacy of gardening clergy like Dr Bartram at Wakes Colne, found strong support in rural elementary schools, where gardening became a vocational study. The handbooks were thorough and of an extremely high standard, written by educators and horticulturists in benevolent alliance. *School Gardening*, first published in 1905 went through several editions, with joint authors, W. E. Watkin, secretary of the East Suffolk Education Authority, and Arthur Sowman, the county lecturer in horticulture. There was also the liberal approach, tinged with feyness, such as *Child Life in Our Schools*, by Mabel A. Brown, which was a manual for infant teaching based on Froebel and Pestalozzi principles: in this nature study is the basis of the school curriculum – 'no subject (was) better calculated to promote right feeling in a child'. Mabel A. Brown was headmistress of such a school, unidentified but on the edge of a substantial town, three quarters of a mile from the sea. She advocated and practised the harmony of lessons inspired by sea and shore life, the seasonal changes in the countryside, and school gardening for even the very smallest pupils. In another book – *The Children's Calendar* of 1909 – she published songs and games for pupils, all based on nature study, seasonal traditions and the work and manufacturing that was the background to their lives.[14]

There is ample evidence of the widespread encouragement of gardening in schools, especially in London: photographs abound of small girls in white smocks tending flower pots on a roof in White Lion Street, Pentonville, in 1912, grammar school girls in pleated gymslips and cloche hats staking lilies in plots in Regent's Park in 1926, infants solemnly grouped around a plane tree planted in their schoolyard, gaggles of small boys, in short grey trousers with snake-buckle belts, enthusiastically digging, raking, hoeing and watering their brick-edged plots. There were also, in those days of endemic tuberculosis, open-air schools where everything was done in a garden setting, with only the flimsiest wooden shelters for refuge from the worst weather.

This vigorous tradition of school gardening developed during the 1920s and 1930s, leaving the vocational aspects – for boys only, in country schools only – behind. With the new schools built on green-field sites during the 1930s and immediately after the war, the syllabus provided scope for the management of their grounds. Middlesex was a leading education authority in this respect: *A Textbook of Gardening for Schools* by Jack Hardy, the county advisory officer, and S. Foxman, head of John Perryn County Secondary School in Acton, first published in 1939, expected a high standard of management via teaching of all aspects of cultivation and propagation which extended into mycology and ento-mology. After the war the thinking was that 'gardening' as a subject did not have the desired technological lilt, so 'Rural Studies' arrived: Messrs Carson and Cotton, rural studies organizers for Hertfordshire and Lin-colnshire respectively, combined on a handbook in 1962 which advocated the school estate run as both garden and farmholding. They observed with feeling that 'the ideal setting for a school is a garden.' Unfortunately, for political and educational thinkers, they were crying in the wilderness. The syllabus was under pressure from the difficulties of managing large classes – the result of the post-war baby boom – and practical subjects, where it was even more difficult to marshall a class of forty pupils into a semblance of order and progress, were pushed aside. My own experience confirms this: I began gardening classes at my junior school, with the task of growing a pot calendula from seed that is a vivid memory, and my first gardening book, a tattered Odhams Press *Practical Gardening and Food Production in Pictures*, still sits on my shelf. But I think the calendula exerts a warm orange glow because it was my only gardening lesson. My senior school had no time for such luxuries, and school grounds assumed the guise of acres of gang-mown grass deserts (osten-sibly for hockey and football but usually empty) or caged tarmacadamed 'playgrounds' for the vast majority of mid-twentieth-century children. The beliefs of the right-thinkers, that to garden and grow things implanted a sympathy with the Earth that is our home, as well as encouraging inner resources and understanding, were abandoned where they were most needed.[15]

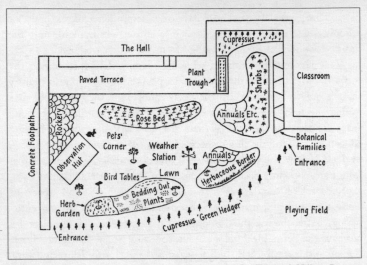

School gardens: a primary school garden built at the Sir Edmund Hillary Primary School, Worksop, as a permanent feature and for the Nottinghamshire Rural Studies Association's Exhibition, 1960.

There are however, small corners of minor domestic history illumined by children gardening. The nine-year-old Wilfred Owen writes to his mother from his grandparents' home at Underdale Road, Shrewsbury, on 19 August 1905: 'Dear Mother, Grandpa has given me as much garden as what you see from the dining room window only where the briks are and I have got about six potatoes planted, I have made another path and on the right side of it is the Vegeatble Garden and on the left is the fruit and the one you saw is the flower. It has just been raining a little for the first time but now it has stopt. We are going to Market this afternoon and I might buy some seeds'.[16] Young Wilfred must have wanted his garden badly to have this temporary plot until his parents settled at Mahim in Monkmoor Road, Shrewsbury, where a considerable part, if not all, of the garden seems to have been his very own territory. Wilfred the gardener was his identity within the family, partly shared with his mother, Susan Owen, who loved wild gardens and for whom he made a fern bank. He attended botany lectures while he was at Reading in 1912, and sought out gardens wherever he

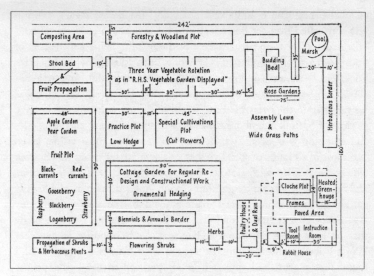

School gardens: a plan for a secondary school garden which serves the syllabus by the Hertfordshire Rural Studies Association, and used as a basis for several schools in the county. Both plans are from S. McB. Carson and R. W. Cotton, *The Teaching of Rural Studies*, 1962.

went; but then, for whatever reason – did he realize that the kind of garden that would satisfy him was far beyond his means? – he put this love away. His last words on the subject seem to have been the wistful sonnet composed in 1913, possibly inspired by a visit to his rich uncle, Edward Quayle:

> When late I viewed the gardens of rich men,
> Where throve my darling blossoms plenteously,
> With others whose rare glories dazed my ken,
> I was not teased with envious misery.
> Enough for me to see and recognize;
> Then bear away sweet names upon my tongue,
> Scents in my breath, and colours in my eyes.
> Their owners watch them die: I keep them young.[17]

The writer Ronald Blythe's first garden taught him to accept limitations, his own as well as the garden's; the plot was beneath a greengage and a walnut tree 'whose roots I encountered when sowing penny packets of lobelia, nasturtium and sweet pea seeds' (Madeline Agar's solution was corrugated iron set three feet into the ground to fend off roots).[18] His garden's 'intricate paths were a prime feature, being constructed of finds from a small abandoned brickworks in the nearby fields. My prize brick was a square sunflower, heavy, tawny, splendid, and was not allowed to be obfuscated by the nasturtiums.' The sunflower brick was his talisman in the overwhelming world of the 'densely ordered' cottage gardens of Suffolk neighbours 'massed with fruit, blooms and vegetables and stunning with scent' which were the families' most visible asset, 'indicator of all kinds of social virtues'.[19] There are terrors in this Suffolk which seems filled with riotous clones of H. E. Bates's Larkin family and Stanley Spencer's mountainous Cookhamites thrown in, all blowsily gardening: such intimidations made Ronald Blythe a writer and only a gardener by inheritance of John Nash's Bottengoms, the clue being that he kept the nasturtiums at bay – the very opposite to gardener Harry Roberts who felt himself at one with Canon Ellacombe: 'if I found that a plant had spread from its position in the border to the middle of the gravel path, where it was obviously more at home, I preferred rather to change the path, than to disturb the plant'. This is the self-confessedly precocious and little more than seven-year-old Harry Roberts, who had been given *Gardening for Children* and his own little strip, who enjoyed 'co-operating' with his mother and accompanying her 'on occasional excursions to fields where she collected in a basket certain special soils for the culture of fastidious flowers',[20] and who also became a collector of butterflies, beetles and wild flowers. Harry Roberts was a contributor to *Gardeners' Chronicle*, author of *A Chronicle of a Cornish Garden* and *English Gardens* in the Collins 'Britain in Pictures' series. It seems that two small boys, a plant and a row of bricks or stones can represent the full spectrum of gardening.

There is often a spark in those who eventually make it professionally that sees them through: when Thomas Mawson was twelve he was given *How to Earn £600 a Year from One Acre of Land* and a part of his family smallholding. He discovered the advice to be flawed, but set to teaching himself to be a garden designer, eventually becoming the President of the Institute of Landscape Architects.[21] Arthur Billitt grew his first pansies from seed at the age of six, and his father dug him a ten-by-ten-feet patch in which to plant them; this became his own garden, edged with 'Princess of Wales' violets which he propagated to make an edging, with some pinks and his star purchase a rose Zephirine Drouhin costing his 'entire wealth' of five shillings.[22] The six-year-old Will Ingwersen definitely had the spark: he found a cast-off box of sickly seedlings of *Gentiana verna* on his father's nursery rubbish dump, took them to his garden, nurtured them back to life and sold them back to his father when supplies were short later in the season. Thus he had the money for a pack of seeds to start something new. Russell Page 'discovered' the flower tent at an agricultural show in his native Lincolnshire, then 'friends and teachers' in the books of Reginald Farrer and Gertrude Jekyll at his local library.[23] He spent all his pocket money on alpines, stole grit and gravel from roadside heaps, cycled for miles to get a basket of leaf-soil and scoured the stoneless countryside for his rockery rocks. Was there some primeval urge to compensate for Lincolnshire by making miniature mountains and developing passions for *Primula farinosa*, the mealy-leaved Birds' eye, pinky-lilac primula, and other natives of mountain grasslands? When he visited a lady living near the Minster in Lincoln, he found her hallway had half the chequerboard of tiles lifted for growing Asiatic primula seedlings, and her dining room draped in ivy garlands brought indoors through holes in the wall. With such romantic possibilities was it any wonder that Russell Page gave up painting for making gardens?

A rock-gardening child is obviously different from a ten-by-ten-feet rows of lettuce and sweet peas child (there is surely a subject for behaviourists here?) Rock gardening means both miniature mountains and a tactile, craft approach, evident a generation after Russell Page in the architect and plantsman Peter Aldington: he began making a rockery in his parents' garden in low-lying Preston, possibly as an echo of his passion for mountaineering, and when the family moved south Peter inherited an ex-Chelsea Show rock garden, probably by the fashionable firm of George C. Whitelegg of Chislehurst, winners of many gold medals in the late 1930s and again after the war. He had always wanted to be an architect, and as soon as architecture allowed he made his wonderful garden at Turn End, Haddenham, in Buckinghamshire, where rocks play a small but significant role; rockeries and alpines are his most enjoyable kind of gardening.[24]

Besides all these horticultural children there are the adventurers:

grottoes were fair game, and there was a fine example at Talacre Abbey in Clwyd, with a lifesize figure of a headless monk and a fire-breathing monster (as long as the fire was lit). The Mostyn children used to lead their new governesses (of which there must have been many) through a maze of paths to the grotto, and then suddenly disappear.[25] Presumably if the governess saw the joke she was accepted. The Mostyn children obviously understood the appeal of the ghoulish; before radio or television, the garden was a rich source of potential horror, or some gardens were, and Aunt Ada Doom's experience of seeing 'something nasty in the woodshed when she was no bigger than a linnet' (blamed for Mrs Starkadder's eccentricity in Stella Gibbons' *Cold Comfort Farm*) was something most healthy children could take in their stride, turn to ridicule, and pass on. In his autobiography *The Crest on the Silver*, Geoffrey Grigson goes into some detail on the layers of meaning of his childhood garden at Pelynt Vicarage in Cornwall. He was conscious of being a child of old loins (his father was sixty when Geoffrey was born in 1905) and of set ways, which meant that his father was 'jealous of the welfare' of the trees and shrubs and would not allow them to be trimmed or cut back, the source of constant neighbourly disputes. When the children came home from school in July they 'drove into a tunnel under the thickest roofs of leaves with a heavy smell of grass and hogweed' to a garden that was damp, luxurious and faintly oppressive, until the grass was scythed in August. It was also beautiful, with everything appearing year after year of its own accord: the rose-scented peonies in the drive June after June, love in a mist amongst the elderly yellow tea roses on the terrace, secret plants that survived here and there and through and over all the rhododendrons which behaved as if they were in their native Himalayas. 'This garden with its varying levels, its freestone walls and its waterfall, provided the symbolic miniatures, the first edition of every possibly adventure and ambition. It seemed boundless to me at one time, with always some new shrubbery to be explored . . . some new tree to be climbed.'[26] And then it became clear, though perhaps only to the outsider, that the garden – in which his elderly father treasures the oaks, redwoods, copper beeches and rhododendrons and will not let them be touched – is the prison of his mother, who hates the scents of the trees in flower and 'had a campaign of hatred' for years against two or three elms 'without ever getting my father to act against them'. His mother went about life along narrow, habitual paths, both in the garden and the village and regarded the darker and higher reaches of the former as 'children's property'. She particularly hated the laurels, into which Geoffrey loved to steer his garden swing from a nearby chestnut tree, to crash into the finer branches; he thought the laurel flowers 'standing up precise and white from the glistening leaves, were one of the first natural excellences of which I was conscious – they have helped to make that translation of Housman's

> We'll to the woods no more
> The laurels are all cut

a poem which is one of my private and intimate properties.'[27]

Alice's adventures can of course be read as horror stories, and her gardens, that of the Red Queen in Wonderland, and The Garden of Live Flowers in *Through the Looking Glass*, are weird places, the product of Lewis Carroll's brilliant, gentle and yet repressed mind. So many children's authors seems to take emotional refuge in the garden of childhood but then turn it into something else. Kate Greenaway's frustrated passion for John Ruskin was poured into her garden in Frognal, Hampstead, and from there into her book illustrations of model, perfect, impotently neat trees and flower beds. This was partly because Ruskin approved of her gardening. 'I will wait at the garden gate – anytime', he wrote to her, raising her hopes (and perhaps his own) but knowing that he would keep the gate firmly shut.[28] Likewise Kenneth Grahame, the distinguished secretary of the Bank of England, emotionally imprisoned in the garden of his happy childhood at The Mount, Cookham Dean, who chose to take his adventures to the river bank.[29] And J. M. Barrie, in the woodland garden at Black Lake Cottage, Tilford, where Peter Pan 'the boy who wouldn't grow up' was born.[30] There is much more to the gardens of childhood than fairy tale and making things grow; they often contain the keys to a harsher adult world.

To return to lighter things: the good Dean of Rochester (so eminently quotable) began his book *Our Garden* in 1899 with the following:

I asked a schoolboy, in the sweet summertide 'What he thought a garden was for?' and he said, Strawberries. His younger sister suggested Croquet, and the elder Garden-Parties. The brother from Oxford made a prompt declaration in favour of Lawn

Tennis and Cigarettes, but he was rebuked by a solemn senior, who wore spectacles, and more black hair than is usual with males, and was told that 'a garden was designed for botanical research, and for the classification of plants'.[31]

The voice of youth seems set for games, and what else can a garden be for? The oldest garden amusement is the swing – once known as Meritot or Merry-trotter. By being pushed or pulled, or by that mysterious but innate skill of bending and thrusting the body into an oscillating motion (a primeval action which, like digging and raking, we can share with our most distant ancestors) the boy or girl begins to fly. (Oh, how much practice learning to swing seemed to need and how short were my permitted stays in the park.) Of course swinging was not confined to children, but full of romantic possibilities – witness Fragonard's *Girl on a Swing*, and John Gay's

> On two near elms the slacken'd cord I hung,
> Now high, now low, my Blouzalinda swung.[32]

Mechanization captured the swing in the early nineteenth century with an aerial wheel with seats hung on ropes. 'This ridiculous method of riding was in vogue for the space of two summers', among people who should have known better, says Joseph Strutt, but – and this may have been one of the great moments of our decadent decline – people knew that they liked to swing without labour, and the swinging moved out of the garden to the fairground.[33]

Joseph Strutt's *Sports and Pastimes of the People of England* was first published in 1801 and revised in 1838 by William Hone. As such an early publication it seems to touch the roots of medieval games (Strutt was a thorough researcher and antiquary of wide interests) which are divided into three, (i) rural exercises, meaning hunting and field sports of the gentry, (ii) rural exercises of the people, much taken with archery, long enforced for military practice, but including slinging stones and weights, hand ball (an ancient game said to have been invented by the Saxons) foot ball, 'goff' and cricket, and (iii) urban pastimes – tournaments, jousts, theatre, minstrelsy, juggling and tumbling and balancing. What becomes clear – as is also implicit in Iona and Peter Opie's researches into children's games and rhymes – is that few of these activities belong in the garden, which was far too precious, and the games too boisterous.

One of the purposes of the Hardenburg basket, wooden or wired ornamental edging for flower beds, which pre-dates Humphry Repton's use
of it at the Brighton Royal Pavilion, was protection. By the end of the
nineteenth century Bayliss's Ornamental Game-Proof Garden Hurdles,
interlocking wire hoops painted green in 6ft lengths, 3ft high, could be
bought for three shillings and ten pence per yard. This was the period
of greatest enthusiasm for games in the garden, which had much to do
with middle-class pride and propriety and the urgings of the manufacturers of croquet and lawn tennis equipment. There was a peak before
the First World War, but with the proto-professional keenness of the
1920s, games started to slip out of the garden again.

Kings led us into garden games: Henry VIII's enthusiasm for real
or royal tennis is legendary (oh, how he would have revelled in Wimbledon, if he was allowed to win) and Charles II's frivolous and lovable
side encouraged his courtiers into long hours of smashing and crashing
with wooden mallets at 'Pall Mall', a game that originated in Italy but
was 'civilized' by the Frenchman Lautier's *Nouveaux Règles pour le Jeu
de Mail* in 1717. The first obsessions with playing surfaces arose with *Jeu
de Mail* (or Pell Mell as Pepys called it, now meaning headlong, reck-
lessly) which required a smoothed earth bed sprinkled with powdered
cockleshells, kept watered to keep it fast, by 'the King's Cockle Strewer'
– surely the origin of Mary, Mary, Quite Contrary, who took cockleshells
to edge her garden? Making allowances for flattery, Edmund Waller's
commentary describes warfare by other means:

> Here a well-polished Mall give us the joy
> To see our Prince his matchless force imploy;
> No sooner has he toucht the flying ball,
> But 'tis already more than half the mall,
> And such a fury from his arm has got
> As from a smoking Culverin 'twere shot.
> May that ill fate my enemies befall
> To stand before his anger or his ball.[34]

The cockleshells proved too difficult for general use and Pall Mall
became a London street. English country gentry preferred to roll their
heavy boxwood balls along the ground, a game of indefinite age when any
surface would do, but exceedingly popular in seventeenth-century gardens
with bowling 'alleys' of smooth grass stiffly hedged to control the balls and

keep the children at bay. Bowling alleys or square greens were made for friendships: the Revd Richardson wrote to Sir Thomas Isham of Lamport on 4 January 1677 of his preference for throwing bowls at Lamport with Will Baxter and Cocus Worlidge 'than losing pistoles in Lombardy, or fishing in yr lake upon Mount Ceny or swelting in your heats of Tiera di Lavoro'.[35] The insular English sportsman was born.

Hoops and pegs had been a feature of *Jeu de Mail* and the love of exuberantly swiping with a mallet was not likely to fade: controlled aggression made its formal debut as Croquet at the 1851 Great Exhibition, developed by Walter Jones Whitmore on his lawns at Chastleton. This was an elitist game in the extreme, and *Croquet Tactics* (1868) by J. H. Walsh, editor of the *Field*, sold only 347 copies. The popularizer was Captain Mayne Reid, who simplified croquet into a garden game. It quickly became a craze, speedily embraced by the young who gave crinoline croquet parties, which demanded especially pretty petticoats and red boots, and enabled much dashing in and out of the rhododendrons.[36] Croquet was the first game played at the All England Club at Wimbledon, and it maintained its superiority over lawn tennis until 1899. The garden game was socially prestigious and could be played by all ages, but the need for a smooth lawn was a deterrent to real mass popularity, so the manufacturers were constantly thinking up variations including table croquet and 'Cozzare' which needed no special shape or size of lawn. Slazenger's were advertising the 'new game' of badminton (derived from the age-old, at least fourteenth-century battledore and shuttlecock) before the First World War, with boxed sets of posts and netting, four racquets and feather shuttlecocks for seventeen shillings and sixpence. There was also Lawn Skittles and Tetherball, also admirably described as Spiropole, in which a ball hung on a long cord on a wooden pole, with two players with racquets vying for control of the winding cord, the first to complete the spiral being the winner. Clock golf, with white painted metal Roman numerals pinned in the grass, and ever more ingenious ways of tethering balls (including balls with parachutes) for golf practice were also garden recreations. Archery – long disdained through long enforcement – also came into Victorian gardens (bowling alleys could be used) as a graceful, rather alluring way of showing off figures and fashions, both male and female, and fulfilled the yearnings of the Romantic movement.

Everything seemed to come in boxed sets, and the most popular boxed set of all was Major Walter Clopton's Wingfield's game of lawn tennis, or 'Sphairistike' from the Greeks, whom he was convinced were the originators of tennis, introduced in 1874. Here was a game needing no special building (as real tennis or squash) which could be played in the beneficial open air, by both sexes, of any age, in (optimistically) any weather and even on ice if the players were equipped with skates. Because of the Greeks Major Wingfield could claim no patent rights on his game, so the sports and general manufacturers took the profit – Harrods, Army & Navy, F. H. Ayres, Hazells, Slazengers, Gamages, Benetfinks of Cheapside and many others popularized lawn tennis. Major Wingfield gave credit to the first tennis party at Nantclwyd (now Clwyd) in December 1873, which had helped him formulate the game's simple rules, and so were spawned tennis parties all over the Empire. Garden designers of the Arts and Crafts period (1880 to 1914) such as M. H. Baillie Scott, Thomas Mawson and even Gertrude Jekyll, designed tennis lawns into their gardens (*Plate 42*).

Ah! The Lawn, that steadily perfected art. The seedsmen were well to the fore with lawn technology; Sutton's printed copiously detailed guides for amateurs, with all the market-research skills which we think of as modern, in the 1850s. They offered seed mixes of fine grasses and clovers for sunny or shaded lawns or cricket grounds, but of fine grasses only for tennis grounds and bowling greens. They had recommendations from Windsor and Osborne, the Crystal Palace, the People's Park in Halifax and even the sandy heights of Aldershot camp, where the desperate engineers had conjured 'very perfect swards' out of barren waste. Sutton's customers needed 'a good, close, velvety turf', perfectly achievable by gardeners and making every man his own groundsman, by following four principal procedures carefully: (i) preparation meant cultivation for 6 to 12 inches, drainage if necessary, rolling, raking, feeding with lime, Peruvian guano and ground bones, then more rolling and fine raking; (ii) sowing was to be done in spring, or from mid-August to mid-September, with only fine fescues, meadow grasses and *Lolium perenne* (rye), then rolled again and when the green frizz had achieved 2 or 3 inches, it was to be cut with a sharp scythe (no mean achievement this); (iii) mowing and rolling was then every ten days, but not a mowing machine for the first six months. Annual weeds could be mowed off, dandelions and daisies that dared appear were to be cut below the soil and salted to death. Regular watering was not mentioned but surely taken for granted; (iv) the lawn thus ready for tennis required the cutting and most of all rolling regimes to be continued, raking and seeding of bare patches in autumn, feeding in spring. The marking-out, with a succession of gadgets which were all basically a bucket on a wheel dispensing white gunge, was customarily the lot of the players.[37]

This ritual of the lawn is an ancient one. Strutt quotes a handed-down memory from the Elvetham masque for Queen Elizabeth in 1591, how 'after dinner, about 3 o'clock, ten of his lordship's (Hertford's) men in a square green court before Her Majestie's window did hang up lines, squaring out the forme of a tennis-court, and making a cross in the middle of this square they (stripped of their doublets) played 5 to 5 with hand ball . . .'[38] Then there was the addictive passion for bowls: 'no other game so provocative of genial mirth, more conducive to sociality and good fellowship . . . as it is only played in pleasant weather, in the open air, and over a green lawn finer and more kindly to tread upon than the most luxurious and costly carpet'. Bowls was open to all 'without regard to skill, sex, age, grade, class, craft or condition. Thus, beginners and adepts, ladies and gentlemen, the maid and the matron, youths in their teens and veterans of three score, the Earl and his tenantry, the lawyer and his client, the representative and his constituent, the baker and the brewer, the delicate and the robust, all there meet and co-mingle in harmony.'[39]

The lawn 'finer and more kindly to tread upon' than the most costly carpet has been the great meeting ground of history, and perhaps that is why it is so prized. The green velvet, the achievement of patient labour and mystical routine, but not dependent upon costliness, became an object of virtue, and it remained a shrine to wily gamesmanship and skills. Other more forceful and boisterous games such as cricket and golf went beyond garden limits (but retained their tiny token fine wickets or 'greens') and in other countries and climates, as well as amongst city children, ball games were played on hard or dirt surfaces. It is suggested that the Victorians prized their lawns in imitation of the lords in their landscape parks, but the velvet green is a much older icon: what is certain is that the seedsmen and gardeners of late nineteenth-century Britain brought lawns to the peak of their perfection.

It was to be keenness for tennis, and the wet summers that made for the greenness of the lawns, that were to precipitate change. In the early 1900s there were a few wet-weather courts in Britain, made of cinders or rolled sand, while abroad hard courts were common, and when the Secretary of the All-England Club, Commander G. W. Hillyard, visited South Africa, he reported that he played upon crushed-up ant-heaps. On his return he happened to meet a Leicester-shire neighbour – the Commander lived at Thorpe Satchville Hall – named Claude Brown, who was in partnership with his cousin, Billy Birkenshaw, exploring alternative uses for a redundant brickyard they had inherited at Syston. This resulted in Claude Brown using crushed bricks to lay a court for Commander Hillyard and his tennis friends to try; it was a great success, playable very soon after heavy rain, clean, kind to the feet and clothes and balls lasted well and did not discolour. At one of the Commander's tennis parties was a lady with a Parisian sunshade which had been waterproofed, so that it was useful in sun and rain, a process the French called 'en-tout-cas'; so that was what Claude Brown called his tennis court company. As far as tennis was concerned En Tout Cas became a legend, celebrities clamoured for the new courts, the Ladies' Champion Mrs Lambert Chambers was thrilled with hers, they were used in clubs all over the country, for hotels, hospitals and companies' clubs, contributing greatly to the popularity of tennis. In the sun-loving and fitness-loving years of the 1930s En Tout Cas were making about a thousand courts a year; they cost £175 and one had even been installed at Buckingham Palace.[40]

Most of the customers for hard courts were private homes, and into the 1920s the court came as part of a package, with a garden designed to receive it, pavings and pergolas to set it in context. The pergola could help to mask the back-stop wire, which prevented the balls from straying into wet vegetation, and sheltered sitting bays for spectators. Large gardens could have both 'red' court and lawn court, and still an ornamen-tal lawn space: however, overwhelmingly, in middle-sized gardens a tennis-sized lawn became the flexible norm, as in the *Daily Mail* Ideal Home Exhibition of 1927 when the architect D. M. McMorran's ideal layout was for a long back garden measuring about 120 feet, into which a 98 × 40 feet tennis lawn could be marked out, allowing for a strip of vegetables and a washing line.[41]

The next garden craze was for a swimming pool, again the result of the sun and fitness-loving 1930s, when stylish, usually rich and keen swimmers had rectangular concrete pools thirty or more feet long and half that width, shelving from 3ft 6 inches to 6 ft 6 inches deep. These were rather serious, grown-up pools; some modernist houses had circular or even kidney-shaped plunge pools, of all one depth, close to a terrace. Interestingly, modernism in the 1930s was a very grown-up design vogue, little influenced by children's needs or places to play, and the garden had to await the post-war period, in particular the affluent 1960s, before it became children's territory.[42]

It is worth pausing for a moment to think about water in the garden. Gertrude Jekyll had no natural water of any kind in her garden at Munstead Wood, and only the tiniest formal pool on the north side of her house so that she could grow water-lilies. There is no water in the garden at Sissinghurst, except for the vestigial moat and the distant lake which Harold Nicolson made to accommodate his eighteenth-century tastes. We know of many watery traditions: the four-fold rills of the *chahar bagh*, the fountains of Rome (Edwin Lutyens thought fountains essentially baroque and would not have them in his gardens: look at the severity of the Trafalgar Square or the New Delhi fountains that he was obliged to design), Dutch canals, landscape lakes, oriental rock falls and moody grottoes. None of these, however, are home-grown traditions which belong in ordinary gardens. Miss Jekyll's Arts and Crafts beliefs extended to saving every drop of rainwater in every garden where she had influence, but this was for the plants, not for frittering away: her day had no re-circulating pumps, which do not seem to appear in gardens until the 1950s.

Pools and patios came to Britain along with the rest of American consumer culture in the post-war years, and in particular they came as garden ideas from California, the fount of all garden-design knowledge at the time. Most influential was the brilliant Thomas Church and the *Sunset Magazine* for which he was design adviser. Considering the basic climatic contrasts between Britain and southern California, or Arizona or Colorado (*Sunset* was a magazine for western living), it always seems to have been the most mighty of marketing achievements. I wonder if we would ever have wanted leisure pools had they not smelt of Hollywood, or had Church not been such a brilliant designer as to make all others wish to emulate him. But, 'ten thousand swimming pools are said to have been constructed in private gardens during the past year', reported the *Architectural Review* in 1964: they cost from £1200 for a big concrete pool and filter system, to £400–900 for fibreglass, or around £300 for a timber-framed and vinyl-lined and usually do-it-yourself construction. In design terms the pool was a monster: very rare indeed (although one was photographed in Farnham) were wide, sunny, sheltered terraces with a view which accommodated a pool perfectly, such as those available along the entire length of the Sierra Nevada. British pools were pushed out into lawns, and were discordant in scale and colour, and were then realized to be dangerous to children, and so were secreted away in sheltered garden rooms, where they were often forgotten. This was far from the Californian ideal, where even the smallest garden would have a large pool, simply because it was a joyful necessity: a rectangular pool against one wall of a Chelsea garden photographed on a sunny day managed to look Californian, but this was rare. Undoubtedly the smartest pools were rectangles or circles; lovely things could be done to incorporate a circular pool into swirls of paving and planting, though the rectangle was always better left plain and unadorned. It was fibreglass that came in curves, something again very Californian: Thomas Church's sinuous blue and white pool set in silvergrey decking, with trees, overlooking San Francisco Bay at Sonoma, ranks very high in the world's beautiful images. But transferred to Surbiton or Solihull too much is lost.

If pools were often to amuse the young, then the patio was their playground. And just what is a Patio? *Sunset* asked. 'Take half a dozen neighbours and 'one or two might agree with the dictionary that it is an enclosed court, walled-in by the house, open to the sky. Someone else will tell you it is a roofless play room located next to the house; and another will contend it is a room of the house itself, with an outer wall missing. Another neighbor may insist that it is a separate structure altogether . . . filled with barbecue gear. Your sixth friend (probably just moved in from some remote part of the country) may not know what you are talking about. A patio? Never heard of it.'[43] That was 1961. Most Britons could never have heard of it either, but in the ensuing thirty years we have acquired patio paving, patio walling, patio furniture, patio planting, patio roses and every other accoutrement. The old terrace was democratized into the patio, and it brought the clean and organized notion of children's play: in the 1960s all the advice to parents, no longer just from the most progressive child specialists, was for clean 'messy' play, the sand-pit, the small pebbled pool, the small tables and benches, the climbing frame or tree, the hamster hutch and the lovely, tricycle-friendly paving that allowed happy sunny hours. It was for brief, ordered modern childhoods; soon they grew up, followed the games pitches and swimming pools out of the garden to the Leisure Centre, and the patio was adapted to sink gardens and supper outdoors.

The last expression of the formative garden concerns children who do not have a clean and toy-filled patio at home. I left Marjory Gill gardening at Bedales: she married Clifford Allen, the pioneering social-ist, later Lord Allen of Hurtwood, in 1921 and was for a time busy with her husband's career and their daughter Polly. She wrote gardening and country pieces and helped with some celebrity socialist gardens, for the Oswald Mosleys and H. G. Wells, and became Chairman of Edward VII's Coronation Planting Committee, but always maintained interests in education and children's welfare. Lord Allen died in March 1939, and Marjory's loss was compounded by the war and the need to earn a living. An absorption in pioneering nursery schools with landscape archi-tect Judith Ledeboer, and what was to become the Children's Film Foundation kept her busy. Immediately the war finished she was drawn into the cause of its child victims and on a lecture tour in Oslo she was taken to see Professor C. Th. Sorensen's housing landscape at Emdrup, where instead of a spacious and beautiful playground he had given the children what they wanted, 'junk yards and building sites where they could mess about with whatever they happened to find'. 'I was completely swept off my feet by my first visit to the Emdrup playground', Marjory Allen wrote, 'I realized I was looking at something quite new and full of possibilities'.[44] The playground had been established in 1943; it allowed the children of the Occupation, unruly and anti-social as they were, to find their own balance and stretch themselves – something Lady Allen believed many children needed – and she wrote about Emdrup in *Picture Post* when she got home. In the early 1950s experimental playgrounds were opened in Camberwell and Clydesdale Road in Kensington, and Lady Allen sought the support of the National Playing Fields Associ-ation for what were now 'adventure playgrounds': others followed, at

Grimsby, Crawley, Lollard Street, Lambeth, and activities developed to 'house-building' and gardening. At Lollard Street trees and shrubs were planted and 'children had gardens of their own with crops of beans and potatoes, and bright patches of marigolds, nasturtiums and giant sunflowers. They learned the art of compost-making, and went round with a barrow collecting vegetable refuse from the Lambeth Walk market.'[45] The London County Council took on play parks and one o'clock clubs for under fives and their mothers, and Lady Allen launched out at the architects and planners for their lack of provision for play, lectures and pamphlets which culminated in her *Planning for Play* published in 1968, a classic manual for all landscape architects.

The causes that Lady Allen espoused evolved many other strands over the ensuing years: she worked on an adventure playground for handicapped children in Chelsea 'the first in England and perhaps the first in the world'[46] which led on to yet more. The Spastics Society established a field studies centre at Churchtown Farm, Llanivery, in Cornwall in 1973 where gardening was to be an important part of the curriculum. The Disabled Living Foundation turned their attentions to therapeutic gardening.

Lady Allen's changing of perceptions of children's play with adventure playgrounds prepared the way for a playground revolution. When I trudged the Wandle Valley from Croydon to the Thames for my book *The Everywhere Landscape* which was published in 1982 most of the school grounds I saw – as indeed most to be seen anywhere – had little to distinguish them from exercise yards at older prisons. Clearly the 'landscape' that surrounded the inner-city child had much to do with why he might grow up fighting, condemned to wall-to-wall tarmac from the age of four, progressing to all-weather pitches in wire cages or an expanse of green desert marked out for football *en masse*. Anything remotely resembling nature was alien, even the daisies that dared to spread their petals in the mowerless intervals were just for trampling, there was neither the time nor inclination for daisy chains.[47] In those days the only chink in the gloom of what was far more than an urban British problem came from California: a lecturer named Robin Moore had shepherded his landscape-design students to digging up the asphalt in a local schoolyard, while asking children and their parents what they would like in its place. The result was a green space with sand, water, gardens, an adventure playground, potting shed, outdoor teaching area and 135 different types of plants, as well as a much better view from the classroom window.[48]

For most of the 1980s the subject of school playgrounds was debated along parallel professional lines in education and landscape architecture, lines that would perhaps never have met but for urban green campaigners and garden historians occasionally being the *alter egos* of the same persona. *Learning Through Landscapes*, an independent charitable trust for the promotion of improvements to school grounds was launched in 1990, to serve England and Wales, with *Grounds for Learning* established in Scotland the following year. With sponsorship from business and industry, and the vital support of teachers who see the outdoor classroom as a help rather than a hindrance in the curriculum race, playgrounds up and down the land have been revitalized. Green deserts have been converted to wild-life gardens and tree nurseries, ponds dug in the tarmac, some of the dreaded tarmac brought to life with mazes, a compass or chess board and other games, hedges and trees planted and treasured, vegetables are planted, tended and eventually eaten for school dinners. The outdoor classroom enriches the teaching of mathematics and art as well as the more usual natural sciences, and extends across the spectrum of childhood through nursery, infant and primary schools, and to schools for children with special needs.[49] Remembering Miss Frances Jane Hope's ministrations amongst the stony yards and streets of Edinburgh a hundred years ago, one new school landscape example is especially appropriate here: in 1989 some of the pupils of High School Yards Nursery School, Flodden Wall, found some stripy caterpillars in their stony playground, and their curiosity encouraged the staff, parents and local community to transform a stony hill slope with trees and wild flowers, and fill the barren yards with planters and outdoor play equipment. High School Yards has become a celebrated example – just as Miss Mabel Brown wished, the small pupils begin their learning surrounded by wild flowers and 'minibeasts' which provide the actual basis for language, experience and self-expression, as well as religious and moral education. High School Yards' garden activities bonds the wider community, and the pupils' doings are featured in a weekly column in the *Edinburgh Evening News*.[50]

Taking the long view, some 200 years on from the Edgeworths' advocacy of garden play, through the massed evidence of almost every biography ever written, we have been unconsciably slow in using the garden as an official tool for childhood development. The educational professionals, no less than the medical profession or churchmen (and I fear that the emphasis is on the 'men') of all denominations, have been reluctant to surrender the territory of children's minds to outside influences. The million-dollar question is, does a school environment of riches and interest, rather than bleak sterility, make any difference? On behalf of *Learning Through Landscapes*, Wendy Titman has recently addressed this big question, talking to schools' staff and pupils to assess the 'hidden curriculum', the way children view their surroundings and react accordingly. For those who require the hard evidence, Wendy Titman has documented this, in *Special Places, Special People*, published in 1994.[51] Her conclusions are shattering to anyone who realizes that, since the 1960s, the basic earthbound connections of our human society have been eliminated from the teaching of children, except for the few pioneering instances that led to the founding of *Learning Through Landscapes*. The evidence is that the children, to whom we so blithely entrust the future, need – far more than they need computer skills or even a sense of history – a contact with the earth and other living creatures through a childhood garden.

CHAPTER ELEVEN

✥

Future Gardens

Trawling the deepest recesses of our gardening past has revealed, as perhaps is habitual with social history, that though the loudest voices urge the following of leaders of fashion, everyman and woman go largely upon their own sweet way. Garden history, a young and callow discipline, has been hitherto obsessed with names and titles, parks and palaces, and is now rapidly converting to more egalitarian concerns, as I have set out to show. At the same time, we have arrived at the end of the twentieth century more deeply doused in an obsession with 'celebrity' than ever, crying ever more loudly for minuscule detailings of the lives of the 'rich and famous' in order to make ourselves, by comparison, feel virtuous and wise, while ostensibly following their lead.

Gardens are not immune from this convoluted idealism, in fact gardens come very high in the tables of media affections and the acreages of display. There is a natural analogy with fashion design, whereby the creations of the catwalks – the annual concoctions of newspapers and magazines for the Chelsea Flower Show – bear little relation to real people or their lives and gardens, but are insidiously prompting our future tastes, nevertheless. I have heard it suggested recently that, as the art-school embrace of fashion design has been such a great British success, a little horticulture should be added to the curriculum so that they could design gardens as well. The catwalk would seem to be an appropriate place for a launch into the future of gardens, especially as the big-name designers are already on their way.

The flower show at Chelsea in 1998 had 'the first-ever Chanel garden', so *Vogue* magazine followed up by asking Karl Lagerfeld of Chanel to sketch his own dream garden: he said it 'would be very different from all the gardens I have now or have had in the past ... I would love a walled garden, with only one opening overlooking an infinite landscape with mountains far away, the walls would frame the sky. This is the only way to avoid making a beautiful view banal. You would have to go and look – if not you wouldn't see anything.' This last aesthetic was actually shared by Gertrude Jekyll: it was part of Arts and Crafts' integrity, was quashed by modernism and scorned by a general desire to sit and enjoy the view ever since. Lagerfeld's retreat, drawn to look like a white, un-padded cell, has an impeccably groomed lawn 'like a carpet' in the centre and at one side, *un escalier d'eau* reminiscent of Chatsworth, a waterfall with steps, also a surrealist tease. His cell is furnished by a couch and one sculpted head. 'It would be difficult for me not to mess it all up, as I do with all my houses and gardens.'[1]

The yearning for minimalist clarity can come with age and the stress of a cluttered life, but contrary to popular belief, the modern garden is not a denial of colour and life. The knitwear and tapestry designer Kaffe Fassett, who transformed our tastes for colourful jumpers, has done the same for quilts, needlepoint, wallpapers and now gardens. He was brought up in California, by the sea, growing squash and watermelon in his own plot, and it was a sea of yellow tulips and forget-me-nots seen in a French park which made him aware that all was not lost in his grey adopted home. In his West Hampstead garden he has covered walls, grounds and pots in a riot of Gaudi-inspired mosaic 'like confetti tossed in the air' and using china and tiles bought at car-boot sales: colours are his challenge and skill, especially the colours of autumn, and he has a passion for crimson, lots of dark red roses, and auriculas. His dream garden would, understandably, be a remembrance of California: pastel colours and crassula, kalanchoe, aloes and other succulents, with lots of 'mouth-watering cabbages and squashes'.[2]

In recent years gardeners in California have had to learn to cope with a serious shortage of water. They have had to be weaned off a passion for roses and English-style lawns in favour of carefully constructed micro-climates of shady pockets which might support a rose or an iris amongst a more general planting of drought-tolerant native succulents. It is not that climates might be shifting or that we are affected by global warming, holes in the ozone layer or El Niño; we simply do not have enough water resources to go on using the refined product of our taps for watering the garden. If I were a young person looking for an enterprise today it would be developing a modernized system for collecting rainwater for every garden owner. The rail still falls; we just seem to have lost our ability to catch it. Though I must begin to apologize for Gertrude Jekyll's becoming the patron saint of this book, she was a stickler for catching rainwater: the houses of architects that she enlightened have competent gutterings to carry water to underground tanks, connected through pipes to further overflow tanks, opened at some point to a safe dipping tank for watering cans. Roofs are no longer just for solar energy but must be water savers as well.

It would seem to be wise to consider the dry or Mediterranean garden, as East Anglian born and bred Beth Chatto has demonstrated to us for years. A visit to her gardens at Elmstead Market outside Colchester[3] might even inspire a wish for a dry garden: in a compact area she runs the gamut from wet to dry (and through shade and sun), from lush ferns, ornamental rhubarbs, bog arums and hostas to her Mediterranean planting of euphorbias, ballota, Jerusalem sage, santolina, salvias and alliums. In one afternoon it is rather like having seven-league-boots, as one passes a steady refinement of forms and characters, and though I went recently with a longstanding love for *Rheums* and their fellows, increasingly dryness becomes of greater attraction. In the spring of 1992 Beth Chatto began to plant her Gravel Garden (on dry gravelly soil where the cars had been parked for twenty-five years). It was ploughed and composted, but was to have no irrigation system, and she does not believe in watering. It is the height of delicacy and enchantment, at any season and different at all seasons; star performers are, in sequence, tulips, alliums and poppies, rising from rivulets of green, purple or gold foliage, 'Good verticals like Kniphofias, Verbascums or flowering grasses often create a screen through which to view lower plants beyond them'. In June sheets of chalk-white daisies and 'honey-scented clouds' of *Crambe cordifolia* catch the light; Mrs Chatto's 'jewel box' of species with small and simple flowers in pinks, purples, crimson, mauve and yellows carry on through the summer, and the autumn can be best of all with tumbled, fluffy grasses, allium seed-heads in variety, silver cineraria, purple euphorbia, set off by vivid blue agapanthus – of which a cobalt blue form of *A. campanulatus* 'Chatto's Blue' is 'home-grown'.[4]

PLATE 26 *The Royal Family at Windsor*, by Rex Whistler, 1939, with the young Princess Elizabeth holding the rake rather in the manner she would one day hold the sceptre. (*see page 274*)

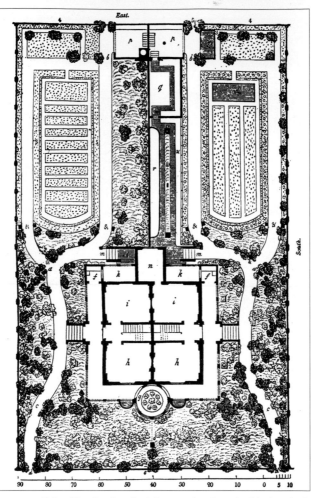

PLATE 27 John Claudius Loudon's layout plan for a double detached villa and gardens, illustrated in *The Suburban Gardener and Villa Companion*, 1838 and built as nos. 3 and 5 Porchester Terrace, Bayswater, London. No. 3, the right-hand house, was the home and office for John and Jane Loudon, no. 5 was tenanted, and the Loudons managed both gardens: the street gates (d) gave onto paths (c) through tunnels of trees (walnut, pear, cherry, lilac) and shrubs (laurels, laburnum, magnolia); the houses shared a conservatory (g) and were surrounded by a wide sitting verandah (f); (h) is the dining-room, (i) the library and (k) the grating which lights the basement kitchen; (n) the office of the *Gardener's Magazine*; the gardens represent alternate designs for working beds of vegetables and flowers, (q) and (r) are glasshouses, and (p) the boiler and tool houses. A landmark of small garden design where Loudon demonstrated that a 50 foot frontage did not deny the garden horticultural variety. The houses survive but not the gardens. (*see pages 117–118*)

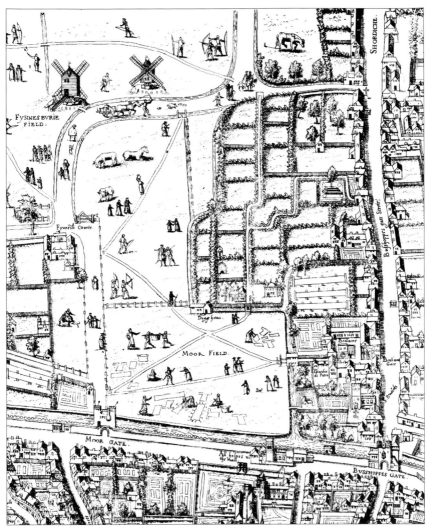

PLATE 28 London, garden city, 1559, showing the area between Moorgate and what is now
Liverpool Street Station, including Finsbury Circus and Finsbury Square, these being the only
fragments of green left between the buildings. The London Wall is prominent at the foot of the
plan, with Moorgate and Bishopsgate marking the present streets of these names: to the south,
within the Wall, are the merchants' houses and gardens of Copthall and Throgmorton streets
and Draper's Gardens and the Austin Friars. North of Moorgate the road appears as a country
lane to Finsbury Square; the parallel lines in the garden on the west may be a rope works, the
name surviving in Ropemaker Street. In the far north-west 'Fynnsburyie Field' with archery and
musketry being practiced, survives in the Honourable Artillery Company's Ground and Bunhill
Fields. Bishopsgate is lined with houses with gardens and orchards, a rope walk and the carefully
hedged enclosures, possibly allotments belonging to a single landlord which represent the size
and shape of the plot now occupied by Liverpool Street and Broad Street Stations. The houses of
Spital Square and Shoreditch are in the north-east corner. The clothmakers, dyers and bleachers
are drying their wares in Moor Fields. (*see page 146*)

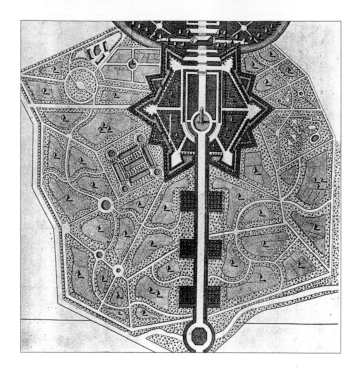

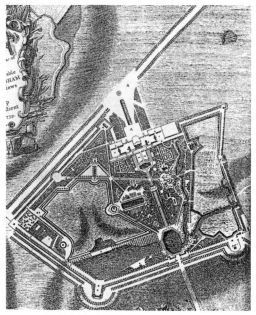

PLATE 29 ABOVE The Military
Garden: Stephen Switzer's
'The Manor of Paston divided
and planted into Rural
Gardens', from *Ichnographia
Rustica*, 1718, and in reality
Grimsthorpe Castle,
Lincolnshire 'fortified' in
woodland. (*see page 86*)

PLATE 30 LEFT Stowe,
Buckinghamshire, the plan
published by Sarah Bridgeman
in 1739 showing the military
basis for Vanbrugh and
Charles Bridgeman's first
schemes, which included
'walls' of trees, bastions,
redoubts, a salient and ha-ha.
(*see pages 91–92*)

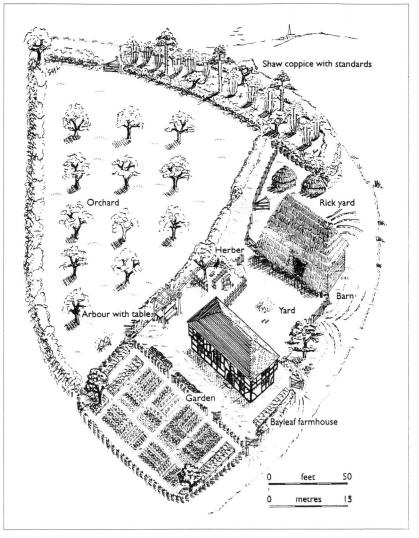

Labels within image:
Shaw coppice with standards
Orchard
Rick yard
Herber
Barn
Arbour with table
Yard
Garden
Bayleaf farmhouse

0   feet   50
0   metres   15

PLATE 31 Bayleaf, a Yeoman's property of *c.*1500, at the Weald and Downland Museum, Singleton, West Sussex, a bird's-eye view of the garden layout: the coppice produces hazel for fencing hurdles and shelters the orchard, where bees are kept. The beds around the house are for herbs and lilies, and the protected beds of the vegetable garden are managed on a sustainable rotation which
parallels that of the arable fields.

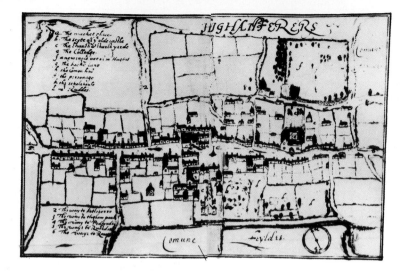

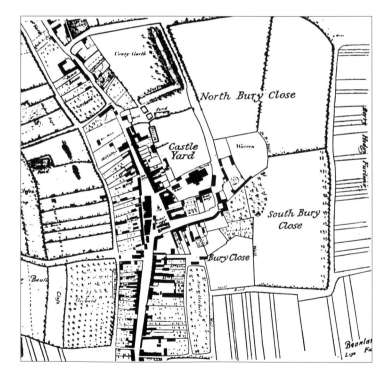

PLATES 32, 33 AND 34 Higham Ferrers, Northamptonshire: the town was surveyed by John Norden in 1591 to produce one of the earliest large-scale maps, used to convince Lord Burghley that such maps had their uses. Higham's stone walls and the route of the A6 from Kettering to Bedford have remained virtually intact for over four hundred years, allowing the church, Chichele College, the market square and many gardens to be identified at intervals in time: in Norden's map (TOP LEFT), in a map of 1789 'OPPOSITE', and in a modern aerial photograph. (*see pages 146–148*)

OPPOSITE: PLATE 35 *Back Garden at Bardfield,* by Edward Bawden, 1933, and PLATE 36 *Garden Path,* by Eric Ravilious, 1934: two artists' views of the garden at Great Bardfield in Essex, which the artists and their wives shared for a while. *(see page 224)*

PLATE 37 Eric Ravilious, the 'Garden' designs for Wedgwood, 1938: a side plate (TOP) and dinner plate showing two of the variety of seasonal vignettes, from the limitedproduction by Wedgwood in 1953.

PLATE 38 ABOVE *Sunday, for Allotments*, by Miriam Macgregor, 1985.

PLATE 39 OPPOSITE *A Lapfull of Windfalls*, by Clare Leighton for *Four Hedges*, 1935, subtitled 'a gardener's chronicle'.

PLATE 40 ABOVE Mary Merrall (1890–1973), an actress, (on the left) seen here modelling a tennis dress with a friend, photographed by Bassano on 14 September 1919. The background shows an elaborate trellis and planting which both contains and shelters the tennis lawn: in the 1920s there was a boom for contractors who could design games lawns into a garden setting.

PLATE 41 RIGHT May Morris (1862–1938), the daughter of William Morris, photographed in her garden c.1920: women's involvement in war work had made comfortable clothing both topical and inevitable, and the London stores were advertising overalls and breeches as 'serviceable' clothes at this time.

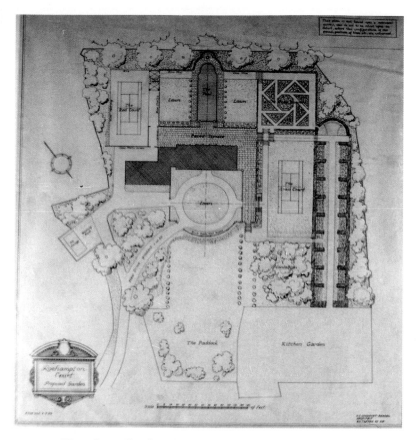

PLATE 42 Harry Stuart Goodhart-Rendel (1887–1959), an architect's concept of a garden for a sport-loving family, for Roehampton Court, London, 1923. Hard court, grass court, swimming pool, croquet and putting lawns, and a pony paddock contribute to the jigsaw puzzle school of design for active lives. The advent of the motor car has subtly modernised the curve of the drive, the turning circle, and the retreat to the 'washing yard' and garage, with a chauffeur's flat. Up until the First World War, the designers still designed for horse transport, so this signifies the acceptance of the motor age for owners who could afford every outdoor amusement with a characteristic 1920s exuberance. It also signifies the deathknell of the private garden as exclusively a place of peace, contemplation and flowers.

PLATE 43 ABOVE *Cardiocrinum giganteum* was a gardening phenomenon, greatly coveted when the first bulbs became available in the 1850s, costing three shillings each (the equivalent of a good prize at a village horticultural show): here it stars in a lavish engraving in the *Gardeners' Chronicle*, 22 December 1894, an unusual event in itself and perhaps a Christmas gift to the readers.

OPPOSITE: PLATE 44 James Pulham's (*c.*1820–98) firm was famous for the artificial rockwork made from clinker set in cement, but so realistically manufactured as to deceive experts, which was used in Battersea Park and the royal garden at Sandringham and many other places. This advertisement is from the 1880s, but the firm continued well into the twentieth century, under his son James R. Pulham (1873–1957) as one of the most famous of contracting names.

PLATE 45 The Kennedy Memorial, Runnymede, Surrey, by Sir Geoffrey Jellicoe, 1964–5: this small woodland garden of refuge is itself the Memorial, leading pilgrims on an allegorical progress through a wicket gate, up the Hill of Difficulty via the winding path of granite setts, to the awful register of the facts on the stone. The craftsmen of the setts, pavings and stone were an integral part of the creative process; Jellicoe's imaginative allegory, the integrity of the craftsmanship and the natural beauty of the small woodland are intended to combine into something greater than the sum of their parts, to carry us beyond the events of 22 November 1963, and into the sunlight of the future. So much could be written on this small designed landscape, on its inspirations and symbolism, and its subject; suffice it to say that it is an immensely powerful exposition of the garden of death.

The delights of the dry gravel garden and attractions of Mediterranean climate zones remind us that we are all now Europeans. We have been Europeans before, right up until the young gentry on the grand tour came home and buried themselves in English landscaped parks. All that coming home, from educational jaunts, from European wars, from Empire-hunting, curtained these islands as if in heavy red velour, in a concentrated isolationism in all things English. All plants and ideas which came home became instantly English, transmogrified as if they had no native roots at all: conversely, *le jardin anglais* was exported and mysteriously became the rage: 'I am at present madly in love with English gardens' wrote Empress Catherine the Great of Russia to Voltaire in 1772, 'with curved lines, gentle slopes, lakes formed from swamps, and archipelagoes of solid earth.'[5] (She added that she despised straight lines and hated fountains that tortured water.) The Elector of Bavaria was equally gratified with Munich's famous Englischer Garten, made by Count Rumford and the army in 1789.[6] *Le jardin anglais* was also the rage in France in the eighteenth and nineteenth centuries.

English gardens invaded the Empire wherever the British went, but the strongest desires and emotions were always attached to coming home, where the climate would allow proper gardening, in comparison with those purposeless struggles in the heat and the dust. All through the Victorian era this intense adoration raised the English garden to symbolic status: was there any other garden at all? Remember how Revd Keble Martin saw only English native flowers on the western front? The English garden was a nationalist icon, even a reason for winning the First World War; Robinson and Jekyll were figures of Empire, and throughout the 1930s and 1940s, through the Second World War, the staple readings of all the English-speaking world were the magazines and books of home. Garden writers such as Beverley Nichols, Eden Phillpotts, E. A. Bowles, Constance Spry, Vita Sackville-West and horticultural columnists were all syndicated across the world: they made little or no concession to this, but wrote steadfastly of their English idylls. Half the world was in a kind of garden prison, forced to regard native plants as mostly weeds, and struggling with hybrid roses and herbaceous borders in alien climates.

This seems amazing to us now, and it is hardly acknowledged: freedom came with the independence of India in 1947 and ensuing relative freedoms of the Commonwealth. South Africa was liberated earlier because of some enlightened celebrations of the Union which included the founding in 1913 of Kirstenbosch Botanic Garden and its outstations specifically to conserve native plants. In Australia there was the remarkable Edna Walling who had gone to Melbourne in 1918 when she was twenty; she designed and made gardens in a Jekyllian manner (that is how they think of her in Australia) through a long life, and undoubtedly came to terms with a variety of habitats. When I first went to Canada, to the lively Civic Garden Centre in Toronto in 1983, I found a warm welcome and response to hearing about Lutyens and Jekyll, but also crowds of gardeners who were dealing with mid-continental extremes of temperature and keenly interested in the American revivals of prairie natives. Toronto gardeners regarded themselves as less fortunate than those of the golden west, Vancouver and British Columbia, with growing conditions 'so like Britain'. This English-garden obsession was equally strong in most parts of America, but the interest in natives – new when I was first there in 1979 – began in California and gradually spread eastwards. All in all I saw so many marvellous gardens in North America that I vowed I would never go there to speak about English gardens again (and consequently wrote my biography of Beatrix Farrand, so that I could go and tell them about a wonderful American gardener).[7]

Having lost an empire and found Europe what do we think of their gardens? Charles Quest Ritson, a rosarian who entered garden writing with a good book on expatriates' gardens around the Mediterranean, has recently exploded on this subject in the *Garden*. In his experience we think European gardens are ghastly, we are not interested, and 'when I tell people I have just written a guide to German gardens, the usual reply is "are there any?"'. His enthusiastic and knowledgeable retort continues: 'people find it hard to believe that anything grown abroad could possibly fare well . . . I am certain we should be buying rhododendrons from Hachman in Holstein; . . . peonies from Klose in Kassel; alpines from Siegfried Geissler in Saxony; fuchsias from Michiels-De Smedt in Antwerp; hibiscus from Osola del Sole in Sicily; fruit trees from Bassi in Cuneo; irises from Innocenti in Tuscany and camellias from Claude Thoby in Loire-Atlantique.'[8] I can only pass on his recommendation of an English-language version of *Pflanzen, Plantes, Plants* (PPP), a Europe-wide plant-finder.

European gardens are sneaking into guides, but fifteen pages out of more than 600 in the current *Good Gardens Guide* seems to confirm Charles's suspicions. There are some 200 wonderful gardens in the Netherlands annual guide, and the Dutch Gardens Society publishes an annual list in English. Since 1992 gardeners in the know have been making their way to the chateau at Chaumont-sur-Loire for the annual summer festival of design. Designs to a set theme are submitted by hundreds of hopefuls and thirty are chosen each March to be built and planted for summer display: Chaumont is setting high and exciting standards, and the director Jean-Paul Pigeat has been quoted as saying they want to awaken young designers to a new style of gardening in France 'escaping *le style anglais*'. Chaumont is an international competition and Britons rarely qualify.[9]

From Chaumont westwards through the Loire Valley, through Tours and Villandry, a journey through paradise for a gardener might end in the heavenly courts of the Abbey of Fontevraud, probably the most interesting restoration of a medieval monastic garden in Europe.[10] Fontevraud was beloved of Plantaganet kings and queens, in the days when Europe was arranged differently, and it is easy to share their appreciation of this warm south, as opposed to the chilly hulks of Windsor, Warwick or the Welsh borders. Fontevraud, founded in 1099 as a complex of monastery, nunnery, hospitals and schools, was a place of benevolence in a warring world, and the emphasis of the gardens is on the medicinal, culinary and practical uses of plants. These are grown in traditional plots, potager and orchards, for their historic uses which are demonstrated and explained. It is a good place for reaching back to the age-old traditions of healing plants and remedies.

The French natural cosmetics company Yves Rocher have been involved at Fontevraud, and the firm also has experimental nurseries in Brittany. The medicinal and curative properties of trees, shrubs and 'weeds' are being rediscovered by chemists working at the frontiers of medicine, or so the press and television constantly tell us, so does this mean that the medical profession is returning to its monastic garden beginnings? Undoubtedly many country general practitioners will vouch for the healing power of a daily walk and gentle gardening, but the hospital sector is less sympathetic. Hospitals are an urban development, single-mindedly devoted to sterile cleanliness, and as such are hardly likely to welcome those 'rich' habitats that were the old breeding grounds for diseases. There has been an understandable resistance to anything as messy as a garden: doctors and nurses who might have gardens at home, kept them as very private retreats, not letting such interests spill over into strictly compartmented professional lives. With the notable exception of King Edward VII Hospital at Midhurst, hospitals and gardens have had little in common, and for most of this century patients have been cured in spite of the hospital environment rather than because of it. Through the King Edward VII connection I have recently been able to raise this subject at another of his foundations, the dynamic think-tank of the medical world, the King's Fund.[11] Searching their records I found a 1967 report by the landscape architect Professor J. St Bodfan Gruffydd on the subject of hospital gardens, the need for these, and the 'gaps' in professional knowledge for designing and building such gardens, even in the opinions of the Fund's long-standing garden advisers, who included Lanning Roper.[12] The Gruffydd report, I regret to say, remains notable for its uniqueness: the Fund has initiated hospital design competitions, landscape architects have designed hospital gardens, but they are the rare exceptions and the examples I have seen are heavily over-designed. They do not have the healing empathy of a garden, the opportunity for frail and hovering human spirits to feel the comforting rhythms of other growing things. The gardener Montagu Don seems to have harnessed all the healing comforts of plants into the Snowdrop Garden at Wythenshawe Hospital's suite for parents who have lost a child – 'the most enlightened and loving piece of hospital treatment' that he had heard of. He overcame the usual difficulties, a shaded, dark space, adorned with concrete pillars, glass wall and manhole covers, and planted honeysuckles, white wisteria, blossoms, roses, and spring bulbs, including snowdrops, with *Nicotiana sylvestris* to succeed them.[13] It is just this kind of gentleness and care that is needed for healing hospital gardens, and we have far to go in their development. Some appropriate hospice gardens have been made – indeed, the hospice movement is enlightened in this way as in so many others: the Children's Hospice in Oxford, St Catherine's Hospice at Crawley, and Trinity Hospice on Clapham Common in south London are notable examples. Hospital art also flourishes: the Chelsea and Westminster Hospital has a vibrant and cheering art collection, which does of course lift everyone's spirits. But, and it is a big but, we humans have occasionally to admit our limitations, and that is when plants and flowers can help.

The ministration of the churches, schools and new hospitals, have been examined for their 'garden' credentials in this book, and found wanting. Society is sometimes leaving such establishments to their prejudices and searching for alternatives elsewhere. There is a present and lively fascination with the Japanese tradition of Zen Buddhist gardens, which promise a contemplative fulfilment, an extra dimension of garden peace. Dharma, the Buddhist word for truth and teachings, is also the word for nature: 'That is because they are the same', says Ajahn Pongsak of the Dhammanaat Foundation conservation project. 'Nature is the manifestation of truth and of the teachings. When we destroy nature we destroy the truth and the teachings. When we protect nature, we protect the truth and the teachings.'[14] Westerners were first won over by the serene beauty of Kyoto's temple gardens of raked sand, symbolic rocks and elegantly branching blossom trees, but now our interest goes deeper, into the Buddhist concept of non-injury to life, which sees deep digging of the soil as overwhelmingly violent: the ornamental solution is raked sand and gravel, and the ethical alternative is compost-layered no-digging cultivation. Reverence and loving kindness embraces all forms of life, animal and vegetable, and non-violence extends towards plants which sustain and shelter life, with especial regard for forest trees with their age and 'wisdom' – which is why gnarled branches or roots are proudly acquired as noble talismans for the garden or courtyard. Sakka, the lord of the gods, was a landscape gardener, and earned god-like status for making parks and gardens, groves, lakes and roads: home life is regarded as a fetter, and Sakka was nobly providing the means of escape, liberation of the spirit, which can be achieved in the smallest court open to the sky. The branching blossom thus points to liberation for the soul, and the cherry blossom is an object of veneration for brightening the returning spring. 'If one of you should ask', says the poet Moto-ori, 'what is the spirit of the Japanese, point to the wild cherry-blossom shining in the sun.'[15] The Buddha is an open-air god who accompanies us into gardens, on country walks and mountain climbs, with a compatibility with nature and natural places that appeals far beyond the chattering classes. Pesticide-free organic growers and meat-refusing teenagers are investigating old understandings rather than discovering anything new. Interestingly, ethically correct practice becomes good practice, much valued by society: pavings laid in sand rather than mired in concrete; delicate 'wild'-sized flowers rather than blowsy doubles; still or subtly bubbling water rather than spouting fountains; gravel as always preferable to tarmacadam or other toxic surfaces; hardwood (silvered oak) rather than stained or creosoted softwoods; subdued earth-tinged greens, blues and browny paints, never pinks or yellows or purples.

The London Ecology Unit has done a great deal of important work on how plants survive in cities, for instance, how trees filter polluted air, modify summer heat and winter cold and how vegetation controls storm water. But the greatest improvement in cities could be said to be in balcony gardens, courtyards and green roofs, the last being the saddest of missed opportunities so far. London's first roof garden came about in a typically Marjory Allen way, when she was flushed with enthusiasm at being elected the first Fellow of the new Institute of Landscape Architects in 1930. She was shopping in Selfridges and by accident or curious design found herself going up to the roof with a liftload of workmen, where she was amazed to discover a vast expanse of sunny emptiness. Thinking of the staff and their lunchtime sandwiches she managed to persuade Gordon Selfridge of the good idea that had struck her, and with Richard Sudell she set to work. They carried a thousand tons of materials up to the roof and in six months had a series of gardens:

an English garden devoted entirely to old-fashioned flowers – stocks, pinks, snapdragons, wallflowers, lupins, lavender and roses. Here fantail pigeons bathed in the formal pool and raised their families in elegant pigeon-houses designed by . . . Julian Trevelyan. There was a rose garden and a lily pool, where two Italian grilles in the sheltering north wall revealed a view of the Hampstead hills. A garden of scents presided over by a beautiful figure of St Francis, led to the sheltered winter garden; and the large water garden was bounded by two long herbaceous borders.

The garden was opened in 1930, Selfridges being congratulated on presenting London with another park. The following year the new Derry & Toms store in Kensington High Street, refused its top storey because the firemen's ladders weren't long enough, hastily constructed its own elaborate oriental-style roof garden. At Selfridges the designers looked after the gardens for three years until the store wanted to use them as selling space for garden equipment, including gnomes – Marjory Allen retorted that it was gnomes or us, and they chose the gnomes. The Selfridges garden soon disappeared, but the Derry & Toms gardens are there still, constantly maintained and much enjoyed.[16]

The next notable roof garden was Geoffrey Jellicoe's for Harvey's store in Guildford High Street in 1956: he designed a garden in the sky, a large sheet of water for maximum reflections, with sinuous islands of planting and stepping stones, all interlocking circles, and all inspired by the first pictures of Earth seen from space. The garden was overlooked by a balcony cafe, enjoyed by shoppers for many years, until it fell foul of safety laws and had to be closed to public access. The garden remains intact, still holding water, and fondly regarded by the long-serving members of the store's staff. Despite the obvious commercial attractions, there has been no continuing tradition of roof gardens, no architect or landscape architect concerned with a shopping mall or superstore having either the inclination or the persuasive ability of Marjory Allen. Corporate roof gardens, Gateway and Mountbatten Houses at Basingstoke, the Scottish Widows' headquarters in Edinburgh, Norman Foster's Willis Faber Dumas building in Ipswich, have all been lauded and awarded but still not started a vogue.

However things are now changing because of a search for improved insulation and energy-saving which has sent architects scurrying back to native traditions of earth building and turf roofs. Planning authorities have also discovered that obtrusive buildings are most easily masked by grassing them into their surroundings: Stuttgart, ever an advanced city, already has regulations demanding the grassing of large flat roofs, other German cities are following and this may well become a European ruling. The Sir Joseph Banks Centre for Economic Botany building at Kew and the extension to the Sainsbury Centre for Visual Arts at the University of East Anglia are both 'grassed-in' buildings. But the technology does not apply only to large buildings: existing house roofs of low pitch can be transformed into rich meadow gardens or beds of houseleeks and other succulents, with great support from local ecologists who see the possibilities of replacing lost habitats from on the ground.

The London Ecology Unit's Building Green approach is most effective in neighbourhood schemes, refurbishments of blocks of flats, or green strategies for whole towns and cities – as yet the only continental examples are in Utrecht, Berlin and Denmark; for the future of our cities, however, surely high-level greening is the answer.[17]

Architects for Peace was set up in the late 1980s with the support of John Darbourne, Richard MacCormac, Richard and Ruth Rogers and Peter Shepheard, among others, to support a proposal for peace gardens and parks as catalysts for understanding 'not only the personal spirit but that of differing cultures'. John Darbourne's foreword to *Places for Peace* recounts how he was discussing the design of a river 'park' in Hanover and was painfully aware of his lack of German: 'However, as we reverted to Latin in discussing the planting, amusingly this universal language became a cultural bridge and even further extended our stunted conversation into its own form of understanding'.[18] Apart from its advocacy of the international currency of plants John Darbourne's *Places for Peace* is the seed of an idea which at the same time recalls the 'secret' garden of retreat and memorial; it seeks to encourage public gardens which are commemorative, celebratory and of everyday use – not necessarily passive, often active, but always with space for contemplation, and an added rhetoric of awareness of 'peace' issues. It discusses commemoration, The Cenotaph and Lutyens, and moves on to Jellicoe's Kennedy Memorial at Runnymede, the only significant step forward since Lutyens's time. The Memorial is the acre of English ground 'forever America', and Sir Geoffrey's design was of the lightest touch, consisting essentially of the path of granite setts in earth that leads to the catafalque incised with the necessary information and those dreadful words 'died by an assassin's hand'. The Kennedy Memorial is a 'Place for Peace' in that it is a commemoration and a warning: 'as professionals and citizens, all we can do today is warn. We cannot afford the luxury of pessimism . . . we must intimate peace and conviviality.' *Places for Peace* naturally finds empathy with Buddhist symbolism, Japanese garden design (another reason for this having revived interest) and Peace Pagodas and the language of plant symbolism. Peace parks and gardens are all over Britain (the most recent being the redemption of the former Greenham Common Airfield, which is now open) as well as worldwide, particularly in Japan and America.[19]

The whole notion of gardens that 'speak' via symbols or messages carved on a stone is evocative of the ancient past, the secret garden of long ago. This is a universally powerful memory and one that human nature prefers to adapt in celebration of living, rather than dying, but it must underly the perennial fascination with sculpture in the garden. Echoing the successes of Mrs Coade, and the divine shepherdesses and gods of Rysbrack and Van Nost, garden sculpture is now enjoying a revival, in part inspired by the internationally famous Goodwood Sculpture Park or Holland's Kroller-Müller collection (which includes the giant's blue trowel stuck in the ground, by Claes Oldenburg) but also supported by a range of new works. The commercial buoyancy of the garden world has made it possible for a whole clutch of artists working in wood, metal, ceramics, glass and plastics to devise lovely pieces for gardens of varying sizes in a range of prices. For the non-horticulturally inclined there is a garden to be proud of – a flock of resin-moulded sheep in the grass, or a brightly coloured, wired dragonfly peering through the bushes – without any 'plants' at all.

The promising future for a garden of messages and amusing sculptures is not the fruit of my crystal-gazing, it already exists and is worshipped by a cognoscenti of artists, photographers and architects. It is a garden whose images are well known through photographs but which is rarely seen: a garden started in 1967, 'hacked out of a barren Lanarkshire hillside' around a gaggle of barn-like buildings, one of which is the artist's home, which approaches the status of hallowed ground through a martyrdom of misunderstanding in a prosaic world. This is, of course, Little Sparta, 'not a rich man's commission' but resembling 'a monastic retreat made by poor members of an Order with their own hands'. Ian Hamilton Finlay's 'garden' is a partly tended, partly wild landscape of sublime views and dominating weather, of mists and rain, or tempestuous winds and skies. It is an intense self-expression, an extension of himself – 'so fitted is he to the environment that I am incapable of picturing his survival outside this domain', his fellow-Scot and frequent visitor Dawn Macleod wrote and 'of course he has created it to contain him, as the form fits the hare.'[20] I imagine Hamilton Finlay with hare-like characteristics (for he is rarely, if ever, photographed) in his lair of boulders, grasses and windswept trees: his minimal intervention into his habitat is in the form of sculptural works with inscriptions that puzzle, surprise or tantalize, and which demand a considerable effort of understanding. The writer Lucius Burkhardt has dared a concise description:

> Through the inscription on a stone of "See Poussin, Hear Lorrain", the pond of a Scottish croft is transformed into a scene from classical painting. The signature of Albrecht Durer on a tablet in the grass evokes complex associations with "The Great Piece of Turf" at the Albertina, Vienna. By using these mediations, Ian Hamilton Finlay draws comparisons between things which are normally considered to be opposites: the garden and the woods; the pond and the sea; the tranquillity of the "charming place" and the battlefields of the Second World War; the virtues of the peasant and the virtues of the French Revolution . . . finally [the] garden mediates on the relation between nature and the spectator. His inscriptions on tree trunks are allusions to both; to arcadian poetry and the motive of cutting one's name in the bark, and to inscriptions in a botanical garden and the labelling of nature . . .[21]

Finlay's 'messages' are all exquisitely worked, carved in stone or wood usually, by a series of collaborative artists, some for the garden, some for commissions and publication by Wild Hawthorn Press.

Finlay is celebrating metaphor, whereas Andy Goldsworthy celebrates nature in the landscape – piles of pebbles, swirls of stones, leaf balls, patterned trees, arches of ice, green-leaved pools. 'Goldsworthy is a natural magician. With nothing up his sleeve but his inventive arms . . . he constructs objects and patterns which are generally ephemeral and often winningly decorative. He plays along with Nature until it reveals its nature.'[22] This is a good description of Goldsworthy's enormous talent; with the notable exception of his dry-stone walled sheep pens, his work is ephemeral, and the photographs do the rest. What is his relevance to gardens? Many gardeners I know are his keenest collectors, his works are so good-natured, so reflective of the magic of nature, they inspire gardeners not just to work – but also to create, because he opens our eyes. Many gardeners find inspiration in conceptual art, and particularly the 'land artists' such as Richard Long and Chris Drury. It is a fellowship of elements and materials which allows gardening inti-

Future Gardens

mately to associate with an art form, as it was once close to modern painting.

Three other artists working on the more exciting landscape fringes may suggest some future garden directions. In France, Bernard Lassus has been restoring for over a decade the former marine arsenal and rigging works for royal ships, the Corderie Royale at Rochefort, now called The Garden of Returns.[23] Rochefort is much declined from great naval days and the purpose is to inspire urban renewal and visitor interest. Bernard Lassus has dug up and re-displayed naval history, using a Second World War blockhouse as the base for the mock-deck of a full-rigged sailing ship – the simulated deck is stocked with 'tontines', containers used to protect exotic plants being brought home. There had always been a sheltered garden tucked away behind the arsenal where Intendant Bégon (after whom the begonia was named) and later Admiral de La Galissonnière had acclimatized exotic plants and flowers. 'The military arsenal was coupled with this "botanical arsenal" [both reverting to the wild until recently] ... the concept of The Garden of Returns implies not only the return of the Corderie to the town, but also its return to a garden.' The tradition of exotic plant imports and Rochefort's purchase of the Millerioux begonia collection prompted the building of greenhouses behind the Corderie in which these could be displayed. New and symbolic plantings soften the lines of the old fortress, and there is a thuya labyrinth of naval battles – 'an act of homage to the warlike and sometimes stormy age of the ships that were fitted out on this site' – and the buildings are put to new cultural uses. Rochefort 'lost its soul on the day that it lost its way to the ocean', writes Lassus, 'but the Corderie can now stand for a new, pluralist attitude to our cultural resources. It offers an arsenal of ideas that seek to link our patrimony with the economic world of the present...'[24]

Martha Schwartz is an American artist with a background in theatre design, who happens to work out of doors. For the last decade she has challenged the landscape profession with her impressive, beautiful and startling works: stylized drumlins grouped elegantly on a courthouse plaza in Minnesota, the revamping of the site of a 1928 Beaux Arts Uniroyal tyre factory which was given a huge oasis of lines of date palms, each (real) palm surrounded at its base by a white concrete 'tyre' – 'the ghosts of tyres past' – which doubles as a seat. In Boston her Bagel

313

Garden is a square double-hedged in sixteen-inch-high box, with purple gravel and precisely set-out weatherproof 'Bagel' rolls alternating with purple ageratum set in brown soil, thus reversing the relationship of ground colour and 'planting'. Some of Martha Schwartz's work is large scale, but most of it targets the personal subconscious, and has elements of human scale. In the summer of 1995, at the deconstructive stage of a new garden on one third of an acre on the New Jersey Shore, the son of the house announced his intention of getting married in the September: the opportunity was taken, as bride and groom were both gardeners, to go to town on a temporary wedding garden, with the approach to the wedding tent along a walkway 'with handsome men' – an avenue of tall potted trees – and a field of empty, blue-painted flower pots. Beyond the ceremonial tent (where bride and groom were surrounded by black-eyed Susans and candles), random yellow circles were painted over the lawn and pool terrace, with a sunflower grove – a grid of potted sunflowers on purple grass. These sauntering areas were en route to the banquet tent, with white-clothed tables set in lines as in a Brueghel painting, and potted orange trees.[25]

The third designer, Kathryn Gustafson, trained in art and graduated to fashion which she found too transient; she made the move to landscape via the 'very, very, contemporary' École Nationale Supérieure du Paysage at Versailles and has done high-profile works in France, at Parc de la Villette in Paris, an environmental park called Imaginary Continents at Terrasson in the Dordogne, and a 1.2-hectare Human Rights Square in the centre of Evry, south-east of Paris. The importance of Gustafson is that her work is vibrant and enthusiastic and expresses both her personal style and total commitment to the job in hand: she uses landscape materials as though they were fashion fabrics, rippling a curvy water stair down the slope at Terrasson, folding and ruching green waves of grass, embroidering the green with ribbons of water rills or jewels of seats, finely made in modernist white concrete. She finds inspiration in the history of the site, and in modern artists such as Isomo Noguchi and David Rabinwitch. She has only worked in a larger-than-garden scale so far but her artistic energy – 'a Herculean figure moving great big pieces of land in the way that Richard Long does, but in a grander way'[26] – and self-identity as an artist who refuses to become enmeshed in a corporate office, mark her as an exciting influence to watch.[27]

To look at any other artists or designers after Ian Hamilton Finlay, Andy Goldsworthy, Bernard Lassus, Martha Schwartz and Kathryn Gustafson would be to travel backwards in time. In graduating from one to another we can see five creative minds suspended at varying heights above the earth: if earthborn design has any lode star to follow it must be this subtle suspension of belief, freed into fantasy and delight. We all have higher thresholds of boredom and belief now.

Earthborn design has almost always had its boots held in the mud and so few practitioners have been able to rise above the constraints of earth-moving, soil-improving, sourcing plants and then spacing them and watering them, to elevation beyond the obvious and banal. The exciting development has been the way conceptual art and perhaps fashion design have come out to meet gardens and landscape with designers who find their fluidity and flexibility becomes one with Mother Nature. (If you want a static set-piece use a stage or exhibition designer.) These five artists exemplify the dual nature of garden making: Finlay and Lassus are the most site-secure, they interpret their ground, every detail of its habitat and history and meld additional interpretations into it for further enchantments. This is garden making at home, the steady familiarizing with the spirit of the place and setting it on display through a series of universal codes or innovative ideas. The intuitive artists on the other hand, Goldsworthy, Schwartz and Gustafson, dance in with magical tread and, out of their own experience allied to what they find, they pierce the heart of a place and enhance it brilliantly.

But do gardens always want to trail in the skirts of high art? What of sustainability, durability, integrity with the earth?

A drive through a home county on a bright May day will confirm the answer: with a head spinning from May blossom, Queen Anne's lace and rape flowers, the beginning of the houses, sprinkled at first, then steadily more intensive, the senses are assaulted by sulphur yellow laburnum draped over shocking pink azaleas, the towering pinks and blushes of rhododendrons reaching the drooping lilacs, houses wreathed in wisteria, fringed in polyanthus and wallflowers of rainbow hues. Nor does it cease with spring, pelargoniums now appear in sizzling iridescent hues like a mixed gaggle of roadworkers and policemen in their flash-jackets. Have we slightly overdone success? The horticultural industry has been very successful: the 1990s has brought the Dutch Perennial

Wave, wave upon wave of more wonderful-looking plants. Nurserymen and designers in one body (and not only Dutch) have enthused about each other's plants. Piet Oudolf writes, 'And then the new range of Sedums ... one can play with colour and shape, which I think is the most important thing of having varieties – one can freely play with colour ... but at the same time you know that those plants are reliable ... we have one of 80 cms in a pink now, and with a purple leaf, and we have a yellow one that's 30 cms, and both are reliable, so that you can play without having to think about the problem, will it do or will it not.'[28]

Do we need carpeting sedums that are 2½ feet tall? Do we need infinite variety or varieties, so that it is impossible to find anything familiar in a sea of novel plants? And that word *reliable* – which to a plantsman means no sins, no running, no hybridizing by accident, no dying within three weeks of taking it home (strangely, it does not in fact seem to mean the last one): there are signs that plant heaven – having lots to chose from – is becoming plant hell: plantsmen speak with pride of how one gene can change a flower, can make a respectable enough looking antirrhinum resemble a distorted aberration.

There is a new battle brewing in the garden world, between the nurserymen and growers and the ecologists. There is a move, supported by the Linnean Society and Flora-for-Fauna, to restore English natives: English Plants for English Gardens. Apparently 56 million trees and shrubs are imported to British gardens every year (out of a total 80 million planted). There is genuine fear for the precious biodiversity of our native flora, and the effect on the food resources that plants provide, in that garden hybrids are notoriously inedible, yet pass these undesirable genes into the wild. The garden of natives has long been a goal of those of a certain refined taste, and one was imagined by Robert Gathorne-Hardy in *The Native Garden* of 1961, with illustrations by John Nash. Now there is a more serious scientific purpose, with a database inspired by the ecologist and entomologist Dr Miriam Rothschild called *The Postcode Plants Database*, which advises nurseries and gardeners on plants that are garden-worthy in their area.

This may save us from the worst genetic disasters, but will surely also spark many arguments about 'what is a native'. For plants have moved about as much as or more than human populations: in America, the 'melting-pot' of plants that now owe settled allegiance to the Stars and Stripes have been amassed into 'the new American garden' by two distinguished gardeners and designers, James van Sweden and Wolfgang von Oehme. They became celebrated for bringing the grasses of steppe, sand-dune and marsh from their shared European backgrounds, into the climatically stressed urban malls of Washington and smart gardens along the eastern seashores: their twenty years of experience has been refined into a planting repertory with a 'point of reference to an American meadow – a place of freedom and ease where wildlife, plant life and human life co-exist in harmony'. Van Sweden and von Oehme have undoubtedly reached an American compromise, a garden for one kind of future and they conclude my search. 'In the American garden we welcome the blurred edges of plants growing together. We encourage the intermixing of species over time such as Black-eyed Susans seeding among the Pennisetum or Fountain grass. Our gardens are low in maintenance (notice "low" not "no"). We do not over-maintain and discourage the unnatural looking "fine toothed-comb" approach. We do not carve shrubs and trees into artificial shapes . . . our gardens must leave room for the occasional glorious mistake. They require a minimum of water after they are established, and we use herbicides and pesticides only as a last resort.'[29]

That such famous and influential designers should reach this happy compromise is worth a round of applause. But individuals are doing this, too, like Rose Irving who has planted a piece of Jamaica (the island she left thirty years ago) in her terrace garden in north London. 'It is as voluptuous as a jungle . . . with shelves heaving under the weight of cacti, ferns, tiger paw begonias and Venus fly-traps while overhead a range of petunias pour from baskets on poles and along arches.' Rose Irving is far from alone: Andreas Demetriou, a Greek Cypriot living in Brixton, has a garden where 'a Persian lilac and a pomegranate flourished alongside discarded buckets, cooking oil cans and paint tins brimming with coriander, loquat, bay grown from a seed of a bay tree in Delphi, basil, rosemary, pansies, bougainvillea, honesty, sage, thyme and fig.'[30]

I am not sure whether it is a cause for laughter or tears that gardens may indeed have to take over from the replication and replacement of the once rich, natural habitats of the earth, but clearly we must cultivate what we once took for granted. Certainly gardens will remain in all the magical guises of memory and present laughter that they have assumed throughout this book, but maybe we shall have to call to mind that they are made of this earth, and it is the only Earth we have. It is not a good omen to promote them as 'exterior decorating', meaningless collections of expensively perfect plants which will die and disappoint.[31] Much better to begin with fingers in the soil, propagating a daisy. It is this, the simplest and yet most precious combination, of us and our soil that bonds us in the pursuit of paradise, with all who have gone before and those yet to come.

GLOSSARY

The garden world loves to debate the definitions of special terms, a maze for the unwary, as well as the Latin nomenclature of plants: in this book Latin plant names have been used for clarity (which is always their purpose) but in conjunction with broadly accepted or common names. What might be called garden jargon seemed to need an easy point of reference, so the following list explains some terms and words as they are used in this book:

Alley, allée, a walk or formerly a ride for horses and small phaetons cut through dense woodland, clipped to smooth edges; originally from French formal gardens, alleys extended vistas and radiated from central circles, *rond-points*. Alleys have soft ground surfaces, sand or turf, and may be covered for shade, *allée en berceau* (c.f. pergola).

Alpine, alpine-scree, alpine house and **rock garden** indicate settings for plants of mountain habitats, from all the world's mountain ranges not just the Alps.

American garden plants, means those introduced from the new colony in seventeenth century, mostly ericaceous (lime-hating) including magnolia, kalmia, pieris, rhododendron, for which special peat beds were made in the nineteenth century.

Aphids is the general term for a large variety of sap-sucking insects with individual appetites for many of the plants that we also like, especially fruits and roses: the clever gardener controls them by care and companion planting to encourage ladybirds and other predators.

Arbour, bower, a shelter made of wood covered with plants from Latin *arbor*, French *arbre* = tree (American Arbor Day for tree planting) see also Herb.

Belvedere, a raised look-out, lantern-tower from the military, see also Gazebo.

Bos, boschi, bosco, bosk, bosket all originate in the sacred groves of classical gardens, meaning thick woodland or shrub planting growing freely in an enclosed garden giving the frisson of wildness.

Canal, a formal usually flat-bottomed length of water in Dutch tradition. Le Nôtre used 'mirrours', reflecting sheets of water at Versailles etc., more sacred .than 'pieces of water', fishponds and reservoirs which were for practical purposes.

Carpet bedding, a term coined by the *Gardeners' Chronicle* for dense plantings of dwarf succulents including sedums, sempervivums, echeverias which were clipped to resemble a Turkish carpet.

Chahar bagh, literally four-fold garden from *bagh* = garden, *chahar* = four, the Islamic interpretation of Eden (c.f. Genesis 2 v.10 'And a river went out of Eden to water the garden; and from thence it was parted, and became into four heads') the four rivers being the Pison, Gihon, Hiddekel (Tigris) and Euphrates, which divided the enclosed garden into four quarters. This is the origin of all formal garden design.

Chinoiserie, a fashion for oriental-style garden buildings derived from early travellers' tales which became more informed in the eighteenth century, especially with Chinese Chippendale red lacquer woodwork. There was no real comprehension of Chinese garden philosophy in the west until the twentieth century, see Maggie Keswick, *The Chinese Garden* etc., 1981.

Clair-voyée, literally see-through, applying to a small opening in a hedge or wall which allows a view to the landscape.

Classification, the internationally recognized ordering of plants by Latin names: genus, genera, defines a group, a surname e.g. *Rosa, Lilium, Quercus* (oak), all with species or Christian names, e.g. *longifolium, longicuspis*, which defines their special character. These two names, genera and species = the binomial, the basic unit of modern taxonomy or classification. Unfortunately taxonomists are constantly revising binomials, a subject of eternal controversy for gardeners. Sub-species, variety, cultivar, form, strain are all applied to plants developed for garden use, giving a 3rd (4th or 5th) Latin name and invariably a proper name e.g. *Rosa filipes* 'Kiftsgate'.

Companion, companionate, gardening is a new term applied to an old tradition of growing plants according to their beneficial effects upon their neighbours whether through the creation of micro-climate or chemical means.

Container gardening originally meant the 1960s development of transplanting young plants into metal, plastic or fibre pots conveniently for long shelf life in garden centres and easy shopping by car as this has become the accepted method of buying plants. The term can also be applied to semi-permanent gardens in tubs, troughs or pots of any kind.

Crazy paving was called by Thomas Mawson 'one of the worst forms of affectation'; in British gardens it undoubtedly came about by default, the breaking up of rectangular paviours, but was a good way of making money out of quarry rubbish! However Gertrude Jekyll approved of random paving with stones of natural shape for unpretentious gardens, especially rougher stones, as her native Bargate sandstone used at Munstead Wood.

Eden, 'the tree garden of delight' is one translation of Genesis, 'And out of the ground made the Lord God to grow every tree that is pleasant to the sight, and good for food; the tree of life also . . . and the tree of knowledge of good and evil.' Endless speculations on the location of Eden have encouraged synonyms with paradise, natural wilderness, benign landscapes.

Exedra is a classical feature, a semi-circular or rectangular bench or recess.

Florist is the name for a specialist grower of (usually) a particular flower, e.g. tulips, auriculas, carnations, anemone and ranunculus were the favourites, the name in popular use when Samuel Gilbert wrote his *Florists Vade-Mecum* in 1682. In Victorian times it was more generally applied to skilled providers of decorative flowers especially in London houses.

Garden, Skeat's Etymological dictionary gives *gardin* (eleventh century Middle English, Old French), the old Saxon *garda* from Anglo-Saxon *geard* = yard; Latin *gardinum* for a low-status Roman garden, c.f. Hortus below, and Old French *jardin*.*

Gazebo, **gaze-about**, a pavilion with a view, the garden version of a belvedere.

Giardino segreto, Italian, enclosed and secret garden.

---

* NB. 'Gardening' is a modern term in cricket for a batsman nervously digging at the crease; 'Garden-shed syndrome' is a psychologists' term for taking refuge from reality.

Gothic, gothick, applied to ornament, buildings etc., refers to the repeated medieval revivals in fashionable taste, which inspired pointed arches, castellations, hermitages, and ruins. These were all romantic revivals *au fond*, inspired by 'the loss of the Romantic House of Stuart' and the Roman Catholic faith. See chapter 2.

Grotto is an artificial cave, derived from Italian Renaissance use in gardens for shade, cooling waters, as well as classical allusion. Grottoes were constructed by specialist builders for eighteenth-century English fashion inspired by Thomas Wright's *Arbours & Grottos*, 1755–8, which added grotesque overtones (Italian *grottesca* = fantastical decorations) and the first intimations of Chinese garden-caves as the abodes of the Immortals.

Ground cover, a term invented in the early twentieth century and popular in the 1960s for plants which smothered out weeds. A pinewood is the ultimate ground cover, but in garden terms the prostrate junipers, the heathers and ground-runners (Lamium or wild strawberry or ivies) were the favourites of this definite style. See chapter 9.

Ha-ha is a ditch, hidden from view from the house, enabling the viewer to comprehend an uninterrupted landscape, with cattle or sheep kept from the close-cut lawn by this device. Developed from the military defensive ditch. See chapter 3.

Herb, herber, herbarium, erbe, all from Latin *herba* = grass, French *erbe*, *erbier* = herb: the Americans still use the absent 'h' i.e. erb garden in pronunciation, one of the seventeenth-century British pronunciations that survives there but not here.

Hortus, another mine of meanings. Pliny used *chortus* for a subsistence garden, *orchatos* for a simple vineyard, but *hortus* became a Latinized word for garden for medieval scholars, *hortus medicus* for a botanic garden, *hortus conclusus* for the Virgin Mary's enclosed garden, so that *hortus* has come to imply a garden where work is part of the pleasure, hence horticultural.

Jardin anglais relates to the French fashion for adopting the natural or neglected look as opposed to their traditional formalism, especially and conveniently for aristocrats returning to neglected gardens after the Revolution: it was applied effectively in Parisian parks, especially les Buttes-Chaumont, completed in 1869, and is a constantly revived inspiration.

Jardinière is an ornamental plant container, usually of high architectural quality.

Knot garden is a formal layout of miniature hedges in the twisted pattern of a knot, hence the symbol of infinity, closely associated with ancient maze symbols. Thomas Hill's *Gardener's Labyrinth* of 1577 suggests thyme or hyssop for 'tying' the knot or knotte; Parkinson (1629) added flowers in a box knot and framework. The idea has been much revived and popularized and by the mid-seventeenth century meant almost any box-edged garden of intricate patterns and flowers. Purists now differentiate and plant both kinds.

Lawn, a term first used in the thirteenth century, especially of the green turf carefully tended in monastic cloisters as conducive to contemplation. Lawns came to symbolize prestige simply because of the labour needed to maintain both levels and angled banks in grand formal gardens before the landscape style e.g. Claremont amphitheatre, and also for a national affection for velvety turf, prized for bowls, the nation's favourite game.

Mazes were moved into gardens as a court fashion for intellectual puzzlement: they were turf and low hedge patterns copying the ancient labyrinths that have persisted in religious and folkloric culture from classical times and possibly earlier: see *Mazes and Labyrinths*, Nigel Pennick, London 1990. Puzzle hedge-mazes in which one gets lost, or trapped, seem to have gradually developed and one was designed for Henry VIII's Nonsuch Palace, which preceded Hampton Court. Mazes are labyrinths, unicursal with a single pathway and no deviations, or multicursal, with many differing paths and dead ends. Knots are only similar in being ancient symbols, and though the two are habitually confused in garden literature their difference thus becomes clear.

Organic gardening is a term confused by history. Organic originally applies to any chemical compound containing carbon, consequently it is prefixed to many compound pesticides, hence organophosphates, very toxic to warm-blooded animals. However organic cultivation was developed on a no-digging basis, using mulches of compost material rich in organic matter of vegetable waste and animal manures, hence organic gardening, of which the main purpose was to avoid using pesticides. See chapter 7.

Paradise garden comes from Persian origin *paradeisos*, meaning the vast controlled and unthreatened territories that emperors such as Cyrus the Great could hunt over and harvest: the word was adopted by the Greeks and Romans as they conquered these hunting territories and imitated them with enclosed parks, thus the origin of park in the west. It should be remembered that for Cyrus 'hunting' meant studying wild animals, as well as the opportunity to roam enjoying wild and cultivated fruits and flowers, the 'paradise' aspect of being lord of all he surveyed. A much-adapted word, Latin *paradisus*, Italian *paradiso*, Hebrew *pardes* (originally, from Liddell Scott Jones, *Greek Lexicon*, *peri* = round, *daiza* = wall). Medieval deer parks were thus a miniature materialization.

Pergola, Latin *pergula* = a projection from a house, often used as a shop or stall, and Latin *peristyle* = an inner colonnaded court of classical houses, also *loggia* = an open-sided gallery or arcade. Garden pergolas are thus latticed or lightly-roofed projections from a house, continuing the hard flooring: as they were extended farther into gardens by Arts & Crafts architects their finished wood structures gave way to growing laburnum or wisteria tunnels, and they merge into alleys.

Pesticides is the general term for chemical agents used against garden undesirables of insect, animal or vegetable origin. The term was first used c.1930 (previous word being pestology). See chapter 7.

Parterre, literally part earth or earth-parts, indicating a pattern cut from turf, leaving bare earth which could be covered with gravels or ground shells. These were a French fashion, and variations on patterns grown in box in Italian Renaissance gardens. With the Italianate and formal revivals of the nineteenth century they were brought to Britain, with turf or box and coloured gravels, or differing kinds of flowers used for the patterns. Fan parterres were the finest, opening to semi-circles divided and decorated like the segments of a fan, the speciality of a former fan painter, W. A. Nesfield, 1793–1881.

Picturesque has three important applications in garden history: (i) the eighteenth-century landscape style was strongly influenced by the paintings of rugged Italian landscapes by Poussin, Claude de Lorrain and Salvatore Rosa making landscape *au naturel* 'picturesque'; (ii) it became known that Claude used a slightly convexed mirror to distort his landscape views and these were manufactured for aesthetic travellers, a smoked mirror for fine days, a silvered version for grey days: Claude glasses held up to frame the mountains of North Wales or the Lakes inspired both rugged rocks, caves and waterfalls as Picturesque features in gardens (and Picturesque gardens in the wild landscape e.g. Hafod) and an aesthetic controversy of the wild versus the contrived, the true beginning of the environmental movement; (iii) the Picturesque framing device was called upon in modernist gardens because the steel frame structure of international modern houses gave endless opportunities for garden pictures to be framed from terraces and garden rooms.

Sharawadgi was the word used by Sir William Temple in *Upon the Gardens of Epicurus* of 1692 to represent what he thought was the Chinese spirit of the perfect garden – 'their greatest reach of Imagination is employed in contriving Figures, where the Beauty shall be great, and strike the Eye, but without any order or disposition of parts, that shall be commonly or easily observed'. Later Sharawadgi was used to describe the irregular before naturalism/wild arrived.

Trellis is a simple lightweight wooden frame for supporting plants which has been used in gardens since medieval times: the French *treillage* is used for trellis taken to high art, especially in French gardens in designs derived from Jacques Androuet du Cerceau, a sixteenth-century architect who travelled in Italy. Du Cerceau's drawings inspired Harold Peto's elaborate Edwardian *treillage* at Easton Lodge, Dunmow (now being restored), and in turn Beatrix Farrand's much photographed barrel-roofed loggia at Dumbarton Oaks, Washington DC. Most of the trellis now marketed has emerged from these sources.

Wild garden, wilderness was a conceit, a stylized imitation in the seventeenth century, with alleys through unclipped trees and bushes to give a taste of adventure to court ladies. It was further exploited in eighteenth-century gardens in contrast to open glades and green hills as overgrown woods sheltering ruins or a hermitage. Gertrude Jekyll designed wildernesses, paddocks or orchards filled with groups of trees and shrubs with mown paths kept cut through long grasses; perennials were also grown in grass as William Robinson advocated. *The Wild Garden* was the title of Robinson's 1870 book advocating native plants in their desired settings (i.e. habitats) which has developed through the twentieth century.

NOTES

Notes for Introduction

1 Stephen Lacey, *Gardens of the National Trust*, 1996, p. 144 on Hill Top's planting.
2 *Macbeth*, Act V Scene 5, for Great Birnam Wood 'a moving grove'.
3 Dame Barbara Cartland's Hertfordshire, *East Anglia Guide*, Hadleigh, Suffolk, 1997, pp. 30–31.
4 Much quoted in garden books, originally Gertrude Stein in *Sacred Emily*.
5 Graham Stuart Thomas, *The Old Shrub Roses*, 1956, 1963 ed., p. 5.
6 Graham Stuart Thomas, *The Manual of Shrub Roses*, Sunningdale Nurseries, Windlesham, Surrey, 5th ed. rev. 1967.
7 Tony Venison, 'Sweet Smell of Success', *Country Life*, 2 September 1993, p. 70.
8 Information from The Royal National Rose Society, *The Gardens of the Rose*, Chiswell Green, St Alban's, Herts, AL2 3NR (tel. 01727 850461 fax 01727 850360 email: mail@rnrs.org.uk).
9 Harold R. Fletcher, *The Story of the Royal Horticultural Society 1804–1968*, 1969, p. 38.
10 Ray Desmond, 'Victorian Gardening Magazines', *Garden History*, vol. v, no. 3, p. 63.
11 Elizabeth Longford, *Victoria R.I.*, 1964, 2nd imp. 1971, p. 145.
12 Fletcher, p. 190–94.
13 Fletcher, p. 190.
14 *William Morris & Kelmscott*, The Design Council, 1981, A. R. Dufty, *Kelmscott*, p. 15.
15 See my *Gardens of a Golden Afternoon*, 1982, for the chapter 'Working Partnership' on Lutyens's and Jekyll's design theories etc.
16 William Robinson, *The Wild Garden*, 1870, reprinted 1983, introduction by Richard Mabey.
17 Robin Moore, *A History of Coombe Abbey*, Jones-Sands Publications, Exhall, Coventry, 1983.
18 See my *Art & Architecture of English Gardens: Designs for the Garden from the Collection of the Royal Institute of British Architects 1609 to the present day*, 1989, pp. 110–11 for the William Miller drawings.
19 David Watkin, *The Rise of Architectural History*, 1980, 1983 ed., p. 172.
20 Dorothy Stroud, *Capability Brown*, 1984 ed., intro. by Christopher Hussey, p. 27.
21 Kay N. Sanecki, letter to the author, 18 March 1997.
22 Westbury Court Garden, Gloucestershire. The National Trust 1986 guide is a model explanation of history and restoration. Pieter de Hooch's *The Game of Ninepins* (Courtauld Institute) is illustrated, p. 29.
23 Mavis Batey, President of the Garden History Society, 'Putting Garden History on the Map' for the *Architectural Association Garden*

Conservation Newsletter no. 21, Spring 1998.

24 Keith Goodway, Chairman of the Garden History Society, 'The Way Ahead' also for the above.

25 Brent Elliott, *Victorian Gardens*, 1986, p. 244.

26 National Council for the Conservation of Plants & Gardens, Annual Directory (1998 ed.) gives complete information on collections, groups, endangered species, plant sales etc., enquiries to The Pines, RHS Garden, Wisley, Woking, Surrey GU23 6QP (tel 01483 211465).

27 See David Green, *Gardener to Queen Anne: Henry Wise (1653–1738) and the Formal Garden*, 1956, and *The Churchills of Blenheim*, 1984, which includes Green's own experiences of the hidden treasure house he found when he started working for the 10th Duke of Marlborough after the war.

28 *Blenheim, Landscape for a Palace*, ed. James Bond and Kate Tiller, 2nd ed., 1997, is a revised report of the 1983 day school.

Notes for ONE : The Purest of Human Pleasures

1 M. V. Ferriolo, 'Homer's Garden' in *Journal of Garden History*, 1989, vol. 9 no. 2, pp. 86–94.

2 *Francis Bacon, Selections* ed. P. E. & E. F. Matheson, Oxford 1922, 1952 ed.

3 Georgia O'Keeffe, *One Hundred Flowers*, afterword by Nicholas Callaway in Callaway Knopf edition, extract in *Artspace Quarterly*, Santa Barbara, winter 1987–8.

4 Walter de la Mare, *Collected Rhymes and Verses*, Faber & Faber 1944, 2nd ed. 1970, p. 273.

5 Robert Louis Stevenson, *A Child's Garden of Verses*, 1885, illus. ed. by Hilda Boswell, nd.

6 Hans Andersen texts from *Fairy Tales and Legends*, illus. Rex Whistler, 1935, 1959 ed.

7 'Gardens of Adonis' from J. G. Frazer, *The Golden Bough*, 1922, 1994 ed., p. 337.

8 Oscar Wilde, 'The Selfish Giant', from *The Happy Prince and Other Tales*, 1888.

9 A. A. Milne, 'The Doormouse and the Doctor', from *When We Were Very Young*, in The Christopher Robin Verses, 1932, 1953 ed.

10 Husain Haddawy introduction to the *Arabian Nights* translated from fourteenth-century Syrian ms., ed. Muhsin Mahdi, 1990.

11 Texts from 1990 ed. as above.

12 Alison Lurie, *Don't Tell the Grown Ups: Subversive Children's Literature*, 1990.

13 Frances Hodgson Burnett, *The Secret Garden*, 1911, quotes from 1987 ed.

14 Song of Solomon, reviews of new translations by Lucille Day, the *Hudson Review*, vol. xlviii, no. 2, 1995 New York.

15 British Museum, *Oriental Gardens*, 1991, p. 47.

16 Naveen Patnaik, *A Second Paradise, Indian Courtly Life 1590–1947*, 1985, p. 43.

17 *Jahanghir's Memoirs* ed. J. H. Beveridge, 1909.

18 Edward Lear's diary quoted in Miles and John Hadfield, p. 114.

19 Sir Robert Ker Porter quoted in Miles and John Hadfield, *Gardens of Delight*, 1964, pp. 113–14.

20 Patnaik, ibid, 73.

21 Patnaik, ibid, 103.

22 John Harvey, *Medieval Gardens*, 1981, p. 44.

23 Raleigh Trevelyan, *Shades of the Alhambra*, 1984, p. 7.

24 Nancy Mitford, *Madame de Pompadour*, 1954, 1970 ed., chapter 3, 'The Ball of the Clipped Yews'.

25 Arthur Calder-Marshall, *The Grand Century of the Lady*, 1976, essay 'Public Pleasures', pp. 49–59.

26 Mollie Sands, *Invitation to Ranelagh 1742–1803*, 1946, title page.

27 Calder-Marshall, ibid, quoting Tobias Smollett, *The Expedition of Humphry Clinker*, p. 49.

28 Fanny Burney, *Evelina*, vol. 2, letter xv, 1994 ed.

29 Guy Williams, *The Royal Parks of London*, 1985, p. 12.

30 Maggie Keswick, *The Chinese Garden, History, Art & Architecture*, 1978.

31 Keswick, p. 32.

32 Keswick, pp. 35–6.

33 Patrick Synge, *Plants with Personality*, 2nd rev. ed. n.d. but c.1948, p. 21 ff.

Notes for TWO : The Secret Garden

1 See Mark Morford, 'The Stoic Garden', *Journal of Garden History*, vol. 7, no. 2, pp. 151–75, and Massimo Venturi Ferriolo, 'Homer's Garden', vol. 9, no. 2, pp. 86–94.

2 Sir Frank Crisp (1843–1919) made an exhaustive collection of manuscript illustrations published as vol. 2 of his *Medieval Gardens*, 1924. See also Harvey, *Medieval Gardens*, 1981.

3 Hon. Alicia Amherst, *A History of Gardening in England*, 1895, p. 7. See also *Saints & She-Devils, Images of Women in the 15th and 16th centuries*, 1987, trans. Sion and van der Wilden, intro. Lene Dresen-Coenders, essay 'Saintly Virgins' by Ellen Muller.

4 Sylvia Landsberg, *The Medieval Garden*, 1995, p. 38.

5 Now that medieval and monastic gardens (Crisp, Harvey, Landsberg etc.) have been brought into focus the ensuing void of garden history, from the Reformation to the Restoration of Charles II yawns more darkly. For this period I used primarily: Christopher Haigh's *English Reformation, Religion, Politics and Society under the Tudors*, 1993; John Bossy, *The English Catholic Community 1570–1850*, 1975; J. T. Cliffe, *The Yorkshire Gentry from the Reformation to the Civil War*, 1969; Alan Haynes, *The Gunpowder Plot*, 1994; Godfrey Anstruther OP, *Vaux of Harrowden, A Recusant Family*, pub. Johns, Newport, Mon., 1953.

6 Roy Strong, *The Renaissance Garden in England*, 1979, is the standard work but deals only in kings, queens and courtiers.

7 Barnaby Googe trans. 'The Popish Kingdom', from Anne Pratt, *St John's Wort*, Friends of the Fitzwilliam Museum Press, Cambridge 1985. See also Eamon Duffy, *The Stripping of the Altars: Traditional Religion in England 1400–1580*, 1992, and Keith Thomas, *Religion and the Decline of Magic*, 1971.

8 Further reading in these directions might begin with William Anderson, *The Green Man, An Archetype of our Oneness with the Earth*, 1990.

9 Evelyn Waugh, *Edmund Campion*, 1935 (comes as a literary delight after all the foregoing substantially heavy history).

10 See John Gerard, *The Autobiography of an Elizabethan*, trans. by Philip Caraman, intro. by Graham Greene, 1951.

11 For these houses see Leanda de Lisle

and Peter Stanford, *The Catholics and their Houses*, 1995.

12 Christopher Hussey, *The Work of Sir Robert Lorimer*, 1931, p. 20.

13 ibid.

14 *Historic Scotland*, guide to Edzell Castle by the late W. Douglas Simpson rev. by Richard Fawcett, HMSO Edinburgh.

15 National Trust for Scotland, *Guide to Pitmedden* by Phil Sked, Eric Robson and Dick Hillson, 1984.

16 Peter Savage, 'Lorimer and the garden heritage of Scotland', *Garden History*, vol. 5, no. 2, Summer 1977 pp. 30–40.

17 ibid, p. 30.

18 Strong, pp. 209–10.

19 Francis Maire of Hardwick, Co. Durham, Autograph 'account of what hath from time to time been done at Hardwick 1550 till 1699' was exhibit 259 in 'The Glory of the Garden' loan exhibition, Sotheby's, 2–28 January 1987.

20 Amherst, p. 32.

21 *The Shell Gardens Book*, ed. Peter Hunt, 1964, p. 87.

22 John Aubrey's curious sketch is reproduced by Sylvia Landsberg p. 21. It seems to show the remains of a walled garden inside another gated wall, about 200 yards square. The Inner 'bower' has a long seat against a wall and a spring which feeds a series of three square pools. Kerry Downes's biography of Vanbrugh 1977, p. 74, refers to the architect's paper, 'Reasons Offer'd for Preserving some Part of the Old Manor' of Woodstock, which is reprinted in J. D. Hunt and P. Willis, *The Genius of the Place*, 1975, pp. 119–21.

23 Fiona Cowell's papers on the Catholic landscape gardener Richard Woods are in *Garden History*, vol.

14, no. 2, Autumn 1986 and vol. 15 nos 1 and 2, Spring and Autumn 1987: also Tim Mowl, 'Air of Irregularity', *Country Life*, 11 January 1990.

24 Strong, p. 206 on William Prynne, a Puritan's opinion of the garden as an aid to devotion, citing Stanley Stewart, *The Enclosed Garden, the Tradition and Image in 17th-century poetry*, Wisconsin U.P., 1966.

25 Strong pp. 206–7. George Wither the Puritan on 'A costly garden in her best array' as the lesson of moral planning and patience: 'Things, to their best perfection come, Not all at once; but, some and some' is accompanied by an illustration of a mighty heavenly hand watering the flowers.

26 Alexander Marshall's album is in the Royal Library at Windsor, but has been published as *Mr Marshall's Flower Album*, intro. John Fisher, preface by Jane Roberts, 1986. See 'Henry Compton as Master of St Cross', Lady O'Neill of the Maine, Hampshire Gardens Trust newsletter 6, Autumn 1987.

27 There is now a museum to Compton and his plants at Fulham Palace; some of his trees also remain, part of his garden is open, part covered by the famous allotments.

28 James Woodforde, *The Diary of a Country Parson 1758–1802*, 1935: entry for 4 September 1783.

29 David Standing, *The Wakes Garden, Selborne*, a short guide.

30 Richard Mabey, *Gilbert White: a biography of the author of* The Natural History of Selborne, 1986, p. 86.

31 ibid, p. 6.

32 ibid, pp. 7–8.

33 ibid, p. 8.

34 Dorothy Gurney (1858–1932), 'The Lord God Planted a Garden': The kiss of the sun for pardon,

The song of the birds for mirth –
One is nearer God's Heart in a garden
Than anywhere else on earth.

35 Piers Dudgeon, *The English Vicarage Garden*, 1991, The garden at Shirley, p. 70.

36 Paul Kleber-Monod, *Jacobitism and the English People 1688–1788*, 1989, p. 289.

37 Revd Charles Kingsley is also in Dudgeon as p. 35 above, and his garden at Eversley was featured in several editions of William Robinson's *The English Flower Garden*, 1883 etc.

38 Brent Elliott, *Victorian Gardens*, p. 152.

39 Dean Samuel Reynolds Hole, *Our Gardens*, 1899, R is for Rosa . . .

40 ibid, p. 71.

41 ibid, chapter one.

42 Hole, *A Book About the Garden*, 1904 on his friend the Hon. Revd John Townshend Boscawen at Lamorran: the Boscawens at Lamorran and Ludgvan are well covered by Piers Dudgeon, who also describes Caunton Grange nr Newark, which is still occupied and gardened by Dean Hole's descendants.

43 Dudgeon, p. 78.

44 Mavis Batey, 'The New Forest' and 'The Picturesque', in *Pleasure Grounds, The Gardens and Landscapes of Hampshire*, ed. Hedley and Rance, Southampton City Art Gallery 1987, (pub. Milestone Publications, 62 Murray Road, Horndean, Hants PO8 9JL), pp. 41–7.

45 E. W. Bovill, *English Country Life 1780–1830*, 1962, 1963 ed., p. 117.

46 ibid.

47 p. 174 of Barbara Jones's classic study, *Follies & Grottoes*, 1953, 2nd ed. rev. 1974; but see also Naomi Miller, *Heavenly Caves, Reflections on the Garden Grotto*, 1982.

48 Jones, ibid.

49 James Stevens Curl, 'Young's Night Thoughts and the origins of the garden cemetery', *Journal of Garden History*, vol. 14, no. 2, Summer 1994.

50 Morford, see note 1 above.

51 Christopher Hussey, *The Life of Sir Edwin Lutyens*, 1950, pp. 372–3, and also *The Letters of Edwin Lutyens*, ed. Percy and Ridley, 1985, p. 349.

52 My *Gardens of a Golden Afternoon*, 1982, p. 136.

53 Lutyens's Irish National War Memorial at Islandbridge, Dublin, is one vast, monumental rose garden, paralleled by many others, including Miss Jekyll's Memorial Garden Cloister (with Herbert Baker) for Winchester School. She also planted the garden memorial at Godalming to J. G. 'Jack' Phillips, the radio officer of the *Titanic*. See my *Lutyens & the Edwardians*, 1996, for the catastrophic effect of the war on Lutyens's morale and designs.

54 *Gardens of a Golden Afternoon*, p. 136 etc.

55 J. G. Frazer, *The Golden Bough, A Study in Magic and Religion*, 1922, 1995 ed., pp. 336–7.

56 ibid.

57 *My Lady's Garden*, planted and grown by Hackleplume, 1921, p. 127.

58 ibid, 'The Glade of Glory', p. 5. Other gardens include the Rose, Pleasaunce, Aquatic, Herb and Physic.

59 ibid, p. 5.

60 The *Gardeners' Chronicle*, 17 November 1894, pp. 591–2.

61 R. C. Turner, 'Mellor's Gardens', *Garden History*, vol. 15, no. 2, Autumn 1987, p. 157 etc.

62 Sheridan Gilley, *Newman and His Age*, 1990, p. 86.

63 W. Keble Martin, *Over The Hills*, 1968.

64 Canon Charles Earle Raven, *English Naturalists from Neckham to Ray*, 1947, and *Natural Religion and Christian Theology*, Gifford Lectures 1951, 1953.

65 Revd Mervyn Wilson letter to the author, 19 November 1997 and related papers.

Notes for THREE :
The Military Garden

1 Siegfried Sassoon, *Siegfried's Journey 1916–20*, 1945 ed., p. 79.

2 See general sources on Egyptian gardens i.e. *Oxford Companion to Gardens*, but also Alix Wilkinson, 'Gardens in Ancient Egypt, their locations and symbolism', *Journal of Garden History*, 1990, vol. 10 no. 4, 199–208. Also Joyce Tyldesley, *Hatchepsut, The Female Pharoah*, 1996.

3 Sir Thomas Browne (1605–82), *The Garden of Cyrus*, 'Not only a Lord of Gardens, but a manual planter thereof: disposing his trees, like his armies in regular ordination', pub. 1690, with *Hydriotaphia, or Urn Burial*.

4 David Stronach, 'Parterres and stone water courses at Pasagardee', *Journal of Garden History*, vol. 14 no. 1, spring 1994, and also 'Pasagardee, a Report on the excavations by the British Institute of Persian Studies 1961–63', 1978.

5 David R. Coffin, *Villa d'Este at Tivoli*, Princeton, 1960, and also *The Villa in the Life of Renaissance Rome*, Princeton, 1979.

6 Christopher Taylor, *The Archaeology of Gardens*, 1983, in the Shire series is the most exciting introduction to these theories: for greater detail see the Council for British Archaeology Research Report no. 78 on garden archaeology. For the developments of the last ten years see *There By Design, Field Archaeology in Parks and Gardens*, ed. Paul Pattison, British Archaeological Reports Series 267, Oxford, 1998.

7 Christopher Duffy, *Siege Warfare*, 1979, p. 250, quotes Tavannes on the 'well-advised governor' removing houses, hedges and ditches from his defences prior to attack. The most well-known European example is the Vienna Ringstrasse, the construction of which formalized (and curtailed) the leisure activities the citizens had enjoyed for centuries on the defensive Glacis.

8 Catherine Morton, *Bodiam Castle, Sussex*, The National Trust, 1981, and also subsequent archaeology by Paul Everson for which there are several references in *There by Design* (above). See also 'Bodiam Castle' in Evans, Salway and Thackray (eds), *The Remains of Distant Times*, pp. 66–72, Society of Antiquaries of London Occasional Paper no. 19, 1996.

9 Colin Platt, *Late Medieval and Renaissance Britain from the Black Death to the Civil War*, The National Trust, 1986, p. 13.

10 My *Vita's Other World, a gardening biography of V. Sackville-West*, 1985, p. 107.

11 Duffy, p. 145.

12 Andrew Saunders, *Fortress Britain*, 1989, p. 76.

13 *The Diary of Thomas Isham of Lamport 1658–81*, trans. Norman Marlow, intro. Sir Gyles Isham, Bart., 1971, p. 220.

14 'A guide to the gardens of St Catherine's College, Oxford', by the Garden Master, Sept. 1986.

15 Clements R. Markham, *A Life of the Great Lord Fairfax, Commander-in-*

Chief of the Army of the Parliament of English, 1870.

16 Andrew Marvell went to Nun Appleton as tutor to Mary Fairfax in 1650, when he was twenty-nine: these stanzas are from 'Upon Appleton House, To My Lord Fairfax'. See also Augustine Birrell, *Andrew Marvell*, 1905.

17 'Upon Appleton House', verse LXXXVII on Mary Fairfax. These stanzas are also published in Hunt and Willis, *The Genius of the Place*, 1975, pp. 70–78, and see also John Dixon Hunt, *Andrew Marvell, His Life and Writings*, 1978.

18 A. Woolrych, *The English Civil War*, 1961, my long treasured copy was used here. It should also be noted that General George Lambert 'The Knight of the Golden Tulip' and Fairfax's sometime ally and friend was also a keen gardener at Wimbledon, and a painter of flowers. Lambert was a friend of Sir Thomas Hanmer, whose (not quite believable) garden book ms. of 1659 was first published in 1933.

19 William Brereton, *Travels in Holland, 1844*, p. 44.

20 David Green, *Henry Wise, gardener to Queen Anne*, pp. 79–80.

21 Green, ibid, p. 79. The site of the Maastricht garden below the curtain wall of Windsor Castle continued to be so named: on 10 May 1708 Queen Anne ordered the 'forming and enlarging' of the canal (Green, p. 80) – earthworks, trees and canal still survive.

22 A. R. Bayley, *The Civil War in Dorset 1642–1660*, 1910.

23 K. Merle Chacksfield, *Glorious Revolution 1688*, Wincanton Press 1988, has description of the surviving ice-house at Charborough Park with the rest of the inscription:

IMMORTAL KING WILLIAM 'to whom we owe our deliverance from Popery and Slavery the expulsion of the tyrant race of STUARTS the restoration of our Liberties security of our Properties and Establishment of National Honor and Wealth', p. 14.

24 An illustration of Wise's gravel pit appeared on the title page of Thomas Tickell, *Kensington Gardens*, 1722, and is illustrated on p. 133, Hunt and Willis, *Genius of the Place*.

25 Sir George Clark, *The Later Stuarts 1660–1714*, Oxford History of England, 1934, 1985 ed., p. 173.

26 *The Life and Opinions of Tristram Shandy, Gentleman* by Laurence Sterne, vol. 1, ed. George Saintsbury, 1894, pp. 96–9, 'Lillabullero' is on p. 165.

27 Madeline Bingham, *Masks and Facades*, 1974, and Laurence Whistler, *The Imagination of Vanbrugh and His Fellow Artists*, 1954, and Kerry Downes, *Vanbrugh*, 1977.

28 See Jellicoe, Lancaster and Goode (eds), *Oxford Companion to Gardens*, 1986, p. 585.

29 G. B. Clarke ed., *Descriptions of Lord Cobham's Gardens at Stowe 1700–50*, Buckinghamshire Record Society no. 26, 1990, p. 11, and also 'Stowe, a guide to the gardens' by Laurence Whistler, Michael Gibbon and George Clarke, Stowe School, 1974 ed.

30 This correspondence is well covered in Charles Saumarez-Smith, *The Building of Castle Howard*, 1990.

31 Winston S. Churchill, *Marlborough, His Life and Times*, 1936, vol. 3, p. 67.

32 M. Bingham, p. 344 and also material in Northampton Record Office, report to March 1966, p. 12

by Dr Paul Hopkins on Holywell 'an out of county' Spencer Estate. In 1685 Marlborough employed William Talman at Holywell and did a great deal of landscape gardening.

33 David Green, *Henry Wise*, p. 99, note on Allingham as a 'Supplement to the new Method of Fortification as Practiced by M. Vauban'.

34 Green, p. 101.

35 Green, ibid, but also his essay on the palace and gardens under Vanbrugh, Hawksmoor and Wise in *Blenheim, Landscape for a Palace*, ed. Bond and Tiller, 2nd ed., 1997.

36 Green, p. 102.

37 The Brompton Park nursery was founded in 1681 by George London and three others, Messrs Lucre, Field and Cooke, and they took Henry Wise into partnership in 1688. They supplied all the great gardens of the day until 1714, when London and Wise relinquished the business to Joseph Carpenter and William Smith.

38 Green, p. 102.

39 For Colonel Armstrong's scheme see David Green and James Bond, 'Blenheim after Vanbrugh, the second phase', in *Landscape for a Palace*.

40 David Green, 'Vanbrugh, Hawksmoor and Wise' as 35 above, p. 69.

41 The Torrington Diaries, containing the tours through England and Wales of the Hon. John Byng, ed. C. Bruyn Andrews, 1936, vol. 3, *A Tour to the North* 1792, p. 159.

42 See my essay 'Frances Wolseley' in *Eminent Gardeners*, 1990.

43 *The Story of Windsor Great Park*, R. J. Elliott, Crown Estate Commissioners n.d. See also Jane Roberts, *Royal Landscape*, 1997, pp. 128–9.

44 Elliott, ibid, p. 15.

45 Ralph Dutton, *The English Garden*, quoted in Green, *Henry Wise*, p. 137.

46 Dorothy Stroud, *Capability Brown*, p. 49 etc.

47 Miles Hadfield, 'History of the Ha-Ha', *Country Life*, 30 May 1963, and John Brushe, 'From Ah! Ah! to Ha Ha: John James, Architect and Garden Designer c.1672–1746', Hampshire Gardens Trust newsletter 1996, and Sally Jeffery, unpub. PhD thesis University of London on John James, 1986.

48 Charles Dickens, *Great Expectations*, chapter 25.

49 Gertrude Jekyll, *Home and Garden*, 1900, pp. 261–3.

50 Ronald Blythe, *Akenfield*, 1969, 1982 ed. Christopher Falconer, gardener, pp. 116–25.

51 John Moore, *Brensham Village*, 1946, part four, The Frost.

Notes for FOUR : Emancipated Gardeners

1 *The Paston Letters* ed. J. Gardner, 6 vols, 1904, rep. 1984. and ed. N. Davis, 2 vols, 1971 and 1976. See also *The Pastons and their England*, H. S. Bennett, 1937.

2 Quoted in Antonia Fraser, *The Weaker Vessel: Woman's Lot in 17th-century England*, 1984, p. 44.

3 Fraser, pp. 45–7.

4 Geoffrey Grigson, *The Englishman's Flora*, Foreword to the 1955 edition, 1987 ed., p. 14.

5 Fraser, chapter 3, 'Crown to her Husband', p. 41: 'I with great thankfulness acknowledge she was my crown and glory . . .' Dr Anthony Walker, *The Holy Life of Mrs Elizabeth Walker*.

6 Grigson, ibid.

7 Keith Thomas, *Religion and the Decline of Magic, Studies in Popular*

Beliefs in Sixteenth- and Seventeenth-Century England, 1971, 1991 ed., chap. 7 and p. 211.

8 Grigson, ibid.

9 John Harvey, *Early Nurserymen*, 1974, plate 9 illustrates Henrietta London's drawings of plants from South Africa from Badminton MS.

10 Harvey, *Early Nurserymen*, appendix VII, 'Letters of Henry Woodman', 1729–33.

11 Harvey, appendix VIII, p. 191, 'Letters of Henry Clark', Harrowby MS.

12 Harvey, p. 103 and p. 199.

13 Harvey, p. 104.

14 Alison Kelly 'Coade Stone in Georgian Gardens', *Garden History* vol. 16, no. 2, autumn 1988.

15 Letters written by the late Rt Hon Lady Luxborough to William Shenstone Esq., 1775, and *Dictionary of National Biography* entry under Knight. Mark Laird, 'Approaches to planting in the late eighteenth century: some imperfect ideas on the origins of the American garden', notes Lady Luxborough as the first to use the term 'shrubbery', *Journal of Garden History* 1991, vol. 11, no. 3, pp. 154–72.

16 *Letters from Georgian Ireland, the correspondence of Mary Delany 1731–68*, ed. Angelique Day, 1991, and *Mrs Delany, her life and her flowers*, Ruth Hayden, 1980.

17 Margaret Anne Doody, *Frances Burney, The Life in the Works*, Rutgers UP, New Jersey, 1988.

18 Introduction by Havelock Ellis to *Men and Manners*, William Shenstone, The Golden Cockerel Press, 1927.

19 ibid, p. xv. See also Shenstone's 'Unconnected Thoughts on Gardening' of 1764 printed in Hunt and Willis, *The Genius of the Place*, 1975, pp. 289–97.

20 Lady Luxborough, letter no. 42 to William Shenstone. G. Tyack, *Warwickshire Country Houses*, 1994, has information on Barrells, the house is a ruin and the park a wilderness (and privately owned). Henrietta's memorial can be found in the evocative little church of Old St Mary's east of Ullenhall.

21 This phrase is used in the DNB entry!

22 Elizabeth Whittle, *The Historic Gardens of Wales, An introduction to parks and gardens in the history of Wales*, CADW/HMSO, 1992, 'This Delicious Solitude', p. 60.

23 David Nokes, *John Gay*, 1996, pp. 44–7.

24 Peter Martin, *Pursuing Innocent Pleasures, the gardening world of Alexander Pope*, 1984, p. 166 etc.

25 Martin, ibid, p. 172.

26 ibid, p. 171.

27 ibid.

28 John Harris, *The Palladians*, 1981, p. 18 and noted in Nokes, *John Gay*, p. 44.

29 Timothy Mowl, *Horace Walpole, The Great Outsider*, 1996; see also Mavis Batey, 'Horace Walpole's Bicentenary', *Garden History Society News* 50, summer 1997, p. 12.

30 Mowl, pp. 239–40.

31 Mowl, p. 240, quoting Walpole, *On Modern Gardening*, 1780.

32 Mowl, p. 239.

33 James Lees-Milne, *William Beckford*, 1979, p. 18.

34 Beckford's house and tower can still be seen in Bath, but the long romantic ride he made between the two, with ornamental buildings, his last garden, remains only in fragments.

35 John Gloag, *Mr Loudon's England*, 1970, p. 61.

36 Gloag, p. 205.

37 Gloag, p. 59.

38 Melanie Louise Simo, *Loudon and the Landscape, from country seat to metropolis 1783–1843*, 1988, pp. 269–70.

39 Simo, above, is the best introduction to the Loudons' enormous output of work, but there is an earlier biography of Jane, *Lady with Green Fingers*, by Bea Howe, 1961.

40 Gloag, p. 216.

41 Simo, p. xiv (introduction).

42 See *Architecture: A Place for Women*, ed. Ellen Perry Berkeley, 1989, for Mariana van Rensselaer as architectural critic etc., and my *Beatrix, The Gardening Life of Beatrix Jones Farrand 1872–1959*, 1995, for the American context of gardening for women.

43 *Notes and Thoughts on Garden and Woodland written chiefly for amateurs* by the late Frances Jane Hope (d. 26 April 1880) of Wardie Lodge in Edinburgh, Lady Associate of the Botanical Society of Edinburgh, ed. Anne J. Hope Johnstone of Annandale, 1881. Many of her pieces appeared in the *Gardener's Chronicle* and the *Garden*.

44 Miss Hope's chapter on 'Flowers for the Poor and the Sick' vividly illustrates how she interpreted her gardening as her particular kind of social work.

45 The making of the garden is described in *Country Life*, vol xxvi, 20 November 1909, p. 701 and see also my essay on Frances Wolseley and her Glynde College in *Eminent Gardeners*, 1990.

46 The latest biography is Sally Festing's *Gertrude Jekyll*, 1991, but see also Richard Bisgrove, *The Gardens of Gertrude Jekyll*, 1992, for analysis of her planting style.

47 The original copy of this catalogue is in the Jekyll Collection, Documents Collection, School of Environmental Design, University of California, Berkeley.

48 For this information on Ellen Willmott I am indebted to three Architectural Association Garden Conservation students of 1996, Charlotte Johnson, Melissa Simpson, Ailsa Wildig, Audrey le Lievre's, *Miss Willmott of Warley Place*, 1980, and current knowledge of the site.

49 The sad affair of *The Genus Rosa* etc., is told in *A Garden of Roses, Watercolours by Alfred Parsons for The Genus Rosa*, essay by Bryan N. Brooke, commentary by G. S. Thomas, 1987.

50 The site of Warley Place garden has long been tended by volunteers from Essex Naturalists' Trust but at the time of writing and re-negotiation of the lease it seems likely that some historic and horticultural conservation management is intended for the future.

51 Dawn Macleod, *Down-To-Earth Women*, Edinburgh, 1982, p. 54.

52 Frederick Eden, *A Garden in Venice*, 1903.

53 Dawn Macleod, *Down-to-Earth Women* covers the horticultural schools for women.

54 Chrystabel Proctor's papers are in the archives of Girton College, Cambridge, see my history of the garden there, *A Garden of Our Own*, Cambridge, 1999.

55 Patricia Jaffe, *Women Engravers*, 1988, p. 5.

56 Eleanour Sinclair Rohde is featured in Macleod, but also Timothy Clark, 'Flashes from a Mirror', *Country Life*, 21 April 1983. For Nymans before the fire see Christopher Hussey's articles in *Country Life*, 10 and 17 September 1932.

57 Elizabeth Coxhead, *Constance Spry*,

A Biography, 1975, p. 99, quoting Spry, *Flowers in House and Garden*, 1937. Gareth Slater of Wiltshire Gardens Trust has recently researched Norman Wilkinson (1882–1934) and found more of his interest in garden design, included in correspondence with the author.

58 Constance Spry's *Flowers in House and Garden*, 1937, includes lists of plants for herbaceous borders in various colour schemes and single colours; the white list is p. 134.

59 Beverley Nichols, *Down the Garden Path*, 1932, foreword to the 1983 ed., p. 5, rep. 1997. As a young man Nichols was a successful journalist and novelist both here and in America. Part of Cecil Beaton's group of beautiful people in the 1920s, he was 'deeply troubled' by his homosexuality and after the end of a serious affair he vowed to live alone for the rest of his life – time and again he admitted that without his gardens he would have perished. He became the most widely known and syndicated garden writer of the twentieth century. Bryan Connon, *Beverley Nichols, A Life*, 1991.

60 Timothy Clark, 'Cottage Garden Pioneer, Margery Fish at East Lambrook Manor', *Country Life*, 7 February 1985; Mrs Margery Fish, obituary by Lanning Roper, *The Times*, 28 March 1969, and the 'Judas weed' and a frank assessment of Mrs Fish in Macleod, pp. 117–28.

Notes for FIVE *: The Rise of the Small Garden*

1 John Betjeman, 'Middlesex', from *A Few Late Chrysanthemums*, 1954, *Collected Poems*, 1958.

2 C. E. Lucas Phillips, *The Small Garden*, 1952, 1971 ed., opening on Presentation, p. 17. In 1979 the author noted that his book had gone through six revisions and seventeen reprintings; the latest copy I have is 1989, published after his death with a note by Barbara Lucas Phillips.

3 M. Aston, 'Gardens and Earthworks at Hardington and Low Ham, Somerset', *Somerset Archaeology and Natural History*, vol. 122, 1978. This paper acknowledges Christopher Taylor's inventories of Cambridgeshire and Northamptonshire for the Royal Commission on Historic Monuments (1968–72) which recognized the consistent formal features as those of gardens, and also suggests many other possible sites in Somerset.

4 Sir Thomas Tresham's Lyveden New Bield near Oundle in Northamptonshire is one of the smaller sites where the development of garden archaeology has revealed the significance of the garden layout, which undoubtedly reflects the Catholic symbolism of the unfinished house. Owned by the National Trust, the roofless house is viewable all the year round, but the garden is only opened occasionally during the summer.

5 Monastic sites have proved useful in the development of garden archaeology because of their consistency of features, which can have no military significance. See Christopher Taylor, *The Archaeology of Gardens*, 1983, and also *The Parks and Gardens of Britain, A Landscape History from the Air*, Edinburgh UP, 1998.

6 Lorna McRobie, Director Gardens and Landscape for English Heritage, article on the development of garden archaeology, *Conservation*

Bulletin, March 1996, issue 28, English Heritage.

7 Taylor, *The Archaeology of Gardens*, 1983, p. 25.

8 Grigson, *The Englishman's Flora*, p. 96.

9 Chysauster Iron Age village, nr Gulval, Penzance, Cornwall (English Heritage, open throughout the summer) is so impressive in its organization that it is impossible to deny its occupants 'gardening' skills. However, the books on ancient settlements pre-date the 'discovery' of garden archaeology so consistently avoid the notion, using other names, toft and garth, for private space. Brian K. Roberts, *Landscapes of Settlement*, 1996, and Françoise Audouze and Olivier Buchsenschutz, *Towns, Villages and Countryside of Celtic Europe*, trans. H. Cleere, 1991.

10 Gay Wilson, 'Early Plants in the Nene Valley', *Nene Archaeology*, 1978, no. 6. Continuing research at Flag Fen, Peterborough, incorporating the Fengate site, is now including the recognition of cultivated plants, Fenland Archaeological Trust, Fourth Drove, Peterborough PE1 5UR. Controlled admission throughout the year. The Iron Age Farm at Butser Hill, near Petersfield in Hampshire, is also developing 'gardens'.

11 Maurice Beresford and John Hurst, *Wharram Percy, Deserted Medieval Village*, 1990, and see also Beresford, *The Lost Villages of England*, 1954.

12 Hangleton in Sylvia Landsberg, *The Medieval Garden*, 1996 and the Weald & Downland Open Air Museum guidebook, ed. Richard Harris, 1998 ed.

13 Landsberg, *The Medieval Garden*, describes her work on Bayleaf in detail, giving sources on medieval plants and collaborations with John Harvey. Two further Harvey references of importance on planting are: 'Henry Daniel, A Scientific Gardener of the Fourteenth Century', *Garden History*, vol. 15 no. 2, Autumn 1987, and 'The Square Garden of Henry the Poet', *Garden History*, vol. 15 no. 1, Spring 1987.

14 Oliver Rackham, *The Illustrated History of the Countryside*, 1994, p. 23.

15 The lilies, added from Dr Landsberg's researches, flower as a vivid reminder of the religious symbolism in an ordinary garden.

16 John Donne, 'Twicknam garden', from *Songs and Sonnets*, 1633–1635, from *Elegies, Songs and Sonnets* ed. H. Gardner, 1965.

17 Mark Girouard, *Robert Smythson and the Elizabethan Country House*, 1983 (orig. *Robert Smythson and the architecture of the Elizabethan Era*, 1967) published and identified these drawings, which are in the RIBA Drawings Collection (British Architectural Library).

18 Robert Greene, from 'Menaphon, Dorons Eclogue joynd with Carmelas', p. 74, the *Penguin Book of English Pastoral Verse*, intro. and ed. John Barrell and John Bull, 1974.

19 Shakespeare, *The Winter's Tale*, Act IV, scene 4.

20 Rowland Parker, *The Common Stream*, 1975, pp. 146–8.

21 Harvey, p. 31.

22 Harvey, *Early Nurserymen*, p. 30.

23 Harvey, ibid, p. 6.

24 Harvey, ibid, pp. 8–10.

25 Winchelsea, from *The Buildings of England*, Sussex, Ian Nairn and Nikolaus Pevsner, 1977 ed., pp. 630–37.

26 P. D. A. Harvey, *Maps in Tudor England*, 1993, p. 31.

27 P. D. A. Harvey, p. 73.

28 Quoted as front jacket illustration, Harvey, ibid.

29 Maurice Beresford, *History on the Ground*, 1957, 1984 ed., chapter 6, 'A Journey to Elizabethan Market Places', p. 154.

30 Beresford, on Higham Ferrers, p. 156 etc.

31 W. G. Hoskins, *The Making of the English Landscape*, 1955, 1971 ed., p. 126.

32 Tom Williamson, *Polite Landscapes*, 1995, quotes Frances Brooke, *History of Lady Julia Mandeville*, 2nd ed., 1763, vol. I, pp. 222–3.

33 Gillian Darley, *Villages of Vision*, 1975, 1978 ed., pp. 35–7.

34 A. G. Clark, *Elton, the History of its Lost and Ancient Buildings*, Stamford, 1992.

35 A. G. Clark, *Dearest Grandpapa, The Hamiltons at Elton Hall 1861–9*, Stamford, 1996, p. 49.

36 A 'popular' American engraving of the 1880s showed a young woman coming out of the garden privy and throwing the contents of the bucket across the yard – it was titled 'Sowing diptheria'. Elisabeth D. Garrett, *The American Family 1750–1870*, Abrams, New York, 1990.

37 John Burnett, *A Social History of Housing 1815–1970*, 1978, pp. 119–20.

38 Gilbert White, *The Natural History of Selborne*, Letter 37, 8 Jan. 1778 to the Hon. Daines Barrington, Folio edition 1962, ed. W. S. Scott, p. 156 ff.

39 Ruth Duthie, *Florists' Flowers and Societies*, 1988 (Shire), p. 15.

40 Just a few of the gems from Richard Morley's *Red Roughs and Copper Kettles, A History of Ditchling Horticultural Society*, Ditchling, 1990. The Ditchling Museum has excellent related exhibits.

41 R. Todd Longstaffe Gowan, 'Proposal for a Georgian Town Garden in Gower Street, The Francis Douce garden', *Garden History*, vol. 15 no. 2, pp. 136–43.

42 R. Todd Longstaffe Gowan, 'James Cochran, Florist and Plant Contractor to Regency London', *Garden History*, vol. 15, no. 1, 1987.

43 No. 4 The Circus, Bath, has a garden reconstructed after excavations (open in summer). See an additional paper, Mark Laird and John H. Harvey, 'The garden plan for 13 Upper Gower Street (Francis Douce garden), a conjectural review of the planting, maintenance etc.', *Garden History*, vol. 25, no. 2, Winter 1997, p. 189.

44 Jane Loudon's 'Short account of the life and writings of John Claudius Loudon', printed as appendix two in Gloag, p. 190.

45 George and Weedon Grossmith, *The Diary of a Nobody*, 1995, ed. Kate Flint.

46 Ebenezer Howard, *Tomorrow: a Peaceful Path to Real Reform*, 1898, re-issued as *Garden Cities of Tomorrow*, 1902, was a case of the right message at the right time, carried forward by the Three Magnets image, instantly understood by many who had never read Howard's books. For influence see *The Anglo-American Suburb* ed. Robert A. M. Stern, Architectural Design Profile, 1981.

47 Darley, *Villages of Vision*, p. 177.

48 *The Art of Building a Home, A collection of lectures and illustrations* by Barry Parker and Raymond Unwin, 1901, intro. p. v.

49 Mervyn Miller and A. Stuart Gray, *Hampstead Garden Suburb*, 1992, p. 72.

50 Diane Haigh, *Baillie Scott, The*

Artistic House, 1995, chapter on 'The Artistic Garden', p. 60.

51 C. B. Purdom, *The Garden City*, 1913, chapter VII, 'Garden City Gardens'.

52 Chas. T. Druery, I discover, was not an entirely innocent small gardener, but a regular contributor to the *Gardener's Chronicle*.

53 For small gardens designed by Mallows, Voysey, Horsley, Hill etc., see my *Art & Architecture of English Gardens*, 1989, illustrations and drawings from the RIBA Collection. For Jekyll's Millmead, see Jekyll and Weaver, *Gardens for Small Country Houses*, 1912, 1981, chapter 1.

54 My *Beatrix, The gardening life of Beatrix Jones Farrand*, 1995, design for a suburban garden, pp. 95–8.

55 Richard Reiss, *The Home I Want*, 1918, 'a little book which may be useful for social reformers to find out what the men who come home from the war WANT', and Mark Swenarton, *Homes Fit for Heroes, The politics and architecture of early state housing in Britain*, 1981.

56 Alan A. Jackson, *Semi-Detached London, Suburban Development, Life and Transport, 1900–39*, 1978, 2nd ed. 1991, pp. 124–6, 'The Hallowed Plot'.

57 Jackson, p. 124.

58 Paul Oliver, Ian Davis et al, *Dunroamin, The Suburban Semi and its Enemies*, 1981, pp. 168–70.

59 David Crouch and Colin Ward, *The Allotment, its landscape and culture*, 1988, pp. 76–7 ff.

60 Lanning Roper, *Successful Town Gardening*, 1957, and my biography, *Lanning Roper and his gardens*, 1987.

61 Sylvia Crowe, *Garden Design*, 1958, 3rd imp. 1965, p. 11.

62 Crowe, ibid, on 'Principles of Design, Unity', p. 81.

63 Crowe, ibid, pp. 85–6.

64 John Brookes, *Room Outside, a new approach to garden design*, 1969.

65 Crouch and Ward, *The Allotment*, p. 78.

66 *Landscape Design*, May 1977, letter to the editor from Mrs E. B. Galloway, Research Fellow, Leisure Gardens Unit, Dept of Geography, University of Birmingham. The Edgbaston Guinea Gardens were registered Grade 2 by English Heritage in 1997, and Warwickshire Gardens Trust is now working on the Hill Close gardens in Warwick.

Notes for SIX : Acquiring Eden

1 Nikolaus Pevsner, *The Englishness of English Art*, 1956, 1978 ed., p. 173.

2 Jane Renfrew, *Food & Cooking in Roman Britain*, English Heritage, 1985, pp. 23–5.

3 A. G. McKay, *Houses, Villas and Palaces in the Roman World*, 1975, chapter 2 on Pompeii and other Italian cities, and a later chapter on European provinces and Britain: this is not primarily garden history but provides wide-ranging clues. An evaluation of Pompeii gardens will be found in 'Nature into Art, Gardens and Landscapes in the Everyday Life of Ancient Rome', Michael Conan, *Journal of Garden History*, vol. 6, no. 4, pp. 348–56.

4 Harvey, *Medieval Gardens*, chapter 1 on legacy of classical gardens, p. 22.

5 Renfrew, ibid, p. 42.

6 Quoted from an early guide to Fishbourne, but see Barry Cunliffe, *Fishbourne, A Roman Palace and its Garden*, 1971.

7 Whittle, *The Historic Gardens of Wales*, pp. 9–10.

8 Prudence Leith-Ross, *The John Tradescants, Gardeners to the Rose*

and Lily Queen, 1984, and also Mea Allan, *The Tradescants*, 1964.

9 Stephen A. Spongberg, *A Reunion of Trees, The Discovery of Exotic Plants and their Introduction into the North American and European Landscapes*, 1990, pp. 17–19.

10 Gary Paul Nabhan, *Enduring Seeds, Native American Agriculture and Wild Plant Conservation*, San Francisco, 1989, p. 87.

11 Michael Foss, *Undreamed Shores, England's Wasted Empire in America*, 1974, has a great deal of material from the John White archive in the British Museum.

12 Leo Marx, *The Machine in the Garden, Technology and the Pastoral Idea in America*, 1964, 1981 ed., chapter 3, p. 77.

13 This whole period is marvellously covered in Spongberg, *A Reunion of Trees*, particularly chapter 1, 'Actively Seeking the Unknown'.

14 Information largely from Alice M. Coats, *Garden Shrubs and their Histories*, 1963.

15 Rosemary Bowden-Smith, *The Chinese Pavilion, Boughton House, Northamptonshire*, 1988.

16 Lawrence James, *The Rise and Fall of the British Empire*, 1994, 1995 ed., p. 142.

17 Robert Hughes, *The Fatal Shore*, 1987, 1988 ed., pp. 9–18, and a further conversation between Hughes and Thomas Keneally broadcast on Today, Radio Four, 24 May 1998.

18 Thomas Rochford and Richard Gorer, *The Rochford Book of Houseplants*, 1961, describes and illustrates all these now accepted curiosities.

19 W. G. J. Kuiters, unpublished thesis on William Paxton 1744–1824, Leiden University, 1992. The drawings of Thomas and William

Daniell are in the RIBA Drawings Collection, with details and commentary upon their travels and patrons. A bibliography includes T. Sutton, *The Daniells: artists and travellers*, 1954, and some of the Sezincote drawings and letters are in my *The Art & Architecture of English Gardens*, 1989.

20 Fletcher, *The Story of the Royal Horticultural Society*, p. 203.

21 Geoffrey and Susan Jellicoe, *The Landscape of Man*, 1975, p. 267.

22 Stephen Lacey, *Gardens of the National Trust*, 1996, on Biddulph Grange, pp. 43–8.

23 Spongberg, ibid, has made good use of the Wilson archive at the Arnold Arboretum and gives an enthralling account of his work and travels.

24 Peter Cox, 'Collectors' Techniques: Then and Now', in *The Rhododendron Story*, ed. Cynthia Postan, 1996.

25 Spongberg, p. 186.

26 Spongberg, p. 182.

27 Spongberg, p. 190.

28 ibid.

29 Reginald Farrer, *My Rock Garden*, 1907, quoted in the *Garden Companion to the Royal Botanic Garden Edinburgh*, 1970.

30 Miles Hadfield, *The Art of the Garden*, 1965, on 'The Inspiration of Mountains', p. 148.

31 E. H. M. Cox, *Wild Gardening*, 1929, chapter 1, 'The Site', p. 17 ff.

32 Cox, ibid, p 18.

33 Cox, ibid, p. 16.

34 Brent Elliott, *Victorian Gardens*, p. 95.

35 George C. Whitelegg, *The Studio Gardens and Gardening*, 1936.

36 Mary Forrest, 'Hooker's Rhododendrons: Their Distribution and Survival', p. 67, in *The Rhododendron Story*, ed. Cynthia Postan, 1996.

37 *The Rhododendron Story, 200 Years of Plant Hunting and Garden Cultivation*, a series of contributions ed. by Cynthia Postan, 1996, is a welcome addition to the literature, offering an essential introduction to this complex subject.
38 Lanning Roper, *The Gardens in the Royal Park at Windsor*, 1959, gives a full account of King George VI's and Queen Elizabeth's great interest in rhododendrons and how this was shared with fellow collectors.
39 Tony Schilling, 'The Road to Everest', part two, in the *Garden*, Journal of the Royal Horticultural Society, vol. 103, part 8, August 1978, pp. 309–14 (part one in July issue).

Notes for SEVEN : Science Lends a Hand

1 Amherst, p. 201.
2 Thomas, *Religion and the Decline of Magic*, p. 35.
3 'Garden Warfare – As it Was', Jim Gould, *Hortus* vol. 4 no. 4, Winter 1990, p. 35.
4 Quoted in *The BMA Guide to Pesticides, Chemicals and Health*, British Medical Association, 1990, 1992 ed., p. 5.
5 BMA guide, ibid. This was the most comprehensive factual background that I found in an exhaustive search through books that the present-day gardener might find.
6 M. B. Green, *Pesticides: Boon or Bane*, 1976, p. 9.
7 Gordon Harrison, *Mosquitoes, Malaria and Man: A History of Hostilities since 1880*, 1978, pp. 218–20.
8 Julian Phillips, *A Short History of ICI at Billingham, The First 60 Years 1917–1977*, 1986, p. 7.
9 The Chrystabel Proctor archive at Girton College, Cambridge, has

interesting material on Second World War 'digging for Victory', and see my *A Garden of Our Own*, a history of Girton College gardens, Cambridge, 1999.
10 Sir Frederick Keeble, *Science Lends a Hand in the Garden*, 1939, p. x.
11 Fletcher, *The History of the RHS*, pp. 281–2.
12 Keeble, ibid, p. 28.
13 Rachel Carson, *The Silent Spring*, 1962, 1988 ed., chapter 11, p. 158.
14 Green, as note 6.
15 *The BMA Guide to Pesticides* is more informative than most other books to be found on this subject, but it raises (and does not answer) the question as to whether any researches show the numbers of cases treated in hospitals and surgeries for the harmful effect of garden chemicals.
16 Roseclear Product Withdrawal Notice addendum to Garden Chemicals Guide, June 1996, British Agrochemicals Association, 4 Lincoln Court, Lincoln Road, Peterborough PE1 2RP.
17 This was in the *Beano* for 31 May 1997, no. 2863.
18 Peter J. Bowler, *The Fontana History of the Environmental Sciences*, 1992, p. 169.
19 Dawn Macleod, *Down-to-Earth Women*, 1982, on Lady Eve Balfour, p. 160.
20 W. E. Shewell-Cooper, *Compost Gardening*, 1972, 1977 ed.
21 Quoted in the Ryton Organic Gardens Guide Book, 1995, Ryton-on-Dunsmore, Coventry CV8 3LG.
22 Jonathan Pickering, 'An Alternative to Peat?' the *Garden*, June 1997, p. 428.
23 However, the *Independent*, 26 July 1998, p. 1, reported that there was little confidence in alternatives to peat and that surveys for the

Department of the Environment showed the use of peat rising by a quarter, to three million tons a year, between 1990 and 1996, as well as the fact that two thirds of peat extracted in Britain came from Sites of Special Scientific Interest.

24 Caroline Holmes, 'The Origins of the Herb Society', in *Herbs*, The Journal of the Herb Society, vol. 22 no. 1, Spring 1997.

25 Kay Sanecki, 'The Work of Margaret Brownlow of Seal Farm', *Herbs*, vol. 22 no. 3, 1997.

26 Gertrude Jekyll, *Wood and Garden*, 1899, reprint 1988, p. 318.

27 Allen Patterson, *Herbs in the Garden*, 1985, 1990 ed., pp. 9–10.

28 ibid, p. 10.

29 Rosemary Verey on her own garden at Barnsley House, in *The Englishwoman's Garden*, ed. Alvilde Lees-Milne and Rosemary Verey, 1980, 1984 ed., p. 139.

30 ibid, p. 141.

31 Sir William Temple's *Gardens of Epicurus*, intro. by A. F. Sieveking, 1908, quoted in Michael Young, *Collins Guide to the Botanical Gardens of Britain*, 1987, p. 99.

32 Lanning Roper, 'Exotic Plants in a Scottish garden (Logan)', *Gardening Illustrated*, January 1952.

33 Information from M. Young, *Guide to Botanical Gardens* and from author's visits to Bath, Bedgebury, Birmingham, Cambridge, Chelsea Physic, Harlow Car, Leicester, Liverpool (Ness), Oxford, Edinburgh, Kew, Wakehurst Place, Winkworth and Westonbirt etc.

34 Information from *The National Plant Collections Directory* 1998 ed. by Linda Cook. Current edition available from The Pines, RHS Garden, Wisley, Woking, Surrey GU23 6QP, tel. 01483 211465.

35 Royal Botanic Gardens Kew, *A Resource for the World*, the new Kew guide, and Plants and People exhibition 1998.

36 Wilfrid Blunt, *The Art of Botanical Illustration*, 1950, rev. edition by William T. Stearn, 1994, p. 276.

37 Stearn's footnote in the above, p. 277.

38 See L. Ponsonby, *Marianne North at Kew Gardens*, 1990.

39 The Fairhaven Garden at South Walsham is open to the public with details advertised in the National Gardens Scheme (Yellow Book).

40 David Scrase, *Flowers of Three Centuries*, 1983, cat. International Exhibitions Foundation, Washington DC. Introduction by Michael Jaffé.

Notes for EIGHT : Is It Art?

1 Rudyard Kipling, 'The Conundrum of the Workshops', 'But the Devil whoops, as he whooped of old: "It's clever, but is it art?"'

2 Quote from Constable in Leslie Parris, *Landscape in Britain c.1750–1850*, The Tate Gallery 1973, p. 96.

3 Graham Reynolds, *Constable: the Natural Painter*, 1965, 1976 ed., p. 50

4 *Life and Correspondence of J. M. W. Turner*, ed. Thornbury, 2nd ed., 1870, pp. 118–19.

5 Judith Bumpus, *Impressionist Gardens*, 1990, p. 10.

6 Bumpus, ibid.

7 Bumpus, ibid, pp 11–13.

8 ibid, p. 9.

9 For how Sargent painted *Carnation Lily, Lily Rose* with the help of gardening friends, see my *Eminent Gardeners*, 1990, essay 'The Henry James Americans'.

10 This is an opinion often recorded by Frances Partridge but I have quoted her from a broadcast interview on

Radio Three, 24 May 1998 at 6.30 p.m.

11 These paintings are all in *The British Landscape 1920–1950*, Ian Jeffrey, 1984.

12 *David Jones: The Maker Unmade* by Jonathan Miles and Derek Shiel, 1995.

13 *Eric Ravilious 1903–42, A Re-assessment of his Life and Work*, Patricia R. Andrew, Towner Art Gallery, Eastbourne, 1986, and Richard Dennis, *Ravilious & Wedgwood, The Complete Wedgwood Designs of Eric Ravilious*, 1995 ed., pub. by Richard Dennis, Shepton Beauchamp, Somerset TA19 0LE.

14 Clare Leighton, *Four Hedges*, 1935.

15 *The Nicholsons: A Story of Four People and their Designs*, York City Art Gallery, 1988.

16 *The Work of Rex Whistler*, Laurence Whistler and Ronald Fuller, 1960, with catalogue raisonné, and Laurence Whistler, *The Laughter and the Urn, The Life of Rex Whistler*, 1985.

17 John Piper, Catalogue of the Tate Gallery exhibition 1983, p. 99.

18 *Cecil Beaton*, ed. Dr David Mellor, Barbican Art Gallery, 1986, *The Role of the Garden in Cecil Beaton's Art* by Ian Jeffrey, p. 81.

19 Richard Morphet, *Cedric Morris*, Tate Gallery 1984, and Ursula Buchan 'Iris and art', in the *Garden*, July 1997.

20 Tony Venison, 'An Artist in the Garden: John Aldridge at Place House, Great Bardfield', *Country Life*, 17 October 1985.

21 *John Nash, The Artist Plantsman*, Tragara Press 1976, and Sir John Rothenstein, *John Nash*, 1983. Quotation from Ronald Blythe, *A Garden of My Own*, the *Observer* Magazine, 4 August 1985.

22 *The Notebooks of Leonardo da Vinci*, arranged, rendered into English,

intro. by Edward MacCurdy, vol. II, a plan for laying out a watergarden, pp. 421–2, and 'Of the lights on dark leaves', p. 314.

23 Gertrude Jekyll, *Home and Garden*, 1900, 1982 ed., 'A Wood Ramble in April, p. 42.

24 Batty Langley, *New Principles of Gardening*, 1728, quoted from Hunt and Willis, *The Genius of the Place*, 1975, p. 178.

25 Sylvia Crowe in *Humphry Repton Landscape Gardener 1752–1818*, George Carter, Patrick Goode, Kedrun Laurie, Sainsbury Centre for the Visual Arts, Norwich, 1982, p. 128.

26 *Humphry Repton*, ibid, essay by Kedrun Laurie, 'First Years', p. 5.

27 ibid, p. 8.

28 ibid, p. 10.

29 *Sketches and Hints on Landscape Gardening: Collected from Designs and Observations now in the possession of the different Noblemen and Gentlemen for whose use they were originally made: The whole tending to establish fixed Principles in the art of laying out Ground*, London, 1795.

30 *Humphry Repton*, ibid, p. 106.

31 Laura Wood Roper, *A Biography of Frederick Law Olmsted*, 1973, p. 292.

32 Percy Cane wrote several books about his own work but the best assessment of him and his career is in Charlotte Johnson's dissertation for The Architectural Association Garden Conservation Course, 1998.

33 Alexander Pope, 'Essay from the Guardian 1713', quoted in Hunt and Willis, p. 204 ff.

34 Thomas Love Peacock, *Headlong Hall*, 1816, 'Mr Milestone was a picturesque landscape gardener of the first celebrity', p. 18 (1940 ed. with *Nightmare Abbey*); he is a caricature of Repton throughout.

35 Ronald Firbank, *Flower Beneath the Foot*, 1923.
36 Frank Muir, *The Oxford Book of Humorous Prose*, 1990, on Amanda M. Ros, pp. 490–91.
37 Reginald Arkell, in *My Garden*, June 1934. Arkell's poems were published as *Green Fingers, More Green Fingers* and *Green Fingers Again* mainly during the 1930s.
38 *My Garden*, ed. Theo Stephens, was published from January 1934.
39 John Hadfield, *Love on a Branch Line*, 1959, pp. 106–7.
40 Sir Geoffrey Jellicoe, foreword to the Christie's sale catalogue of Sir Frederick Gibberd's watercolour collection, October 1994.
41 Sir Frederick's garden is now managed by The Gibberd Garden Trust, Marsh Lane, Old Harlow, Essex, tel. 01279 442112, frequently open, as in current guides.
42 Marion Whybrow, *The Leach Legacy, The St Ives Pottery and its influence*, Bristol, 1996, and Tom Cross, *Painting the Warmth of the Sun, St Ives Artists 1939–1975*, 1995.
43 *The Tale of Genji*, trans. by Arthur Waley, 1925–33: gardens are an essential part of the Lady Murasaki's life, particularly in chapter XII, 'Mirage'; see also *The Pillow Book of Sei Shonagon*, trans. and ed. Ivan Morris, 1967, p. 62 and p. 80.
44 *Gardener's Chronicle*, 15 December 1894, 'A Chrysanthemum exhibition in Japan'.
45 Cane and Charlotte Johnson, n. 32 above.
46 Russell Page, *The Education of a Gardener*, 1962, 1985 ed.
47 Sylvia Crowe, *Garden Design*, 1958, 1965 ed., p. 88.
48 See my *Lanning Roper and His Gardens*, 1987.
49 'David Hockney at Sixty', interview with Richard Cork, BBC Radio Four, 1 May 1997.
50 Jane Brown, 'The Brotherhood of Ruralists', *Hortus* no. 9, Spring 1989.
51 See Nicholas Usherwood, *The Brotherhood of Ruralists*, 1981.
52 David Inshaw's *The Badminton Game* is in the Tate Gallery: see also Christopher Neve, *One Moment One Summer*, David Inshaw, 'Recent Paintings', *Country Life*, 4 October 1984.

Notes for NINE : Labour of Love

1 Noel Kingsbury, 'On the Trail of the Lonesome Pineapple', *Country Life*, 4 December 1997, pp. 88–91.
2 Rudyard Kipling and C. R. L. Fletcher, 'The Glory of the Garden', printed in Sotheby's catalogue to the Loan Exhibition in Association with the Royal Horticultural Society, 1986–7. Originally in *A History of England*, 1911.
3 Blanche Henrey, *No Ordinary Gardener, Thomas Knowlton's Life and Letters 1691–1781*, ed. A. O. Chater, 1986.
4 Hannah Clarke's memories from *Country Voices, Life and lore in farm and village*, ed. Charles Kightly, 1984, pp. 159–62.
5 Kipling and Fletcher, ibid.
6 Loudon quoted in Hadfield, *Gardens of Delight*, pp. 35–6, from 1822 Encyclopaedia
7 David Green, *Henry Wise*, p. 11.
8 Daphne Bennet, *Emily Davies and the Liberation of Women 1830–1921*, 1990, for her early life.
9 V. Sackville-West, *Country Notes*, 1939, a collection of pieces from various journals etc., the two essays 'Gardens and Gardeners' and 'Gardeners' pp. 96–110 are an

excellent summation of characteristics of the late Victorian and First World War periods.

10 Jane Brown, *Beatrix*, p. 39.

11 Griswold and Weller, *The Golden Age of American Gardens*, p. 99.

12 ibid.

13 William Cobbett, *The English Gardener*, 1829, chapter 2 on enclosing, laying out.

14 Edward Blore, 'Designs for Worsley Hall near Manchester', 1841, two vols. in RIBA Drawings Collection, British Architectural Library, an epitome of the thorough practice of building a working garden establishment. The drawings for kitchen garden and melon pits are in my *Art and Architecture of English Gardens*, pp. 96–7.

15 Sources include *Historic Garden Tools, Catalogue of an exhibition at the Museum of Garden History*, ed. Christopher Thacker and Francesca Greenoak, 1990, essay 'Our Knowledge of Garden Tools' by Christopher Thacker, and Kay N. Sanecki, *Old Garden Tools*, Shire Album 41, 1997. There is a fine collection of tools at Normanby Hall Country Park, Scunthorpe, North Lincolnshire (tel. 01724 720588) which also has a working kitchen garden.

16 Humphrey Denham (Humphrey John), *The Skeptical Gardener*, 1940, 1949 ed., chapter 17 'The Gardener's Armoury', p. 197.

17 ibid, p. 196.

18 Brent Elliott, *Victorian Gardens*, 1986, especially the chapter 'Art and Nature', pp. 87–93 and also the gardeners in Brent Elliott's *Brief Lives* in *The Garden*, particularly 'John Fleming: trendsetter', February 1992.

19 Joan Morgan and Alison Richards, *A Paradise Out of a Common Field*, 1990, pp. 197–9.

20 Blythe, *Akenfield*, pp. 118–19.

21 Hazel le Rougetel, 'Roses for the Queen, The Floral Artistry of R. F. Felton', *Hortus*, vol. 7, no. 3, Autumn 1993, pp. 86–92.

22 Charles Wade's *Haphazard Notes* quoted in David Ottewill, *The Edwardian Garden*, 1989, p. 137.

23 Frances Wolseley quoted in my essay on her in *Eminent Gardeners*, pp. 30–31.

24 *Country Voices*, p. 162.

25 Blythe, p. 116.

26 C. Falconer quoted in Blythe, p. 123.

27 Cecil Beaton, *Ashcombe, The Story of a Fifteen Year Lease*, 1949, p. 94.

28 ibid.

29 ibid, pp. 98–9.

30 Tricia Vaughan, unpub. notes on 'Dig for Victory, The Home Front 1939–45', copy in author's possession.

31 ibid.

32 V. Sackville West, *The Garden*, 1946, pp. 118–19.

33 Ted Humphris, *Garden Glory*, 1969.

34 Arthur Billitt, *The Story of Clack's Farm*, 1981.

35 Brenda Colvin, 'Gardens to Enjoy' in *Gardens and Gardening, The Studio Annual* 1952, pp. 9–23.

36 Roy Hay, *Gardening the Modern Way*, 1962, a model of current thinking.

37 Alan Bloom, *Prelude to Bressingham*, Lavenham, 1975.

38 For the Puddles and Ayres's see *The Gardener's Garden*, ed. Jerry Harpur, 1985, which also has Brian Hutchinson of Castle Howard's piece on founding the P.G.G., pp. 86–9.

39 Susan Campbell on 'Writing a history of kitchen gardens' in *AA Garden Conservation Newsletter* no. 17, Winter 1996. See also S.

Campbell, *Cottesbrooke*, 1987, and *Charleston Kedding*, 1997. And also, Jennifer Davies, *The Victorian Flower Garden*, 1991, and *The Victorian Kitchen Garden*, 1987.

Notes for TEN : The Formative Garden

1 Elizabeth Longford, *Victoria RI*, 1964, 2nd imp. 1971, p. 28.
2 See Morgan and Richards, *A Paradise Out of a Common Field*, chapter 10 on the conditions of apprentice gardeners: many boiler houses included a sleeping 'shelf' with a bed of straw for the duty apprentice, or the boys slept with straw pallets on wooden flooring just above the boiler room for warmth in winter. With coal–fired stoves, or erratic steam contraptions, this was extremely dangerous, and the perils of this apprentice life were many.
3 The Hole childhood at Caunton Manor near Newark is quoted from Hadfield, *Gardens of Delight*, 1964, pp. 26–7.
4 Augusta de Lacy Lacy, 'The Child's Garden' in the *Garden*, 14 January 1905, part of a regular column.
5 See previous refs. to 'Gardeners' essay in *Country Notes*, and also my *Vita's Other World*, 1985, for the garden world of her childhood at Knole.
6 *Vita's Other World*, pp. 57–9.
7 The letter in full is in *The Letters of Edwin Lutyens*, ed. Clare Percy and Jane Ridley, 1985, 24 July 1904, pp. 111–12, and see also my *Lutyens and the Edwardians*, 1996, pp. 77–83.
8 Madeline Agar, *A Primer of School Gardening*, 1909, intro. by Miss J. F. Dove MA, headmistress of Wycombe Abbey School.
9 Marjory Allen and Mary Nicholson,

Memoirs of an Uneducated Lady, 1975, especially on Bedales, pp. 40–45.
10 Dora Russell, *The Tamarisk Tree*, vol. 2, *My School and the Years of War*, 1981.
11 See Reginald Snell, *From the Bare Stem, Making Dorothy Elmhirst's Garden at Dartington Hall*, Exeter 1989.
12 Michael Young (Lord Young of Dartington), *The Elmhirsts of Dartington: the Creation of a Utopian Community*, 1982, and my *Beatrix, The Gardening Life of Beatrix Jones Farrand*, chapter on Atlantic 'cousins' – the gardens of Dumbarton Oaks and Dartington Hall.
13 Stowe was one of a few exceptions to the following notes of neglect by schools. Stowe's historic landscape was safely guarded for years, especially by its resident historian (on the teaching staff) George B. Clarke.
14 These two books by Mabel A. Brown are in full: *Child Life in Our Schools, A manual for the infant teacher based on principles of Pestalozzi and Froebel*, 1906, 4th ed. 1911, and *The Children's Calendar of Song, Game and Verse, Month by month rhymes, songs, games etc. to inspire work*, 1909.
15 The photographs and all the books mentioned were lent to me by Wendy Titman, an international consultant on children's environmental experience and opportunity, author of *Special Places for Special People*, published by the World Wide Fund for Nature, 1994, and a guiding hand to Learning Through Landscapes. Just when I arrived at this chapter, Wendy was revealed as my neighbour! She will write the definitive book on this untold story.

16 Wilfred Owen, *Collected Letters*, ed. Harold Owen and John Bell, 1967, p. 21.

17 *The Poems of Wilfred Owen*, ed. and intro. Jon Stallworthy, 1993, p. 46.

18 Agar, *Primer of School Gardening*, p. 1.

19 Ronald Blythe, 'A Garden of My Own', *Observer*, 4 August 1985.

20 Harry Roberts, *English Gardens*, 1944, 3rd imp. 1947, pp. 10–11.

21 David Mawson, 'Thomas Mawson at Wood', p. 106 in *Devon Gardens*, ed. S. Pugsley, 1994.

22 Arthur Billitt, *The Story of Clack's Farm*, 1981, p. 9.

23 Russell Page, *Education of a Gardener*, 1985, pp. 14–16.

24 For Peter Aldington's house and garden see *Turn End, A Garden and Three Houses*, words by Jane Brown, photographs by Richard Bryant, 1999.

25 Whittle, *Gardens of Wales*, p. 70.

26 Geoffrey Grigson, *The Crest on the Silver*, 1950, pp. 33–7.

27 Grigson, ibid, p. 35.

28 Rodney Eugen, *Kate Greenaway, A Biography*, 1981, pp. 136–8.

29 Kenneth Grahame, *The Golden Age*, 1895, and *Dream Days*, 1898, both have idyllic gardens of childhood in their story settings, as the preludes to *The Wind in the Willows*, 1908.

30 J. M. Barrie's reluctance to grow up can be tracked through his many biographies, including those by Denis Mackail, 1941, Cynthia Asquith, 1954, and Janet Dunbar, 1970, and especially in Andrew Birkin's *J. M. Barrie and The Lost Boys*, 1987.

31 Samuel Reynolds Hole, *Our Garden*, 1899, p. 3.

32 Joseph Strutt, *The Sports and Pastimes of the People of England*, 1801, 1838 ed., quoting John Gay, p. 302.

33 ibid.

34 Guy Williams, *The Royal Parks of London*, pp. 25–9 on origins of Pall Mall.

35 *The Diary of Thomas Isham of Lamport 1658–81* (kept by him in Latin from 1671–1673) trans. Norman Marlow, intro. and notes by Sir Gyles Isham Bart., 1971, p. 130. See also Phil Pilley ed., *The Story of Bowls from Drake to Bryant*, 1987.

36 A. E. Gill, *Croquet: The Complete Guide*, 1988.

37 From Sutton's Spring Catalogue and Amateur's Guide, 1858.

38 Strutt, ibid, p. 95.

39 Pilley, ibid, p. 19 quoting *A Manual of Bowl Playing*, 1864.

40 Information in the author's possession from the En Tout Cas archive by kind permission of Colin Brown, ETC Holdings Ltd., Melton Mowbray.

41 D. H. McMorran, Daily Mail Ideal Home and Garden 1927 plan in the RIBA Drawings Collection, illustrated in my *Art and Architecture of English Gardens*, p. 221.

42 Elisabeth Beazley, 'The Private Pool', *Architectural Review*, October 1974.

43 Sunset Magazine, *Patio Book*, rev. ed. 1961, Lane Book Company, Menlo Park, California, p. 9.

44 Allen and Nicholson, ibid, p. 196.

45 ibid, p. 244.

46 ibid, p. 257.

47 Jane Brown, *The Everywhere Landscape*, 1982, pp. 15–30.

48 Robin Moore, 'Before and after Asphalt' in Bloch and Pellegrini eds., *The Ecological Context of Children's Play*, and *Childhood's Domain – Play and Place in Childhood Development*, 1986.

49 Jane Stoneham, *Grounds for Sharing, A guide to developing special school*

sites, Learning Through Landscapes, Winchester, 1996.

50 Kate Kenny, *Grounds for Learning, A celebration of school site developments in Scotland*, Learning Through Landscapes, 1996, pp. 79–81. (Learning Through Landscapes, Third Floor, Southside Offices, The Law Courts, Winchester, SO23 9DL.)

51 Wendy Titman, *Special Places; Special People, The hidden curriculum of school grounds*, World Wide Fund for Nature/Learning Through Landscapes, 1994. (WWF UK, Panda House, Weyside Park, Godalming, Surrey GU7 1XR.)

Notes for ELEVEN : Future Gardens

1 Karl Lagerfeld, quoted in *Vogue*, June 1998, no 2399, vol. 164, p. 181.

2 Kaffe Fassett, 'An easy pattern to follow', *Daily Mail Weekend*, 30 May 1998.

3 Beth Chatto, The Beth Chatto Gardens descriptive guide, Elmstead Market, Colchester, Essex, 1998 ed. The gardens are open Mon.–Sat., 9a.m.–5p.m. from 1 March–31 October, and 9a.m.–4p.m Mon.–Fri. in winter; closed on Sundays and Bank Holidays.

4 ibid, pp. 17–18. See also Beth Chatto, *The Dry Garden*, 1978, and paperback 1998.

5 See Priscilla Roosevelt, *Tatyana's Garden, Life on a Russian Country Estate*, 1995.

6 W. J. Sparrow, 'Count Rumford', *Architectural Review*, March 1958, p. 161.

7 Only since about 1980 have Canada, Australia and South Africa seemed to throw off this Anglicization and come to appreciate their own native plants. The NCCPG are also now concentrating upon the distinctive plant inheritance from these regions in British gardens.

8 Charles Quest Ritson, 'Benefits of a broader outlook', the *Garden*, March 1998. Also *The English Garden Abroad*, 1992.

9 The design festival is held annually at the Chateau of Chaumont-sur-Loire, 17 km from Blois (tel. 002 54 20 99 22, fax. 002 54 20 99 24). These particulars from Joy Larkom, *'Le Style français'*, the *Garden*, September 1997.

10 Gillian Mawrey, 'The Medieval Gardens at Fontevraud Abbey', *Hortus* no. 7, Autumn 1988. Fontevraud Abbey is open all the year except for some winter holidays: tel. 002 41 51 71 41.

11 This came about after Surrey County Council arranged to celebrate the 150th anniversary of Gertrude Jekyll's birth with a seminar on her wider interests: Bill Lucas, then Director of Learning Through Landscapes, three holders of National Plant Collections, Chris Hallsworth (bergenias), Noreen Jardine (digitalis) and Jeff Yates (primulas), the flower arranger Julia Clements, Richard Bisgrove on 'Memorials, Graves and Cemeteries', and Richard Hannay, of Land Use Consultants, designer of Park House garden for disabled and partially sighted people at Horsham, and Sir Francis Avery Jones on 'Plants, Gardens and Health' were the speakers. To my great regret we have never followed up with the publication of these papers nor pursued the subjects.

12 Author's notes and correspondence from the King's Fund archives, 11–13 Cavendish Square, London W1M 0AN.

13 Montagu Don, 'Maternal rest', *Observer Life*, February 1996.

14 'Compassion with Wisdom, teaching people about themselves', Martine Batchelor and Kerry Brown ed., *Buddhism & Ecology*, 1992, p. 98.

15 John McKean, *Places for Peace*, 1989, p. 43.

16 Allen and Nicholson, pp. 100–101.

17 Jacklyn Johnston and John Newton, *Building Green, A Guide to using Plants on Roofs, Walls and Pavements*, n.d. London Ecology Unit, c.1995.

18 *Places for Peace*, ibid, Foreword, John Darbourne CBE BA(Arch) MLA(Harv) RIBA AILA.

19 ibid, pp. 2–3.

20 Dawn MacLeod, 'Return to Stonypath', *Hortus*, no. 13, Spring 1990, pp. 63–72.

21 Lucius Burckhardt 'Minimal Intervention', p. 103 in *The Unpainted Landscape, Essays and Texts* by Simon Cutts et al, Coracle Press, 1987.

22 David Reason, 'A Hard Singing of Country', *Unpainted Landscape*, ibid, p. 52 see also Andy Goldsworthy, *Wood*, 1996.

23 'The Garden of Returns' in 'The landscape approach of Bernard Lassus', part II, trans. etc. by Stephen Bann, *Journal of Garden History*, vol. 15 no. 2, Summer 1995, pp. 67–106.

24 ibid, pp. 80–84.

25 Martha Schwartz, *Transfiguration of the Commonplace*, ed. Heidi Landecker, Spacemaker Press, Washington/Cambridge, Mass., 1997.

26 'Kathryn Gustafson, Art into Landscape', Ruth Slavid, *The Architect's Journal*, 21 Nov. 1996.

27 Kathryn Gustafson is now working at the new Botanic Garden of Wales, on the old site of Paxton's Middleton Hall in Carmarthenshire. The gardens will open in 2000.

28 Piet Oudolf, 'Perennials as building elements' from *Perennial Preview*, report of the symposium Perennial Perspectives, Arnhem, 19 and 20 June 1996, Perennial Perspectives Foundation, contact Rob Leopold, Postbox 1414, 9701 BK Groningen, The Netherlands.

29 Wolfgang Oehme and James van Sweden, *Bold Romantic Gardens, The New World Landscapes of Oehme and van Sweden*, with Susan Rademacher Frey, Acropolis Books, 13950 Park Center Road, Herndon, Virginia 22071, 1991, pp. 39–51.

30 Jane Owen, 'Why transplants can work', *The Times Weekend*, 13 June 1998.

31 Robin Lane Fox, 'Just add water . . .', *Financial Times*, 11–12 July 1998.

FURTHER READING

Baines, C., *The Wild Side of Town: How You Can Help and Enjoy the Wildlife Around You* (1986)

Bisgrove, R., *The Gardens of Gertrude Jekyll* (1992)

Blunt, W., and Steam, W. T., *The Art of Botanical Illustration* (1994)

Brown, J., *A Garden and Three Houses: the Story of Architect Peter Aldington's Garden and Three Village Houses* (1999)

Crouch, D., and Ward, C., *The Allotment, its landscape and culture* (1988)

Crowe, S., *Garden Design* (1981)

Dudgeon, P., *The English Vicarage Garden* (1991)

Elliott, B., *Victorian Gardens* (1986)

Fairbrother, N., *Men and Gardens* (1956)

Fairbrother, N., *New Lives New Landscapes* (1970)

Festing, S., *Gertrude Jekyll* (1991)

Flowerdew, Bob, *Complete Book of Companion Gardening* (1993)

Girouard, M., *Sweetness and Light, The Queen Anne Movement 1860–1900* (1977)

Green, D., *Gardener to Queen Anne, Henry Wise (1653–1738)* and *The Formal Garden* (1956)

Hadfield, M., and Hadfield, J., *Gardens of Delight* (1964)

Harvey, J. H., *Early Nurserymen* (1974)

Harvey, J. H., *Medieval Gardens* (1981)

Henrey, B., *No Ordinary Gardener, Thomas Knowlton's Life and Letters, 1691–1781*, ed. Chater (1986)

Humphris, Ted, *Garden Glory* (1969)

Hunt, J. D., and Willis, P., *The Genius of the Place* (1975)

Jackson, A. A., *Semi-Detached London: Suburban Development, Life and Transport, 1900–39* (1991)

Jones, B., *Follies and Grottoes* (1974)

Keswick, M., *The Chinese Garden, History, Art and Architecture* (1978)

Landsberg, S., *The Medieval Garden* (1995)

Leighton, C., *Four Hedges* (1935, 1991)

MacLeod, D., *Down-to-Earth Women, Those Who Care for the Soil* (1982)

Minter, S., *The Healing Garden. A Natural Haven for Emotional and Physical Well-Being* (1993)

Morgan, J., and Richards, A., *A Paradise Out of a Common Field: The Pleasures and Plenty of the Victorian Garden* (1990)

Mowl, T., *Horace Walpole: The Great Outsider* (1996)

Oliver, P., Davies, I., and others, *The Suburban Semi and its Enemies* (1981)

Ottewill, D., *The Edwardian Garden* (1989)

Page, R., *The Education of a Gardener* (1962, 1985)

Postan, C., ed. *The Rhododendron Story. Two Hundred Years of Plant Hunting and Garden Cultivation* (1996)

Roberts, J., *Royal Landscape. The Gardens and Parks of Windsor* (1995)

Robinson, W., *The Wild Garden* (1870, 1983)

Simo, M., *Loudon and the Landscape, From Country Seat to Metropolis 1783–1843* (1988)

Spens, M., *The Complete Landscape Designs and Gardens of Geoffrey Jellicoe* (1994)

Spongberg, S., *A Reunion of Trees, The Discovery of Exotic Plants and their Introduction into the North American and European Landscapes* (1990)

Taylor, C., *The Archaeology of Gardens* (1983)

Taylor, C., *The Parks and Gardens of Britain. A Landscape History from the Air* (1998)

Thomas, K., *Man and the Natural World. Changing Attitudes in England 1500–1800* (1983)

Thomas, K., *Religion and the Decline of Magic. Studies in Popular Beliefs in Sixteenth and Seventeenth-Century England* (1971, 1991)

Tunnard, C., *Gardens in the Modern Landscape* (1938, 1948)

Verey, R., *Classic Garden Design. How to Adapt and Recreate Garden Features of the Past* (1984)

Williamson, T., *Polite Landscapes* (1995)

INDEX

Fairfax, Thomas, 3rd Baron 87–8, 96
Fairhaven, Henry Broughton, Lord 15, 218
Fairhaven Trust garden, South Walsham 218
Falconer, Chris 101, 102, 259, 262
Far Eastern gardens 176–81
Farges, Paul 182
Farm Journal and Farmers' Wife 196
Farnham, Surrey 251
Farrand, Beatrix 158, 279, 304
Farrand, Max 119
Farrer, Reginald 183, 186, 285
fashion design 300–1
Fassett, Kaffe 301
Fat Hen 138
Fatal Shore, The (Hughes) 179
Fawcett, Ted 18
Faxon, Charles 218
Felton, Robert 259
Feng Shui 44
Fengate, Peterborough 138
fenitrothion 200
Fergusson, James 218
fertilisers, nitrogenous 196, 199
Festival of Britain (1951) 46–7, 48, 234
Field, Marshall III 250
Finlay, Ian Hamilton 311–12, 315
Finnis, Valerie (later Scott) 129
Firbank, Ronald 232
First World War (1914–18) 159, 244, 247, 253, 261, 303
Fish, David Taylor 74
Fish, Margery 17, 133
Fish, Walter 133
Fishbourne, Suss 137, 171–2
fishponds, clearing 194
Fisons company 199
Fitzwilliam Museum, Cambridge 59, 218, 219
Flag Fen, Peterborough 138
Fleming, George 256
Fleming, John 257
Fletcher, C R L 244
Flora-for-Fauna 316
floral clocks 257
floribunda roses 5
Flower Artists of Kew (Stearn) 218

Flower Missions 122
flowers
  arranging 132, 262–3
  for blind people 122
  for decoration 258–60
  liturgy and 56–7
  military 103–4
  as natal familiars 28–9
  selling 260
Flowers in House and Garden (Spry) 131
Flowers of the World (Johns) 80n
Fonthill, Wilts 116, 220
Food & Cooking in Roman Britain (Renfrew) 170–1
Food, Ministry of 200
food chain 203
Food Programme (radio series) 205
Foote, Maria 19
Ford, Ann 108
Ford, William 108
Forest Lawns, Los Angeles 71
Forrest, George 183, 189, 214
Forster, E M 233
Forsyth, Alexander 253
Forsyth, William 212
Forsyth, William senior 9
Fortune, Robert 177–9
Foss, Michael 174–5
Foster, Myles Birket 142, 221
Foster, Norman 309
Fothergill, John 176
Four Hedges (Leighton) 130–1
Fox, Robin Lane 24
Fox, Wilfred 214
Foxman, S 281
Foxton, Cambs 144
Fragonard, Jean Honoré 288
France, gardens 305
Franklin, Benjamin 176
Fraser, Antonia 106
Frazer, George 72
Fremont, Col John 176
French Impressionists 222–3
Friar Park, Henley 51
Frick, Elizabeth 235
fritillary 56
Frognal, London 287
front gardens 164

Mutis, Jose Celestino 176
My Garden: an Intimate Magazine for Garden Lovers 232–3
My Lady's Garden (Hackleplume) 72–3
My Own Garden . . . (Loudon) 275
My Rock Garden (Farrer) 186

Nabhan, Gary 174
names, plant 176
Namur, siege (1695) 90
Nash, John 109, 149, 218, 225–6, 284, 316
Nash, Paul 223–4
national collections 216
National Council for the Conservation of Plants and Gardens (NCCPG) 20–1, 168, 190
National Garden Festivals 48–9
National Gardens Scheme 16, 168, 262
National Peatlands Conservation Council 205
National Playing Fields' Association 296
National Trust, The 5, 8, 13, 17, 18, 20, 81, 181, 269
National Trust for Scotland 58
Native Garden, The (Garthorne-Hardy) 316
native plants 316–17
Natural History of Selborne (White) 63
Naturalis Historia (Pliny) 170
nature, art and 311–15
Nature Conservancy 200
NCCPG. *see* National Council for the Conservation of Plants and Gardens
Neckham, Abbot 79
Neolithic gardens 138
Nesfield, W A 14, 227
Nesfield, William Eden 14
Netherlands gardens 305
Nettlefold, John 215
Nevill, Lady Dorothy 129
New Earswick, Yorks 154–5, 159
New English Art Club 223–4
New Monthly magazine 63
New Orchard and Garden, A (Lawson) 107
New Principles of Gardening (Langley) 250

New York Botanic Gardens 215
Newark, Notts 86
Newman, John Henry 78
Nichols, Beverley 133, 234, 303
Nicholson, Ben 234, 236
Nicholson, J M 215
Nicholson, Nancy 225
Nicholson, Rosemary 19
Nicolson, Harold 133, 264, 294
Nicolson, Nigel 133
Night Thoughts (Young) 70
'No Dig Garden' 204
Noguchi, Isomo 314
Nokes, David 113
Norden, John 146
Normanby Hall, Lincs 272
Normans 85
North, Marianne 217–18
North Green Plants 240
Northern Horticultural Society 216
Nost, John van 311
Nowell, Lawrence 146
Nunappleton, Yorks 87–8, 103
nunnery gardens 53
Nur Jahan 36
Nurseries 231
  Japanese plants 236
Nurserywomen 107–8, 125, 126, 132
Nymans, Sussex 15, 17, 59

Oates Memorial Trust 64
Oatlands, Surrey 69, 116
O'Keeffe, Georgia 28, 133
Old Garden Roses (Bunyard) 4
Old Wardour, Wilts 85
Oldenburg, Claes 311
Olmsted, Frederick Law 119, 230
On Gardens (Bacon) 245
On Modern Gardening (Walpole) 115
On the Making of Gardens (Sitwell) 232
'One Thousand Years of British Gardening' exhibition (1979) 20
Opie, Iona 29, 288
Opie, Peter 29, 288
orchids 265
organic gardening 204–5, 323
Osborne House, IOW 273
Oudolf, Piet 316

Index